W9-AUQ-874

Space Shuttle Tragedy

"The Columbia is lost." Those words from Mission Control at the Johnson Space Center told the terrible story. Seventeen years after *Challenger* exploded after lift-off, the space shuttle *Columbia* broke up in the sky above Texas. It had traveled 6 million miles through outer space.

The catastrophic accident happened as the spaceship was preparing to land at the Kennedy Space Center in Florida on February 1, 2003. Pieces of the shuttle were scattered over several states.

All seven astronauts aboard the shuttle died. In a televised speech to the nation, President George W. Bush said news of the shuttle tragedy had brought "great sadness to our country." Six Americans and the first Israeli astronaut ever to journey into space died in the tragic accident. They were: Rick D. Husband, the shuttle's commander; William C. McCool; Michael P. Anderson; David M. Brown; Kalpana Chawla; Laurel Clark and Israeli astronaut Ilan Ramon. Americans mourned these brave heroes.

Rick D. Husband · William C. McCool · Laurel Clark · Kalpana Chawla · David M. Brown · Michael P. Anderson · Ilan Ramon

9

SHOWDOWN IN IRAQ

It was the most dangerous game of hide and seek in history. In 2003, U.N. weapons inspectors combed Iraq, looking nuclear, chemical or biological weapons. The U.S. and Great Britain accused Iraq of concealing weapons of mass destruction. Weapons inspectors reported that Iraq was beginning to cooperate—somewhat. However, the U.S. remained convinced that Iraqi leader Saddam Hussein had to go. President Bush called for a full-scale military action against Iraq to remove the weapons and remove Saddam from power.

Not everyone was in favor of a war with Iraq. Across the nation—and throughout the world—people protested against war. France, Russia, China and Germany urged President Bush to give weapons inspectors more time before launching an attack.

President Bush claimed that Iraq's weapons posed a serious threat to U.S. security—especially if the weapons fell into the hands of terrorists. He said the U.S. could not wait for a potential crisis to become a real one. In 2003, American, British and Australian troops invaded Iraq.

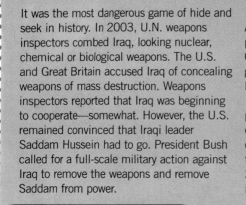

TIME FOR KIDS
ALMANAC 2004

with
FACT MONSTER™

Beth Rowen
Editor

Curtis Slepian
Managing Editor

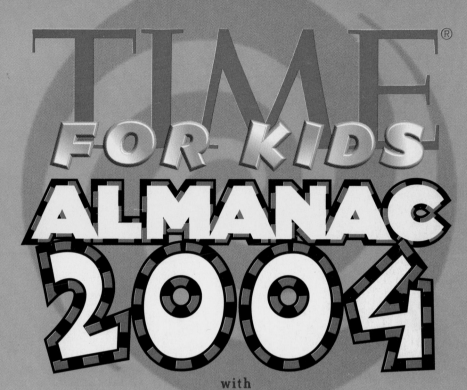

FACT MONSTER™
from **Information Please**®
a Pearson Education Company
http://www.factmonster.com
Unless otherwise noted, all information in
this book comes from FactMonster.com

TIME FOR KIDS online

AOL Keyword: TFK
When you go to
www.timeforkids.com
use this special TFK Password: TFKNEWS

TIME FOR KIDS ALMANAC 2004

with FACT MONSTER

INFORMATION PLEASE

EDITOR: Beth Rowen
CONTRIBUTORS: Christine Frantz, Holly Hartman, Ann-Marie Imbornoni, Erin Martin, Michael Morrison
FACT-CHECKING AND PROOFREADING: Christine Frantz
DESIGNER: Sean Dessureau
INDEXING: Marilyn Rowland
EDITORIAL DIRECTOR: Borgna Brunner
VICE PRESIDENT AND GENERAL MANAGER: George Kane

TIME FOR KIDS

GROUP PRESIDENT: Leanna Landsmann
PRESIDENT, TIME LEARNING VENTURES: Keith Garton
EDITOR: Curtis Slepian
COPY EDITOR: Peter McGullam
PHOTOGRAPHY EDITOR: Sandy Perez
MAPS: Joe Lertola
ART DIRECTION AND DESIGN: Raúl Rodriguez and Rebecca Tachna for R studio T

TIME INC. HOME ENTERTAINMENT

PRESIDENT: Rob Gursha
VICE PRESIDENT, BRANDED BUSINESSES: David Arfine
VICE PRESIDENT, NEW PRODUCT DEVELOPMENT: Richard Fraiman
EXECUTIVE DIRECTOR, MARKETING SERVICES: Carol Pittard
DIRECTOR, RETAIL & SPECIAL SALES: Tom Mifsud
DIRECTOR OF FINANCE: Tricia Griffin
MARKETING DIRECTOR: Kenneth Maehlum
ASSISTANT MARKETING DIRECTOR: Ann Marie Doherty
PREPRESS MANAGER: Emily Rabin
RETAIL MANAGER: Bozena Bannett
BOOK PRODUCTION MANAGER: Jonathan Polsky

SPECIAL THANKS: Robert Dente, Anne-Michelle Gallero, Peter Harper, Suzanne Janso, Robert Marasco, Natalie McCrea, Gina Di Meglio, Mary Jane Rigoroso, Steven Sandonato, Niki Whelan

SPECIAL THANKS TO IMAGING: Patrick Dugan, Eddie Matros, Angelo Papadopoulos, Jerome Bush

All Fact Monster material copyright © 2003 by Pearson Education, Inc. All rights reserved worldwide. Fact Monster® and Information Please® are registered trademarks of Pearson Education. Visit our kids' reference site at **www.factmonster.com**.

All TIME For Kids material copyright © 2003 Time Inc. All rights reserved.

Published by TIME For Kids Books
Time Inc.
1271 Avenue of the Americas
New York, New York 10020

All rights reserved. No part of this book may be reproduced in any form or by any electronic or mechanical means, including information storage and retrieval systems, without permission in writing from the publisher, except by a reviewer, who may quote brief passages in a review.

For information about permissions to reproduce selections from this book in print or electronic form, write to Fact Monster/Information Please, Permissions, Pearson Education, 160 Gould Street, Needham, MA 02494.

ISSN: 1534-5718
ISBN: 1-929049-97-8

"TIME For Kids" is a trademark of Time Inc.

We welcome your comments and suggestions about TIME For Kids Books. Please write to us at:
TIME For Kids Books
Attention: Book Editors
PO Box 11016
Des Moines, IA 50336-1016

If you would like to order any of our hardcover Collector's Edition books, please call us at 1-800-327-6388 (Monday through Friday 7:00 a.m.-8:00 p.m. or Saturday 7:00 a.m.-6:00 p.m. Central Time).

Did you know
that a baseball
bat is about 1
meter long?

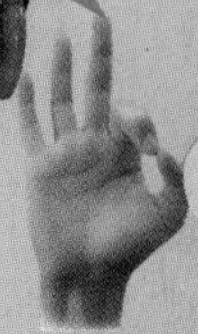

Visit all the nations of the world.

Who's News

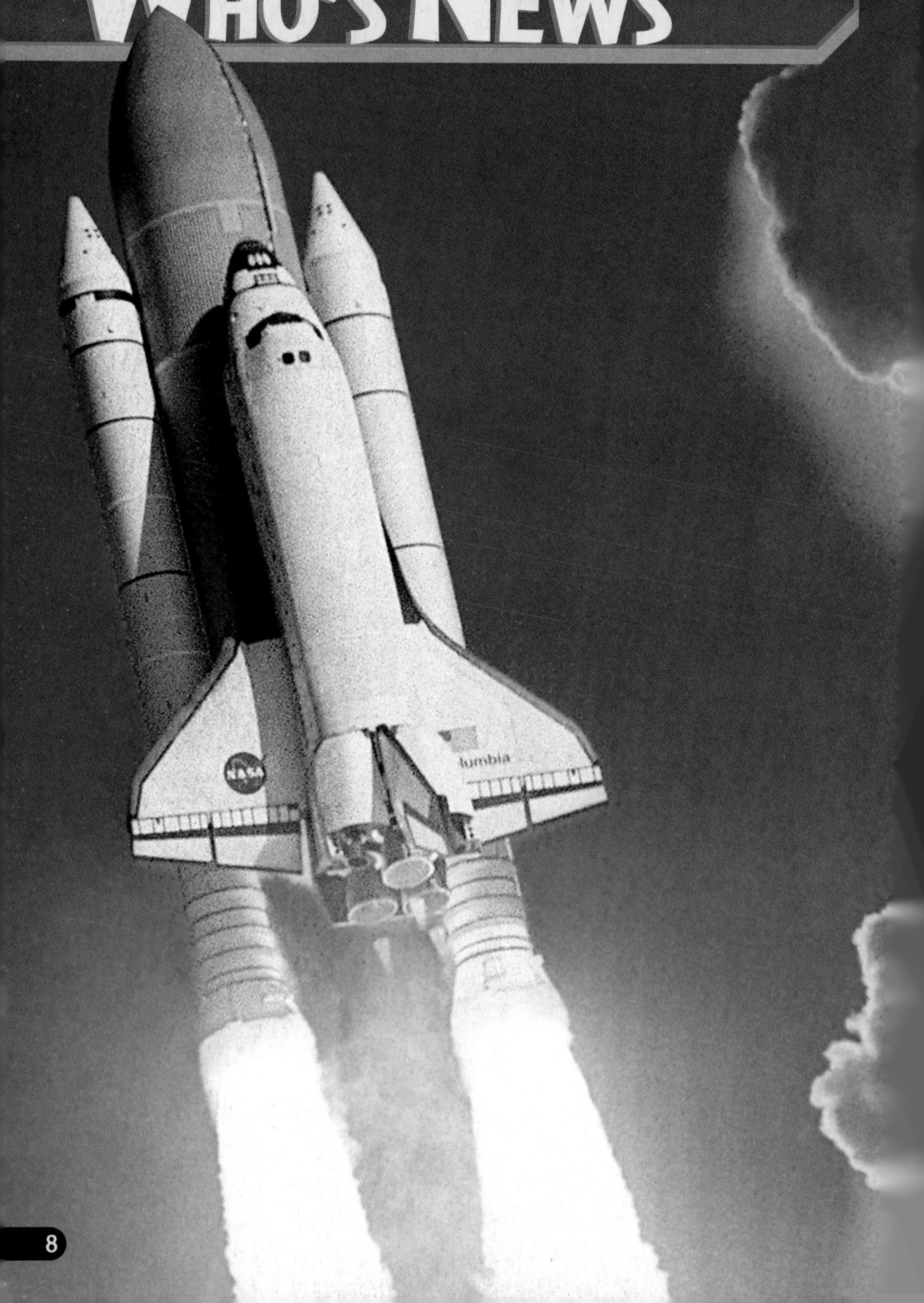

THIN ICE?

ANTARCTIC MELTDOWN?

Is Antarctica melting? Recent events make some scientists think so. The rocky continent at the bottom of the world is covered in ice up to three miles thick. Its ice holds 75% of the Earth's freshwater. If it all melted, global sea levels would rise 200 feet! Some of this ice is beginning to crumble into the sea. Recently, giant icebergs have broken off the Ross Ice Shelf in the southern part of the pole. Some environmentalists worry that this meltdown is a sign that the whole planet is heating up. They blame this global warming on increasing air pollution. Other scientists are saying this melting is nothing to worry about—that it has happened in cycles throughout history. Scientists do agree that Antarctica's ice is a clue to our planet's condition. That's why a NASA satellite called ICEsat is in orbit. It is measuring changes in the ice sheets covering Antarctica and Greenland. More than ever, scientists are keeping their eyes on the ice.

THE "MIRACLE" TWINS

Guatemalan twins **Maria Teresa** and **Maria de Jesus Quiej-Alvarez** didn't face much of a future when they were born in July 2001. They were joined at the head, their skulls fused together. In August 2002, they traveled to California where surgeons performed a risky operation to save the toddlers. A 50-member surgical team worked 22 hours to separate the two sisters. Six months later, the girls were finally well enough to go home. Doctors say their futures looks bright.

A crowd that included Guatemala's First Lady, Evelyn de Portillo, greeted the "Little Marias." One well-wisher told a reporter: "These little girls make all of Guatemala smile."

Seventh Heaven

So this is what perfection looks like! In January 2003, America's Queen of the ice, **Michelle Kwan,** 22, turned in a flawless performance at the U.S. Figure Skating Championships in Dallas, Texas. Fancy footwork earned Kwan her sixth-straight national title and seventh overall. In March, Kwan won the World Figure Skating Championships, which took place in Washington, D.C. It was her fifth world title. Kwan says she hasn't ruled out another run for Olympic gold: "I still feel at my prime. If you love it, why not continue?"

LeBron James

Hoop sensation **LeBron James** is making a big leap! The 18-year-old James is jumping straight from St. Vincent–St. Mary High School (Akron, Ohio) to the NBA. As a senior, the 6 foot, 8-inch, 240-pound James was widely considered the best high school player in the U.S. Scouts say his scoring, rebounding and passing skills make him a can't-miss pro. Is James the first player to skip college for the NBA? No way! All-stars Kobe Bryant (Lower Merion High School; Ardmore, Pennsylvania), Kevin Garnett (Farragut Academy; Chicago, Illinois) and Tracy McGrady (Mount Zion Christian Academy; Durham, North Carolina) all went from high school directly to the pros. Many experts think James has a great "shot" to play at their level.

13

What a Kick!

For soccer lovers, the **World Cup** is the World Series and Super Bowl rolled into one. Held every four years, it determines the best soccer team on the planet. In the men's 2002 World Cup, played in Japan and South Korea, the U.S. team did far better than expected. It advanced to the quarterfinals for the first time since 1930. The U.S. played a strong game against Germany but lost 1-0. The good showing by the U.S. gave American soccer fans hope and other teams something to worry about: Has a sleeping giant awakened?

The Real Deal

Keeping it real is the biggest trend in television. From the *Survivor* series and *Fear Factor* to *The Family*, *Married by America* and *Joe Millionaire,* reality TV seems to be taking over the airwaves. One of the most popular TV reality shows has been *American Idol.* The show gives amateur singers a chance to be heard and judged by millions of viewers. Kelly Clarkson was the winner of the first *American Idol* contest. More than 50,000 people auditioned for the 2003 show. Talk about a noteworthy competition!

WELL, IT'S ABOUT TIME!

The wait was finally over for **Harry Potter** fans. In June 2003, the fifth book in the series finally arrived in bookstores. It is titled *Harry Potter and the Order of the Phoenix.* "I am so excited," said Phillip Weekes, 10, of London, England. The 896-page volume is not only longer than previous books, but the type is also smaller. That didn't stop the book from becoming an immediate best seller. In fact, it went to the top of Amazon.com's best-seller list six months before it was published!

TERRIFIC TOYS

Toymakers from all over the world introduced new products at the 100th International Toy Fair, held in New York City in 2003. Among the hottest toys this year are stackable battle figures called NakNakes and NeoPets, small "pets" that light up and move. Other new fun products include a portable personal video player, super-thin radios and watches that use ultra-flat batteries, a **K'NEX roller coaster** and SpongeBob toys galore.

Beyoncé Knowles

Destiny is calling for Beyoncé Knowles. Only 22 years old, her list of accomplishments keeps growing. The lead singer of **Destiny's Child** co-writes many of its songs and has also co-written songs for movies, including *Scooby-Doo* and *Charlie's Angels*. The Houston-area native made her movie debut as Foxxy Cleopatra in *Austin Powers in Goldmember*. Now she's filming another movie, *The Fighting Temptations*, with Cuba Gooding Jr. As if that weren't enough, in 2003 the diva produced her first solo album, *Dangerously in Love*. It sounds like Beyoncé has a date with destiny!

17

Screen Superheroes

It's
the year of
super movies—
superhero movies, that is. First,
Daredevil hit the silver screens.
Ben Affleck played the sightless masked
avenger fighting injustice. The misunderstood
mutants of *X-Men* have returned in the sequel, *X2*.
Wolverine, Storm and newcomers Mystique and Nightcrawler
show off some amazing powers. The Hulk also explodes from comic books
to the big screen. Cool computer-generated graphics make the Incredible Hulk
look...incredible!

Some of 2003's other grand openings include the Hobbit-forming *The Lord of the Rings: The Return of the King;* there are two sequels (yes, two!) to *The Matrix: Reloaded* and *Revolutions.* A new visual technology called "virtual cinematography" makes viewers forget about the original *Matrix*'s slow-motion effects. Disney's *Pirates of the Caribbean* is another special-effects fest. Based on the popular park ride, it gives audiences a yo-ho-ho good time. Although based on a book, *The Cat in the Hat* is just as much fun as a ride. Mike Myers plays the cat who has a purr-fectly good time making life miserable for two children stuck inside the house on a rainy day.

and Super Effects

Alien Invasion

ver the past 200 years, thousands of foreign plant and animal species have settled in the U.S. Most travel into the country with humans. Some nonnative species were brought here on purpose. Others slipped in accidentally with cargo on boats or planes.

Some of these nonnative species have become invasive. This means that their introduction has caused environmental, economic or health problems in our country. The Asian long-horned beetle turned up in Brooklyn, New York, six years ago and has

The northern snakehead can reach a length of three feet and weigh more than 15 pounds.

since traveled to Chicago, Illinois. The wood-chomping beetles have killed thousands of healthy trees.

Many foreign species have no natural enemies in their new environment. This allows them to spread rapidly and threaten the survival of native species. "In eastern Africa, the [invasive] Nile perch has caused the extinction of 300 species of fish," says Guy McPherson, an ecologist at the University of Arizona. In 2002, the northern snakehead from Southeast Asia turned up in a lake in Maryland. Scientists feared that the snakehead, which can flop from pond to pond across small pieces of land, would have a similar effect on U.S. waterways.

No one wants to keep out all foreign species. Many scientists are saying we should be more practical. Instead of trying to wipe out all foreign species, we should figure out which new creatures are desirable and which are undesirable.

Most nonnative species are harmless. Some are even beneficial to the environment. The European honeybee, for example, is important in agriculture. It provides pollination for valuable crops.

Plants and animals do have a special place in their original environments. "Native species have a role in the ecosystem that they evolved into," says researcher Faith Campbell. "There's a balance."

The U.S. and other countries around the world are doing what they can to preserve this balance. Most wildlife officials agree that we may not be able to stop the invasions. But we can work to protect healthy native species from harmful foreign ones.

By Kathryn R. Hoffman

America's Most Unwanted

FROM **TFK** MAGAZINE

Researchers say that humans have brought about 50,000 foreign species into the U.S. Here is a look at some of our uninvited guests.

ZEBRA MUSSEL

This invader from Eastern Europe has caused problems in the Great Lakes for years. Now, zebra mussels are threatening waterways in northern Virginia. They upset the food chain in lakes and damage the pipes of power plants and water systems.

NUTRIA

This rodent was brought here from South America for the fur trade. By digging and gnawing at grasses, it has ruined 100,000 acres of marshland in Louisiana and 8,000 acres in Maryland.

ASIAN LONG-HORNED BEETLE

These pests came to the U.S. from China—where they're also a problem. Most beetles only munch on dead or dying trees, but these bugs prefer healthy wood!

COQUI

This frog is beloved in Puerto Rico but is seen as an annoying pest in Hawaii. The noisy coquis (ko-kees) compete with the islands' rare birds for food and eat insects that pollinate flowers.

CARP

The Mississippi River is teeming with several kinds of carp from Asia. They compete with native fish for food and threaten the fishing industry. Some leap into boats and hit boaters on the head!

Reptiles are cold-blooded.

ANIMAL GROUPS

Almost all animals belong to one of two groups, **vertebrates** or **invertebrates**. Adult vertebrates have a spinal column, or backbone, running the length of their bodies; invertebrates do not. Vertebrates are often larger and have more complex bodies than invertebrates. However, there are many more invertebrates than vertebrates.

VERTEBRATES

Reptiles are cold-blooded and breathe with lungs. They have scales, and most lay eggs. Reptiles include turtles and tortoises, crocodiles and alligators, snakes and lizards.

Fish breathe through gills and live in water; most are cold-blooded and lay eggs (although sharks give birth to live young).

Amphibians are cold-blooded and live both on land (breathing with lungs) and in water (breathing through gills) at different times. Three types of amphibians are frogs and toads, salamanders and caecilians. Caecilians are primitive amphibians that resemble earthworms. They are found in the tropics.

Frogs are amphibians.

Dinosaurs were reptiles, although some scientists believe that some dinosaurs were warm-blooded.

Birds are warm-blooded animals with feathers and wings. They lay eggs, and most birds can fly. Some, including penguins and ostriches, cannot fly.

Mammals are warm-blooded and are nourished by their mothers' milk. Most are born live, but the platypus and echidna are hatched from eggs. Most mammals also have body hair.

Platypuses are mammals.

INVERTEBRATES

Sponges are the most primitive of animal groups. They live in water, are sessile (do not move from place to place) and filter tiny organisms out of the water for food.

Echinoderms, including starfish, sea urchins and sea cucumbers, live in seawater and have external skeletons.

Worms come in many varieties and live in all sorts of habitats—from the bottom of the ocean to the inside of other animals. They include flatworms (flukes), roundworms (hookworms), segmented worms (earthworms) and rotifers (philodina).

Mollusks are soft-bodied animals, some of which live in hard shells. They include snails, slugs, octopuses, squid, mussels, oysters, clams, scallops and cuttlefish.

Arthropods are the largest and most diverse of all animal groups. They have segmented bodies supported by a hard external skeleton (or exoskeleton). Arthropods include insects, arachnids (spiders and their relatives) and crustaceans (such as shrimp and lobster).

Coelenterates are also very primitive. Their mouths, which take in food and get rid of waste, are surrounded by stinging tentacles. Some coelenterates are jellyfish, corals and sea anemones.

The oyster is a mollusk.

Sea anemones do not have backbones.

Warm-blooded and Cold-blooded Animals

Warm-blooded animals regulate their own body temperatures; their bodies use energy to maintain a constant temperature. Cold-blooded animals depend on their surroundings to establish their body temperatures.

Snakes are cold-blooded.

Extinct, Endangered and Threatened Species

Many species of animals are disappearing from our planet. **Extinct** means that the entire species has died out and can never return. **Endangered** animals are those in immediate danger of becoming extinct. **Threatened** species are likely to become endangered in the future.

Humans are largely responsible when animals become extinct, endangered or threatened. Here are some of the things that can lead animals to become endangered.

Destruction of Habitat

Humans destroy precious habitat—the natural environment of a living thing—when they fill swamps and marshes, dam rivers and cut down trees to build homes, roads and other developments.

Pollution

Oil spills, acid rain and water pollution have been devastating for many species of fish and birds.

Hunting and Fishing

Many animals are over-hunted because their meat, fur and other parts are very valuable.

Introduction of Exotic Species

When animals or plants arrive into a new habitat from a foreign place, they sometimes introduce diseases that the native species can't fight. "Exotic" species can prey on the native species, and often have no natural enemies.

mountain gorilla

coho salmon

northern spotted owl

California condor

There are 1,072 endangered and threatened species of animals in the world. The list includes:

- 342 species of mammals, such as the red wolf, the right whale and the mountain gorilla

- 273 species of birds, such as the California condor, the whooping crane and the northern spotted owl

- 126 species of fish, such as coho salmon

- 115 species of reptiles, such as the green sea turtle

whooping crane

Source: U.S. Fish and Wildlife Service

red wolf

Classifying Animals

There are billions of different kinds of living things (organisms) on Earth. To help study them, biologists have created ways of naming and classifying them according to their similarities and differences. The system most scientists use puts each living thing into seven groups, organized from most general to most specific. Therefore, each kingdom is composed of phylums, each phylum is composed of classes, each class is composed of orders, and so on.

From largest to smallest, the groups are:

Kingdoms are huge groups, with millions of kinds of organisms in each. All animals are in one kingdom (called Kingdom Animalia); all plants are in another (Kingdom Plantae). It is generally agreed that there are five kingdoms: Animalia, Plantae, Fungi, Prokarya (bacteria) and Protoctista (organisms that don't fit into the four other kingdoms, including many microscopic creatures).

Species are the smallest groups. In the animal kingdom, a species consists of all the animals of a type who are able to breed and produce young of the same kind.

Kingdom
Phylum
Class
Order
Family
Genus
Species

TIP

To remember the order for classification, keep this silly sentence in mind: **King Philip came over for good soup.**

A Sample Classification:

The Gray Wolf

Kingdom: Animalia includes all animals

Phylum: Chordata includes all vertebrate, or backboned, animals

Class: Mammalia includes all mammals

Order: Carnivora includes all carnivorous, or meat-eating, mammals

Family: Canidae includes all dogs

Genus: Canis includes dogs, foxes and jackals

Species: lupus the gray wolf

Animal Names: Male, Female and Young

ANIMAL	MALE	FEMALE	YOUNG
Bear	Boar	Sow	Cub
Cat	Tom	Queen	Kitten
Cattle	Bull	Cow	Calf
Chicken	Rooster	Hen	Chick
Deer	Buck	Doe	Fawn
Dog	Dog	Bitch	Pup
Duck	Drake	Duck	Duckling
Elephant	Bull	Cow	Calf
Fox	Dog	Vixen	Cub
Goose	Gander	Goose	Gosling
Horse	Stallion	Mare	Foal
Lion	Lion	Lioness	Cub
Pig	Boar	Sow	Piglet
Sheep	Ram	Ewe	Lamb
Swan	Cob	Pen	Cygnet

Did You Know?

Many animals can regenerate—that is, grow new parts of their bodies to replace those that have been damaged. Lizards, planarians (flatworms), sea cucumbers, sponges and starfish are a few of these amazing creatures.

A herd of elephants

GAGGLES, CLUTTERS, PRIDES AND OTHER ANIMAL GROUP NAMES

Ants: colony
Bears: sleuth, sloth
Cats: clutter, clowder
Cattle: drove
Crows: murder
Ducks: brace, team
Elephants: herd
Elk: gang
Fish: school, shoal, draught
Foxes: leash, skulk
Geese: flock, gaggle, skein

Goats: trip
Gorillas: band
Hens: brood
Horses: pair, team
Hounds: cry, mute, pack
Kangaroos: troop
Kittens: kindle, litter
Lions: pride
Oxen: yoke
Oysters: bed
Parrots: company

Pigs: litter
Ponies: string
Rabbits: nest
Seals: pod
Sheep: drove, flock
Swans: bevy, wedge
Toads: knot
Turtles: bale

Source: James G. Doherty, general curator, The Wildlife Conservation Society

For more types of animal names, www.FACTMONSTER.COM

Talk Like a Zoologist

Although these words sound scientific, they are commonly used to describe animal families or behavior.

- **Marsupials** are families of mammals, such as kangaroos and opossums, whose females carry their young in an external pouch.

- **Monotremes** are the rare mammals (the platypus and the echidna) that lay eggs.

- **Nocturnal** animals, like owls, are active at night.

- **Diurnal** animals, like squirrels, are awake during the day.

- **Pinnipeds** are aquatic mammals, such as seals and walruses, with flippers.

- **Quadrupeds**, like cows, are animals with four feet.

- **Bipeds**, such as humans and gorillas, walk upright on two legs.

- **Primates** include humans and their closest relatives. They share flexible arms and legs, agile fingers and relatively big brains.

- **Cetaceans** are ocean mammals, including whales and dolphins.

- **Rodents**, like squirrels, have large front teeth for gnawing and cheek teeth for chewing.

- **Arachnids**, such as spiders, scorpions, mites and ticks, are arthropods.

Kangaroos are marsupials.

Cows are quadrupeds.

Spiders are arachnids.

Seals are pinnipeds.

Zoo Websites

Would you like to see amazing pictures or catch up on animal news? Through the American Zoo and Aquarium Association website, you can visit hundreds of zoos and aquariums online!

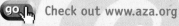

go Check out www.aza.org

The Big Sleep
Hibernation and Estivation

When weather conditions get tough, some animals pack up and head for better climates. Others dig in and wait for things to get better. To protect themselves, they may go into a state of inactivity called hibernation (in cold climates) or estivation (in hot climates).

When an animal goes into a state of inactivity, body processes like breathing and heartbeat slow down greatly, allowing the animal to conserve energy and go without food or water for long periods of time. Animals do not grow when they hibernate or estivate.

Woodchucks, chipmunks, groundhogs, skunks and some bears hibernate. Many amphibians and reptiles and some insects, snails and fish estivate.

Amazing Animal Facts

A chameleon can move its eyes in two different directions at the same time.

Dolphins sleep at night just below the surface of the water. They frequently rise to the surface for air.

A cockroach can live for up to a week without its head.

An albatross can sleep while flying. It can catch some shut-eye cruising at 25 miles an hour.

Amazon ants (red ants found in the western U.S.) steal the larvae of other ants to keep as slaves. The slave ants build homes for and feed the Amazon ants, who don't do anything but fight. They depend completely on their slaves for survival.

The hummingbird is the only bird that can hover and fly straight up, down or backward!

A leech is a worm that feeds on blood. It will pierce its victim's skin, fill itself with three to four times its own body weight in blood and not feed again for months.

Lovebirds are small parakeets who live in pairs. Male and female lovebirds look alike, but most other male birds have brighter colors than the females.

Only female mosquitoes bite. Females need the protein from blood to produce their eggs.

A slug has four noses.

Despite its long neck, the giraffe has only seven neck bones— the same number as a person.

Woodpeckers' heads are filled with pockets of air that cushion their head bones as they drill for food

TFK TOP 5 LONGEST-LIVING ANIMALS

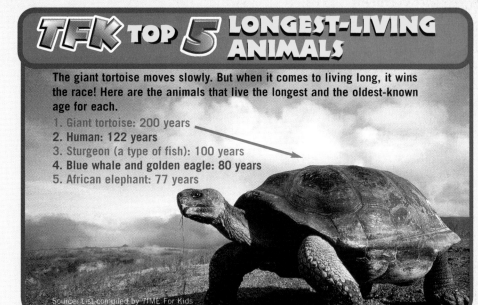

The giant tortoise moves slowly. But when it comes to living long, it wins the race! Here are the animals that live the longest and the oldest-known age for each.

1. Giant tortoise: 200 years
2. Human: 122 years
3. Sturgeon (a type of fish): 100 years
4. Blue whale and golden eagle: 80 years
5. African elephant: 77 years

Source: List compiled by TIME For Kids

Calling All Animal Scientists

A person who specializes in the study of animals is called a zoologist. Zoologists who study certain kinds of animals have their own names.

Anthropologists study human beings.

Entomologists study insects.

Herpetologists study reptiles and amphibians.

Ichthyologists specialize in fish.

Malacologists study mollusks, such as snails and clams.

Mammalogists specialize in mammals.

Nematologists study roundworms.

Ornithologists study birds.

Ethologists study animal behavior.

Animal Gestation & Longevity

Here's a look at the average gestation (the time an animal spends inside its mother) and longevity (life span) of certain animals.

Animal	Gestation (days)	Longevity (years)
Cat	52-69	10-12
Cow	280	9-12
Dog	53-71	10-12
Guinea pig	58-75	3
Hamster	15-17	2
Hippopotamus	220-255	30
Horse	329-345	20-25
Kangaroo	32-39	4-6
Lion	105-113	10
Parakeet	17-20	8
Rabbit	30-35	6-8
Wolf	60-63	10-12

Source: James G. Doherty, general curator, The Wildlife Conservation Society.

CARBON COPIES

The cloning craze began in 1996, when scientists in Scotland astonished the world by announcing that they had successfully cloned an adult sheep. They called her clone Dolly.

A clone is a copy of another living thing. Instead of having two sets of genes, from a mother and a father, a clone has genes from just one parent. Genes are the instructions inside cells that determine the traits of a living thing. All non-cloned, naturally created mammals, including humans, have genes from two parents.

Scientists hope that animal cloning will someday save lives. Cloned pigs could provide organs to transplant into humans. Cow clones could be used to make life-saving medicines. In addition, cloning may help to preserve some of the world's fastest-disappearing species.

Here are some other animals that have been created in a laboratory.

● In 1997, not long after Dolly was born, scientists in Oregon announced that they had cloned a pair of rhesus monkeys, named Neti and Ditto. The monkeys were created from DNA taken from cells of developing monkey embryos.

● Scientists in Blacksburg, Virginia, cloned five piglets from an adult pig in 2000. They dubbed the newborns Millie, Christa, Alexis, Carrel and Dotcom.

● Also in 2000, Japanese scientists cloned a baby bull from a bull that was a clone itself. It was the first time a large mammal was re-cloned.

● In 2001, scientists in Italy produced the first surviving clone of a baby mouflon—an endangered wild sheep found in Corsica and in Cyprus.

● In February 2002, Texas scientists introduced the world's first cloned cat. They named her "cc," short for carbon copy.

Dolly is a genetic copy of an adult sheep.

Fish Facts

How many fish species are there?

An estimated 20,000 species exist. But there may be as many as 20,000 more.

What is the world's largest fish?

The largest fish is the whale shark, which grows to more than 50 feet in length and may weigh several tons.

What is the smallest fish?

The smallest fish is the **tiny goby,** an inhabitant of fresh-to-brackish waters in Luzon, Philippines. It grows to only a half inch at adulthood.

How long do fish live?

Some fish live just a few weeks or months (some of the small reef fishes); others live up to 100 years (sturgeons). Scientists have learned that in temperate (moderately warm) waters, there are many species that live 10 to 20 years.

Do some fish give birth to living young instead of laying eggs?

Yes, many do. These are called viviparous fishes. The sea perches of the Pacific Coast, for example, give birth to living young of considerable size. Several kinds of sharks produce living young.

Do fish breathe air?

Yes, but not directly into the lungs as mammals do. Actually, fish breathe oxygen, not air. As water passes over a system of extremely fine gill membranes, fish absorb the water's oxygen content.

Do sharks prey on people?

Sharks rarely pose a danger to humans. But humans are a risk to sharks! Fishermen kill millions of sharks every year. About 75 shark species are in danger of becoming extinct. Often, when an attack on a human occurs, the shark has mistaken the human for a fish. A human is too bony to be a good meal for a shark.

How many shark attacks have occurred in the U.S.?

According to the International Shark Attack File, there have been a total of 855 shark attacks in the U.S. That's not many, considering that tens of thousands of people come in close contact with sharks each year while swimming, surfing or boating.

MYSTERY PERSON

CLUE 1: I was born in England in 1820. At an early age, I was concerned about how poorly horses were treated in my country.

CLUE 2: My only book, *Black Beauty*, became a children's classic.

CLUE 3: Published in 1877, it is the moving tale of a horse's life told from the horse's point of view. The book made people aware of the mistreatment of animals.

WHO AM I?

(See Answer Key that begins on page 340.)

The Color Wheel

A color wheel shows how colors are related.

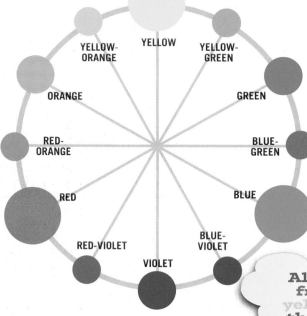

Red, yellow and **blue** are the **primary** colors. Primary colors are the most basic colors. You can't make them by mixing any other colors.

Orange, green and **violet** are the **secondary** colors. A secondary color is made by mixing two primary colors. For instance, if you mix red and yellow, you get orange. That is why orange is between red and yellow on the color wheel.

What goes between primary and secondary colors? **Intermediate**, or tertiary, colors are made by mixing a primary color and a secondary color. **Red-orange, yellow-orange** and **yellow-green** are some intermediate colors.

All those colors from just red, yellow and blue— that's awesome!

Values

The lightness or darkness of a color is called its **value**. You can find the values of a color by making its tints and shades.
- **Tints** are light values that are made by mixing a color with white. Pink is a tint of red.
- **Shades** are dark values that are made by mixing a color with black. Maroon is a shade of red.

Try It Yourself!

Making a color wheel is a good way to understand how colors work. Start with red, yellow and blue paint. Then, mix the secondary and intermediate colors. Finally, you can make tints and shades by mixing black and white with the colors you've made.

go → For more on colors, www.FactMonster.com

The World of Art

A **mosaic** is a picture or design made by gluing together small stones, pieces of glass or other hard materials. In ancient times, grand homes sometimes had mosaic floors.

From prehistoric cave paintings to graffiti art today, **painting** has always been a part of human life. Some of the world's best-known artists, such as Michelangelo and Picasso, were painters.

Photography was invented almost 200 years ago. We see photographs every day in newspapers and magazines, on billboards and buses, and in museums and galleries. Ansel Adams and Mathew Brady were famous photographers.

For thousands of years, people all over the world have made **masks** to use in rituals, work, theater and just for fun. Have you ever made a mask from a paper bag?

Drawing is everywhere—in newspapers, books, posters and more. It is an art by itself, but it is also the starting point for other arts, such as painting or sculpture.

In prehistoric times, people wore **jewelry** even before they wore clothing. Jewelry has been created using everything from berries to gold.

People have made **sculpture** from materials such as clay, marble, ice, wood and bronze. Some artists today create sculptures that move with the wind. Alberto Giacometti and Louise Nevelson were important sculptors.

There are as many uses for **baskets** as there are ways to make them. Archaeologists have found 7,000-year-old farming baskets in Egypt.

People have been **weaving** since the Stone Age. Tapestries and rugs in every color have brought warmth and beauty to walls and floors.

As technology changes, the tools artists use change too. **New media** includes video, performance, computer imagery and installation (where an entire room may be made into a work of art).

Figure, a 1939 painting by Pablo Picasso

This mask was carved by the Kaigani Haidi, a Native American tribe from the Pacific Northwest.

Louise Nevelson created this artwork called *Abstract Sculpture.*

Major Types of PAINTING

How many of these types of paintings have you tried? Some paintings combine types. For example, a portrait might also include details of a still life.

A **landscape** is an outdoor scene. An artist can paint land, water, clouds, air and sunlight.

A **portrait** is an image of a person or an animal. Besides showing what someone looks like, a portrait often captures a mood or personality.

A **real life** scene captures life in action. It could show anyplace where living goes on.

A **religious work of art** shares a religious message.

A **still life** shows objects. It reveals an artist's skill in painting shapes, light and shadow.

TFK TOP 5 FAVORITE CRAYOLA CRAYON COLORS

When Crayola introduced its crayons in 1903, there were just eight colors in the box. Now there are more than 100 colors, so they come in a much bigger box!

1. BLUE
2. PURPLE HEART
3. CERULEAN
4. BLIZZARD BLUE
5. HOT MAGENTA

Source: Crayola Color Census 2000

Abstract Expressionism

A style developed in the mid-20th century, abstract expressionism emphasized form and color rather than an actual subject. Jackson Pollock and **Willem de Kooning** were abstract expressionists.

Baroque

A form of art and architecture that was popular in Europe in the 17th and early 18th centuries, baroque art was very ornate, dramatic and realistic. The Palace of Versailles near Paris is considered the greatest example of baroque architecture. Peter Paul Rubens and **Rembrandt** were baroque painters.

Cubism

Cubism stressed basic abstract geometric forms and often presented the subject from many angles at the same time. Pablo Picasso was a cubist painter.

Impressionism

Impressionism developed in France during the late 19th century. The impressionists tried to capture an immediate visual interpretation of their subjects by using color rather than lines. Claude Monet and **Pierre Auguste Renoir** were impressionist painters.

Pop Art

THE MELODY HAUNTS MY REVERIE.

Pop art emerged in England and the U.S. after 1950. Pop artists use materials from the everyday world of popular culture, such as comic strips, canned goods and science fiction. Andy Warhol and **Roy Lichtenstein** were pop artists.

Romanticism

Romanticism was popular in the early 19th century. Romantic artists produced exotic, emotional works that portrayed an idealized world and nostalgia for the past. William Blake was a member of the romantic school of painters.

TFK MYSTERY PERSON

CLUE 1: I was born in 1912. I grew up in Hollywood and became a fan of movie comedies. I also loved to draw.
CLUE 2: I am an award-winning animator and was part of the loony art team that gave life to Bugs Bunny, Daffy Duck and friends.
CLUE 3: I created the original drawings of Wile E. Coyote and Road Runner and worked on hundreds of animated films, including the original *How the Grinch Stole Christmas*.

WHO AM I?

(See Answer Key that begins on page 340.)

BOOKS

Book Awards

The **Caldecott Medal** honors an outstanding American picture book.

2003 winner: *My Friend Rabbit,* **Eric Rohmann, writer and illustrator**

The **Newbery Medal** honors an outstanding example of children's literature. The Newbery winner is not a picture book.

2003 winner: *Crispin: The Cross of Lead,* **Avi**

The **Coretta Scott King Awards** recognize black authors and illustrators whose works have promoted an understanding and appreciation of all cultures.

2003 winners:
Writer: Nikki Grimes, *Bronx Masquerade*
Illustrator: E.B. Lewis, *Talkin' About Bessie: The Story of Aviator Elizabeth Coleman*

- **2002 National Book Award for Young People's Literature** *The House of the Scorpion,* **Nancy Farmer**

- **2002 Boston Globe Horn Book Award**

- Fiction and Poetry *Lord of the Deep,* **Graham Salisbury**

- Nonfiction *This Land Was Made for You and Me,* **Elizabeth Partridge**

- Picture Book *"Let's Get a Pup!" Said Kate,* **Bob Graham, writer and illustrator**

TFK TOP 5 BEST-SELLING CHILDREN'S BOOKS

The Poky Puppy may not be fast, but sales of the book have been brisk for years. It's the best-selling hardcover children's book of all time! Here's a list of books that have been trying to catch up to it.

Title	Copies sold
1. *The Poky Little Puppy* (1942)	14,898,341
2. *The Tale of Peter Rabbit* (1902)	9,380,274
3. *Tootle* (1945)	8,560,277
4. *Green Eggs and Ham* (1960)	8,143,088
5. *Harry Potter and the Goblet of Fire* (2000)	7,913,765

Source: *Publisher's Weekly,* through the end of 2001

Top Titles of
2002

Don't know what to read while you wait for the next installment in the Harry Potter series? Check out these highly acclaimed books.

Abarat
by Clive Barker
After a difficult day at school, Candy Quackenbush wanders into a field where she is transported to Abarat, a magical world of 25 islands.

Action Jackson
by Jan Greenberg and Sandra Jordan
"Action painter" Jackson Pollock splattered, dribbled and swirled paint around on his canvases. Follow the painter as he creates a new masterpiece, *Number 1, 1950*, also called *Lavender Mist*.

Coraline
by Neil Gaiman
A girl unlocks a door in her home and finds herself in a creepy alternate universe that eerily parallels her own life.

Fields of Fury: The American Civil War
by James M. McPherson
McPherson uses photographs, illustrations, newspaper articles and maps to explain the major battles and important figures in the biggest war fought on U.S. soil.

The Frogs Wore Red Suspenders
by Jack Prelutsky
Playful and prolific poet Prelutsky offers 28 poems linked by the common theme of U.S. geography.

A House Called Awful End, Vol. 1
by Philip Ardagh
Outrageous adventures abound when 11-year-old Eddie moves in with his Mad Uncle Jack and Mad Aunt Maud after his parents get sick and turn yellow.

Hush
by Jacqueline Woodson
A 12-year-old girl must create a new life when her family enters the witness-protection program after her father testifies against two fellow police officers.

Stand Tall
by Joan Bauer
Twelve-year-old Tree stands 6 feet, 3 inches tall—and he's still growing. But his height is the least of his problems when his parents get divorced.

Summerland
by Michael Chabon
A mystical baseball scout recruits an 11-year-old boy to save the world from an evil schemer named Coyote.

The Thief Lord
by Cornelia Funke
Two trouble-prone boys escape to Venice, Italy, and find themselves entangled with the Thief Lord, a boy who steals from the rich to buy clothes for his poor friends.

go For more Harry Potter fun, go to www.FACTMONSTER.COM

Types of Literature

Here are some examples of kinds of fiction (made-up stories) and nonfiction (books about real-life events and people).

An **autobiography** is the story of a person's life written or told by that person.
Example: *Bill Peet: An Autobiography*

A **biography** is the story of a person's life written or told by another person.
Example: *Eleanor,* by Barbara Cooney

A **fable** is a story that teaches a moral or a lesson. It often has animal characters.
Example: "The Tortoise and the Hare"

A **folktale** is a story that has been passed down, usually orally, within a culture. It may be based on superstition and feature supernatural characters. Folktales include fairy tales, tall tales, trickster tales and other stories passed down over generations.
Example: "Hansel and Gretel"

A **legend** is a story that has been handed down over generations and is believed to be based on history, though it typically mixes fact and fiction. The hero of a legend is usually a human.
Example: King Arthur and the Roundtable

A **myth** is a traditional story that a particular culture or group once accepted as sacred and true. It may center on a god or supernatural being and explain how something came to be, such as lightning or music or the world itself.
Example: The Greek story of the Titan Prometheus bringing fire to humankind

Did You Know?

Most of the European fairy tales that delight readers today were collected and written down by Wilhelm and Jakob Grimm in the early 1800s.

He PICTURED a New Museum

For many years, toddlers around the world have curled up at bedtime with *The Very Hungry Caterpillar.* Eric Carle's popular picture book has sold more than 12 million copies! The caterpillar, the grouchy ladybug and other Carle creatures have a new home. The Eric Carle Museum of Picture Book Art opened in November 2002 in Amherst, Massachusetts. Art by Maurice Sendak and Leo Lionni were on display in its first year. "It's a place of learning and enjoyment," says Carle, 73.

Awesome Animal Books

Since the days of Aesop's fables, animal stories have brought readers closer to the animal kingdom while pointing up truths about the human world.

Arabel's Raven by Joan Aiken
Always hungry and often cranky, Arabel's pet raven Mortimer brings endless trouble.

Babe the Gallant Pig by Dick King-Smith
Yes, it's that Babe—the movie star—as he first appeared, in this wacky British novel.

Capyboppy by Bill Peet
In this true story, a giant rodent takes over a family's home—and pool.

Charlotte's Web by E.B. White
What would happen if a clever spider could weave not only webs, but words?

The Cricket in Times Square by George Selden
Street-smart Tucker Mouse and Harry Cat befriend a musical country cricket.

Fantastic Mr. Fox by Roald Dahl
Mr. Fox creates an underground world with splendid feasts.

Julie of the Wolves by Jean Craighead George
On a lengthy solo journey, an Eskimo girl is accepted by a pack of wolves.

Misty of Chincoteague by Marguerite Henry
This classic portrays real events on Chincoteague Island, where wild horses swim.

Mrs. Frisby and the Rats of NIMH by Robert C. O'Brien
A field mouse encounters a colony of lab rats with humanlike intelligence.

The Wind in the Willows by Kenneth Grahame
Mole leaves hibernation for adventures with brave Rat, shy Badger and impossible Toad.

Books Inside and Out

Inside

Leaves: Each sheet of paper is a leaf.

Pages: Each side of a leaf is a page.

Front matter: The pages before the main text, including the title page

Title page: The page at the beginning of a book. It lists the title, the author's or editor's name and the publication and copyright information.

Text: The main part, or core, of a book

Back matter: The pages following the text, including the index

Endpapers: The pages between the cover and body of a book. They may be plain, colored or printed, such as with a map.

Outside

Dust jacket: The paper cover

Cover or case: The outside binding

Spine: The narrow "backbone" of the book. It's the part you see if the book is standing or lying in a bookshelf.

Reference Books: You Could Look It Up

Atlas
A book of maps with or without text
Example: *Rand McNally Atlas of the Earth's Resources*

Biographical Index
A book of information about people who are well known in a particular field
Example: *Who's Who*

Dictionary
Definitions, spellings and pronunciations of words, arranged in alphabetical order
Example: *The American Heritage Dictionary*

Encyclopedia
Information on just about every subject arranged in alphabetical order
Example: *Encyclopædia Britannica*

Guidebook
Information and directions, often for travelers
Example: *Let's Go Europe*

Thesaurus
Synonyms, or near synonyms, for words as well as related terms
Example: *Roget's Thesaurus*

Yearbook/Almanac
Current information on a wide range of topics. You're reading one now.

TFK PUZZLES & GAMES

Harry and Hogwarts

How well do you know Harry and his Hogwarts chums?

1. What subject does Professor McGonagall teach?
   a. Transfiguration
   b. History of Magic
   c. Defense Against the Dark Arts

2. What was the first name of Hufflepuff's founder?
   a. Hilda
   b. Helen
   c. Helga

3. To which house at Hogwarts did Harry's father belong?
   a. Hufflepuff
   b. Gryffindor
   c. Slytherin

4. How did Harry get to Diagon Alley after he fled the Dursleys?
   a. He took the Knight Bus
   b. He was driven by car
   c. He walked

5. Who sent Harry the firebolt?
   a. Professor McGonagall
   b. Profesor Dumbledore
   c. Sirius Black

6. Which Hogwarts professor was once a death eater?
   a. Trelawney
   b. Snape
   c. McGonagall

(See Answer Key that begins on page 340.)

TFK SPOTLIGHT

Strange new worlds!

Have you ever heard of a train traveling to the North Pole? Or rhinos charging through a living room? If so, then you're already a fan of Chris Van Allsburg, the author and illustrator of *The Polar Express* and *Jumanji*. "I like writing stories about strange things happening in the everyday world," says Van Allsburg. His new book, *Zathura*, takes readers out of this world! In *Zathura*, two brothers play a game that sweeps their house into outer space. "If you have an active imagination," he said, "the world is a much more interesting place!"

ZATHURA
BY CHRIS VAN ALLSBURG

TFK MYSTERY PERSON

CLUE 1: I was born in 1898 in Ireland. I fought in World War I when I was 19 years old.

CLUE 2: When I returned home from the war, I became very interested in writing. I published many essays and became an expert on literature.

CLUE 3: I later became famous for writing a series of books, including *The Lion, the Witch and the Wardrobe*, about an imaginary land called Narnia.

WHO AM I?

(See Answer Key that begins on page 340.)

FROM **TFK** MAGAZINE

Keeper of the Flame

Charlie DeLeo helps Lady Liberty shine bright!

By Laura C. Girardi

T he Statue of Liberty has welcomed immigrants to America since October 28, 1886. Its torchlights have safely guided boats into New York Harbor and proudly declared the freedom our nation has to offer. Charlie DeLeo has helped Lady Liberty light the way for newcomers for more than 30 years. The native New Yorker has been changing the nearly 800 lights that illuminate the statue and Liberty Island, where the 152-foot-tall statue stands.

DeLeo has made about 2,500 trips to the top of the statue's flame, both the original glass-and-copper one and the current golden flame that replaced it in 1986. He replaces burned-out lights and removes bird droppings from its tippy top! DeLeo used to climb and vacuum skinny iron girders inside the statue.

DeLeo was never afraid to go out on a limb for the statue. "I wanted to give something back to this beautiful lady, whom I love so much," he says. Although he was shocked while out on the torch during a thunderstorm and twice fell several feet from the girders, DeLeo has managed to avoid major injury at work. He appears in an upcoming film about his life, *Charlie DeLeo, Keeper of the Flame*.

Architects and Their Masterpieces

An architect designs homes, libraries, museums and other structures and environments. Here are some famous modern architects and their signature creations.

● **R. Buckminster Fuller** (1895–1983) An engineer and a poet, Fuller was known for his revolutionary designs that were both innovative and efficient. He developed the Dymaxion principle, which called for using the least possible amount of material and energy in construction and manufacturing. His most famous creation was the geodesic dome.

● **Frank Gehry** (b. 1929) Many of Gehry's designs are oddly shaped and made from a variety of materials, such as corrugated metal and chain-link fencing. His best-known project is the Guggenheim Museum in Bilbao, Spain.

The words of Martin Luther King Jr., are etched on the Civil Rights Memorial.

...UNTIL JUSTICE AND RIGHTEOU...

● **Michael Graves** (b. 1934) Graves is known for his postmodernist, often colorful projects. Postmodernism is a playful style of art and architecture that was developed after 1970. He also designs furniture and home accessories. Graves designed the Walt Disney Company headquarters in Burbank, California.

● **Maya Lin** (b. 1959) Lin earned fame when, as a student at Yale, she won a contest to design the Vietnam Veterans Memorial in Washington, D.C. She also designed the **Civil Rights Memorial** in Montgomery, Alabama.

● **I.M. Pei** (b. 1917) Born in China and educated in the U.S., Pei has designed landmarks all over the world. He often incorporates marble, concrete and glass into his geometrically precise designs. Among his most famous designs are the **Rock-and-Roll Hall of Fame and Museum** in Cleveland, Ohio, the expansion of the Louvre in Paris and the John F. Kennedy Library in Boston, Massachusetts.

● **Frank Lloyd Wright** (1869-1959) Wright is widely considered the greatest American architect. He developed the Prairie style of architecture in Chicago. The Prairie style features low horizontal lines, earth tones and protruding overhangs. Although he mostly designed homes and furniture, Wright also designed the Oak Park Unity Temple near Chicago and the Larkin Office Building in Buffalo, New York.

The Rock-and-Roll Hall of Fame and Museum is a magnet for music lovers.

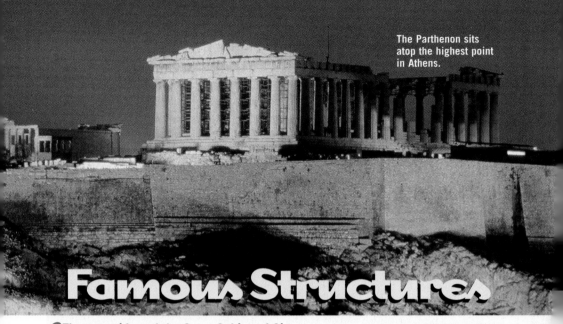

The Parthenon sits atop the highest point in Athens.

Famous Structures

●**The pyramids and the Great Sphinx of Giza,** near Cairo, are some of the wonders of ancient Egyptian architecture.

●**The Parthenon of Greece,** built on the Acropolis in Athens, was the chief temple to the goddess Athena. It is believed to have been completed by 438 B.C.

●**The Colosseum of Rome,** the largest and most famous of the Roman amphitheaters, was opened for use in A.D. 80.

●**The Pantheon** at Rome was begun in 27 B.C. It has served for 20 centuries as a place of worship.

●**The Tower of London** is a group of buildings covering 13 acres. The central White Tower was begun in 1078.

●**The Vatican** is a group of buildings in Rome that includes the residence of the Pope. The Basilica of St. Peter, the largest church in the Christian world, was begun in 1450.

●**The Eiffel Tower** in Paris was built in 1889. It is 984 feet high (1,056 feet including the television tower).

Pharaohs were buried in Egyptian pyramids.

- The white marble **Taj Mahal** (built 1632-1650) at Agra, India, was built by Shah Jahan as a tomb for his wife.

- The 12th-century temples at **Angkor Wat** in Cambodia are surrounded by a moat and have walls decorated with sculpture.

- The **Great Wall of China** (begun 228 B.C.), designed as a defense against nomadic tribes, is so big and long that it can be seen from space!

- The **Alhambra** in Granada, Spain, is considered one of the greatest masterpieces of Muslim architecture. Construction of the palace and fortress began in 1248. It was finished in 1354.

- San Francisco's **Golden Gate Bridge,** completed in 1937, is one of the most recognizable structures in the U.S.

- The massive standing stones of **Stonehenge** are located in the south of England. Begun some 5,000 years ago, their purpose remains a mystery.

- **Machu Picchu** is an Inca fortress in the Andes Mountains of Peru. It is believed to have been built in the mid-15th century.

- **The Duomo,** with its pink, white and green marble façade, is a symbol of the Renaissance. Construction on the cathedral in Florence, Italy, began in 1296, and it was completed 200 years later.

For more about famous structures around the world, www.FACTMONSTER.COM

The Seven Wonders
of the Ancient World

Since ancient times, people have put together many **"seven wonders"** lists. Below are the seven wonders that are most widely agreed upon as being on the original list.

1. Pyramids of Egypt
A group of three pyramids located at Giza, Egypt, was built around 2680 B.C. Of all the Ancient Wonders, only the pyramids still stand.

2. Hanging Gardens of Babylon These terraced gardens, located in what is now Iraq, were supposedly built by Nebuchadnezzar II around 600 B.C. to please his queen.

3. Statue of Zeus (Jupiter) at Olympia The sculptor Phidias (fifth century B.C.) built this 40-foot-high statue in gold and ivory. It was located in Olympia, Greece.

4. Temple of Artemis (Diana) at Ephesus This beautiful marble structure was begun about 350 B.C. in honor of the goddess Artemis. It was located in Ephesus, Turkey.

5. Mausoleum at Halicarnassus This huge above-ground tomb was erected in Bodrum, Turkey, by Queen Artemisia in memory of her husband, who died in 353 B.C.

6. Colossus at Rhodes This bronze statue of Helios (Apollo), about 105 feet high, was the work of the sculptor Chares. Rhodes is a Greek island in the Aegean Sea.

7. Pharos of Alexandria The Pharos (lighthouse) of Alexandria was built during the third century B.C. off the coast of Egypt. It stood about 450 feet high.

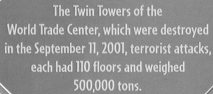

Did You Know?

The Twin Towers of the World Trade Center, which were destroyed in the September 11, 2001, terrorist attacks, each had 110 floors and weighed 500,000 tons.

Impressive Lengths and Heights

Tallest Building	World: Petronas Towers 1&2, in Kuala Lumpur, Malaysia, 88 stories, 1,483 feet high
	U.S.: Sears Tower, in Chicago, Illinois, 110 stories, 1,450 feet high
Tallest Tower	Canadian National Tower, Toronto, Canada, 1,815 feet high
Longest Vehicle Tunnel	Laerdal. Laerdal–Aurland, Norway, 15.2 miles long
Longest Bridge	World: Akashi Kaikyo, Hyogo, Japan, main span* of 6,529 feet
	U.S.: Verrazano-Narrows, Lower New York Bay, main span* of 4,260 feet

*The main span of a bridge is the longest distance between two supports.

TFK TOP 5 HIGHEST DAMS

NAME	RIVER AND COUNTRY	HEIGHT
1. Rogun	Vakhsh, Tajikistan	1,099 ft.
2. Nurek	Vakhsh, Tajikistan	984 ft.
3. Grande Dixence	Dixence, Switzerland	935 ft.
4. Inguri	Inguri, Georgia	892 ft.
5. Vaiont	Vaiont, Italy	859 ft.

The Rogun Dam provides hydroelectric power.

TFK MYSTERY PERSON

CLUE 1: I was born in Canada in 1929. I moved to Los Angeles in 1947, where I began studying architecture.

CLUE 2: I am now one of the most famous architects in the world. I design buildings that curve and swoop and tilt.

CLUE 3: I have designed buildings in Prague, Czech Republic; Berlin, Germany; and New York City.

WHO AM I?

(See Answer Key that begins on page 340.)

47

CALENDARS

Measuring Years

The calendar most Americans use is called the Gregorian calendar. In an ordinary year this calendar has 365 days, which is about the amount of time it takes Earth to make one trip around the Sun.

Earth's journey takes slightly more than a year. It takes about 365 days, 5 hours, 48 minutes and 46 seconds. Every fourth year these extra hours, minutes and seconds are added up to make another day. When this happens, the year has 366 days and is called a **leap year.**

Groups of Years

- Olympiad: 4 years
- Decade: 10 years
- Score: 20 years
- Century: 100 years
- Millennium: 1,000 years

Seasons

In the Northern Hemisphere, the year is divided into four seasons. **Each season begins at a solstice or an equinox.**

It's Different Down South

In the Southern Hemisphere, the dates (and the seasons) are reversed. The summer solstice (still the longest day of the year) falls around December 21, and the winter solstice is around June 21. So when it's summer in North America, it's winter in South America (and vice versa).

SPRING

●The spring equinox brings the start of spring, around March 21. At the equinox, day and night are of about equal length.

SUMMER

●The summer solstice, which happens around June 21, has the longest daylight time. It's also the first day of summer.

Months

Months are based roughly on the cycles of the moon. A lunar (moon) month is 29½ days, or the time from one new moon to the next.

But 12 lunar months add up to just 354 days—11 days fewer than in our calendar year. To even things out, these days are added to months during the year. As a result, most months have 30 or 31 days.

To figure out how many days are in a month, **remember:** "30 days have September, April, June and November. All the rest have 31, except February, which has 28."

The Names of the Months

January was named after **Janus**, protector of the gateway to heaven.

February was named after **Februalia**, a time period when sacrifices were made to atone for sins.

March was named after **Mars**, the god of war, signifying that fighting interrupted by the winter could be resumed.

April is from **aperire**, Latin for "to open" (buds).

May was named after **Maia**, the goddess of growth of plants.

June is from **Junius**, Latin for the goddess Juno.

July was named after **Julius Caesar**.

August was named after **Augustus**, the first Roman Emperor.

September is from **septem**, Latin for seven.

October is from **octo**, Latin for eight.

November is from **novem**, Latin for nine.

December is from **decem**, Latin for ten.

FALL

● Fall begins at the fall equinox, around September 21. Day and night are of about equal length.

I can't believe that when it's summer in the U.S., it's winter in Australia.

WINTER

● The winter solstice, around December 21, has the shortest daylight time and officially kicks off winter.

The Jewish Calendar

The Jewish calendar is counted from 3761 B.C. Nisan is considered the first month, although the new year begins with Rosh Hashanah, on the first of Tishri, which is the seventh month. **The year 2004 is the Jewish year 5764-5765.** In 2004, the Jewish New Year begins on September 16.

Months	Number of days
NISAN	30
IYAR	29
SIVAN	30
TAMMUZ	29
AV	30
ELUL	29
TISHRI	30
HESHVAN	29 or 30
KISLEV	29 or 30
TEVET	29
SHEVAT	30
ADAR	29 or 30
ADAR SHENI*	29

*Additional month in leap year only

The Islamic Calendar

The Islamic calendar is based on a lunar year of 354 days. Each month begins about two days after the new moon. The Islamic calendar is counted from A.D. 622. **The year 2004 is the Islamic year 1424-1425.** In 2004, the Islamic New Year begins on February 22.

Months	Number of days
MUHARRAM	29 or 30
SAFAR	29 or 30
RABI I	29 or 30
RABI II	29 or 30
JUMADA I	29 or 30
JUMADA II	29 or 30
RAJAB	29 or 30
SHA'BAN	29 or 30
RAMADAN	29 or 30
SHAWWAL	29 or 30
DHU'L-QA'DAH	29 or 30
DHU'L-HIJJAH	29 or 30

Hindu (Indian National) Calendar

The Indian National calendar was introduced in 1957 in a push for all of India to use the same calendar. However, some older calendars are still used. Indian National years are counted from A.D. 78. **The year 2004 is the Indian National year 1925-1926.** In 2004, the Hindu New Year begins on March 21.

Months	Number of days
CAITRA	30 or 31
VAISAKHA	31
JYAISTHA	31
ASADHA	31
SRAVANA	31
BHADRA	31
ASVINA	30
KARTIKA	30
AGRAHAYANA	30
PAUSA	30
MAGHA	30
PHALGUNA	30

The Chinese Calendar

The Chinese year is divided into 12 months of 29 or 30 days. Each year is named after one of 12 animals. The Chinese New Year is celebrated at the second new moon after the winter solstice and falls between January 21 and February 19 on the western calendar. In the year 2004, the Chinese year 4702 begins. It will be the **Year of the Monkey.**

Fill in the years below, then answer the questions.

1. The year 2005 is named for which animal?

   — — — — — — —

2. People born in 1988 are said to be

   — — — — — — — — —

3. 1999 was the Year of the

   — — — — —

BONUS: WHEN IS THE NEXT YEAR OF THE ROOSTER?

RAT popular	OX dependable	TIGER brave	RABBIT nice	DRAGON energetic	SNAKE wise	HORSE cheerful	GOAT artistic	MONKEY smart	ROOSTER hard working	DOG loyal	PIG good students
1960	1961	1962	1963	1964	1965	1966	1967	1968	1969	1970	1971
1972	1973			1976	1977	1979		1980			1983
1984		1986				1990	1991		1993		1995
	1997			2000	2001	2002					2007

(See Answer Key that begins on page 340.)

BIRTHSTONES

MONTH	STONE
JANUARY	GARNET
FEBRUARY	AMETHYST
MARCH	AQUAMARINE OR BLOODSTONE
APRIL	DIAMOND
MAY	EMERALD
JUNE	PEARL, ALEXANDRITE OR MOONSTONE
JULY	RUBY OR STAR RUBY
AUGUST	PERIDOT OR SARDONYX
SEPTEMBER	SAPPHIRE OR STAR SAPPHIRE
OCTOBER	OPAL OR TOURMALINE
NOVEMBER	TOPAZ OR CITRINE
DECEMBER	TURQUOISE, LAPIS LAZULI, BLUE ZIRCON OR BLUE TOPAZ

Source: Jewelry Industry Council

THE ZODIAC

Twelve constellations, together called **"the Zodiac,"** form a circle around Earth. As Earth revolves around the Sun, a different part of the sky becomes visible, and each month a different one of these 12 constellations can be seen above the horizon.
The word *Zodiac* means "circle of figures" or "circle of life."

Aries
The Ram
March 21 •
April 19

Pisces
The Fish
Feb. 20 •
March 20

Aquarius
The Water
Bearer
Jan. 20 •
Feb. 19

Taurus
The Bull
April 20 •
May 20

Gemini
The Twins
May 21 •
June 20

Capricorn
The Sea
Goat
Dec. 22 •
Jan. 19

Cancer
The Crab
June 21 •
July 22

Sagittarius
The Archer
Nov. 22 •
Dec. 21

Leo
The
Lion
July 23 •
Aug. 22

Scorpio
The
Scorpion
Oct. 23 •
Nov. 21

Virgo
The Virgin
Aug. 23 •
Sept. 22

Libra
The Scales
Sept. 23 •
Oct. 22

Days

A day is measured by how long it takes Earth to rotate (turn) once, which is 24 hours.

The names of the days are based on seven celestial bodies—the Sun, the Moon, Mars, Mercury, Jupiter, Venus and Saturn. The ancient Romans believed these bodies revolved around Earth and influenced its events.

Europe used the Roman names. But some languages, including English, used Germanic versions of the names of four of the Roman gods: Tiw, the god of war, replaced Mars; Woden, the god of wisdom, replaced Mercury; Thor, the god of thunder, replaced Jupiter; and Frigg, the goddess of love, replaced Venus.

THE NAMES OF THE DAYS OF THE WEEK

Latin	Old English	English	German	French	Italian	Spanish
Dies Solis	Sun's Day	Sunday	Sonntag	dimanche	domenica	domingo
Dies Lunae	Moon's Day	Monday	Montag	lundi	lunedì	lunes
Dies Martis	Tiw's Day	Tuesday	Dienstag	mardi	martedì	martes
Dies Mercurii	Woden's Day	Wednesday	Mittwoch	mercredi	mercoledì	miércoles
Dies Jovis	Thor's Day	Thursday	Donnerstag	jeudi	giovedì	jueves
Dies Veneris	Frigg's Day	Friday	Freitag	vendredi	venerdì	viernes
Dies Saturni	Seterne's Day	Saturday	Samstag	samedi	sabato	sábado

DAYS OF THE WEEK and HEAVENLY BODIES

SATURN — Saturday
SUN — Sunday
MOON — Monday
VENUS — Friday
MARS — Tuesday
JUPITER — Thursday
MERCURY — Wednesday

TFK

MYSTERY PERSON

CLUE 1: I was the Queen of Egypt from 51 to 30 B.C. The details of my life have inspired dozens of plays, books and movies.

CLUE 2: My brother and I became joint rulers after our father's death. I was only 17 years old! I became the sole ruler in 47 B.C.

CLUE 3: I won the hearts of two powerful Roman leaders, Julius Caesar (whom the month of July is named after) and Mark Antony.

WHO AM I?

(See Answer Key that begins on page 340.)

Internet Timeline

1969 The Internet era begins. Four universities in the U.S. are connected in a communications network created by the Advanced Research Project Agency (ARPA). It is called ARPANET.

1972 Electronic mail is introduced.

1976 Presidential candidate Jimmy Carter and running mate Walter Mondale use e-mail to plan campaign events. Queen Elizabeth sends her first e-mail—the first state leader to do so.

1982 The word "Internet" is used for the first time.

1984 Writer William Gibson coins the term "cyberspace." The Domain Name System (DNS) is established. Network addresses are identified by extensions such as .com, .org and .edu.

1985 Quantum Computer Services, which later changes its name to America Online, launches. It offers e-mail, electronic bulletin boards, news and other information.

1988 A virus called the Internet Worm temporarily shuts down about 10% of the world's Internet servers.

1989 The World (world.std.com) debuts as the first provider of dial-up Internet access for consumers.

1991 The World Wide Web is introduced to the public as a text-only interface. It marks the dawn of the Internet! Gopher provides point-and-click navigation on the Internet.

1993 Mosaic, the first graphics-based web browser, is launched.

1994 Marc Andreessen and Jim Clark start Netscape Communications. They introduce the Navigator browser. The White House launches its website, *www.whitehouse.gov.* The first shopping sites are established. Companies market their products via e-mail, and the term "spamming" is introduced.

1995 CompuServe, America Online and Prodigy start providing dial-up Internet access. Sun Microsystems releases the Internet programming language called Java. The Vatican launches its own website, *www.vatican.va.*

1997 The NASA website broadcasts pictures taken by *Pathfinder* on Mars and smashes Internet traffic records. The broadcast generates 46 million hits in one day.

1999 College student Shawn Fanning invents Napster, a computer application that allows users to swap music over the Internet. The number of Internet users worldwide reaches 150 million.

2000 The computer viruses Love Bug and Stages wreak havoc with computers worldwide.

2001 About 9.8 billion electronic messages are sent each day.

2002 58.5% of the U.S. population (about 164 million people) use the Internet. Worldwide, there are 544 million users.

55

Computer Milestones

1945 ----> The computer age begins with the debut of ENIAC (Electronic Numerical Integrator and Calculator). It is the first multipurpose computer.

1975 ----> The MITS Altair, a PC-building kit, hits stores.

----> Bill Gates and Paul Allen establish Microsoft.

1976 ----> Steven Jobs and Stephen Wozniak start Apple Computer.

1977 ----> Apple Computer introduces the Apple II computer.

1978 ----> Floppy disks replace older data cassettes.

1981 ----> IBM introduces a complete desktop PC.

1983 ----> TIME magazine names the PC "Man of the Year."

1984 ----> The user friendly Apple Macintosh goes on sale.

1985 ----> Microsoft launches Windows.

1992 ----> The Apple PowerBook and IBM ThinkPad debut.

1996 ----> Palm releases the PalmPilot, a hand-held computer also called a "personal digital assistant."

Apple II computer

TIME
MACHINE OF THE YEAR
The Computer Moves In

PalmPilot

TFK PUZZLES & GAMES

Video-Game Invasion!

Over the last 30 years, video games have gone through incredible changes. Can you draw a straight line from each game system to the year it came out? Each line will go through one or more letters in the middle of the page. The leftover letters will spell out the name of the only game played on the first-ever home video-game system: Magnavox's Odyssey, which was introduced in 1972.

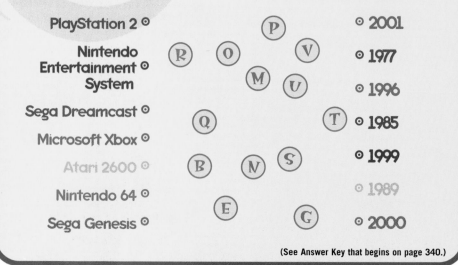

PlayStation 2 ⊙

Nintendo Entertainment System ⊙

Sega Dreamcast ⊙

Microsoft Xbox ⊙

Atari 2600 ⊙

Nintendo 64 ⊙

Sega Genesis ⊙

Ⓟ Ⓥ Ⓡ Ⓞ Ⓜ Ⓤ Ⓠ Ⓣ Ⓑ Ⓝ Ⓢ Ⓔ Ⓖ

⊙ 2001
⊙ 1977
⊙ 1996
⊙ 1985
⊙ 1999
⊙ 1989
⊙ 2000

(See Answer Key that begins on page 340.)

What Kids Do Online

	AGE	PERCENT OF TOTAL U.S. POPULATION*
Schoolwork	5–9	**46.9%**
	10–13	**76.6%**
	14–17	**86.1%**
E-mail	5–9	**43.2%**
	10–13	**63.8%**
	14–17	**82.1%**
Play Games	5–9	**66.4%**
	10–13	**64.7%**
	14–17	**61.0%**
Listen to the Radio or Watch Movies	5–9	**11.0%**
	10–13	**17.9%**
	14–17	**26.9%**
Chat Rooms	5–9	**5.6%**
	10–13	**16.0%**
	14–17	**34.2%**

*People under age 25

Source: NTIA and ESA, U.S. Dept. of Commerce

How Many Kids Are Online?

AGE	PERCENT OF TOTAL U.S. POPULATION
2001 3–4	**14.3%**
5–9	**38.9%**
10–13	**65.4%**
14–17	**75.6%**

Source: NTIA and ESA, U.S. Dept. of Commerce

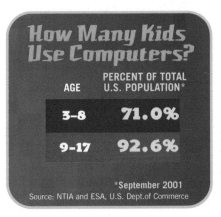

How Many Kids Use Computers?

AGE	PERCENT OF TOTAL U.S. POPULATION*
3–8	**71.0%**
9–17	**92.6%**

*September 2001
Source: NTIA and ESA, U.S. Dept.of Commerce

Short Cuts

In e-mails and online, people often use **acronyms** or abbreviations, called e-mailese. Do you know the correct meaning for each e-mail term?

1. PIR
 a. Parent in room
 b. Please ignore rowdies

2. BTW
 a. Browse the web
 b. By the way

3. ICBIGBA
 a. I can't believe I gave bagels away
 b. I can't believe I got booted again

(See Answer Key that begins on page 340.)

What's a Domain?

Did you ever wonder what those funny endings are in Internet addresses—like ".com"? They're part of the domain. The domain is the name of a network or computer that is linked to the Internet. You can find the domain in an e-mail address after the @ sign. The e-mail address for the First Lady, for example, is first.lady@whitehouse.gov. You can see that "whitehouse.gov" is the domain. The ending of a domain tells you what type it is.

    .com = commercial
    .gov = government
    .org = organization
    .edu = educational institution

Many countries have an official extension or country code that appears at the end of a URL (website address) or e-mail address. The extension identifies where the host website or network is located. For example, the web address for the Nobel e-Museum is http://www.nobel.se. The extension ".se" indicates that the information on the Nobel site originates in Sweden. These are some other examples.

    .fr = France
    .in = India
    .it = Italy
    .jp = Japan
    .pe = Peru
    .zr = Zaire

Smiley City

Sometimes when you're sending an e-mail to a friend, you want to use more than just words. That is the perfect time to include a smiley. Smileys, also called emoticons, can show your feelings about a person or subject, or just add a touch of fun.

:-)	smiling
;-)	winking
:-(	frowning
:'-(	crying
:-P	tongue sticking out
:-D	ha ha
:-O	oh no!
:-\	doubtful
d:-)	wearing a cap
8-)	wearing glasses
:-*	here's a kiss
(::()::)	Band-aid
=^..^=	cat
><)))">	fish
@-->--	rose
^^^^^:-	snake

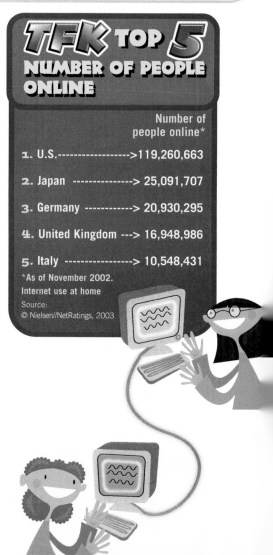

TFK TOP 5
NUMBER OF PEOPLE ONLINE

	Number of people online*
1. U.S.	>119,260,663
2. Japan	> 25,091,707
3. Germany	> 20,930,295
4. United Kingdom	> 16,948,986
5. Italy	> 10,548,431

*As of November 2002.
Internet use at home
Source:
© Nielsen//NetRatings, 2003

Safety Rules!
Online Safety

The Internet is a great research tool. It can also be a fun, fascinating place to hang out. But just like the real world, the virtual world has important rules to follow. Keep a copy of these guidelines near your computer:

■ I will not give out personal information such as my address, telephone number, parents' work address or telephone number or the name and location of my school without my parents' permission.

■ I will tell my parents right away if I come across any information that makes me feel uncomfortable.

■ I will never agree to get together with someone I "meet" online without first checking with my parents. If my parents agree to the meeting, I will be sure that it is in a public place and will bring my mother or father along.

■ I will never send anyone my picture or anything else without first checking with my parents.

■ I will not respond to any messages that are mean or in any way make me feel uncomfortable. It is not my fault if I get that sort of message. I will tell my parents right away about the message so that they can contact the online service.

■ My parents and I will agree to rules for going online. We will decide upon the time of day, the length of time and appropriate areas for me to visit.

Source: National Center for Missing and Exploited Children

Did You Know?

The first multipurpose computer, ENIAC, set speed records with an amazing 5,000 additions per second. Computers have come a long way since—a laptop today can do 500,000,000 additions per second!

TFK
MYSTERY PERSON

CLUE 1: I became interested in computers when I was 13 years old. My school had an early computer called the ASR-33, and I've been hooked ever since.
CLUE 2: I co-founded Microsoft Corp., a multibillion-dollar personal-computer software company, in 1975.
CLUE 3: I am now the richest man in the world.

WHO AM I?
(See Answer Key that begins on page 340.)

DANCE & THEATER

From earliest times people have used dance for a variety of purposes—to entertain, to celebrate, to convey beliefs and feelings and just for the sheer fun of it.

Almost every culture in the world has used dance as a means of expression. Argentina, for example, is the home of the sultry ballroom dance called the **tango**, which evokes a passionate mood.

Traditional African dances often form part of religious ceremonies or mark important events. **Square dances**, which developed in colonial America, became an opportunity for farmers to gather socially with their often far-flung neighbors.

Dance is both a part of everyday life and an art performed on stage in front of an audience. Some of the most common forms of dance performance are **ballet, modern dance** and **Broadway musical dance**.

Types of Dance

Some Popular Dance Crazes

Boogie-woogie
Cakewalk
Cha-cha
Fandango
Fox-trot
Frug
Funky chicken
Hustle
Jitterbug
Jive
Lindy hop
Macarena
Rumba
Shimmy
Twist

Ballet

Ballet was first created in 16th-century Italy. Each position and step in ballet is carefully worked out. Many ballets convey a feeling of delicate beauty and lightness—ballet dancers' graceful motions seem airy and effortless, and much of the movement is focused upward, as if the dancers are reaching for the stars. Toe (or pointe) shoes allow ballerinas to dance on their toes and appear to defy gravity.

Modern dance

Modern dance, created in the 20th century, was a rejection of the traditions of ballet. It went against what was viewed as ballet's rigid steps, limited emotional expression and dainty sense of beauty. Modern dance steps often seem informal, and modern dancers don't mind if a step looks rough as long as it expresses the truth.

The waltz

is a romantic ballroom dance in which the couple revolves in circles to a beat of three. The Viennese waltz is the most famous.

Flamenco

is a fiery, emotional dance that originated in Spain and is characterized by hand clapping and fast, rhythmic foot stamping.

ative American dance

ften ceremonial or religious, calling on the its for help in farming or hunting or giving n thanks for rain or for victory in war.

Hip-Hop

was developed by teenagers in New York City's South Bronx in the 1970s. It brings together driving rhythm, athletic moves and urban style.

The Five Ballet Positions

first position   second position   third position   fourth position   fifth position

Classic Ballets

Because many ballets take their stories from folklore, they can feel like fairy tales told through dance. Here are some favorites. The date the ballet was first performed is in parentheses.

Coppélia (1870)

A doll is so exquisitely beautiful and lifelike that she wins the heart of a village boy. Saint-Léon choreographed *Coppélia* and Léo Delibes wrote the music.

Giselle (1841)

A young girl spends her days dancing and gathering flowers until love brings tragedy. Jean Coralli and Jules Perrot choreographed *Giselle*, and Adolphe Adam wrote the music.

The Nutcracker (1892)

The nutcracker doll Clara receives for Christmas leads the way into an enchanted world. Lev Ivanov choreographed *The Nutcracker* and Peter Ilyich Tchaikovsky wrote the music.

Ondine (1958)

A curious young water nymph pays an unforgettable visit to the land of mortals. Frederick Ashton choreographed *Ondine* and Hans W. Henze composed the music.

The Sleeping Beauty (1890)

One fairy's curse and another fairy's gift mark the destiny of a young princess. Marius Petipa choreographed *The Sleeping Beauty* and Peter Ilyich Tchaikovsky wrote the music.

Swan Lake (1877)

Under a magic spell, the swan Odette becomes a human each night—and falls in love. Lev Ivanov and Marius Petipa choreographed *Swan Lake* and Peter Ilyich Tchaikovsky wrote the music.

TFK TOP 5 LONGEST-RUNNING SHOWS ON BROADWAY

SHOW	OPENING—CLOSING DATES	PERFORMANCES
1. Cats	October 1982—September 2000	7,485
2. Les Misérables	March 1987—present	6,556
3. The Phantom of the Opera	January 1988—present	6,259
4. A Chorus Line	July 1975—April 1990	6,107
5. Oh! Calcutta!	September 1976—August 1989	5,959

Source: League of American Theatres and Producers, Inc. As of January 2003

Favorite Musicals

Here are some of Broadway's most adored musical extravaganzas. All of them feature snappy song-and-dance numbers. The date the musical opened on Broadway is in parentheses.

Annie (1977)
In *Annie*, set in New York City during the Depression, a spunky girl and her scruffy dog move from a dismal orphanage to the mansion of millionaire Daddy Warbucks.

Oklahoma! (1943)
Oklahoma! was the first collaboration between composer Richard Rodgers and lyricist Oscar Hammerstein II. In this rollicking musical, a Southern farm girl must choose between two suitors who both want to escort her to a social.

Fiddler on the Roof (1964)
Fiddler on the Roof takes place in Russia in 1905. The main character, a Jewish milkman, deals with discrimination, poverty and a world changing before his eyes.

The King and I (1951)
Anna, a British nanny, takes a job in Bangkok, Thailand, caring for and teaching the king's children. Anna and the king fall in love, and she persuades him to embrace democracy.

The Sound of Music (1959)
The Sound of Music was a Broadway success years before it hit the big screen. The musical was based on the real-life Von Trapp family and their charming nanny, Maria, who brought music and adventure into the family's somewhat stodgy home.

TFK
MYSTERY PERSON

CLUE 1: I was born in 1962 and was a huge fan of theater at an early age.
CLUE 2: I have starred in many plays on Broadway, such as *The Producers* and *Biloxi Blues*.
CLUE 3: You might be familiar with some of my movies, too. I starred in *Inspector Gadget* and *Ferris Bueller's Day Off*.

WHO AM I?
(See Answer Key that begins on page 340.)

One Weird Dinosaur!

By Dina El Nabli

A fossil with four wings stuns scientists

Imagine a dinosaur small and light enough to glide from tree to tree. Now imagine it with four wings! Scientists in China have proof that such creatures existed about 130 million years ago. They found fossils of four-winged dinosaurs in China's Liaoning province, northeast of Beijing.

The dinosaur was about the size of a pheasant. It had one set of feathered wings on its forelimbs (front legs) and another on its hind (back) legs. Even its long tail was covered with feathers. Researchers named it *Microraptor gui*. (*Microraptor* means small predator; *gui* honors Chinese paleontologist Gu Zhiwei.) The discovery was announced in the science journal *Nature*.

Paleontologists are fascinated by the unique fossil find. "It would be a total oddity—the weirdest creature in the world of dinosaurs and birds," said Luis Chiappe, a paleontologist at the Natural History Museum of Los Angeles County in California.

The discovery is reviving a hot scientific debate over two theories of how dinosaurs may have evolved into modern birds. The first theory says the ancestors of birds lived on the ground but used wings to increase their running speed.

The second theory says that bird ancestors lived in trees and used wings to glide from tree to tree. Flying evolved from gliding.

The new fossil strongly supports the second theory. Scientists believe *Microraptor gui* was a glider that moved like today's flying squirrels.

The *Microraptor* belongs to a large category of lightweight, meat-eating dinosaurs called theropods. Its closest known relatives may be *Dromaeosaurs* (dro-me-uh-sawrs), which had feathers but did not fly.

Paleontologist Xing Xu, who led the discovery team, says *Microraptor* is the best example yet of the transition from dinosaurs to birds. Mark Norell, a paleontologist at the American Museum of Natural History, told TFK that the fossils bring up new questions about how animals began to fly. "The origin of flight is a lot more complex than we thought it was," he says.

How Are Dinosaurs Classified?

The word **dinosaur** comes from *Dinosauria,* which means "terrible lizards." Dinosaurs belong to a group of reptiles called ***Archosauria*** (ruling reptiles). They are classified into **two orders,** based on the shape of their pelvises (hip areas).

Dinosaurs

Saurischian (lizard hipped)

All Saurischian dinosaurs had lizardlike pelvises. In a lizard pelvis, an arch in the front points forward, which makes the animal's rear end very stable. Saurischians

included both carnivores and herbivores. Neither chewed their food much. Saurischian carnivores gulped down meat in chunks, and Saurischian herbivores swallowed plant material in a wad called a bolus.

Saurischians included *Allosaurus* (different lizard), *Apatosaurus* (deceptive lizard), formerly called *Brontosaurus,* and *Tyrannosaurus* (tyrant lizard).

Ornithischian (bird hipped)

All Ornithischian dinosaurs had pelvises similar to those of modern birds. In a bird pelvis, an arch in the front points backward, which allows room for a longer digestive tract that makes digestion easier. Ornithischians were herbivores. They chewed their food well. Most of them had cheeks, just as a cow or a human does, which would

help them to chew their food neatly.

Ornithischians included *Iguanodon* (iguana tooth), *Hadrosaur* (bulky lizard), *Stegosaurus* (plated lizard) and *Triceratops* (three-horned face).

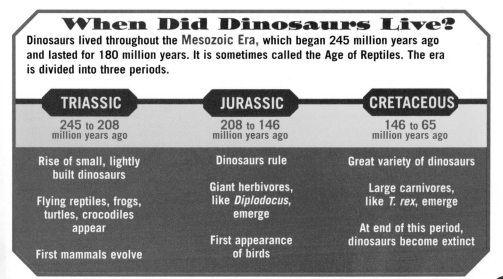

When Did Dinosaurs Live?

Dinosaurs lived throughout the Mesozoic Era, which began 245 million years ago and lasted for 180 million years. It is sometimes called the Age of Reptiles. The era is divided into three periods.

TRIASSIC	JURASSIC	CRETACEOUS
245 to 208 million years ago	208 to 146 million years ago	146 to 65 million years ago
Rise of small, lightly built dinosaurs	Dinosaurs rule	Great variety of dinosaurs
Flying reptiles, frogs, turtles, crocodiles appear	Giant herbivores, like *Diplodocus,* emerge	Large carnivores, like *T. rex,* emerge
First mammals evolve	First appearance of birds	At end of this period, dinosaurs become extinct

DINO

HALL OF FAME

Ornithomimus

LARGEST DINOSAUR

Seismosaurus (seismic lizard)

Cretaceous Period

Found: New Mexico

Although larger creatures may yet be found, for now *Seismosaurus* would probably win the largest-dino award. It measured about 120 feet (36 meters) from head to tail and about 18 feet (5.5 meters) high. It had a whiplike tail and four short, stout legs.

SMALLEST DINOSAUR

Compsognathus (pretty jaw)

Jurassic Period

Found: Germany, France and Portugal

The smallest-known dinosaur was about the size of a chicken and weighed around 6.5 pounds (3 kg). It had a long tail, moved quickly on two skinny legs and ate meat.

LONGEST NECK

Mamenchisaurus (Mamenchin lizard)

Jurassic Period

Found: China

The neck of *Mamenchisaurus* was an amazing 46 feet (14 meters) long. This herbivore probably used its long neck to reach into forests, where its 12-ton body couldn't fit. But hold that medal: the recently discovered *Sauroposeidon* may have had an even longer neck.

FASTEST

Ornithomimus (bird mimic)

Cretaceous Period

Found: Western U.S. and Mongolia

Resembling an ostrich, this dinosaur was estimated to run at a speed of 40 to 50 miles per hour (64 to 80 km). It was 6 to 8 feet (1.8 to 2.4 meters) tall and had two long legs, a long tail and a beak.

SMARTEST

Troodon (wounding tooth)

Cretaceous Period

Found: North America and Asia

Troodon had the largest brain-to-body ratio of all known dinosaurs. It is believed to have been as intelligent as modern-day birds. A meat-eater, it was about 6 feet (1.75 meters) tall and ran quickly on two narrow legs.

Compsognathus

Ankylosaurus

DUMBEST

Stegosaurus (plated lizard)

Jurassic Period

Found: U.S., Europe, India, China and Africa

The *Stegosaurus* had a brain the size of a walnut. If brain-to-body ratio indicates intelligence (or lack of!), this three-ton herbivore wasn't a mental giant.

EARLIEST DINOSAUR

Eoraptor lunensis (dawn thief)

Triassic Period

Found: Argentina

The earliest-known dinosaur was *Eoraptor*. This small carnivore walked on two feet some 227 million years ago.

FIRST DISCOVERED

Iguanodon (iguana tooth)

Triassic Period

Found: North America, Europe and Asia

In 1822 an Englishwoman, Mary Mantell, found some large teeth and bones that were determined to be unlike any known reptile. The fossil creature was named *Iguanodon* because its teeth looked like those of the modern iguana.

BEST DEFENSE

Ankylosaurus (bent/crooked lizard)

Cretaceous Period

Found: Montana, U.S. and Alberta, Canada

Ankylosaurus was the most heavily armored of all dinosaurs, with bony plates, studs and spikes lining its entire back. It even had spikes on its eyelids! Its tail had a thick knob of bone at the end, which was probably used as a club.

MOST FAMOUS

Tyrannosaurus rex (tyrant lizard)

Tyrannosaurus rex

Cretaceous Period

Found: North America and Asia

Tyrannosaurus rex certainly ran the show during the Cretaceous Period. As the world's best-known dinosaur, this regal beast still rules in the popular imagination.

DINO
Fact & Fiction

When did the dinosaurs first appear on Earth?

The oldest-known dinosaur fossils were found in Argentina and Brazil. They are about 230 million years old. The most primitive of these, *Eoraptor*, was a small, meat-eating dinosaur. Because *Eoraptor*'s skeleton shows some advanced skeletal features, older dinosaurs may yet be found.

Were dinosaurs social animals?

Some dinosaurs were social creatures. New evidence indicates that they traveled together and that some may even have migrated. Grouped *Hadrosaur* nest sites have been found with badly crushed eggshells and skeletons of baby dinosaurs (with slightly worn teeth) still in the nests. This suggests that some babies stayed in their nests after hatching and probably were fed by their parents.

Did people and dinosaurs live at the same time?

No! After the dinosaurs died out, nearly 65 million years passed before people appeared on Earth. However, small mammals were alive at the time of the dinosaurs. Many scientists who study dinosaurs now think that birds are direct descendants of one line of carnivorous dinosaurs, and some say that birds represent modern living dinosaurs.

When did dinosaurs become extinct?

Dinosaurs became extinct about 65 million years ago (at the end of the Cretaceous Period), after living on Earth for about 165 million years. The dinosaurs' long period of dominance makes them unqualified successes in the history of life on Earth.

Where did dinosaurs live?

Paleontologists, scientists who study fossils, now have evidence that dinosaurs lived on all of the continents. At the beginning of the age of dinosaurs, the continents that we now know were arranged together as a single supercontinent called Pangaea. During the 165 million years that dinosaurs lived on Earth, this supercontinent slowly broke apart. Its pieces then gradually spread across the globe.

Why did dinosaurs become extinct?

There are dozens of theories. Throughout the Mesozoic Era, individual dinosaur species were evolving and becoming extinct for various reasons. The massive extinction at the end of the Cretaceous Period exterminated the last of the dinosaurs. There is now evidence that a meteorite impact was at least the partial cause for this extinction. Other factors may include volcanic gases, climatic cooling, sea-level change, low reproduction rates, poison gases from a comet or changes in Earth's orbit or magnetic field.

Source: The United States Geological Survey

Toothy Theropod

With teeth like a bunny and a body like a *Tyrannosaurus rex*, the fossil found in China was one goofy-looking dinosaur! Scientists reported the strange discovery in *Nature* magazine. They called it *Incisivosaurus* (in-sigh-see-vo-sore-us) because of its long incisor teeth.

The creature belongs to a group of theropod—or two-legged—dinosaurs known as oviraptors. Other oviraptors had birdlike beaks. But *Incisivosaurus* had a long skull with two large front teeth. The discovery challenges the idea that all theropods were carnivores. Scientists believe that with its big, buck teeth, this dinosaur munched plants. And that's not the only theory about theropods that's changed.

A recent study that said theropod dinosaurs were speedy creatures has been stopped in its tracks. Some scientists aren't so sure that these dinos had the legs to even chase down live prey. Many scientists now argue, for example, that *T. rex* was a slow mover, lumbering along at 10 miles an hour.

The scientists calculated that a 6-ton *T. rex* would need giant leg muscles—taking up about 80% of its body mass—to hit high speeds.

On the other hand, speed didn't matter so much to *Incisivosaurus*. Since it was an herbivore, it didn't have to run too fast to catch its next meal.

Nothing But the Tooth

Meat-eating **carnivores,** such as *Tyrannosaurus rex,* have sharp, pointy teeth that can tear apart animal flesh. In contrast, plant-eating **herbivores,** such as *Plateosaurus,* have dull, flat teeth— excellent tools for grabbing and grinding plants.

Tyrannosaurus rex

Plateosaurus

TFK MYSTERY PERSONS

CLUE 1: We are two of the most famous explorers of all time.

CLUE 2: In 1804, the United States didn't know much about the western part of its country. So President Thomas Jefferson asked us to explore the land all the way to the Pacific Ocean and report back with our findings.

CLUE 3: It took nearly three years. But during our trip, we discovered several new animals. We also found fossils of animals that lived during the age of dinosaurs.

WHO ARE WE?

(See Answer Key that begins on page 340.)

DISASTERS

Disasters can be natural occurrences, such as floods and earthquakes; human mistakes, such as shipwrecks; or acts of violence, such as terrorism. Here are two recent disasters

September 11, 2001

One of the worst events of all time was the September 11, 2001, terrorist attack against the U.S. Hijackers who are believed to have been members of the al-Qaeda terrorist group crashed two commercial jets into the Twin Towers of the World Trade Center in New York City. Another hijacked plane crashed into the Pentagon in Washington, D.C., and a fourth in a field in rural Pennsylvania. The total number of people who died in the attacks reached 3,044, including the hijackers. That's more than the number of people who died in the Japanese attack on Pearl Harbor in 1941.

Pennsylvania Coal Miners

In 2002, disaster struck Quecreek, Pennsylvania, when nine coal miners were stranded 240 feet below ground in a cold, dark, wet mineshaft. The miners kept warm by huddling together after millions of gallons of cold water from an adjacent mine rushed into their site. But tragedy was averted when all of the miners were rescued in good health and spirits 77 hours after their ordeal began.

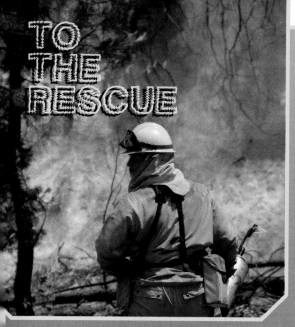

TO THE RESCUE

When disasters occur in the U.S., the Federal Emergency Management Agency (FEMA) steps in to help victims find a place to live if their homes were damaged or destroyed. FEMA also helps to repair homes and public buildings that have been damaged. The agency is part of the executive branch of the government.

FEMA also teaches people how to prepare for natural calamities and offers tips for people to make their homes as safe and as disaster-resistant as possible. Here are some ways to make disasters less disastrous.

ASSEMBLE A DISASTER KIT

According to the American Red Cross, your disaster kit should include:

- First-aid kit and essential medications
- Canned food and a can opener
- At least three gallons of water for each person in the house
- Warm clothing, rainwear and bedding or sleeping bags
- A battery-powered radio, a flashlight and extra batteries
- Special items for babies, the elderly or disabled family members
- Written instructions for how to turn off the electricity, gas and water in your home
- A place to go if told to evacuate. Choose several alternatives.

BE PREPARED FOR A FIRE

- Install a smoke alarm outside each bedroom and on each level of your home. Test the batteries monthly and replace them twice a year.
- Make sure you have at least one fire extinguisher in your home.
- Plan two ways to escape from each room.
- Choose a place for family members to meet outside.
- Practice "stop, drop and roll"—which you do if your clothes catch fire.

••• OR AN EARTHQUAKE

- Bolt or strap cupboards and bookcases to the walls.
- Choose a safe place in every room—under a sturdy table or desk or against an inside wall where nothing can fall on you—where you will go during an earthquake.
- Practice "drop, cover and hold on" at least twice a year. Drop under a sturdy desk or table, cover your eyes by pressing your face against your arm and hold on. If there's no table or desk nearby, sit on the floor against an inside wall away from windows, bookcases or tall furniture.
- Strap your gas water heater to a nearby wall. This will keep it from falling on someone or starting a fire from a broken gas main.

Here are some disastrous accidents that made history.

A *Titanic* Disaster
April 15, 1912

They called it "unsinkable." But on its maiden voyage, the British luxury steamship *Titanic* collided with a massive iceberg southeast of Newfoundland. The ship began to fill with icy water. Less than three hours later, the 883-foot-long *Titanic* turned on end and then slipped into the ocean. More than 1,500 people died.

The Fall of the *Hindenburg*
May 6, 1937

The German blimp, or airship, *Hindenburg* burst into flames 200 feet over its intended landing spot at New Jersey's Lakehurst Naval Air Station. Thirty-five people on board the flight were killed, along with one crewman on the ground. The majestic ship turned into a ball of flames on the ground in only 34 seconds.

The bow of the *Titanic*, on the ocean floor near Newfoundland

The *Challenger* Explosion January 28, 1986

The *Challenger* space shuttle exploded 73 seconds after liftoff, killing all seven aboard—six NASA astronauts and Christa McAuliffe, a schoolteacher who was to be the first civilian in space. A booster fuel leak had ignited, causing the explosion. Millions of people who had tuned in to watch the launch on television saw the tragedy unfold.

Nuclear Disaster at Chernobyl April 26, 1986

In the worst nuclear disaster in history, a reactor blew at a nuclear power plant in Chernobyl, Ukraine. The explosion released eight tons of radioactive material over part of the Soviet Union, eastern Europe, Scandinavia and later western Europe. Total casualties are unknown, but estimates run into the thousands.

The *Exxon Valdez* Oil Spill March 24, 1989

The *Exxon Valdez* oil tanker hit an undersea reef and tore open, spilling 11.2 million gallons of crude oil into Alaska's Prince William Sound. The worst oil spill in U.S. history, it killed millions of birds, fish and other wildlife. Cleanup efforts began late and ended up costing billions of dollars.

Train Tragedy in India June 6, 1981

The driver of a train carrying more than 500 passengers braked to avoid hitting a cow. The train plunged off a bridge into the Baghmati River near Mansi, India. The death toll numbered 268 passengers, and at least 300 more were missing.

Devastating Runway Collision March 27, 1977

A Pan American Boeing 747 and a KLM Boeing 747 collided on a runway in Santa Cruz de Tenerife, Canary Islands. All 249 people aboard the KLM plane and 333 of the 394 aboard the Pan Am jet were killed. The total of 582 is the highest death toll for any type of aviation disaster.

Fiery Explosion in Canada
December 6, 1917

A Belgian steamship collided with the French ammunition ship *Mont Blanc* in Halifax Harbor, Nova Scotia. The *Mont Blanc* was carrying more than 2,500 tons of explosives. The collision ignited the explosives, causing about 1,600 deaths and destroying the northern part of Halifax Harbor.

The Chicago Fire
October 8, 1871

The legendary fire consumed 17,450 buildings, killed 250 people and caused $196 million in damage.

The Chicago fire burned down 2,000 acres of the city.

Soccer Disaster
May 24, 1964

More than 300 soccer fans were killed and more than 500 injured in Lima, Peru, when rioting broke out over an unpopular ruling by a referee in a Peru vs. Argentina soccer game. It is the worst soccer disaster on record.

Riots that take place at soccer games are not that uncommon.

73

Earthquakes and Tidal WAVES

An earthquake is a trembling movement of Earth's crust. The movement causes vibrations to pass through and around Earth in waves, just as ripples are created when a pebble is dropped into water. Volcanic eruptions, landslides and explosions can also cause the ground to tremble.

A tidal wave is a huge sea wave that follows an earthquake or volcanic eruption. *Tsunami* is the Japanese word for a tidal wave caused by an undersea earthquake.

WORST
EARTHQUAKE *IN* HISTORY
- **Where: Near East & Mediterranean Sea**
- **When: 1201**
- **This quake took an estimated 1 million lives.**

A MONSTER

WAVE WALLOPS JAPAN
- **Where: Honshu, Japan**
- **When: 1933**
- **A deadly *tsunami* killed 3,000 people on the island of Honshu. The tidal wave, caused by an earthquake, sank 8,000 ships and destroyed 9,000 homes.**

WHAT CAUSES A QUAKE?

Earth's crust is not a solid sphere like a billiard ball. It has a crust made of pieces that slowly shift. A fault is a weak line below the surface, where two pieces of the crust meet. An earthquake happens when two pieces crash together or move in opposite directions. A quake begins at a point called the focus. Vibrations traveling outward from the focus are called seismic waves. The areas closest to the focus are hit hardest.

Did You Know?
The Richter scale is no longer the most commonly used measurement of the intensity of an earthquake. It proved to be imprecise in measuring the biggest earthquakes. Moment magnitude is now the most widely used scale. It is based on the size of the fault on which an earthquake occurs and the amount of land that slips during an earthquake.

An earthquake that struck Mexico in 2003 reduced to rubble this home in the town of Colima.

What Makes a
VOLCANO
Blow Its Top?

A volcanic eruption occurs when molten rock, ash and steam pour through a vent in Earth's crust. Volcanoes can be active (erupting), dormant (not erupting at the present time) or extinct (no longer able to erupt). Some volcanoes explode. Others are slow-flowing fountains of lava, which is hot fluid rock. Here are two of the most famous eruptions.

MOUNT VESUVIUS
Italy A.D. 79
The eruption of Mount Vesuvius buried the towns of Pompeii and Herculaneum under 20 feet of ash and lava, killing thousands of people. The ash that buried the town and the people also preserved them. The work of uncovering the ancient cities began in 1748 and continues to this day.

KRAKATAU
Indonesia 1883
The greatest explosion in modern times occurred when Krakatau erupted. The roar of the explosion was heard over one-thirteenth of the surface of Earth. The eruption wiped out 163 villages, killing 36,380 people.

TFK TOP 5
WORST YEARS FOR DISASTROUS TORNADOES

The U.S. has more tornadoes than any other country: about 1,000 a year! Most are not so serious. But each year, about 38 tornadoes get rated very strong to violent on a scale of wind speed. Here are the worst years for powerful tornadoes.

1) **1975:** 116 strong tornadoes
2) **1965:** 75 strong tornadoes
3) **1957:** 64 strong tornadoes
4) **1973** and **1976:** 59 strong tornadoes
5) **1971:** 56 strong tornadoes

Source: National Climatic Data Center, NOAA

Strong tornadoes can cause deaths and property damage.

Storms in 2003 caused the streets of Wertheim, Germany, to flood.

DEVASTATING FLOODS

A flood happens when a body of water rises and overflows onto dry land. Floods are most often caused by heavy rain, melting ice and snow or a combination of these.

- **Where: Pennsylvania**
- **When: 1889**
- The Johnstown Flood is one of the worst disasters in U.S. history. After a rainstorm, a dam 74 miles upriver from Johnstown broke. One out of 10 people in the path of the flood died—2,000 people were killed in less than an hour.

- **Where: Italy**
- **When: 1966**
- After heavy rain, the Arno River overflowed, flooding the streets of Florence. Art in the city's famous museums was damaged. In two days, more than 100 people died, and the city was covered with half a million tons of mud, silt and sewage.

DESTRUCTIVE AVALANCHES

An avalanche is any quick movement of snow, ice, mud or rock down a mountain or slope. Avalanches can reach speeds of more than 200 miles per hour! An avalanche might be triggered by an earthquake, human disturbance or extreme rain.

- **Where: Washington State**
- **When: 1910**
- The worst snowslide in U.S. history occurred in the Cascade Mountains in Wellington, Washington, when 118 people were trapped in a snowbound train. An avalanche then swept them to their deaths in a gorge 150 feet below the tracks.

- **Where: Peru**
- **When: 1962**
- When tons of ice and snow slid down Huascaran Peak in the Andes Mountains, nearly 4,000 people were killed. It is considered the world's worst avalanche.

This dry lake bed is in Panamint Valley, California.

DROUGHTS and Famines

Droughts are long periods of insufficient rain that can ruin crops and deplete water supplies. Droughts may lead to famines—extreme food shortages that cause people to die of starvation.

- Where: **Egypt**
- When: **1200-1202**
- **The Egyptians relied on the annual flooding of the Nile River for growing crops. After a shortage of rain, however, the Nile didn't rise. People were unable to grow food and began to starve to death. As many as 110,000 people died as a result of the famine.**

- Where: **Northern China**
- When: **1959-1961**
- **The world's deadliest famine killed about 30 million people in China. News of the famine was not revealed to the rest of the world until 1981, some 20 years later.**

EPIDEMICS

An epidemic occurs when a disease affects a large number of people in one area or when a disease spreads to areas that are not usually associated with the disease.

- What: **Bubonic plague, also called black death**
- Where: **Europe**
- When: **1347-1351**
- **The disease spread rapidly throughout Europe. About 25 million people, or about one-quarter of Europe's population, died of bubonic plague.**

- What: **Spanish influenza**
- Where: **United States**
- When: **March-November 1918**
- **An outbreak of Spanish influenza killed more than 500,000 people. It was the worst single U.S. epidemic. The outbreak was considered a pandemic because it also struck throughout the world.**

For more on disasters of all kinds, **go** www.FACTMONSTER.COM

TFK
MYSTERY PERSON

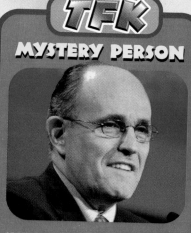

CLUE 1: I was born in Brooklyn, New York, in 1944. I entered politics soon after graduating from New York University Law School.
CLUE 2: In 1993, I ran for mayor of New York City and won. I was re-elected in 1997.
CLUE 3: In 2001, TIME magazine named me Man of the Year for helping to keep New York City together after the terrorist attack of September 11, 2001.

WHO AM I?
(See Answer Key that begins on page 340.)

Too Dry!

By Martha Pickerill

Across the nation in 2002, Americans were choked by one of the worst droughts anyone can remember. According to experts, only two others in the past 100 years have been as bad.

A drought occurs when a region gets less rain than usual and water supplies fall short. Unlike a tornado, hurricane or other weather disaster, a drought sneaks up and does its damage slowly. The current drought began in 1998.

Because farmers and ranchers can't stay in business without water for crops and animals, the pain of drought hits them first. Western corn and wheat crops, Massachusetts's cranberry bogs and Georgia's pecan crop were all hit hard.

Over the summer, many states declared water emergencies. Officials in some areas banned washing cars, filling swimming pools and watering lawns. Even schools have been affected by the drought. In York, Pennsylvania, kids are using paper plates in their cafeterias so that no one will have to wash dishes. A soccer league in Pennsylvania ended its season a month early because the school district closed its parched fields. In Mayer, Arizona, schoolkids are sipping water from bottles instead of fountains, because local wells dried up.

One of the worst things about 2002's drought was its impact on the nation's forests. In Oregon, Arizona and other western states, dry conditions have contributed to raging wildfires. More than 6 million acres went up in flames.

Drought experts say that if Americans save more water when rain is plentiful, we will be able to make it through droughts without severe shortages. Americans use about 27 billion gallons of water a day. If we want to avoid long-term water shortages, Americans will have to change their water-wasting ways.

The 2002 Drought

MAP KEY
- Drought areas
- At risk for drought
- Recovering from drought
- No drought

Map courtesy of the National Drought Mitigation Center

Waste Not, Water Not

Here are some simple ways you and your family can cut back on water use.

- Don't pour water down the drain. Instead, use it to water your plants or garden.

- Fix dripping faucets. One drop per second wastes 2,700 gallons of water per year!

- Take shorter showers and turn off the water while you lather up.

- Turn off the water while brushing your teeth or washing your face.

- Run dishwashers only when they are fully loaded. The light-wash feature uses less water.

- When hand-washing dishes, use two containers—one with soapy water for washing and the other with plain water for rinsing.

- Don't water your lawn too much. Grass only needs to be watered about once a week in the summer. Lawns can go two weeks without water after a heavy rain.

- Make sure sprinklers—if you must use them—are aimed at grass and plants, not at pavement or houses.

Other Environmental Dangers

The **greenhouse effect** is the term used to describe the warming of the atmosphere that happens when certain gases let in sunlight and prevent heat from escaping. This is similar to the way the glass in a greenhouse works. This warming upsets the atmosphere's natural balance.

The **ozone layer**, a thin sheet of an invisible gas called ozone, surrounds Earth about 15 miles above its surface. Ozone protects us from the Sun's harmful rays. In recent years, scientists have learned that the amount of ozone in the atmosphere is decreasing, probably due to man-made gases called chlorofluorocarbons (CFCs) and certain chemicals. As the ozone level decreases, we are in greater danger of damage by the Sun.

Pollution is the contamination of air or water by harmful substances. One source of pollution is **hazardous waste**—anything thrown away that could be dangerous to the environment, such as paint, oven cleaner, furniture polish and pesticides. These materials can seep into water supplies and contaminate them.

Another source of pollution is **acid rain**, which occurs when rainwater is contaminated with pollutants such as sulfur dioxide and nitrogen oxide. These gases come from fuels being burned at high temperatures, as in car exhausts. When acid rain falls, it can damage wildlife, contaminate drinking water and erode buildings and monuments.

Major Biomes of the World

Have you visited any **biomes** lately? A biome is a large community of plants and animals that is supported by a certain type of climate.

A polar bear crosses a frozen sea.

Arctic Tundra

Where: The Arctic tundra is a cold, treeless area of low, swampy plains in the far north around the Arctic Ocean.

Special features: This is Earth's coldest biome. The Arctic tundra's frozen subsoil, called permafrost, makes it impossible for trees to grow.

What lives there? Animals that live in this biome include polar bears, arctic foxes, caribou and gray wolves. Plants that you might find include small shrubs and the lichen that covers the tundra's many rocks.

Coniferous Forest

Where: The coniferous-forest biome is south of the Arctic tundra. It stretches from Alaska across North America and across Eurasia.

Special features: These forests consist mainly of cone-bearing trees such as spruce, hemlock and fir. The soil is not very fertile, because there are no leaves to decompose and enrich it.

What lives there? Some animals that thrive in this biome are ermine, moose, red foxes, snowshoe rabbits and great horned owls.

Desert

Where: About one-fifth of Earth's land surface is desert. Deserts are found on every continent except Europe. There are two kinds: hot and dry (such as the Sahara) and cold and dry (such as Antarctica).

Special features: Lack of water and intense heat or cold make this biome unfriendly for most life forms.

What lives there? Most of the plants you'll see in the hot desert are types of cactuses. A few animals—mainly reptiles, such as snakes and lizards, and amphibians, such as frogs and toads—are adapted to the hot desert. Another famous hot-desert animal is the camel. Emperor penguins are well-known animals living at the edge of the Antarctic desert.

Deciduous Forest

Where: This biome is in the mild temperate zone of the Northern Hemisphere. Major regions are found in eastern North America, Europe and eastern Asia.

Special features: Deciduous trees lose their leaves in fall. The natural decaying of the fallen leaves enriches the soil and supports all kinds of plant and animal life.

What lives there? Oak, beech, ash and maple trees are typical, and many types of insect and animal life abound. In the U.S., the deciduous forest is a home for many animals including deer, American gray squirrels, rabbits, raccoons, bears and woodpeckers.

A raccoon roams in Florida.

Grasslands

Where: Grasslands are known throughout the world by different names. In the U.S. they are called prairies.

Special features: Grasslands are places with hot, dry climates that are perfect for growing food. This inland biome is made of vast areas of grassy field. It receives so little rain that very few trees can grow.

What lives there? The U.S. prairies are used to graze cattle and to raise cereal crops. There is little variety of animal life. Today, common grassland animals include the prairie dog and the mule deer in North America, the giraffe and the zebra in Africa and the lion in Africa and Asia.

Mountains

Where: Mountains exist on all the continents. Many of the world's mountains lie in two great belts. The Circum-Pacific chain runs from the west coast of the Americas through New Zealand and Australia, and through the Philippines to Japan. The Alpine-Himalayan system stretches from the Pyrenees in Spain and France through the Alps, and on to the Himalayas before ending in Indonesia.

Colorado is home to mountain goats.

Special features: A mountain biome is very cold and windy. The higher the mountain, the colder and windier the environment. There is also less oxygen at high elevations.

What lives there? Mountain animals that have adapted to the cold, the lack of oxygen and the rugged landscape include the mountain goat, sheep and puma. Lower elevations are commonly covered by forests, while very high elevations are usually treeless.

Did You Know?

An ecosystem is a community of plants and animals in an environment that supplies them with the raw materials they need, such as nutrients and water. An ecosystem may be as small as a puddle or as large as a forest.

Rain Forests

Where: Tropical rain forests are found in Asia, Africa, South America, Central America and on many of the Pacific islands. Almost half are in Brazil.

Special features: Tropical rain forests receive at least 70 inches of rain each year and have more species of plants and animals than any other biome. The thick vegetation absorbs moisture, which then evaporates and falls as rain.

A rain forest grows in three levels. The canopy, or tallest level, has trees between 100 and 200 feet tall. The second level, or understory, contains a mix of small trees, vines and palms, as well as shrubs and ferns. The third and lowest level is the forest floor, where herbs, mosses and fungi grow.

What lives there? The combination of heat and moisture makes the tropical rain forest the perfect environment for more than 15 million plants and animals. Some of the animals of the tropical rain forest are the anteater, jaguar, lemur, orangutan, macaw, sloth and toucan. Among the many plant species are bamboo, banana trees and rubber trees.

For more about biomes, www.FACTMONSTER.com

81

Energy and the Earth

Energy is the power we use for transportation, for heat and light in our homes and for the manufacture of all kinds of products. There are two sources of energy: renewable and nonrenewable.

Nonrenewable Sources of Energy

Most of the energy we use comes from fossil fuels, such as coal, natural gas and petroleum. Once these natural resources are used up, they are gone forever. Uranium is another nonrenewable source, but it is not a fossil fuel. Uranium is converted to a fuel and used in nuclear power plants.

The process of gathering fossil fuels can be harmful to the biomes from which they come. Fossil fuels are put through a process called combustion in order to produce energy. Combustion releases pollution, such as carbon monoxide and sulfur dioxide, which may contribute to acid rain and global warming.

Renewable Sources of Energy

Renewable sources of energy can be used over and over again. Renewable resources include solar energy, wind, geothermal energy, biomass and hydropower. They generate much less pollution—both in gathering and production—than nonrenewable sources.

- **Solar energy** comes from the Sun. Some people use solar panels on their homes to convert sunlight into electricity.

- **Wind turbines,** which look like giant windmills, generate electricity.

- **Geothermal energy** comes from the Earth's core. Engineers extract steam or very hot water from the Earth's crust and use the steam to generate electricity.

- **Biomass** includes natural products such as wood, manure and corn. These materials are burned and used for heat.

- Dams and rivers generate **hydropower.** When water flows through a dam, it activates a turbine, which runs an electric generator.

Wind turbines in Altamont, California, produce electricity.

Did You Know?

Fossil fuels are called fossil fuels because over many millions of years, heat from the Earth's core and pressure from rock and soil have reacted with the fossils (or remains) of dead plants and animals to form fuel.

Top Energy Producers and Consumers

The United States, Russia and China are the world's leading energy producers and energy consumers. In 2000, these countries produced 38% and consumed 41% of the world's total energy.

Country	Amount of energy produced in 2000	Amount of energy consumed in 2000
United States	71.6 quadrillion Btu*	98.8 quadrillion Btu
Russia	43.3 quadrillion Btu	28.1 quadrillion Btu
China	34.9 quadrillion Btu	36.7 quadrillion Btu

*"Btu" is the abbreviation for British thermal unit. One Btu is nearly equal to the amount of energy released when a wood match is burned.
Source: Energy Information Administration, Dept. of Energy

Remember the Three R's of the Environment
Reduce Reducing waste is the best way to help the environment.
Reuse Instead of throwing things away, find ways to use them again.
Recycle Recycled items are new products made out of the materials from old ones.

TFK TOP 5 MOST COMMON TREES IN THE U.S.

April 26 is Arbor Day. More than 1 million trees were planted in the U.S. on the first Arbor Day in 1872. In 2002, Americans celebrated the holiday by planting more than 18 million trees! Here are the most common trees in the country. Are any of them growing in your backyard?

1. silver maple **2.** black cherry **3.** box elder

4. eastern cottonwood **5.** black willow

Source: American Forests

TFK MYSTERY PERSON

CLUE 1: I was born in Massachusetts, and I traveled West in the early 1800s with a bag of seeds, planting thousands of apple trees.
CLUE 2: My dream was to have apple trees growing everywhere so that no one would go hungry.
CLUE 3: Because of this, I was known as Johnny Appleseed.

WHO AM I?
(See Answer Key that begins on page 340.)

FASHION

CLOTHES ENCOUNTERS
FASHION THROUGH THE DECADES

1900s

- corsets for tiny waists
- tight collars
- lots of lace
- long, lightweight "duster" coats
- upswept hair
- narrow shoes for both men and women
- straw "boater" hats for men
- feathered hats for women

1910s

- bathing costumes
- lace-up boots
- decorated stockings
- narrow "hobble" skirts
- trenchcoats
- beaded handbags
- Middle Eastern patterns
- V-neck sweaters

1920s

- drop-waist "flapper" dresses
- cloches (close-fitting hats) for women
- baggy flannel trousers for men
- long, wide coats
- costume jewelry
- T-strap shoes
- sheer stockings
- bobbed hair

1930s

- hats worn at an angle
- patterned sweaters
- one-piece wool bathing suits
- long, flowing gowns
- sandals
- fox-fur collars
- wide overcoats for men
- rectangular wristwatches

1940s

- matching skirts and sweaters
- fur muffs
- rolled-up blue jeans
- narrow "drainpipe" trousers
- the "pompadour" hairstyle
- sleek evening dresses
- cork-soled "wedgie" shoes
- baggy pull-on sweaters
- Hawaiian shirts for men

1950s

- white T-shirts
- motorcycle jackets
- pedal pushers (capri pants)
- Bermuda shorts
- poodle skirts
- saddle shoes
- full skirts with petticoats
- strapless evening gowns

1960s

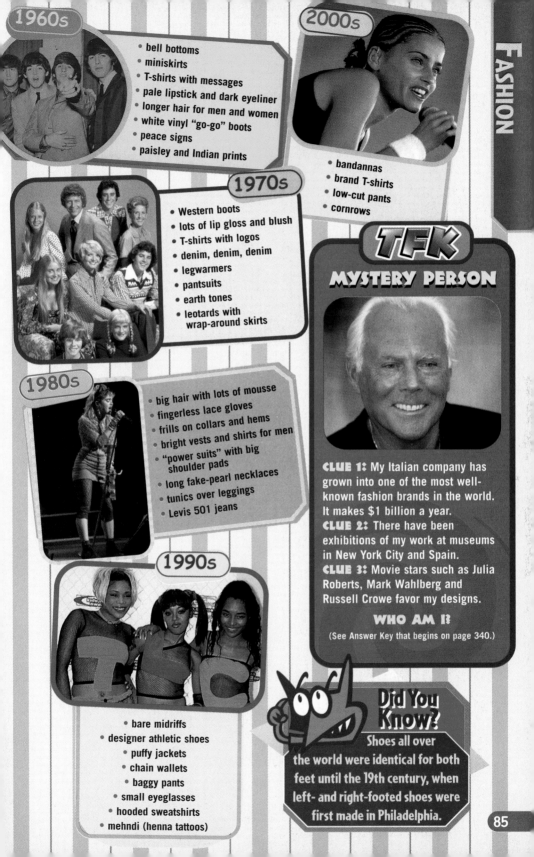

- bell bottoms
- miniskirts
- T-shirts with messages
- pale lipstick and dark eyeliner
- longer hair for men and women
- white vinyl "go-go" boots
- peace signs
- paisley and Indian prints

2000s

- bandannas
- brand T-shirts
- low-cut pants
- cornrows

1970s

- Western boots
- lots of lip gloss and blush
- T-shirts with logos
- denim, denim, denim
- legwarmers
- pantsuits
- earth tones
- leotards with wrap-around skirts

1980s

- big hair with lots of mousse
- fingerless lace gloves
- frills on collars and hems
- bright vests and shirts for men
- "power suits" with big shoulder pads
- long fake-pearl necklaces
- tunics over leggings
- Levis 501 jeans

1990s

- bare midriffs
- designer athletic shoes
- puffy jackets
- chain wallets
- baggy pants
- small eyeglasses
- hooded sweatshirts
- mehndi (henna tattoos)

TFK

MYSTERY PERSON

CLUE 1: My Italian company has grown into one of the most well-known fashion brands in the world. It makes $1 billion a year.

CLUE 2: There have been exhibitions of my work at museums in New York City and Spain.

CLUE 3: Movie stars such as Julia Roberts, Mark Wahlberg and Russell Crowe favor my designs.

WHO AM I?

(See Answer Key that begins on page 340.)

Did You Know?

Shoes all over the world were identical for both feet until the 19th century, when left- and right-footed shoes were first made in Philadelphia.

A Historic Journey

Lewis and Clark's big adventure began 200 years ago

On January 18, 1803, President Thomas Jefferson asked Congress to approve a daring mission. He wanted to send a team of explorers from the Mississippi River to the Pacific Ocean for the first time. Its cost to taxpayers: $2,500.

Congress agreed, and by the following year Meriwether Lewis and William Clark were leading a 33-member "Corps of Discovery" on an expedition into the Wild West.

Over the next few years, Americans will mark the 200th anniversary of Lewis and Clark's mission. The bicentennial celebration began in January 2003 at Thomas Jefferson's historic home, Monticello, in Virginia. All 11 states along the Lewis and Clark trail

BY
MARTHA
PICKERILL

are staging events and inviting visitors to see the sights as the explorers saw them.

In 1803, the land west of the Mississippi was known only to the dozens of tribes of American Indians who had lived there for centuries, some European settlers and traders who worked along the Missouri River. Jefferson hoped that the Missouri would lead to a Northwest Passage, a river that would provide an easy route to the Pacific Ocean. He also wanted to improve relations with the Indians by sending peaceful explorers.

The urge to explore the West was driven by another big event in 1803: the Louisiana Purchase. Jefferson agreed to pay France $15 million for a huge chunk of western land. He was eager to explore this land, and, he wrote, "enlarge our knowledge of the geography of our continent."

Lewis, 29, was Jefferson's neighbor and had been his secretary. After the President asked him to lead the mission, Lewis got his old army pal, William Clark, 33, to join him.

There were misunderstandings on the trek, but only one violent conflict

FROM TFK MAGAZINE

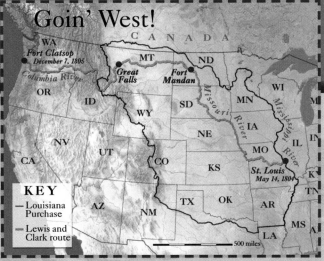

Goin' West!

CANADA

WA
Fort Clatsop
December 7, 1805

Columbia River

OR

ID

NV

CA

UT

AZ

NM

MT

Great
Falls

Fort
Mandan

ND

WY

SD

NE

CO

KS

TX

OK

Missouri River

MN

IA

MO

St. Louis
May 14, 1804

AR

LA

WI

M

IL

IN

Mississippi River

K

TN

MS

A

KEY
— Louisiana Purchase
— Lewis and Clark route

500 miles

The trail now runs through 11 states. Of course, in 1803, there were no states west of the Mississippi.

alone. That's how he became the first to see the massive Rocky Mountains and the Great Falls of the Missouri.

Lewis was also the first between the explorers and Indians. In fact, a Shoshone guide named Sacagawea (sac-uh-juh-wee-uh) was a vital member of the crew.

Clark is often described as the warmer, friendly one of the pair. Lewis liked to scout ahead of the team

to realize that no river flowed straight to the Pacific. To reach the coast, the explorers had to cross mountains and haul boats over land. But despite the lack of a Northwest Passage, generations of Americans have declared the mission a success.

IMPORTANT EXPLORERS

985 Erik the Red (Viking) settled in Greenland

1000 Leif Eriksson (Viking) explored Labrador and Newfoundland in Canada

1271 Marco Polo (Italian) explored China

1325-1349 Ibn Batuta (Arab) explored Africa, Middle East, Europe, parts of Asia

1488 Bartolomeu Dias (Portuguese) rounded South Africa's Cape of Good Hope

1492 Christopher Columbus (Italian) arrived in the West Indies

1498 Vasco da Gama (Portuguese) explored the coast of India

1513 Ponce de León (Spanish) reached Florida

1519-1521 Hernando Cortés (Spanish) conquered Mexico

1519-1522 The expedition led by Ferdinand Magellan (Portuguese) circled the globe

1532-1533 Francisco Pizarro (Spanish) conquered Peru

1535-1536 Jacques Cartier (French) sailed up Canada's St. Lawrence River

1539-1542 Hernando de Soto (Spanish) explored the southeastern U.S.

1541 Francisco Orellana (Spanish) explored the Amazon River

1607 John Smith (British) settled Jamestown, Virginia

1609-1610 Henry Hudson (British) explored the river, strait and bay that bear his name

1769 James Cook (British) explored New Zealand

1804-1806 Meriwether Lewis and William Clark (American) explored the northwest U.S.

1855 David Livingstone (Scottish) reached Victoria Falls in East Africa

1909 Robert E. Peary (American) reached the North Pole

1911 Roald Amundsen (Norwegian) reached the South Pole

The SEVEN Continents

CONTINENT	APPROX. AREA	HIGHEST POINT	LOWEST POINT
Africa	11,608,000 square miles (30,065,000 sq km)	Mount Kilimanjaro, Tanzania, 19,340 feet (5,895 m)	Lake Assal, Djibouti, 512 feet (156 m) below sea level
Antarctica	5,100,000 square miles (13,209,000 sq km)	Vinson Massif, 16,066 feet (4,897 m)	Ice covered 8,327 feet (2,538 m) below sea level
Asia (includes the Middle East)	17,212,000 square miles (44,579,000 sq km)	Mount Everest, Tibet/Nepal, 29,035 feet (8,850 m)	Dead Sea, Israel/Jordan, 1,349 feet (411 m) below sea level
Australia (includes Oceania)	3,132,000 square miles (8,112,000 sq km)	Mount Kosciusko, Australia, 7,316 feet (2,228 m)	Lake Eyre, Australia, 52 feet (16 m) below sea level
Europe (Ural Mountains divide Europe from Asia)	3,837,000 square miles (9,938,000 sq km)	Mount Elbrus, Russia/Georgia, 18,510 feet (5,642 m)	Caspian Sea, Russia/Kazakhstan, 92 feet (28 m) below sea level
North America (includes Central America and the Caribbean)	9,449,000 square miles (24,474,000 sq km)	Mount McKinley, Alaska, U.S., 20,320 feet (6,194 m)	Death Valley, California, U.S., 282 feet (86 m) below sea level
South America	6,879,000 square miles (17,819,000 sq km)	Mount Aconcagua, Argentina, 22,834 feet (6,960 m)	Valdes Peninsula, Argentina, 131 feet (40 m) below sea level

Source: WorldAtlas.com

The FIVE Oceans

In spring 2000, the International Hydrographic Organization delimited (marked the boundaries of) a fifth ocean. The new ocean, called the Southern Ocean, surrounds Antarctica and extends north to 60 degrees south latitude. It is the fourth-largest ocean, bigger only than the Arctic Ocean.

OCEAN	AREA	AVERAGE DEPTH
Pacific Ocean	60,060,700 square miles (155,557,000 sq km)	13,215 feet (4,028 m)
Atlantic Ocean	29,637,900 square miles (76,762,000 sq km)	12,880 feet (3,926 m)
Indian Ocean	26,469,500 square miles (68,556,000 sq km)	13,002 feet (3,963 m)
Southern Ocean	7,848,300 square miles (20,327,000 sq km)	13,100-16,400 feet* (4,000-5,000 m)
Arctic Ocean	5,427,000 square miles (14,056,000 sq km)	3,953 feet (1,205 m)

*Official depths of the Southern Ocean in dispute.

FAMILIES
of Countries

People aren't the only things with relatives; countries have them, too. Families of countries exist for several reasons, such as location, trade or politics.

BALKANS

The Balkans refers to the southeasternmost peninsula of Europe. It includes all or most of Slovenia, Croatia, Bosnia and Herzegovina, Albania, Serbia and Montenegro (formerly Yugoslavia), Macedonia, Bulgaria and European Turkey. Southeast Romania and northern Greece are also part of the Balkans.

CENTRAL AMERICA

Central America refers to the seven countries of North America between Mexico and South America: Belize, Costa Rica, El Salvador, Guatemala, Honduras, Nicaragua and Panama.

LATIN AMERICA

Latin America refers to all countries south of the United States—the nations of Central and South America and Mexico.

THE MIDDLE EAST

These countries of western Asia, northern Africa and the Arabian Peninsula are related geographically: Bahrain, Egypt, Iran, Iraq, Israel, Jordan, Qatar, Kuwait, Lebanon, Oman, Saudi Arabia, Syria, Turkey, the United Arab Emirates and Yemen.

NATO COUNTRIES

The North Atlantic Treaty Organization (NATO), formed in 1949, has one goal: to protect democratic systems of government. Today, the member countries are: Belgium, Bulgaria, Canada, Czech Republic, Denmark, Estonia, France, Germany, Greece, Hungary, Iceland, Italy, Latvia, Lithuania, Luxembourg, the Netherlands, Norway, Poland, Portugal, Romania, Slovakia, Slovenia, Spain, Turkey, the United Kingdom and the United States. Bulgaria, Estonia, Latvia, Lithuania, Romania, Slovakia and Slovenia were admitted to NATO in November 2002.

POLYNESIA

Polynesia, which means "many islands," is a collective term for the islands of the east-central Pacific Ocean, which include Cook, Easter, Pitcairn, Samoa, Tahiti and Tuvalu, as well as the Hawaiian islands.

SOUTHEAST ASIA

The countries that make up Southeast Asia are: Brunei, Indonesia, Cambodia, Laos, Malaysia, Myanmar (formerly called Burma), Vietnam, Singapore and Thailand.

The Lines on a Map

The equator divides Earth into halves, or **hemispheres**. The Northern Hemisphere is the half of Earth between the North Pole and the equator. The Southern Hemisphere is the half of Earth between the South Pole and the equator.

Earth can also be divided into the Eastern Hemisphere and the Western Hemisphere. The Western Hemisphere includes North and South America, their islands and the surrounding waters. The Eastern Hemisphere includes Asia, Africa, Australia and Europe.

Latitude measures distance from the equator. Latitude is measured in degrees and shown on a map by lines that run east and west.

Longitude measures distance from the prime meridian, an imaginary line on a map that runs through Greenwich, England. Longitude is measured in degrees and shown on a map by lines that run north and south.

Together, the lines of latitude and the lines of longitude form a grid on which it is possible to locate any place on Earth.

The **Tropic of Cancer** is a line of latitude that is one-quarter of the way from the equator to the North Pole. During the summer solstice, the Sun is directly overhead this line.

The **Tropic of Capricorn** is a line of latitude that is one-quarter of the way from the equator to the South Pole. During the winter solstice, the Sun is directly overhead this line.

ARCTIC CIRCLE

LINE OF LONGITUDE

TROPIC OF CANCER

LINE OF LATITUDE

EQUATOR

TROPIC OF CAPRICORN

ANTARCTIC CIRCLE

Three-quarters of the way between the equator and the North Pole lies the **Arctic Circle**. Above this imaginary line is the Arctic region. It is known as the Land of the Midnight Sun because in summer the Sun never sets.

The **Antarctic Circle** lies three-quarters of the way between the equator and the South Pole.

RECORD BREAKERS

LARGEST CONTINENT
Asia: 17,212,000 square miles
(44,579,000 sq km)

SMALLEST CONTINENT
Australia: 3,132,000 square miles
(8,112,000 sq km)

HIGHEST MOUNTAIN
Mount Everest: Himalayan Mountains,
Nepal/Tibet, 29,035 feet (8,850 m) above
sea level

LOWEST POINT ON LAND
The Dead Sea: Israel/Jordan, 1,349 feet
(411 m) below sea level

LARGEST LAKE
Caspian Sea: 152,239 square miles
(394,299 sq km)

LARGEST FRESHWATER LAKE
Lake Superior: U.S./Canada,
31,820 square miles (82,414 sq km)

DEEPEST LAKE
Lake Baikal: Russia, 5,315
feet (1,620 m)

Salto Angel is the world's tallest waterfall.

DEEPEST OCEAN
Pacific Ocean: average depth, 13,215 feet
(4,028 m); deepest point, 36,198 feet
(11,033 m)

LARGEST OCEAN
Pacific Ocean: 60,060,700 square miles
(155,557,000 sq km)

SMALLEST OCEAN
Arctic Ocean: 5,427,000 square miles
(14,056,000 sq km)

LARGEST ISLAND
Greenland: 839,999 square miles
(2,175,600 sq km)

LARGEST PENINSULA
Arabia: 1,250,000 square miles
(3,237,500 sq km)

LONGEST MOUNTAIN RANGE
The Andes: South America, more than
5,000 miles (8,000 km)

LONGEST RIVER
The Nile: Africa, 4,145 miles (6,670 km)

SHORTEST RIVER
The Roe: Montana, U.S., 201 feet (61 m)

HIGHEST WATERFALL
Angel (Salto Angel): Venezuela, 3,212
feet (979 m) high

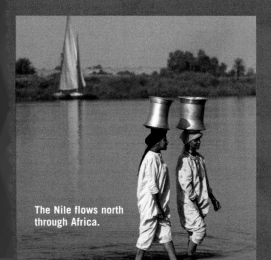

The Nile flows north through Africa.

EXTREME Points of the U.S.

Extreme	Latitude	Longitude	Distance*
Northernmost point: Point Barrow, Alaska	71°23' N	156°29' W	2,507 miles (4,034 km)
Easternmost point: West Quoddy Head, Maine	44°49' N	66°57' W	1,788 miles (2,997 km)
Southernmost point: Ka Lae (South Cape), Hawaii	18°55' N	155°41' W	3,463 miles (5,573 km)
Westernmost point: Cape Wrangell, Alaska (Attu Island)	52°55' N	172°27' E	3,625 miles (5,833 km)

*From the geographic center of the U.S. in Castle Rock, South Dakota

Explore The Past!

1000 Leif Eriksson was a Viking. He traveled to North America, which he named Vineland.

1271 Marco Polo was born in Venice, Italy. His adventures took him to China.

1325 Ibn Batuta was born in Morocco. He traveled to the Middle East and China.

1492 Christopher Columbus was born in Genoa, Italy. He traveled to North America.

In October, we celebrate the adventures of Christopher Columbus, a famous explorer who changed the course of history. Study the timeline to learn about other explorers who changed history. Then answer the questions by filling in the circle next to the correct answer.

1. Marco Polo's adventures happened
- ○ about 100 years after Columbus.
- ○ about 500 years before Columbus.
- ○ about 220 years before Columbus.

2. Leif Eriksson went to North America
- ○ about 500 years before Columbus.
- ○ about 1,000 years before Columbus.
- ○ about 400 years after Columbus.

3. Ibn Batuta's journeys occurred
- ○ about 300 years after Eriksson.
- ○ about 100 years after Columbus.
- ○ about 500 years after Polo.

(See Answer Key that begins on page 340.)

92

The Roof of the World

In 1852 scientists declared Mount Everest the world's highest mountain. This announcement captured the international imagination, and soon the idea of reaching the summit of the "roof of the world" was viewed as the ultimate geographic feat.

It wasn't until 101 years later that someone achieved the lofty goal. On May 29, 1953, Edmund Hillary, a New Zealand beekeeper, and Tenzing Norgay, an acclaimed Sherpa climber, became the first to reach the roof of the world. The dangers of climbing Everest, which measures 29,035 feet, include avalanches, crevasses, ferocious winds up to 125 miles per hour, sudden storms, temperatures of minus 40°F and oxygen deprivation. Climbers spend months getting used to the climate. They usually attempt Everest only in May and October, avoiding the winter snows and the summer monsoons.

Here are some other Everest firsts:

First American to summit Everest: James Whittaker in 1963
First woman to summit Everest: Junko Tabei (Japanese) in 1975
Oldest person to summit Everest: Sherman Bull, 64, (American) in 2001
Youngest person to summit Everest: Temba Tsheri, 16, (Nepalese) in 2001
First blind person to summit Everest: Erik Weihenmayer (American) in 2001

TFK TOP 5 DESERTS

Deserts are the driest places on the planet, with only about 10 inches of rain a year. Some deserts are hot, like the Sahara in Africa, and some are cold, like the Gobi in Asia. Deserts are found in every continent except Europe. Here are the largest deserts in the world.

1. **Sahara (Africa)**—3,500,000 square miles (9,065,000 sq km)
2. **Arabian (Asia)**—1,000,000 square miles (2,600,000 sq km)
3. **Australian**—570,000 square miles (1,476,000 sq km)
4. **Gobi (Asia)**—500,000 square miles (1,295,000 sq km)
5. **Kalahari (Africa)**—225,000 square miles (582,700 sq km)

Source: Information compiled by Time For Kids

TFK MYSTERY PERSON

CLUE 1: In 1927, I became the first pilot to complete a nonstop *solo* flight across the Atlantic Ocean. (The first flight across the Atlantic included two British aviators in 1919.)
CLUE 2: My grandson marked the 75th anniversary of my flight by taking the same transatlantic flight in 2002.
CLUE 3: My nickname was "Lucky Lindy."

WHO AM I?
(See Answer Key that begins on page 340.)

GOVERNMENT

THE Constitution

★ ★ ★ ★ ★ ★

In 1787 leaders of the states gathered to write the Constitution—a set of principles that told how the new nation would be governed. The Constitution went into effect in 1789.

The Constitution begins with a famous section called the preamble. The preamble says that the U.S. government was created by the people and for the benefit of the people:

We the people of the United States, in order to form a more perfect Union, establish justice, insure domestic tranquility, provide for the common defense, promote the general welfare and secure the blessings of liberty to ourselves and our posterity, do ordain and establish this Constitution for the United States of America.

The leaders of the states wanted a strong and fair national government. But they also wanted to protect individual freedoms and prevent the government from abusing its power. They believed they could do this by having three separate branches of government: the Executive, the Legislative and the Judicial. This separation is described in the first three articles, or sections, of the Constitution.

The Constitution was originally made up of seven articles.

ARTICLE I Creates the Legislative Branch—the House of Representatives and the Senate—and describes its powers and responsibilities.

ARTICLE II Creates the Executive Branch, which is led by the President, and describes its powers and responsibilities.

ARTICLE III Creates the Judicial Branch, which is led by the Supreme Court, and describes its powers and responsibilities.

ARTICLE IV Describes the rights and powers of the states.

ARTICLE V Explains how amendments (changes or additions) can be made to the Constitution.

ARTICLE VI Says the Constitution is "the supreme law of the land."

ARTICLE VII Tells how the Constitution would be ratified (approved and made official) by the states.

THE Bill OF Rights

As Article V shows, the authors of the Constitution expected from the beginning that amendments, or changes and additions, would be made to it. There are now **27 amendments**.

The first 10 amendments are known as the Bill of Rights. They list individual freedoms promised by the new government. The Bill of Rights was approved in 1791.

AMENDMENT I Guarantees freedom of religion, speech and the press.

AMENDMENT II Guarantees the right of the people to have firearms.

AMENDMENT III Says that soldiers may not stay in a house without the owner's agreement.

AMENDMENT IV Says that the government cannot search people and their homes without a strong reason.

AMENDMENT V Says that every person has the right to a trial and to protection of his or her rights while waiting for a trial. Also, private property cannot be taken without payment.

AMENDMENT VI Says that every person shall have the right to "a speedy and public trial."

AMENDMENT VII Guarantees the right to a trial in various types of legal cases.

AMENDMENT VIII Outlaws all "cruel and unusual punishment."

AMENDMENT IX Says that people have rights in addition to those listed in the Constitution.

AMENDMENT X Says that the powers the Constitution does not give to the national government belong to the states and to the people.

Other Notable Amendments

Amendment XIII (approved 1865) Declares slavery illegal.

Amendment XV (approved 1870) Says the right to vote cannot be denied because of race.

Amendment XVI (approved 1913) Gives Congress the power to tax incomes.

Amendment XIX (approved 1920) Grants women the right to vote.

Amendment XXII (approved 1951) Says that a President may serve no more than two four-year terms.

Amendment XXIV (approved 1964) Forbids poll taxes—money paid for the right to vote—in national elections.

Amendment XXV (approved 1967) Says the Vice President becomes President if the President leaves office early.

Amendment XXVI (approved 1971) Lowers the voting age to 18.

The Constitution was signed by the nation's leaders in Philadelphia.

For the complete Constitution, including all the amendments, www.FACTMONSTER.COM

THE
Legislative Branch

The Legislative Branch is made up of the two houses of Congress—the **Senate** and the **House of Representatives**. The most important duty of the Legislative Branch is to make laws. Laws are written, discussed and voted on in Congress.

There are **100 Senators** in the Senate, two from each state. Senators are elected by their states and serve six-year terms. The Vice President of the U.S. is considered the head of the Senate, but does not vote in the Senate unless there is a tie. The Senate approves nominations made by the President to the Cabinet, the Supreme Court, federal courts and other posts. The Senate must ratify all treaties by a two-thirds vote.

There are **435 Representatives** in the House of Representatives. The number of Representatives each state gets is based on its population. For example, California has many more Representatives than Montana. When Census figures determine that the population of a state has changed significantly, the number of Representatives in that state may shift proportionately. Representatives are elected by their states and serve two-year terms. The Speaker of the House, elected by the Representatives, is considered the head of the House.

Both parties in the Senate and the House of Representatives elect leaders. The leader of the party that controls the house is called the majority leader. The other party leader is called the minority leader.

Did You Know?

In November 2002 President Bush approved a new cabinet-level office called the Department of Homeland Security to protect the country against terrorism. The new department unites 22 different agencies and 170,000 employees. The Secret Service and the Coast Guard are just a few of the agencies that come under the new department.

President George W. Bush signs a proclamation as supporters look on.

THE
Executive Branch

The President is the head of the Executive Branch, which makes laws official. The President is elected by the entire country and serves a four-year term. The President approves and carries out laws passed by the Legislative Branch. He appoints or removes Cabinet members and officials.

THE PRESIDENT

THE VICE PRESIDENT

He negotiates treaties and acts as head of state and Commander-in-Chief of the armed forces.

The Executive Branch also includes the **Vice President** and other officials, such as members of the **Cabinet**. The Cabinet is made up of the heads of the 15 major departments of the government.

The Cabinet gives advice to the President about important matters.

THE CABINET

Secretary of Agriculture	Secretary of Commerce	Secretary of Defense	Secretary of Education	Secretary of Energy

Ann Veneman

Donald Evans

Donald Rumsfeld

Rod Paige

Spencer Abraham

Secretary of Health and Human Services	Secretary of Housing and Urban Development	Secretary of the Interior	Attorney General	Secretary of Labor

Tommy Thompson

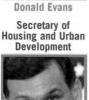
Melquiades Martinez

Gale Norton

John Ashcroft

Elaine Chao

Secretary of State	Secretary of Transportation	Secretary of the Treasury	Secretary of Veterans' Affairs	Secretary of Homeland Security

Colin Powell

Norman Mineta

John W. Snow

Anthony Principi

Tom Ridge

THE Judicial Branch

The Judicial Branch oversees the court system of the U.S. Through court cases, the Judicial Branch explains the meaning of the Constitution and laws passed by Congress. **The Supreme Court** is the head of the Judicial Branch. Unlike a criminal court, the Supreme Court rules whether something is constitutional or unconstitutional—whether or not it is permitted under the Constitution.

On the Supreme Court there are **nine Justices,** or judges: eight associate Justices and one Chief Justice. The judges are nominated by the President and approved by the Senate. They have no term limits. The Supreme Court is the highest court in the land. Its decisions are final, and no other court can overrule those decisions. Decisions of the Supreme Court set precedents—new ways of interpreting the law.

Chief Justice William Rehnquist, center, and the eight associate Justices

SIGNIFICANT SUPREME COURT DECISIONS

1803 *Marbury v. Madison*
The first time a law passed by Congress was declared unconstitutional

1857 *Dred Scott v. Sanford*
Declared that a slave was not a citizen, and that Congress could not outlaw slavery in U.S. territories

1896 *Plessy v. Ferguson*
Said that racial segregation was legal

1954 *Brown v. Board of Education*
Made racial segregation in schools illegal

1966 *Miranda v. Arizona*
Stated that criminal suspects must be informed of their rights before being questioned by police

Famous Female Firsts!

Draw a line from each person on the left to the phrase on the right that describes her accomplishment.

Jeannette Rankin

Hillary Clinton

Hattie Caraway

Frances Perkins

Shirley Chisholm

First woman to hold a Cabinet post

First woman member of Congress

First black woman elected to the U.S. House of Representatives

First woman elected to Senate

First First Lady elected to Senate

(See Answer Key that begins on page 340.)

One Big Party

In the November 2002 midterm elections, the Republican Party won control of the Senate and held on to its majority in the House of Representatives. This marks the first time in 50 years that Republicans have control of the White House and both houses of Congress.

Powers of the Government

Federal Government	State Government	Federal and State Government
★ Print money	★ Issue licenses	In addition to their unique powers, both the Federal Government and state governments have the power to:
★ Regulate interstate (between states) and international trade	★ Regulate intrastate (within the state) businesses	
★ Make treaties and conduct foreign policy	★ Conduct elections	★ Collect taxes
	★ Establish local governments	★ Build roads
★ Declare war	★ Ratify amendments to the Constitution	★ Borrow money
★ Provide an army and a navy		★ Establish courts
★ Establish post offices	★ Take measures for public health and safety	★ Make and enforce laws
★ Make laws necessary and proper to carry out these powers	★ May exert powers the Constitution does not delegate to the federal government or prohibit the states from using	★ Charter banks and corporations
		★ Spend money for the good of the people
		★ Take private property for public use, with fair payment

Source: The U.S. Government Printing Office

Checks AND Balances

The system of checks and **balances** is an important part of the Constitution. With checks and balances, each of the three branches of government can limit the powers of the others. This way, no one branch becomes too powerful. Each branch "checks" the power of the other branches to make sure that the power is balanced among them. How does this system of checks and balances work?

The process of how laws are made (see the following page) is a good example of checks and balances in action. First, the **Legislative Branch** introduces and votes on a bill. The bill then goes to the **Executive Branch**, where the President decides whether he thinks the bill is good for the country. If so, he signs the bill, and it becomes a law.

If the President does not believe the bill is good for the country,

he does not sign it. This is called a veto. But the Legislative Branch gets another chance. With enough votes, the Legislative Branch can override the Executive Branch's veto, and the bill becomes a law.

Once a law is in place, the people of the country can test it through the court system, which is under the control of the **Judicial Branch**. If someone believes a law is unfair, a lawsuit can be filed. Lawyers then make arguments for and against the case, and a judge decides which side has presented the most convincing arguments. The side that loses can choose to appeal to a higher court, and the case may eventually reach the highest court of all, the Supreme Court.

If the Legislative Branch does not agree with the way in which the Judicial Branch has interpreted the law, it can introduce a new piece of legislation, and the process starts all over again.

How A Bill Becomes A Law

★ ★ ★ ★ ★ ★

1 A member of Congress introduces a bill.

When a Senator or Representative introduces a bill, it is sent to the clerk of the Senate or House, who gives it a number and title. Next, the bill goes to the appropriate committee.

2 Committees review and vote on the bill.

Committees specialize in different areas, such as foreign relations or agriculture, and are made up of small groups of Senators or Representatives.

The committee may reject the bill and "table" it, meaning it is never discussed again. Or it may hold hearings to listen to facts and opinions, make changes in the bill and cast votes. If most committee members vote in favor of the bill, it is sent back to the Senate and the House for debate.

3 The Senate and the House debate and vote on the bill.

Separately, the Senate and the House debate the bill, offer amendments and cast votes. If the bill is defeated in either the Senate or the House, the bill dies.

Sometimes, the House and the Senate pass the same bill, but with different amendments. In these cases, the bill goes to a conference committee made up of members of both houses of Congress. The conference committee works out differences between the two versions of the bill.

Then the bill goes before all of Congress for a vote. If a majority of both the Senate and the House votes for the bill, it goes to the President for approval.

You're Grounded

The President, Vice President and other U.S. officials can be impeached—that is, formally charged with "high crimes and misdemeanors." Such crimes and misdemeanors include bribery, perjury, treason and abuse of power.

Under the Constitution, only the House of Representatives has the power to impeach a federal official. If a majority of the House votes for impeachment, then the Senate holds a trial and votes on whether to convict the official. If two-thirds of the Senate votes for conviction, the official will be removed from office.

Only two Presidents have been impeached: Andrew Johnson and William Clinton. However, neither was convicted by the Senate.

4 The President signs the bill—or not.

If the President approves the bill and signs it, the bill becomes a law. However, if the President disapproves, he can veto the bill by refusing to sign it.

Congress can try to overrule a veto. If both the Senate and the House pass the bill by a two-thirds majority, the President's veto is overruled and the bill becomes a law.

How THE President Gets Elected

★ ★ ★ ★ ★ ★ ★ ★

STEP BY STEP on the Campaign Trail

1 Candidate announces plan to run for office.

This announcement launches the candidate's official campaign. Speeches, debates and baby-kissing begin.

2 Candidate campaigns to win delegate support.

The first stage of a presidential campaign is the nomination campaign. At this time the candidate is competing with other candidates in the same party, hoping to get the party's nomination. The candidate works to win delegates—representatives who pledge to support the candidate's nomination at the national party convention—and to persuade potential voters in general.

3 Caucuses and primary elections take place in the states.

Caucuses and primaries are ways for the general public to take part in nominating presidential candidates.

At a caucus, local party members gather to nominate a candidate. A caucus is a lively event at which party leaders and activists debate issues and consider candidates. The rules governing caucus procedures vary by party and by state.

A primary is more like a general election. Voters go to the polls to cast their votes for a presidential candidate (or delegates who will represent that candidate at the party convention). A primary election is the main way voters choose a nominee.

4 Nominee for President is announced at national party convention.

There are two primary political parties in the U.S.—the Democratic Party and the Republican Party. The main goal of a national party convention is to unify party members. Thousands of delegates gather to rally support for the party's ideas and to formally nominate party candidates for President and Vice President.

After the convention, the second stage of the presidential campaign begins: the election campaign. In this stage, candidates from different parties compete against each other as they try to get elected President.

5 Citizens cast their votes.

Presidential elections are held every four years on the Tuesday after the first Monday of November.

Many Americans think that when they cast their ballot, they are voting for their chosen candidate. Actually, they are selecting groups of electors in the Electoral College.

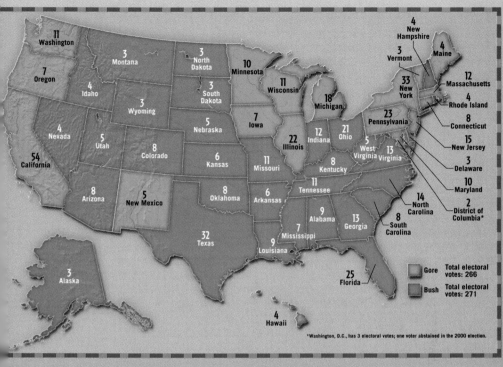

Electoral College votes by state in the 2000 election.

6 The Electoral College casts its votes.

Some of the Founding Fathers wanted Congress to elect the President. Others wanted the President to be elected by popular vote. The Electoral College represents a compromise between these ideas.

Every state has a number of electors equal to its number of Senators and Representatives. In addition, there are three electors for the District of Columbia. In the 2000 election there were 538 electors. Laws vary by state, but electors are usually chosen by popular vote. An elector may not be a Senator, Representative or other person holding a U.S. office.

In most cases, the electoral votes from a particular state go to the candidate who leads the popular vote in that state. (Only Maine and Nebraska divide electoral votes among candidates.) This "winner takes all"

system can produce surprising results; in the elections of 1824, 1876, 1888 and 2000, the candidate who had the greatest popular vote did not win the greatest Electoral College vote, and so lost the presidency.

On the first Monday after the second Wednesday in December, the electors cast their ballots. At least 270 electoral votes are required to elect a President. If this majority is not reached, the House of Representatives chooses the President.

7 The President is inaugurated.

On January 20, the President enters office in a ceremony know as the Inauguration and takes the presidential oath: "I do solemnly swear (or affirm) that I will faithfully execute the office of President of the United States, and will to the best of my ability, preserve, protect, and defend the Constitution of the United States."

PARTY ANIMALS

The **Democratic donkey** was first associated with Democrat Andrew Jackson's 1828 presidential campaign. His opponents called him a jackass (a donkey), and Jackson decided to use the image of the strong-willed animal on his campaign posters. Later, cartoonist Thomas Nast used the Democratic donkey in newspaper cartoons and made the symbol famous.

Nast invented another famous symbol— the **Republican elephant**. After the Republicans lost the White House to the Democrats in 1877, Nast drew a cartoon of an elephant walking into a trap set by a donkey. He chose the elephant to represent the Republicans because elephants are intelligent but easily controlled.

Democrats today say the donkey is smart and brave, while Republicans say the elephant is strong and dignified.

Who can vote?

Anyone who is
1. 18 years of age
2. a citizen of the U.S. and meets the residency requirements of his or her state.

Who can be a Senator?

Anyone who is
1. at least 30 years old
2. a citizen of the U.S. for at least 9 years
3. a resident of the state where he or she is elected

Who can be a Representative?

Anyone who is
1. at least 25 years old
2. a citizen of the U.S. for at least 7 years
3. a resident of the state where he or she is elected

Who can be President?

Anyone who is
1. a natural-born citizen of the U.S.
2. at least 35 years of age
3. a resident of the U.S. for at least 14 years

Did You Know?

In November 2002 Representative Nancy Pelosi, a Democrat from California, was elected House Minority Leader, making her the first woman to lead a political party in Congress.

The Presidential Succession

Who would take over if the President died, resigned or was removed from office? The list of who's next in line is known as presidential succession.

★ The Vice President
★ Speaker of the House
★ President pro tempore of the Senate
★ Secretary of State
★ Secretary of the Treasury
★ Secretary of Defense
★ Attorney General
★ Secretary of the Interior
★ Secretary of Agriculture
★ Secretary of Commerce
★ Secretary of Labor
★ Secretary of Health and Human Services
★ Secretary of Housing and Urban Development
★ Secretary of Transportation
★ Secretary of Energy
★ Secretary of Education
★ Secretary of Veterans' Affairs

Two members of the current Cabinet cannot become President because they were not born in the U.S. Can you name them?

(See Answer Key that begins on page 340.)

TFK MYSTERY PERSON

CLUE 1: I was born in Windsor Locks, Connecticut, in 1919. I started my political career when I was 33 years old.
CLUE 2: From 1970-1974, I served in the U.S. House of Representatives.
CLUE 3: In 1974, I won election as governor of Connecticut. I was the first woman in U.S. history to be elected governor.

WHO AM I?

(See Answer Key that begins on page 340.)

105

FROM TFK MAGAZINE

The New GYM

BY RITU UPADHYAY

It's a sunny day, and 9-year-old Liza Parisaca pulls on a life vest and cautiously climbs into the bobbing sailboat. Today, the first-time sailor will learn how to tack, or change course, on the boat.

This isn't a sailing trip. It's gym class for fourth and fifth graders at Riverside Elementary School in Miami, Florida. Riverside is one of many schools around the country that has begun adding fun, new activities to gym classes.

In these schools, gym class is no longer about lining up and choosing dodgeball teams. A new physical education (P.E.) movement helps kids find activities they'll enjoy so much that they'll stay active for the rest of their lives. The activities include yoga, cycling, martial arts, dance, kickboxing, in-line skating, using treadmills and even sailing and kayaking. The goal is to teach children sports and workouts that they can enjoy outside of school.

The movement comes in response to studies that show kids are less active than ever before. A recent report released by the Institute of Medicine said American kids and adults need much more exercise. The report calls for at least an hour a day of some type of physical activity.

Yet fewer than one in four children get even 20 minutes of vigorous activity daily. One in four kids gets no physical education in school, claims P.E. 4 Life, a group that promotes fitness for kids.

The government has launched its own program to get America's children moving. The campaign, called "Verb: It's What You Do," shows kids ages 9 to 13 fun ways to get active. "Verb means action, and action is the focus of this campaign," said Tommy Thompson, secretary of the Department of Health and Human Services.

It is part of President Bush's Healthier U.S. program. "Better health is an important national goal," said the President. "A healthier America is a stronger America."

Gym classes now emphasize lifelong fitness habits, not competition.

Fitness Tips

Want to feel good, have fun and stay healthy? Here are some tips from Judy Young, executive director of the National Association for Sport and Physical Education.

Get moving: Exercise at least an hour every day. Kick a soccer ball, go for a family walk, practice a dance with a friend—whatever! Try new and varied activities so you work different muscles in your body.

Stick with it: Do one of your daily physical activities for at least 10 minutes at a time. Increase the time as you get stronger.

Set limits: Don't spend more than two hours a day sitting and playing computer games or watching TV.

Fuel up: Eat a balanced diet that includes grains, fruits and vegetables, dairy and lean meat or other protein foods. It's okay to have sweets sometimes, but never instead of a meal. Drink plenty of water every day.

Have fun: Exercise is more fun with a partner. Invite a friend or family member the next time you're ready for active play.

Exercise—It's Good for You

Exercise is not only fun, it's also good for your body, mind and overall well-being. Kids who exercise on a regular basis often do better in school, sleep better, don't feel as tired, are less likely to get hurt while exercising and are stronger than less-active kids. Exercise can also relieve stress and improve your mood.

There are two types of exercise, **aerobic** and **anaerobic.** When you do aerobic exercise, you increase your heart rate and the flow of oxygen-rich blood to your muscles. Aerobic exercises include running, swimming, biking, playing soccer, dancing and skiing. Aerobic exercise builds endurance and burns fat and calories.

When you do anaerobic exercise, such as weight-lifting or push-ups, which involve short bursts of effort, you build strength and muscle mass.

Indoor Exercise
Stuck inside with energy to burn? Here are some ways you might exercise.

- Dance to your favorite music
- See how long you can hula hoop
- Practice jump-rope tricks
- Run up and down stairs
- Set up an obstacle course

107

Smoking Stinks

Even though you may see stars smoke in movies, in music videos or on television, there's nothing cool or glamorous about smoking. Smoking stinks—literally! It makes breath, hair and clothes smell like smoke. It's expensive. It raises blood pressure and causes shortness of breath. It can cause bronchitis, emphysema, asthma and chronic coughing. Smokers run slower and can't run as far as nonsmokers.

And, most important, it kills. Each year, about 500,000 Americans die from smoking-related illnesses. Smokers are 10 times more likely to get cancer than nonsmokers. People who smoke one pack of cigarettes a day reduce their life expectancy by about six years.

Cigarettes contain nicotine, a highly addictive drug. Nicotine is also a poison that's used in bug spray. Arsenic, formaldehyde, hydrogen, cyanide, tar and carbon monoxide are some of the other poisons found in cigarettes. No wonder smoking is linked to heart disease and cancer.

People who have smoked one pack of cigarettes a day for two years have spent about $3,240 on cigarettes!

It's Hip to Be Clean

Think taking drugs will make you hip? Think again. Drugs, including alcohol, can seriously harm your body. They impair judgment, and people high on drugs often do things they would never do when sober, such as commit crimes or engage in dangerous behavior that could hurt themselves or other people. Kids who use drugs usually do poorly in school and are more likely to drop out of school than kids who don't.

Drug abuse can kill brain cells, damage the liver and cause heart failure. It can also lead to depression. Once people start using drugs, they need more and more to feel their effects. This leads to addiction and increases the chances of overdosing.

Prescriptions: Just for You

Prescription medicines are also drugs. They are good drugs because they kill bacteria and infections and make you feel better when you're sick. When a doctor prescribes a drug, it's important that you finish the medicine and follow the doctor's directions about taking the drug. You should never share your prescription medicine with anyone, even if he or she has the same symptoms as you. Some people are allergic to certain medications, and taking the medicine can make them very ill.

Did You Know?

Smokeless tobacco (chewing or spitting tobacco) is not safe! It can cause bleeding gums and mouth sores that never heal. It may lead to cancer. It also contains nicotine and can become addictive.

The Food Pyramid:
Healthy or Not?

The food pyramid, created by the U.S. Department of Agriculture (USDA), debuted in 1992. It recommends the number of servings of each food group a person should eat each day to stay healthy.

But in recent years, doctors and scientists have studied the food pyramid and have begun to question just how helpful—and healthful—the guidelines really are. In fact, the USDA itself is reevaluating the food pyramid.

The pyramid indicates that people should eat between 6 and 11 servings of grains a day. Grains include bread, pasta and cereals. One serving equals one slice of bread or one-half cup of cooked rice or pasta. By recommending so many bread products, which are usually low in fat, the USDA has been promoting a low-fat diet.

But many experts now believe that a low-fat diet that's high in sugar (most processed grains, such as white flour, are made out of forms of sugar like glucose and fructose) has actually led to an increase in obesity and heart problems.

Some doctors now contend that a diet higher in fat—with the fat coming from nuts, cheeses, some oils (such as olive oil), poultry, eggs and some lean red meat—will keep people trimmer and healthier than a high-carbohydrate, low-fat diet.

This food pyramid is from 1992. It calls for a diet high in carbohydrates and low in fats. Since 1992, scientists have learned more about our nutritional needs. Based on this data, a new pyramid would emphasize a diet high in protein, fruits, vegetables and whole grains.

So what should you eat? Eat a variety of foods from all five food groups—grains, vegetables, fruit, dairy and fats and oils. But when eating grains, try to avoid white bread and pasta and instead eat whole-grain foods, such as whole-wheat bread, crackers and pasta. They contain more natural nutrients and are high in fiber, which helps to lower cholesterol and may protect against some cancers.

Try to eat less red meat, such as hamburgers and steak, and more fish, nuts and cheese. You won't go wrong eating lots of fruits and vegetables. No one is questioning their nutritional value. In fact, many vegetables have been found to reduce the risk of getting cancer, and fruits are a great source of many vitamins, like vitamin C.

Finally, avoid junk foods, such as soda, candy and potato chips. These foods provide little or no nutritional value. Instead, choose healthy snacks, such as fruit, nuts and yogurt.

Did You Know?

Boys age 9-18 need about 2,800 calories a day. Girls age 9-18 need about 2,200 calories a day.

Your Body

If you could peek inside your own body, what would you see? Hundreds of bones, miles of blood vessels and trillions of cells, all of which are constantly working together.

Skin

MAIN JOB: To protect your internal organs from drying up and to prevent harmful bacteria from getting inside your body
HOW MUCH: The average person has about six pounds of skin.

Main layers:
- **Epidermis:** Outer layer of skin cells, hair, nails and sweat glands
- **Dermis:** Inner layer of living tissue, containing nerves and blood vessels

Bones

DID YOU KNOW? The largest bone in the body is the femur, or thighbone. In a 6-foot-tall person, it is 20 inches long. The smallest is the stirrup bone, in the ear. It is .1 inch long.
MAIN JOB: To give shape and support to your body
HOW MANY: At birth you had more than 300 bones in your body. As an adult you'll have 206, because some bones fuse together.

Kinds of Bones
- **Long** bones are thin; they are found in your legs, arms and fingers.
- **Short** bones are wide and chunky; they are found in your feet and wrists.
- **Flat** bones are flat and smooth, like your shoulder blades.
- **Irregular** bones, like the bones in your inner ear and the vertebrae in your spine, come in many different shapes.

Joints

DID YOU KNOW? Bones don't bend. It is the joint that allows two bones next to each other to move.
MAIN JOB: To allow bones to move in different directions

Ligaments

MAIN JOB: To hold joints together. These bands of tough tissue are strong and flexible.

Muscles

MAIN JOB: To make body movement possible
HOW MANY: Your body has more than 650 muscles.

Kinds of Muscles
- **Skeletal** muscles help the body move. You have about 400 skeletal muscles.
- **Smooth** muscles are located inside organs, like the stomach.
- **Cardiac** muscle is found only in the heart.

Tendons

MAIN JOB: To hold your muscles to your bones
DID YOU KNOW? Tendons look like rubber bands.

Viscera

This term refers to the organs that fill your body's chest and abdominal cavity.
MAIN JOB: To provide your body with food and oxygen and to remove waste
HOW MANY: The viscera include the trachea (windpipe), lungs, liver, kidneys, gallbladder, spleen, stomach, large intestine, small intestine and bladder.

Glands

MAIN JOB: To manufacture substances that help your body to function

Kinds of Glands
- **Endocrine** glands make hormones, which tell the different parts of your body when to work.
- **Oil glands** keep your skin from drying out.
- **Salivary** glands make saliva, which helps to digest and swallow food.
- **Sweat** glands make perspiration, which regulates your body temperature.

Cells

DID YOU KNOW? There are 26 billion cells in a newborn baby and 50 trillion cells in an adult.

MAIN JOB: To perform the many jobs necessary to stay alive, such as moving oxygen around your body, taking care of the fuel supply and waste removal

Some Different Cells

- **Bone** cells help to build your skeleton by producing the fibers and minerals from which bone is made.
- **Fat** cells contain fat, which is burned to create energy.
- **Muscle** cells are organized into muscles, which move body parts.
- **Nerve** cells pass nerve messages around your body.
- **Red** blood cells carry oxygen around your body.
- **White** blood cells fight disease.

Body Count

- The five senses are sight, hearing, smell, touch and taste.

- Your body contains eight pints of blood.

- You use 14 muscles to smile and 43 to frown.

- Kids have 20 first teeth. Adults have 32 teeth.

- Most people shed 40 pounds of skin in a lifetime.

- Your body is 70% water.

- An **eyelash** lives about 150 days before it falls out.

- You blink your eyes about 20,000 times a day.

- Your heart beats about 100,000 times a day.

- When you sneeze, air rushes through your **nose** at a rate of 100 miles per hour.

- Humans breathe 20 times per minute, more than 10 million times per year and about 700 million times in a lifetime.

- You have about **100,000 hairs** on your head.

- Your **tongue** has four taste zones: bitter (back), sour (back sides), salty (front sides) and sweet (front).

Your Body's Systems

Circulatory System

The circulatory system transports blood throughout the body. The heart pumps the blood and the **arteries** and **veins** transport it. Blood is carried away from the heart by arteries. The biggest artery, called the **aorta,** branches from the left side of the heart into smaller **arteries,** which then branch into even smaller vessels that travel all over the body. When blood enters the smallest of these vessels, which are called **capillaries,** it gives nutrients and oxygen to cells and takes in carbon dioxide, water and waste. The blood then returns to the heart through **veins.** Veins carry waste products away from cells and bring blood back to the heart, which pumps it to the lungs to pick up oxygen and eliminate waste carbon dioxide.

Digestive System

The digestive system breaks down food into protein, vitamins, minerals, carbohydrates and fats, which the body needs for energy, growth and repair. After food is chewed and swallowed, it goes down a tube called the **esophagus** and enters the **stomach,** where it is broken down by powerful acids. From the stomach the food travels into the **small intestine,** where it is broken down into nutrients. The food that the body doesn't need or can't digest is turned into waste and eliminated from the body through the **large intestine.**

Endocrine System

The endocrine system is made up of glands that produce **hormones,** the body's long-distance messengers. Hormones are chemicals that control body functions, such as metabolism and growth. The **glands,** which include the pituitary gland, thyroid gland, adrenal glands, pancreas, ovaries and testes, release hormones into the bloodstream, which then transports the hormones to organs and tissues throughout the body.

Immune System

The immune system is our body's defense system against infections and diseases. It works to respond to dangerous organisms, such as viruses or bacteria, and substances that may enter the body. There are **three** types of response systems in the immune system.

- **The *anatomic response* physically prevents dangerous substances from entering your body. The anatomic system includes the skin and the mucous membranes.**
- **The *inflammatory system* eliminates the invaders from your body. Sneezing and fever are examples of the inflammatory system at work.**
- **The *immune response* is made up of white blood cells, which fight infection by gobbling up toxins, bacteria and other threats.**

Muscular System

The muscular system is made up of tissues that work with the skeletal system to control movement of the body. Some muscles—like the ones in your arms and legs—are **voluntary,** meaning that you decide when to move them. Other muscles, like the ones in your stomach, heart and intestines, are **involuntary.** This means they're controlled by the nervous system and hormones, and you often don't even realize they're at work.

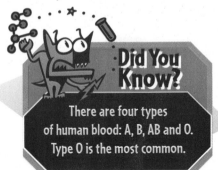

Did You Know?

There are four types of human blood: A, B, AB and O. Type O is the most common.

Nervous System

The nervous system is made up of the brain, the spinal cord and nerves. The nervous system sends and receives nerve impulses that tell your muscles and organs what to do. There are three parts of your nervous system that work together.

•The **central** nervous system consists of the brain and spinal cord. It sends out nerve impulses and receives sensory information, which tells your brain about things you see, hear, smell, taste and feel.

•The **peripheral** nervous system includes the nerves that branch off from the brain and the spinal cord. It carries the nerve impulses from the central nervous system to the muscles and glands.

•The **autonomic** nervous system regulates involuntary action, such as heartbeat and digestion.

Respiratory System

The respiratory system brings air into the body and removes carbon dioxide. It includes the nose, trachea (windpipe) and lungs. When you inhale, air enters your **nose** and goes down the **trachea.** The trachea branches into two bronchial tubes, which go to the **lungs.** These tubes branch off into even smaller bronchial tubes, which end in air sacs. Oxygen follows this path and passes through the air sacs and blood vessels and enters the blood stream. At the same time, carbon dioxide passes into the lungs and is exhaled.

Skeletal System

The skeletal system is made up of **bones, ligaments** and **tendons.** It shapes the body and protects organs. The skeletal system works with the muscular system to help the body move.

TFK
MYSTERY PERSON

CLUE 1: I was born in 1875 in Alsace, which is now part of France.
CLUE 2: As a young man, I studied music and religion. At age 30, I decided to become a doctor.
CLUE 3: I devoted my life to providing health care for needy people in West Africa. In 1952, I won the Nobel Peace Prize.

WHO AM I?
(See Answer Key that begins on page 340.)

For more about the body and its systems, go to www.FACTMONSTER.COM

WHO KILLED KING TUT?

TWO MODERN DETECTIVES TRY TO CRACK AN OLD CASE

A golden throne shows King Tutankhamen and his wife (top). The gold "death mask" covered the head of the boy king's mummy.

Egypt's boy king, **Tutankhamen** (toot-ong-kah-men), died more than 3,300 years ago. But questions about his death persist. Why would the tomb of someone so important be so small? Why was his mummy prepared in a sloppy way? And why did a Pharaoh (fair-oh), or king, who had the best nutrition and medical care of the time, die so young?

Two former police detectives recently reopened Tut's case, hoping to solve the ancient mystery. After many months of research, Greg Cooper and Mike King say they have proof that the 18-year-old Tut was murdered. They also claim to have a short list of suspects. Now they want to prove it to the world.

Cooper and King started by digging through books and photos of Tut's tomb. Then they traveled to Egypt for more sleuthing. At first, everyone was a suspect. "We looked at the entire Egyptian empire," Cooper says. "But we quickly narrowed our focus."

Doctors consulted by the detectives confirmed earlier theories that Tut may have been a victim of foul play. X rays showed a possible blood clot and breaks in the thin bones above Tut's eyes. These findings suggest he may also have suffered a violent blow to the head. The X rays also revealed a

A Gallery of Suspects:

FROM TFK MAGAZINE

Detectives Greg Cooper and Mike King focused their investigation on people who had easy and frequent access to King Tut and who might have had a reason to want him dead. Here are the final four suspects:

- Did Tut's wife (and half sister), Ankhesenamen, plot his murder? The detectives believe that she loved him too much to harm him.

- Tut's prime minister, Ay, had the most to gain from killing the king. In fact, he won the throne and ruled Egypt after Tut's death. Is Ay the guilty one?

- As head of the army, Horemheb had the power to kill the king. But did he have a motive?

- Was Maya, the royal treasurer, loyal to King Tut?

Mike King (left) and Greg Cooper search King Ay's tomb for clues to Tut's death.

new clue. Tut had a condition affecting his neck. He couldn't turn his head without moving his torso. It would have been very easy to sneak up and attack Tut from behind.

Scientists who study ancient Egypt say that Cooper and King's theory is based more on guesswork than on facts. "Do we know he was murdered? Absolutely not," says Egyptologist Rita Freed.

Freed says that tomb paintings, used to find suspects, weren't always realistic. Other problems: Tut's medical report is 77 years old. The X ray is 34 years old. Back then, doctors didn't have the equipment we have now to detect certain diseases and genetic defects.

What really happened to Tut? These detectives have interesting new guesses, but for now the truth remains buried with the boy king.

TFK MYSTERY PERSON

CLUE 1: I was born in Spain in 1451. In 1474, I became queen.
CLUE 2: Under my rule, Moors (Muslims) were driven from Granada, their last stronghold in Spain.
CLUE 3: I gave Christopher Columbus money for his voyage to the New World in 1492.

WHO AM I?

(See Answer Key that begins on page 340.)

Ancient History

10,000–4000 B.C.	In Mesopotamia, settlements develop into cities and people learn to use the wheel.
4500–4000 B.C.	Earliest-known civilization arises in Sumer.
3000–2000 B.C.	The rule of the pharaohs begins in Egypt. King Khufu completes construction of the Great Pyramid at Giza (ca.* 2680 B.C.), and King Khafre builds the Great Sphinx of Giza (ca. 2540 B.C.).
3000–1500 B.C.	The Indus Valley civilization flourishes in what is today Pakistan. In Britain, Stonehenge is erected.
1500–1000 B.C.	Moses leads the Israelites out of Egypt and delivers the Ten Commandments. Chinese civilization develops under the Shang Dynasty.
1000–900 B.C.	Hebrew elders begin to write the books of the Hebrew Bible.
900–800 B.C.	Phoenicians establish Carthage (ca. 810 B.C.). The *Iliad* and the *Odyssey* are composed, probably by the Greek poet Homer.
800–700 B.C.	The first-recorded Olympic games (776 B.C.) take place.
700–600 B.C.	Lao-tse, Chinese philosopher and founder of Taoism, is born around 604 B.C.
600–500 B.C.	Confucius (551-479 B.C.) develops his philosophy in China. Buddha (ca. 563-ca. 483 B.C.) founds Buddhism in India.
500–400 B.C.	Greek culture flourishes during the Age of Pericles (450-400 B.C.); the Parthenon is built in Athens as a temple of the goddess Athena (447-432 B.C.).
400–300 B.C.	Alexander the Great (356-323 B.C.) destroys Thebes (335 B.C.), conquers Tyre and Jerusalem (332 B.C.), occupies Babylon (330 B.C.) and invades India.
300–250 B.C.	The Temple of the Sun is built at Teotihuacán, Mexico (ca. 300 B.C.).
250–200 B.C.	The Great Wall of China is built (ca. 215 B.C.).
100–31 B.C.	Julius Caesar (100-44 B.C.) invades Britain (55 B.C.) and conquers Gaul (France) (ca. 50 B.C.). Cleopatra rules Egypt (51-31 B.C.).
44 B.C.	Julius Caesar is murdered.

*"ca." is an abbreviation for "circa,"
which means "around."

World History A.D. 1–999

1-49 Life of Jesus Christ (ca. 1-30). Emperor Kuang Wu Ti founds Han dynasty in China. Buddhism introduced to China.

50-99 Jews revolt against the Romans; Jerusalem destroyed (A.D. 70).

100-149 The great emperor Hadrian rules Rome (A.D. 117-138).

150-199 The earliest Mayan temples are built in Central America.

200-249 Goths invade Asia Minor (ca. A.D. 220).

250-299 Mayan civilization (A.D. 250-900) has advances in art, architecture and science.

300-349 Constantine the Great (rules A.D. 312-337) unites eastern and western Roman empires, with new capital at Constantinople (A.D. 330).

350-399 Huns (Mongols) invade Europe (ca. A.D. 360).

400-449 St. Patrick returns to Ireland (A.D. 432) and brings Christianity to the island.

450-499 Vandals destroy Rome (A.D. 455).

500-549 Arthur, semi-legendary king of the Britons, is killed around 537.

550-599 After killing about half the European population, plague subsides (594).

600-649 Muhammad, founder of Islam, flees from Mecca to Medina (the *Hegira*, 622). Arabs conquer Jerusalem (637) and destroy the Alexandrian library (641).

650-699 Arabs attack North Africa (670) and destroy Carthage (697).

700-749 Arab empire extends from Lisbon to China (by 716).

750-799 City of Machu Picchu flourishes in Peru.

800-849 Charlemagne is crowned first Holy Roman Emperor in Rome (800).

850-899 Russian nation is founded by Vikings under Prince Rurik (855-879).

900-949 Vikings discover Greenland (ca. 900). Arab Spain under Abd al-Rahman III becomes center of learning (912-961).

950-999 Erik the Red establishes first Viking colony in Greenland (982).

117

World History 1000–1499

ca. 1000–1300	The Pueblo period of Anasazi culture flourishes; cliff dwellings are built.
ca. 1000	Viking raider Leif Eriksson reaches North America.
ca. 1008	Murasaki Shikibu finishes *The Tale of Genji*, the world's first novel.
1066	William of Normandy invades England, crowned William I (the Conqueror).
1096	Pope Urban II launches the First Crusade, one of at least eight European military campaigns between 1095 and 1291 to take the Holy Land from the Muslims.
ca. 1150	The temple complex of Angkor Wat is completed in Cambodia.
1211	Genghis Khan invades China, captures Peking (1214), conquers Persia (1218) and invades Russia (1223).
1215	King John is forced by barons to sign the Magna Carta, limiting royal power.
1231	The Inquisition begins as the Catholic Church fights heresy; torture is used.
1251	Kublai Khan governs China.
1271	Marco Polo of Venice travels to China; visits court of Kublai Khan (1275-1292).
1312–1337	The Mali Empire reaches its height in Africa under King Mansa Musa.
ca. 1325	Aztecs establish Tenochtitlán on the site of modern Mexico City.
1337–1453	In the Hundred Years' War, English and French kings fight for control of France.
1347–1351	At least 25 million people die in Europe's Black Death (bubonic plague).
1368	The Ming Dynasty begins in China.
ca. 1387	Geoffrey Chaucer writes *The Canterbury Tales*.
1428	Joan of Arc leads the French against the English.
1438	The Incas rule in Peru.
1450	Florence, Italy, becomes the center of Renaissance art and learning.
1453	The Turks conquer Constantinople, thus beginning the Ottoman Empire.
1455	Johannes Gutenberg invents the printing press.
1462	Ivan the Great rules Russia until 1505 as first czar.
1492	Christopher Columbus reaches the New World.

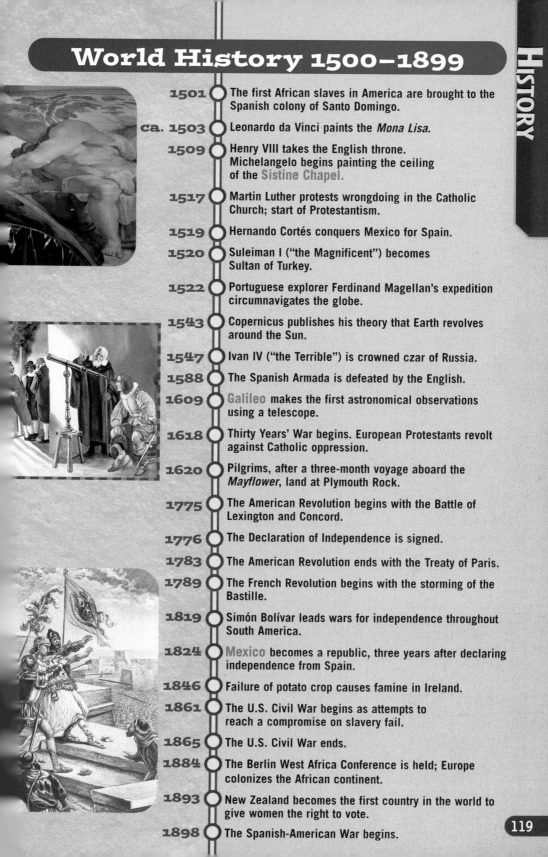

World History 1500–1899

1501 The first African slaves in America are brought to the Spanish colony of Santo Domingo.

ca. 1503 Leonardo da Vinci paints the *Mona Lisa*.

1509 Henry VIII takes the English throne. Michelangelo begins painting the ceiling of the Sistine Chapel.

1517 Martin Luther protests wrongdoing in the Catholic Church; start of Protestantism.

1519 Hernando Cortés conquers Mexico for Spain.

1520 Suleiman I ("the Magnificent") becomes Sultan of Turkey.

1522 Portuguese explorer Ferdinand Magellan's expedition circumnavigates the globe.

1543 Copernicus publishes his theory that Earth revolves around the Sun.

1547 Ivan IV ("the Terrible") is crowned czar of Russia.

1588 The Spanish Armada is defeated by the English.

1609 Galileo makes the first astronomical observations using a telescope.

1618 Thirty Years' War begins. European Protestants revolt against Catholic oppression.

1620 Pilgrims, after a three-month voyage aboard the *Mayflower*, land at Plymouth Rock.

1775 The American Revolution begins with the Battle of Lexington and Concord.

1776 The Declaration of Independence is signed.

1783 The American Revolution ends with the Treaty of Paris.

1789 The French Revolution begins with the storming of the Bastille.

1819 Simón Bolívar leads wars for independence throughout South America.

1824 Mexico becomes a republic, three years after declaring independence from Spain.

1846 Failure of potato crop causes famine in Ireland.

1861 The U.S. Civil War begins as attempts to reach a compromise on slavery fail.

1865 The U.S. Civil War ends.

1884 The Berlin West Africa Conference is held; Europe colonizes the African continent.

1893 New Zealand becomes the first country in the world to give women the right to vote.

1898 The Spanish-American War begins.

World History 1900–

1903 The Wright brothers fly the first powered airplane at Kitty Hawk, North Carolina.

1904 The Russo-Japanese War begins as competition for Korea and Manchuria heats up.

1909 U.S. explorers Robert E. Peary and Matthew Henson reach the North Pole. The National Association for the Advancement of Colored People (NAACP) is founded in New York City.

1912 The *Titanic* sinks on its maiden voyage; more than 1,500 drown.

1914 World War I begins.

1917 U.S. enters World War I. Russian Revolution begins.

1918 World War I fighting ends. A worldwide flu epidemic strikes; by 1920, nearly 20 million are dead.

1919 Mahatma Gandhi begins his nonviolent resistance against British rule in India.

1924 Joseph Stalin begins his rule as Soviet dictator, which lasts until his death in 1953.

1929 In the U.S., stock market prices collapse and the Depression begins.

1933 Adolf Hitler is appointed German chancellor; Nazi oppression begins. Franklin Delano Roosevelt is inaugurated U.S. President; he launches New Deal.

1937 The Nazis open their first concentration camp (Buchenwald); by 1945, the Nazis had murdered some 6 million Jews in what is now called the Holocaust.

1939 World War II begins.

1941 A Japanese attack on the U.S. fleet at Pearl Harbor in Hawaii (December 7) brings U.S. into World War II. Manhattan Project (atomic bomb research) begins.

1945 War ends in Europe on V-E Day (May 8). The U.S. drops the atomic bomb on Hiroshima, Japan (August 6), and Nagasaki, Japan (August 9). The war ends in the Pacific on V-J day (September 2).

1947 The U.S. Marshall Plan is proposed to help Europe recover from the war. India and Pakistan gain independence from Britain.

1948 The nation of Israel is proclaimed.

1949 The North Atlantic Treaty Organization (NATO) is founded. Communist People's Republic of China is proclaimed by Chairman Mao Zedong. South Africa sets up apartheid (a policy of discrimination against nonwhites).

1950 Korean War begins when North Korean Communist forces invade South Korea. It lasts for three years.

1957 Russians launch *Sputnik I*, the first Earth-orbiting satellite; the Space Age begins.

1963 Martin Luther King Jr. delivers his "I have a dream" speech in Washington, D.C. President Kennedy is shot and killed by a sniper in Dallas, Texas.

1965 U.S. planes begin combat missions in Vietnam War.

1967 Israeli and Arab forces battle; Six-Day War ends with Israel occupying Sinai Peninsula, Golan Heights, Gaza Strip and the east bank of the Suez Canal.

1969 *Apollo 11* astronauts take man's first walk on the moon.

1973 Vietnam War ends with signing of peace pacts. The Yom Kippur War begins as Egyptian and Syrian forces attack Israel.

1979 Muslim leader Ayatollah Khomeini takes over Iran; U.S. citizens seized and held hostage.

1981 Scientists identify the AIDS virus.

1989 Thousands rallying for democracy are killed in Tiananmen Square, China. After 28 years, the Berlin Wall that divided Germany is torn down.

1990 South Africa frees Nelson Mandela, who was imprisoned 27 years. Iraqi troops invade Kuwait, setting off nine-month Persian Gulf War.

1991 The Soviet Union breaks up after President Mikhail Gorbachev resigns. In Yugoslavia, Slovenia and Croatia secede; a four-year war with Serbia begins.

1994 South Africa holds first interracial national election; Nelson Mandela elected President.

2000 Elections in Yugoslavia formally end the brutal rule of Slobodan Milosevic.

2001 Hijackers crash two jetliners into New York City's World Trade Center and another into the Pentagon. A fourth hijacked plane crashes 80 miles outside Pittsburgh, Pennsylvania. In response to the Sept. 11 terrorist attacks, U.S. and British forces launch bombing campaign against the Taliban government and al-Qaeda terrorist camps in Afghanistan.

2002 U.S. and British troops defeat the Taliban in Afghanistan; Hamid Karzai elected its President. United Nations weapons inspectors begin searching for weapons of mass destruction in Iraq.

For a year-by-year guide from 1900 onward, www.FactMonster.com

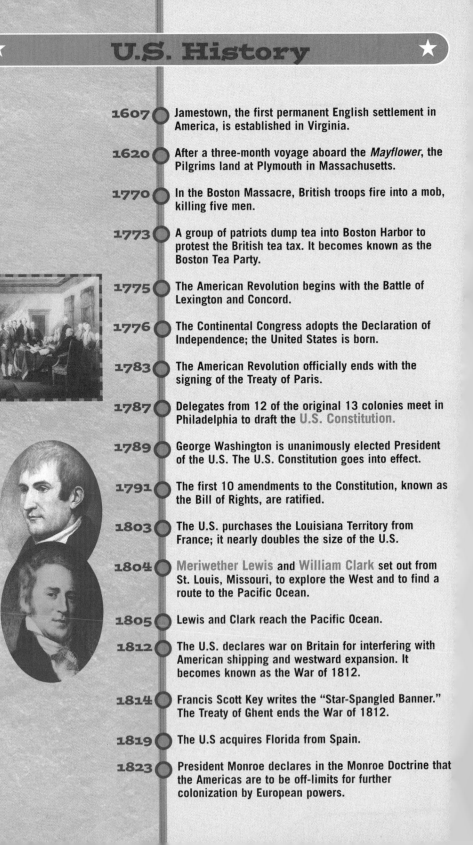

1607 Jamestown, the first permanent English settlement in America, is established in Virginia.

1620 After a three-month voyage aboard the *Mayflower*, the Pilgrims land at Plymouth in Massachusetts.

1770 In the Boston Massacre, British troops fire into a mob, killing five men.

1773 A group of patriots dump tea into Boston Harbor to protest the British tea tax. It becomes known as the Boston Tea Party.

1775 The American Revolution begins with the Battle of Lexington and Concord.

1776 The Continental Congress adopts the Declaration of Independence; the United States is born.

1783 The American Revolution officially ends with the signing of the Treaty of Paris.

1787 Delegates from 12 of the original 13 colonies meet in Philadelphia to draft the U.S. Constitution.

1789 George Washington is unanimously elected President of the U.S. The U.S. Constitution goes into effect.

1791 The first 10 amendments to the Constitution, known as the Bill of Rights, are ratified.

1803 The U.S. purchases the Louisiana Territory from France; it nearly doubles the size of the U.S.

1804 Meriwether Lewis and William Clark set out from St. Louis, Missouri, to explore the West and to find a route to the Pacific Ocean.

1805 Lewis and Clark reach the Pacific Ocean.

1812 The U.S. declares war on Britain for interfering with American shipping and westward expansion. It becomes known as the War of 1812.

1814 Francis Scott Key writes the "Star-Spangled Banner." The Treaty of Ghent ends the War of 1812.

1819 The U.S acquires Florida from Spain.

1823 President Monroe declares in the Monroe Doctrine that the Americas are to be off-limits for further colonization by European powers.

1836 Texas declares its independence from Mexico. The Texan defenders of the Alamo are all killed in a siege by the Mexican Army.

1838 More than 15,000 Cherokee Indians are forced to march from Georgia to Indian Territory in present-day Oklahoma. About 4,000 die from starvation and disease along the "Trail of Tears."

1845 Texas joins the U.S.

1846 The U.S. declares war on Mexico to gain territory in the Southwest.

1848 The Mexican War ends; the U.S. gains territory comprising present-day California, Nevada, Utah, most of New Mexico and Arizona and parts of Colorado and Wyoming.

1849 Gold is discovered at Sutter's Mill in California.

1854 Congress establishes the territories of Kansas and Nebraska. Tensions rise between those who want them to be free states and those who want them to be slave states.

1857 Abolitionist John Brown and 21 followers try to spark a slave revolt by capturing a government arms depot in Harpers Ferry, West Virginia.

1860 Following the election of Abraham Lincoln as President, South Carolina secedes from the U.S.

1861 More Southern states secede from the U.S. and form the Confederate States of America, with Jefferson Davis as President. The Civil War, a conflict between the North (the Union) and the South (the Confederacy) over the expansion of slavery, begins when the Confederates attack Fort Sumter in Charleston, South Carolina.

1863 Lincoln issues the Emancipation Proclamation, freeing slaves in the Confederate states.

1865 The Civil War ends with the surrender of Confederate general Robert E. Lee to Union general Ulysses S. Grant. Lincoln is assassinated by John Wilkes Booth in Washington, D.C. The 13th Amendment to the Constitution is ratified, prohibiting slavery.

1867 The U.S. purchases Alaska from Russia.

1869 The Central Pacific and Union Pacific railroads are joined at Promontory, Utah, creating the first transcontinental (cross-country) railroad.

1890 ● The last major battle of the Indian Wars occurs at Wounded Knee in South Dakota.

1898 ● The U.S.S. *Maine* is blown up in Havana harbor, which leads the U.S. to declare war on Spain. As a result of the Spanish-American War, the U.S. acquires Puerto Rico, Guam and the Philippines.

1917 ● The U.S. enters World War I by declaring war on Germany and Austria-Hungary.

1919 ● The 19th Amendment to the Constitution is ratified, giving women the right to vote.

1929 ● The U.S. stock market crashes, and the Great Depression begins.

1933 ● President Franklin Roosevelt's economic recovery measures, known as the New Deal, are enacted by Congress.

1941 ● Japan attacks the U.S. naval base at Pearl Harbor, Hawaii, leading to the U.S.'s entry into World War II.

1945 ● Germany surrenders, marking the end of World War II in Europe. The U.S. drops two atomic bombs on Japan. Japan surrenders, and World War II ends in the Pacific.

1950 ● The Korean War begins as the U.S. sends troops to defend South Korea against communist North Korea.

1953 ● The Korean War ends.

1954 ● The Supreme Court decision *Brown v. Board of Education of Topeka, Kansas*, declares that racial segregation of schools is unconstitutional.

1955 ● Rosa Parks refuses to sit at the back of the bus. Martin Luther King Jr. leads a black boycott of the Montgomery, Alabama, bus system.

1963 ● President Kennedy is assassinated in Dallas, Texas.

1965 ● The first U.S. combat troops arrive in South Vietnam.

1968 ● Martin Luther King Jr. is assassinated in Memphis, Tennessee.

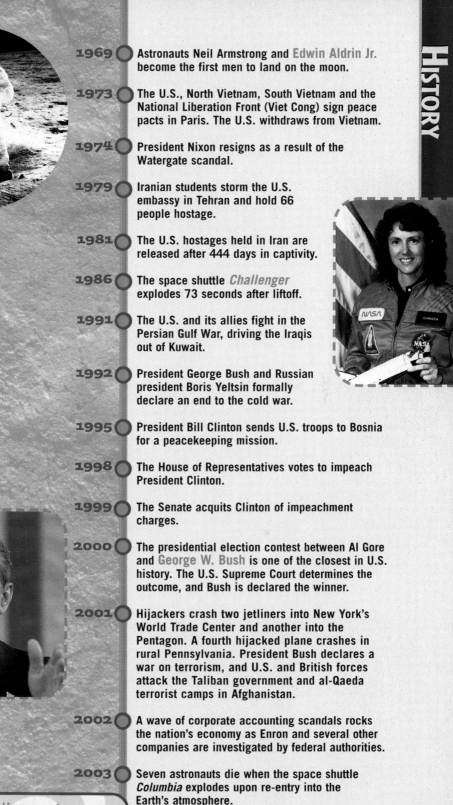

1969 Astronauts Neil Armstrong and Edwin Aldrin Jr. become the first men to land on the moon.

1973 The U.S., North Vietnam, South Vietnam and the National Liberation Front (Viet Cong) sign peace pacts in Paris. The U.S. withdraws from Vietnam.

1974 President Nixon resigns as a result of the Watergate scandal.

1979 Iranian students storm the U.S. embassy in Tehran and hold 66 people hostage.

1981 The U.S. hostages held in Iran are released after 444 days in captivity.

1986 The space shuttle *Challenger* explodes 73 seconds after liftoff.

1991 The U.S. and its allies fight in the Persian Gulf War, driving the Iraqis out of Kuwait.

1992 President George Bush and Russian president Boris Yeltsin formally declare an end to the cold war.

1995 President Bill Clinton sends U.S. troops to Bosnia for a peacekeeping mission.

1998 The House of Representatives votes to impeach President Clinton.

1999 The Senate acquits Clinton of impeachment charges.

2000 The presidential election contest between Al Gore and George W. Bush is one of the closest in U.S. history. The U.S. Supreme Court determines the outcome, and Bush is declared the winner.

2001 Hijackers crash two jetliners into New York's World Trade Center and another into the Pentagon. A fourth hijacked plane crashes in rural Pennsylvania. President Bush declares a war on terrorism, and U.S. and British forces attack the Taliban government and al-Qaeda terrorist camps in Afghanistan.

2002 A wave of corporate accounting scandals rocks the nation's economy as Enron and several other companies are investigated by federal authorities.

2003 Seven astronauts die when the space shuttle *Columbia* explodes upon re-entry into the Earth's atmosphere.

For TFK timelines, go to
www.timeforkids.com/timelines

HOLIDAYS

Federal Holidays

In the U.S., there are **10** federal holidays set by law. Four of these holidays are set by date. The other six are set by a day of the week and month. Most of these are celebrated on Mondays to create three-day weekends.

New Year's Day
January 1

New Year's Day has its origin in ancient Roman times, when sacrifices were offered to Janus, the two-faced Roman god who looked back on the past and forward to the future.

Martin Luther King Jr. Day
Third Monday in January

This holiday honors the civil rights leader. It has been a federal holiday since 1986.

Washington's Birthday
Third Monday in February

Although this holiday is sometimes called Presidents' Day to honor both George Washington and Abraham Lincoln, the federal holiday is officially Washington's Birthday.

Memorial Day
Last Monday in May

Memorial Day originated in 1868 as a day when the graves of Civil War soldiers would be decorated. Later, it became a holiday dedicated to the memory of all war dead.

Independence Day
July 4

The Declaration of Independence was adopted on July 4, 1776. It declared that the 13 colonies were independent of Britain.

Big balloons are part of the fun at the Macy's Thanksgiving Day parade.

TFK TOP 5
HOLIDAYS FOR CANDY SALES

Americans buy about 20 million pounds of candy corn a year, plus tons of candy bars and fruit chews! Check the graph to see how much Americans spend on holiday sweets.

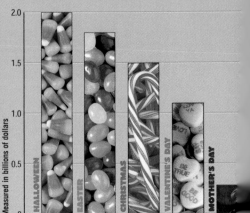

Measured in billions of dollars

2.0
1.5
1.0
0.5
0

HALLOWEEN · EASTER · CHRISTMAS · VALENTINE'S DAY · MOTHER'S DAY

Source: National Confectioners Association

Labor Day
First Monday in September
Labor Day, a day set aside in honor of workers, was first celebrated in New York in 1882 under the sponsorship of the Central Labor Union.

Columbus Day
Second Monday in October
Columbus Day honors Christopher Columbus's landing in the New World in 1492.

Veterans' Day
November 11
Veterans' Day honors all men and women who have served America in its armed forces.

Thanksgiving
Fourth Thursday in November
The first American Thanksgiving took place in 1621, to celebrate the harvest reaped by the Plymouth Colony after a harsh winter.

Christmas Day
December 25
The most popular holiday of the Christian year, Christmas is celebrated as the anniversary of the birth of Jesus.

go For more on these holidays and others
www.FACTMONSTER.COM

TFK PUZZLES & GAMES

Pumpkin Patch Match!
Only two of these jack-o-lanterns are exactly alike. Put an X on both of them. Then answer the questions below.

1. Count all the triangles. How many did you find? _____

2. Count all the ovals. How many did you find? _____

3. Now count all the circles. Write the number that you found. _____

4. How many different kinds of shapes are carved into the pumpkins? _____

(See Answer Key that begins on page 340.)

Other FUN Holidays

Groundhog Day
February 2
Legend has it that on this morning if a groundhog can see its shadow, there will be six more weeks of winter.

Mardi Gras
Last day before Lent
"Mardi Gras," or "Fat Tuesday," is a time of carnivals and parades before Ash Wednesday starts the Christian season of Lent.

Valentine's Day
February 14
Named for the third-century martyr St. Valentine, this day is celebrated with candy, cards and other tokens of love.

Mother's Day
Second Sunday in May
Having a day to honor mothers goes back at least as far as 17th-century England, when Mothering Sunday began.

Father's Day
Third Sunday in June
This U.S. holiday honoring fathers began in 1910 in Spokane, Washington.

Halloween
October 31
Halloween is celebrated with jack-o-lanterns, costumes and the telling of ghost stories.

Kwanzaa
December 26 through January 1
Kwanzaa, an African-American holiday, honors the values of ancient African cultures.

Christian Holidays 2004

Ash Wednesday
February 25
The first day of Lent

Easter
April 11
The resurrection of Jesus

Pentecost
May 30
The feast of the Holy Spirit

First Sunday in Advent
November 28
The start of the Christmas season

Christmas Day
December 25
The birth of Jesus

Thanksgiving Feast

We don't have an exact menu for the first Thanksgiving, but historians know it featured ducks, geese, turkey, deer and Indian corn. The feast probably also included lobster, codfish, rabbit, Dutch cheese, wild berries, melons and pumpkin. Contrary to legend, popcorn was not served at the first Thanksgiving.

All Jewish and Muslim holidays begin at sundown the day before they are listed here.

Jewish Holidays 2004

Purim
March 7
The feast of lots

Passover
April 6
The feast of unleavened bread

Shavuot
May 26
The feast of first fruits

Sukkot
September 30
The feast of the tabernacles

Rosh Hashanah
September 16
The Jewish New Year

Simchat Torah
October 8
The rejoicing of the law

Yom Kippur
September 25
The day of atonement

Hanukkah
December 8
The festival of lights

Muslim Holidays 2004

Eid al-Adha
February 2
The festival of sacrifice

Muharram
February 22
The Muslim New Year

Mawlid al-Nabi
May 2
The prophet Muhammad's birthday

Ramadan
begins October 15
The month of fasting

Eid al-Fitr
November 14
Ramadan ends

Bastille Day
July 14 in France

Americans have the 4th of July; the French have Bastille Day. On July 14, 1789, a group of Parisians stormed the Bastille, a fortress and prison in France. The people of Paris considered it a symbol of the oppressive power of the monarchy. The uprising proved that power belonged to the people rather than the king. The event marked the beginning of the French Revolution.

The French recognize Bastille Day as the end of the monarchy and the beginning of the modern republic. Today, Parisians celebrate this national holiday with a grand military parade up the Champs Élysées, colorful arts festivals and lively parties.

TFK MYSTERY PERSON

CLUE 1: Born in Atlanta and raised in the South, I was one of the most important civil rights leaders.
CLUE 2: I devoted my life to teaching nonviolent ways of achieving civil rights for blacks, and I won the Nobel Peace Prize in 1964.
CLUE 3: The third Monday in January is named after me and is now a federal holiday.

WHO AM I?
(See Answer Key that begins on page 340.)

Testing, Testing

By Elizabeth Siris

Paige Donahoo is both scared and excited as she waits for April to come. That's when she and all third graders in Texas will take state reading and math tests. Her teacher has spent a lot of time getting Paige's class ready.

Soon every third grader in U.S. public schools will face the kind of tests Paige is preparing for. So will older students. The No Child Left Behind Act, signed by President Bush in 2002, says that by 2005, schools must begin giving yearly reading and math tests to students in grades three through eight. Each state will set the standards for what students need to know.

The new tests will not only measure how kids are doing, they will also be used to evaluate schools and help them do a better job. The $26.5 billion bill will make money available to failing schools in poor areas and reward successful schools. Schools had better use the money to improve test scores or staff members could lose their jobs.

Many Americans agree that testing is the best way to ensure that kids are getting an education that meets state standards. But critics of the new law worry that teachers will become so focused on preparing kids for math and reading tests that school will become boring and other subjects will be neglected.

That has already begun to happen in some places. California student Tessa Wooden recently had to prepare for tests during gym!

Like it or not, state tests are a fact of life. "But kids need to understand that the tests are only a snapshot of what they know," says Natalie Roca, a testing expert for Miami-Dade County Schools in Florida. "You prepare year-round. You do your homework."

Remember, it's not just what happens on test day but what happens every day that counts.

President Bush greets students in Washington, D.C.

Parents in Ohio protest against testing.

NO MOR TEST

How to Study for Tests

Tests are a way for you and your teacher to measure how well you have learned the material covered in class. Think of them as a challenge!

BEFORE THE TEST

1. If possible, find out what material the test will cover and what type of test it will be (multiple choice, true or false, short answer or essay).

2. Study at a time when you are alert and not hungry or sleepy.

3. Don't wait until the last minute! Short, daily study sessions are better than cramming the night before the test.

4. Set a goal for each study period. If you are being tested on three chapters, set up four study sessions—one for each chapter and one for a review of all three.

5. Repeat, repeat, repeat! Read and reread your notes and the key parts of the textbook.

6. While reviewing your notes, cover them up and summarize them out loud.

GROUP STUDY

Working in a group can be a great way to study. Here's one plan for getting the most out of it.

1. First, compare your notes and review old homework.

2. Next, drill each other on facts you need to memorize. For example: What are the four stages of a butterfly's life cycle?

3. Lastly, take the time to discuss "why" questions. For example: Why do monarch butterflies migrate?

Remember—be prepared!
A study group is a place to share your understanding of a subject. The other people in the group aren't there to teach you facts you should already know.

STUDY TIPS

☛ Use your notes to make an outline of the main ideas.

☛ Make a timeline of important dates.

☛ Make flashcards for studying key events or vocabulary.

☛ Have someone test you.

Ten Tips for Taking Tests

1. Read the instructions carefully. Never assume you will know what they will say! Ask the teacher if you are unsure about anything.

2. Read the entire test through before starting. Notice the point value of each section. This will help you to pace yourself.

3. Answer the easiest questions first, then the ones with the highest point value. You don't want to spend 20 minutes trying to figure out a two-point problem!

4. Keep busy! If you get stuck on a question, come back to it later. The answer might come to you while you are working on another part of the test.

5. If you aren't sure how to answer a question fully, try to answer at least part of it. You might get partial credit.

6. Need to guess on a multiple-choice test? First, eliminate the answers that you know are wrong. Then take a guess. Because your first guess is most likely to be correct, you shouldn't go back and change an answer later unless you are certain you were wrong.

7. On an essay test, take a moment to plan your writing. First, jot down the important points you want to make. Then number these points in the order you will cover them.

8. Keep it neat! If your teacher can't read your writing, you might lose points.

9. Don't waste time doing things for which you will not receive credit, such as rewriting test questions.

10. Leave time at the end to look over your work. Did you answer every question? Did you proofread for errors? It is easy to make careless mistakes while taking a test.

AFTER THE TEST

☛ Read the teacher's comments carefully and try to learn from your mistakes.

☛ Save tests to review for end-of-term tests.

Homework TIP

Keep your homework out of reach of pets and younger siblings.

The Dewey Decimal System

Homework TIP

Don't put off your homework until the last minute.

Imagine walking into a house where room after room is filled with shelves, all packed with books in no specific order. Imagine trying to find the one book you want! That's what happened every day to Melvil Dewey, an American librarian who lived from 1851 to 1931. He became so unhappy trying to help people find books that he invented the Dewey Decimal System of Classification, which is still used in libraries today. The system numbers books by their subject matter in the following way.

000-099	General Works (encyclopedias, magazines, almanacs)
100-199	Philosophy and Psychology
200-299	Religion and Mythology
300-399	Social Science
400-499	Language
500-599	Math and Science
600-699	Medicine and Technology
700-799	Arts and Entertainment
800-899	Literature
900-999	History and Geography

TFK PUZZLES & GAMES

Rhyme Time

This seaside scene is full of things that rhyme. We've circled pail and sail, but there are at least nine more rhyming pairs. Circle them and write down the words on a piece of paper. BONUS: Write a poem using the rhyming pairs you found.

(See Answer Key that begins on page 340.)

Tips for Writing Essays

Homework TIP

Do your homework in a quiet, well-lit room.

Come Up with a Good Topic

1. First, choose a subject that interests you. Let's say you like dogs. That's a good place to start.

2. Then try to narrow the subject down to something you can write about knowledgeably. Let's say you have a beagle and you know a lot about beagles based on your experience as a dog owner.

3. Now come up with a statement about your topic. "Beagles are the best breed of dog." This will be your main idea, or thesis statement.

4. Answer the question "why" at least three times. Why are beagles the best? Some answers might be, "beagles are smart" or "beagles are neither too small nor too big—they're just right."

5. Wrap it up. Write a brief conclusion that sums up the points you have made. "Clearly, beagles are best because they're smart and they're just the right size."

Brainstorm

1. Brainstorming is one way to develop your topic. It is a good way to let ideas you didn't know you had come to the surface.

2. Write down whatever comes into your head about your topic. Don't worry about organizing your thoughts just yet.

3. Keep writing for a short but specific amount of time—maybe five minutes. Don't stop to correct spelling or grammar errors.

4. After a few minutes, read through what you have written. Chances are you came up with some new ideas.

Organize Your Ideas

Develop an outline to organize your ideas. An outline shows your main ideas and the order in which you are going to write about them. Here is a sample outline.

Recycling
Reduce, Reuse, Recycle

1. Introduction

2. Recycling is good for the Earth.
   a. Recycling reduces the amount of trash at landfills.
   b. Recycling helps to save energy and natural resources.
   c. Recycling reduces pollution.

3. Recycling is an interesting way to learn about the environment.
   a. Making paper from recycled products uses up to 50% less energy than making it from trees.
   b. Plastic is made out of petroleum, so when people recycle plastic, they are helping to conserve a nonrenewable resource.

4. My personal experience recycling
   a. I started a recycling program at my school.
   b. I enjoyed learning about how trash is used after I recycle it.
   c. One of my chores is to separate the trash into recyclables and nonrecyclables.

5. Conclusion

Revise the First Draft

Try to set aside your draft for a day or two before revising. This way you can see it with fresh eyes and notice any problems. You may decide you need to develop your ideas in more detail, give more evidence to support your claims or delete material that you consider unnecessary. You may also reword sentences.

Read your paper out loud. This sometimes makes it easier to identify writing that is awkward or unclear. Have somebody else read the paper and tell you if there's anything that's unclear or confusing.

Proofread the Final Draft

Look for careless errors such as misspelled words and incorrect punctuation and capitalization. If you type your paper on a computer, print out a copy to proofread. Don't rely on spell checkers and grammar checkers—they don't always catch errors!

How to Write a Narrative Essay

The first important thing to remember about a narrative essay is that it tells a story. You may write about:

* An experience or event from your past
* A recent or an ongoing experience or event
* Something that happened to somebody else, such as a parent or a grandparent

> **Learning something new can be a scary experience. One of the hardest things I've ever had to do was learning how to swim. I was always afraid of the water, but I decided that swimming was an important skill that I should learn.**

The second important thing is that in a narrative essay the story should have a point. In the final paragraph, you should come to a conclusion about the story you told.

> **Learning to swim was not easy for me, but in the end my efforts paid off. Now when I am faced with a new situation I am not so nervous. I may feel uncomfortable at first, but I know that as my skills get better, I will feel more and more comfortable.**

The conclusion is where the author reflects on the larger meaning of the experience described. In this case, the author concludes that learning to swim has helped her to feel more confident about herself in new situations. The idea that self-confidence comes from conquering your fears is something that anyone can relate to. It is the point of this essay.

GET PERSONAL!

The writing in an essay should be lively and engaging. Try to keep the reader's interest by adding details or observations. Sharing your thoughts invites the reader into your world and makes the story more personal and more interesting.

Homework TIP

Turn off the TV while you do your homework.

Tackle a Descriptive Essay

The purpose of a descriptive essay is to describe a person, place or thing in such vivid detail that the reader can easily form a mental picture. You may accomplish this by using words that create a mood, making interesting comparisons and describing images that appeal to the senses.

I have always been fascinated by carnival rides. My first experience with a carnival ride was a Ferris wheel at a local fair. It was huge, smoky and noisy. Ever since that first impression years ago, these rides have reminded me of mythical beasts carrying off their screaming passengers. Even the droning sound of their engines brings to mind the great roar of a fire-breathing dragon.

Mood Words The author uses words that create excitement, like "fascinated," "great roar" and "fire-breathing dragon."

Interesting Comparisons One way the author makes his subject interesting is by comparing the Ferris wheel to a mythical beast.

Sensory Details The author uses his senses for details about how the Ferris wheel looks, sounds and feels. The ride is "huge, smoky and noisy" and its engines "drone."

Like other essays, a descriptive essay should be well organized. This essay began with a general statement—that the author has always been fascinated by carnival rides. The body is made of paragraphs that describe the subject. The conclusion restates the main idea—in this case, that the author continues to find carnival rides fascinating.

A trip on the Ferris wheel never fails to thrill me. The fascination I have for Ferris wheels comes back with each and every ride.

How to Write a Persuasive Essay

The purpose of a persuasive essay is to convince the reader to agree with your viewpoint or to accept your recommendation for a course of action. For instance, you might argue that the salaries of professional athletes are too high. Or you might recommend that vending machines be banned from your school cafeteria. A successful persuasive essay will use evidence to support your viewpoint, consider opposing views and present a strong conclusion.

> **Some people worry that adopting a school uniform policy would be too expensive. However, there are ways to lessen the cost. For example, in Seattle, Washington, local businesses pay for uniforms at South Shore Middle School. In Long Beach, California, graduating students donate or sell their old uniforms to other students.**

Use evidence to support your viewpoint. Statistics, facts, quotations from experts and examples will help you to build a strong case for your argument. Appeal to the reader's sense of logic by presenting specific and relevant evidence in a well-organized manner.

Consider opposing views. Try to anticipate the concerns and questions that a reader might have about your subject. Responding to these points will give you the chance to explain to the reader why your viewpoint or recommendation is the best one.

Present a strong conclusion. All your evidence and explanations should build toward a strong ending in which you summarize your view in a clear and memorable way. The conclusion in a persuasive essay might include a call to action.

TIP: Use a pleasant and reasonable tone in your essay. Sarcasm and name-calling weaken an argument. Logic and fairness will help to keep it strong.

Homework TIP

Take short breaks when you have a long assignment.

Spelling Tips

This may be the best-known spelling rule:

> *i* before *e*, except after *c* (or when sounded like *ay* as in *neighbor* and *weigh*)
> Examples: IE words: *believe, field*
> CEI words: *ceiling, deceit*
> EI words: *freight, reign*

Silent *e* helps a vowel say its name.

This means that when a word ends with a vowel followed by a consonant and then silent *e*, the vowel has a long sound. For example, the *a* in *rate* has a long *a*. The *a* is short in *rat*. The *i* in *hide* is long. The *i* is short in *hid*.

When two vowels go walking, the first one usually does the talking.

This means that when there are two vowels in a row, the first has a long sound and the second is silent. For example, the *o* in *coat* is long, and the *a* is silent.

Make sure that you are pronouncing words correctly.

This can help you to avoid some common spelling errors, such as *canidate* instead of *candidate*, *jewelery* instead of *jewelry*, and *libary* instead of *library*.

Make up funny memory aids.

For example, do you have trouble remembering which has two s's—*desert* (arid land) or *dessert* (a sweet treat)? Remember that with dessert, you'd like two of them. Similarly, do you have trouble remembering how to spell *separate*? Remember that there's *a rat* in the middle.

Break a word into syllables.

Look for prefixes, suffixes and roots. Practice each short part and then the whole word.

> *dis-ap-pear-ing*
> *tra-di-tion-al*

After you break apart a word, ask yourself: How is this word like other words I know? Spelling the word *traditional* may make you think of spelling *functional* and *national*. Finding patterns among words is one of the best ways to learn spelling.

How to Write a

Book reports are a way to show how well you understood a book and to tell what you think about it. Many teachers have their own rules about what should be in a book report, so be sure to check with your teacher. Here are some general guidelines.

INTRODUCTION

The introduction starts your report and captures the reader's attention. It should include:

☞ **The title and author of the book**

☞ **Some information about the book (but don't give away the ending)**

☞ **What kind of story it is—adventure, fantasy, animal, nonfiction, biography?**

BODY

This is where you describe the main parts of the story: theme, plot, setting and characters. Then you can give your opinions about the book.

☞ The **theme** is the most important message in the story. An example might be the importance of friendship. Tell what you think the theme is and why you do. Lessons learned by the main character are often important clues to the theme.

☞ The **plot** is the series of events in the book. In your book report, you should explain the main event or conflict in the plot. What events lead up to it? What happens as a result?

Be careful not to re-tell the whole plot in detail—you will need room in your report to write about other things. Just say enough about the plot so that the rest of your report will make sense. If the plot has a big mystery or a surprise, be careful not to give away the ending.

☞ The **setting** is the time and place of the story. Is it set a long time ago, now or in the future? Does it take place in another country or in an imaginary place?

☞ The **characters** are people, animals and creatures in the book. The main character is called the protagonist. Who are the other characters? Do they help or hinder the protagonist?

Homework TIP

Try to do your homework at the same time and in the same place every day.

Book Report

An important part of a book report is giving your opinion or telling what you thought about the book. Some questions you might want to answer are:

☞ Did you like the story? Why or why not?

☞ What was the best part of the book? Why?

☞ How did the story make you feel? Did you feel different emotions at different points?

☞ Would you recommend the book to friends?

☞ Would you read other books by the author?

☞ What new things did you learn from the book?

CONCLUSION

The conclusion sums up your report. It tells your overall opinion of the book and the most important thing you want readers to know about it.

Mrs. Coverlet's Magicians
A Spellbinding Story

The babysitter has been in bed for weeks, and Toad says it's because he put a spell on her. Could it be true? That's the question that runs through *Mrs. Coverlet's Magicians* by Mary Nash. This hilarious novel tells about the troubles that Toad, his sister Mary and his brother Malcolm get into while the one adult in the house lies asleep.

I loved this book because whenever people said Toad's ideas were silly, he found a surprising way to prove them wrong. For example, when Toad announced that he could find a Christmas tree to chop down, Malcolm and Molly laughed, because there are no woods near their town. But soon afterward, Toad led them into the old marsh and began to make a very strange-looking wand.

How to Write a Research Paper

Writing a research paper involves all of the steps for writing an essay plus some additional ones. To write a research paper you must first do some research, that is, investigate your topic by reading about it in different sources, including books, magazines, newspapers and the Internet. The information you gather is used to support the points you make in your paper.

Writing a research paper also involves documenting your sources of information in footnotes or endnotes. This way, the reader knows where you got your information and can judge whether it is reliable.

Eight Steps to a Great Research Paper

1. Find your topic. Try to pick a topic that's fun and interesting. If your topic genuinely interests you, chances are, you'll enjoy working on it.

2. Look for sources. Take a trip to the library. Use the electronic catalog or browse the shelves to look for books on your topic. If you find a book that is useful, check the bibliography (list of sources) in the back of that book for other books or articles on that topic. Ask a librarian if you need help finding sources.

Keep a list of all the sources that you use. Include the title of the source, the author, publisher and place and date of publication.

3. Read your sources and take notes. After you've gathered your sources, begin reading and taking notes.

Use 3 x 5 index cards, writing one fact or idea per card. This way related ideas from different sources can be easily grouped together. Be sure to note the source and the page number on each card.

Homework TIP

Don't eat messy snacks while doing your homework.

4. Make an outline. Organize your index cards by topic, then develop an outline to organize your ideas. An outline shows your main ideas and the order in which you are going to write about them. (See page 135 for a sample outline.)

5. **Write a first draft.** Every essay or paper is made up of three parts: the introduction, the body and the conclusion.

☞ The introduction is the first paragraph. It often begins with a general statement about the topic and ends with a more specific statement of your main idea.

☞ The body of the paper follows the introduction. It has a number of paragraphs in which you develop your ideas in detail. Limit yourself to one main idea per paragraph and use examples and quotations to support your ideas.

☞ The conclusion is the last paragraph of the paper. Its purpose is to sum up your points—leaving out specific examples—and to restate your main idea.

6. **Use footnotes or endnotes.** These identify the sources of your information. If you are using footnotes, the note will appear on the same page as the information you are documenting, at the bottom (or foot) of the page. If you are using endnotes, the note will appear together with all other notes on a separate page at the end of your report, just before the bibliography.

There are different formats, so be sure to use the one your teacher prefers.

The National Beagle Club held its first show in 1891.[1]

[1] Samantha Lopez, *For the Love of Beagles* (New York: Ribbon Books, 1993), p. 24.

7. **Revise your draft.** After you've completed your first draft, you'll want to make some changes. (See page 135 for general tips.) Also remember that in a research paper, it's important to check that you have footnotes or endnotes wherever they are needed.

8. **Proofread your final draft.** When you are happy with your revision, print it and check spelling, punctuation and grammar. It is good to do this more than once, checking for different kinds of mistakes each time.

DON'T COPY THIS!

Plagiarism means using someone else's work as your own. If you take words or ideas from a source without giving credit, you are plagiarizing. When you copy something directly from a book without putting it in your own words, put quotation marks around it so that you know it is an exact quotation. This will help you avoid plagiarism.

How to Write a Biography

A biography is the story of a life. Biographies can be just a few sentences long, or they can fill an entire book. Biographers (people who write biographies) use primary and secondary sources.

※ Primary sources convey first-hand experience. They include letters, diaries, interview tapes and other accounts of personal experience.

※ Secondary sources convey second-hand experience. They include articles, textbooks, reference books and other information sources.

To write a biography, you should:

1. Select a person you find interesting.

2. Find out the basic facts of the person's life. You might want to start by looking in an encyclopedia.

3. Think about what else you would like to know about the person.

※ What makes this person special or interesting?

※ What kind of effect did he or she have on the world?

※ What are the adjectives you would use to describe the person?

※ What examples from the person's life show those qualities?

※ What events shaped or changed this person's life?

And Furthermore: Transition Words and Phrases

Transition words and phrases help establish clear connections between ideas and ensure that sentences and paragraphs flow together smoothly, making them easier to read. Use the following words and phrases in the following circumstances.

To indicate more information:	To indicate an example:	To indicate a cause or reason:	To indicate a result or an effect:
Besides	For example	As	Accordingly
Furthermore	For instance	Because	Consequently
In addition	In particular	Because of	Finally
In fact	Particularly	Due to	Therefore
Moreover	Specifically	Since	Thus

Homework TIP

Don't study if you are hungry. You won't be able to concentrate.

144

Giving Credit Where It Is Due:
Putting Together a
Bibliography

A bibliography is a list of the sources you used to get information for your report. It is included at the end of your report. You will find it easy to prepare your bibliography if you keep track of each source you use as you are reading and taking notes.

When putting together a final bibliography, list your sources (texts, articles, interviews and so on) in alphabetical order by authors' last names. Sources that don't have authors should be alphabetized by title. There are different formats for bibliographies, so be sure to use the one your teacher prefers.

General Guide for Bibliographies

Book
Author (last name first). *Title of the book.* City: Publisher, Date of publication.
Dahl, Roald. *The BFG.* New York: Farrar, Straus and Giroux, 1982.

Encyclopedia
Encyclopedia title, edition, date. Volume number, "Article title," page numbers.
Encyclopædia Britannica, 1997. Volume 7, "Gorillas," pp. 50-51.

Magazine
Author (last name first), "Article Title." *Name of magazine.* Volume number, (Date): page numbers.
Jordan, Jennifer, "Filming at the Top of the World." *Museum of Science Magazine.* Volume 47, No. 1 (Winter 1998): p. 11.

Newspaper
Author (last name first), "Article title." *Name of newspaper*, city, state of publication. (Date): edition if available, section, page number(s).
Powers, Ann, "New Tune for the Material Girl." *The New York Times*, New York, N.Y. (3/1/98): Atlantic Region, Section 2, p. 34.

Person
Full name (last name first). Occupation. Date of interview.
Smeckleburg, Sweets. Bus driver. April 1, 2002.

CD-ROM
Disc title: version, date. "Article title," pages if given. Publisher.
Compton's Multimedia Encyclopedia: Macintosh version, 1995. "Civil rights movement," p. 3. Compton's Newsmedia.

Internet
Author (last name first) (date). "Article title." Date work retrieved, name and url of website.
Brunner, Borgna (2001). "Earthquakes!" Retrieved January 27, 2003, from www.infoplease.com/spot/earthquake1.html.

Doing Research on the Internet

Homework TIP

Do math assignments in pencil.

The Internet has become a convenient tool for finding information on just about anything. Here are some things to keep in mind when you're doing research on the Internet.

> **Choose your keywords carefully.** The more words you use, the more specific your search will be. For example, if you use the keyword "animals," you will find sites with all kinds of information about animals. If you use the keywords "endangered animals," you will find sites with information on that particular topic. If you don't find what you want, try using different keywords.

> **Know your source!** Anybody can put up information on the Internet and call himself an expert. The information you read on someone's home page may be incorrect. The websites of government sources, schools, and magazine and newspaper publishers are more accurate. If you use other sources, verify the information in a book or on another website.

> **Search in different ways.** Just as one encyclopedia at the library may not have all the information you want, one search engine may not have just what you are looking for. If you don't find what you want through one search, try another.

Here is a list of websites that you might find useful.

Back | Forward | Reload | Home | Search | Netscape | Images | Print

Netsite:

WebMail | Contact | People | Yellow Pages | Download | Ch

Search Engines
Ask Jeeves Kids: *www.ajkids.com*
Google: *www.google.com*
Yahooligans!: *www.yahooligans.com*

Kids
Fact Monster: *www.factmonster.com*
Sports Illustrated For Kids: *www.sikids.com*
Time For Kids: *www.timeforkids.com*

News
BBC Interactive: *www.bbc.co.uk*
CNN Interactive: *www.cnn.com*
The New York Times: *www.nytimes.com*
The Washington Post: *www.washingtonpost.com*

Government Sites
Census Bureau: *www.census.gov*
Department of the Treasury: *www.ustreas.gov*
Environmental Protection Agency (EPA): *www.epa.gov*
Federal Bureau of Investigation: *www.fbi.gov*
FedStats (statistics) for Kids: *www.fedstats.gov/kids.html*
House of Representatives: *www.house.gov*
National Weather Service: *www.nws.noaa.gov*
Senate: *www.senate.gov*
U.S. Postal Service: *www.usps.gov*
White House: *www.whitehouse.gov*

Conducting an Interview

Books, magazines and the Internet aren't the only sources for research. Conducting an interview can be a great way to learn about a subject, too! You may learn unexpected things, and you'll feel like a reporter.

BEFORE THE INTERVIEW

Make a list of questions you plan to ask. What would you like to learn about? Let's say the person you're interviewing worked at the World Trade Center during the September 11 terrorist attacks. You could ask the person to explain how she escaped from the building. You could ask her to describe the rescue effort. How did she feel after the towers fell? Does that person feel safe now?

You should try to avoid asking "yes" or "no" questions. You'll get much more interesting answers if your questions require an explanation. For example, instead of asking, "Were you scared?" ask, "What terrified you most?" or "What was the most frightening part of the experience?"

DURING THE INTERVIEW

1. If the person gives you permission, tape-record the interview. Even if you tape the interview, you should take notes so that you'll remember important points.

2. At the beginning of the interview, ask when and where the person was born. This will save you from having to backtrack and figure out dates later.

3. Don't interrupt or correct the person you are talking to. People sometimes remember things wrong. That's okay—you can check dates and facts later. The important thing is to hear about the person's impressions and feelings.

4. Listen carefully. Something the person says may inspire you to ask a question you hadn't planned. For example, the person may say that she hopes New York officials decide against rebuilding the Twin Towers. You could ask why. You might ask what she envisions for the site.

AFTER THE INTERVIEW

Look back over the questions your prepared before the interview. Did the interview help to answer them? If you are going to do an oral report, think about how you will present your information. You might talk about what you had hoped to get out of the interview, and what you learned from it that was unexpected. You could also talk about the difference between reading a book and getting a personal view.

How to Give an
Oral Report

In many ways, planning an oral report is similar to planning a written report.

☛ **Choose a subject that is interesting to you.** What do you care about? What would you like to learn more about? Follow your interests, and you'll find your topic.

☛ **Be clear about your purpose.** Do you want to persuade your audience? Inform them about a topic? Or just tell an entertaining story?

An oral report also has the same three basic parts as a written report.

☛ The **introduction** should "hook" your audience. Catch their interest with a question, a dramatic tale or a personal experience that relates to your topic.

☛ The **body** is the main part of your report and will take up most of your time. Make an outline of the body so that you can share information in an organized way.

☛ The **conclusion** is the time to summarize and get across your most important point. What do you want the audience to remember?

It's important to really know your subject and be well organized. If you know your material well, you will be confident and able to answer questions. If your report is well organized, the audience will find it informative and easy to follow.

Think about your audience. If you were listening to a report on your subject, what would you want to know? Too much information can seem overwhelming, and too little can be confusing. Organize your outline around your key points, and focus on getting them across.

Remember—enthusiasm is contagious! If you're interested in your subject, the audience will be interested, too.

Practicing your report is a key to success. At first, some people find it helpful to go through the report alone. You might practice in front of a mirror or in front of your stuffed animals. Then try out your report in front of a practice audience—friends or family. Ask your practice audience:

☛ Could you follow my presentation?

☛ Did I seem knowledgeable about my subject?

☛ Was I speaking clearly? Could you hear me? Did I speak too fast or too slow?

If you are using visual aids, such as posters or overhead transparencies, practice using them while you rehearse. Also, you might want to time yourself to see how long your report actually takes. The time will probably go by faster than you expect.

Homework TIP

Make sure you write down your homework assignme in class.

3. Report!

Stand up straight. Hold your upper body straight, but not stiff, and keep your chin up. Try not to distract your audience by shifting around or fidgeting.

Make eye contact. You will seem more sure of yourself, and the audience will listen better, if you make eye contact during your report.

Use gestures. Your body language can help you make your points and keep the audience interested. Lean forward at key moments, and use your hands and arms for emphasis.

Use your voice effectively. Vary your tone and speak clearly. If you're nervous, you might speak too fast. If you find yourself hurrying, take a breath and try to slow it down.

Nerves!

Almost everyone is nervous when speaking before a group. Many people say public speaking is their Number 1 fear. Being well prepared is the best way to prevent nerves from getting the better of you. Also, try breathing deeply before you begin your report, and remember to breathe during the report. Being nervous isn't all bad—it can help to keep you on your toes!

One last thing!

Have you prepared and practiced your report? Then go get 'em! Remember: you know your stuff, and your report is interesting and important.

TFK TOP 5

BOOKS TEACHERS RECOMMEND TO KIDS

The hottest books these days are the Harry Potter titles. But it seems the Potter books haven't worked their magic on teachers. Here are the top books that teachers recommend to kids:

1. *Charlotte's Web* by E.B. White

2. *The Polar Express* by Chris Van Allsburg

3. *Green Eggs and Ham* by Dr. Seuss

4. *The Cat in the Hat* by Dr. Seuss

5. *Where the Wild Things Are* by Maurice Sendak

Source: National Education Association

TFK MYSTERY PERSON

CLUE 1: Born to former slaves in 1875, I spent my life making sure African Americans got the right to an education.

CLUE 2: I founded the Daytona Normal and Industrial Institute for Negro Girls in 1904.

CLUE 3: I served as an adviser on African American affairs to President Franklin Roosevelt.

WHO AM I?
(See Answer Key that begins on page 340.)

INVENTIONS

COOLEST NEW INVENTIONS

Throughout history, inventors' ideas have transformed the way we live. Imagine a world without telephones, televisions or computers! Every year inventive minds dream up gadgets and gizmos that make our lives easier—at least a lot more fun. Here are some of the biggest new ideas.

BOWWOW! WOW!

Wonder what your dog is really thinking? Takara, a Japanese toymaker, claims it can translate barking into words with its new gadget, Bowlingual. A microphone attaches to a dog's collar, and a receiver "translates" his yelps and growls into phrases like "I can't stand it," "How boring," and "I'm lonely." How does it work? Animal experts collected and interpreted dog noises. When a dog barks, the sound is matched to the ones translated earlier. For now, the translator is available only in Japan. That's ruff.

THREE-WHEELER

This isn't your kid brother's tricycle! The Trikke (pronounced "trike") has three wheels, which make the Trikke more stable than the Razor scooter. After pushing off with one foot, the rider uses the side-to-side rocking motion used by in-line skaters to keep it going. The Trikke sells for $200 to $300.

MODEL CAR

What will the car of the future look like? This one has no engine. It doesn't need gasoline. There isn't even a steering wheel. Best of all, it doesn't pollute the air!

The controls for the Hy-wire car were inspired by aircraft cockpits. The car has a small color screen and two hand grips in place of a steering wheel. To drive, just grab the grips and twist right to go faster. Move the grips up or down to turn left or right. Squeeze them to stop.

The Hy-wire is powered by chemical reactions between hydrogen and oxygen. The only thing this car releases is water vapor.

General Motors says the Hy-wire could be on the road by 2010.

FLY RIGHT

The Power Air Surfer is not a plain plane. It's a new radio-controlled toy airplane from Hasbro that's almost impossible to crash. Its two 32-inch wings and double propellers make it super stable, even when floating down from 100 feet up.

A SMALL WORLD

In 1997, a team of Japanese engineers imagined a computer so powerful that it could keep track of every environmental event in the world at once. On March 11, 2002, they switched on the Earth Simulator for the first time. A virtual twin of our home planet was born.

Located in Yokohama, Japan, the Earth Simulator is the size of four tennis courts. It cost around $350 million to build. After climate data from satellites and ocean instruments go in, the simulator creates a computer model of the planet. Scientists have already completed a forecast of ocean temperatures for the next 50 years.

Now we need not wait 10 or 20 years to see how our actions will affect our world. By digitally copying Earth, we might just be able to save it.

TOTALLY TOUGH BUBBLES

With Catch-a-Bubble, you can blow bubbles that last about five minutes instead of just a few seconds. The secret is a chemical that toughens when it touches air. These thick-skinned bubbles can be held, tossed and—carefully, carefully—stacked together.

超高解像度全球海洋シミュレーションの結果

海面温度分布

ea Surface Temperature: date = OCT / 17

75S-75N, Resolution: 0.1 degree for horizontal, 54 levels for vertical
1500cpus(188nodes) used

60E   120E   180   120W   60W

0   2   4   6   8   10   12   14   16   18   20   22   24   26   28

ROBO-VAC

Geniuses at the Massachusetts Institute of Technology have created Roomba, a robot that vacuums. The $200 robot zips under furniture. Sensors keep it from bumping into walls or falling down the stairs. When it finishes, Roomba beeps proudly, then turns itself off.

go → Vote for your favorite at
www.timeforkids.com/inventions

Great Ideas from Great

ca. 3800–3600 B.C.	Wheel
ca. A.D. 100	Paper
1608	Telescope
1709	Piano
1829	Braille
1831	Lawn mower
1839	Rubber
1849	Safety pin
1850	Refrigerator
1867	Dynamite / Fluorescent lamp / Typewriter
1869	Vacuum cleaner
1870	Chewing gum
1876	Telephone
1877	Phonograph (record player)
1888	Handheld camera / Ballpoint pen
1891	Zipper
1893	Motion pictures (movies)
1899	Aspirin / Tape recorder
1901	First transatlantic radio signals
1904	Ice-cream cone
1907	Plastic
1908	Model T car
1909	Toaster
1911	Oreo cookies
1913	Moving assembly line

MINDS

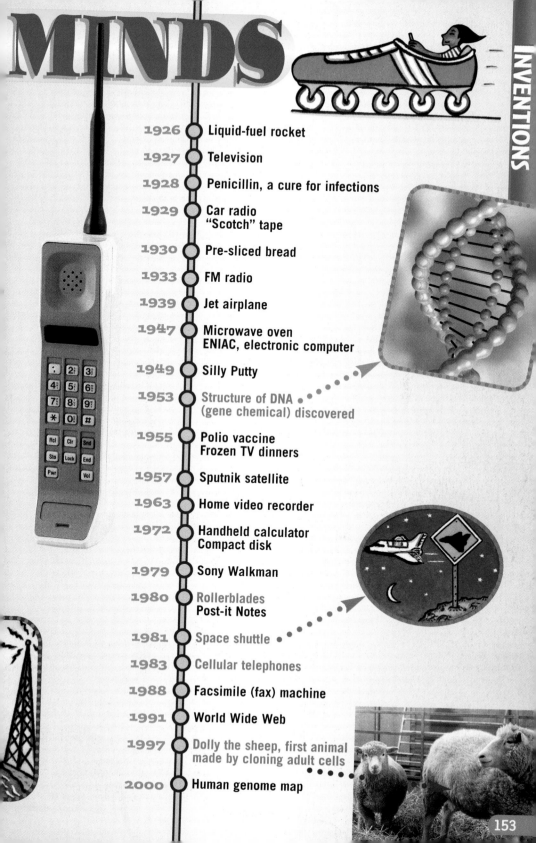

1926	Liquid-fuel rocket
1927	Television
1928	Penicillin, a cure for infections
1929	Car radio "Scotch" tape
1930	Pre-sliced bread
1933	FM radio
1939	Jet airplane
1947	Microwave oven ENIAC, electronic computer
1949	Silly Putty
1953	Structure of DNA (gene chemical) discovered
1955	Polio vaccine Frozen TV dinners
1957	Sputnik satellite
1963	Home video recorder
1972	Handheld calculator Compact disk
1979	Sony Walkman
1980	Rollerblades Post-it Notes
1981	Space shuttle
1983	Cellular telephones
1988	Facsimile (fax) machine
1991	World Wide Web
1997	Dolly the sheep, first animal made by cloning adult cells
2000	Human genome map

153

The year 2003 marks the 100th anniversary of flight.

Did You Know?

Aviation has come a long way since 1903. Today's 747s typically travel at a cruising speed of about 490 knots, or 564 miles per hour.

THE WRIGHT STUFF

ORVILLE AND WILBUR WRIGHT, bicycle mechanics from Dayton, Ohio, worked painstakingly for four years to build the world's first heavier-than-air, power-driven airplane. Between 1899 and 1902, they tested several gliders (motorless planes). After gliding a record 620 feet in 1902, Orville and Wilbur built the 1903 Flyer, a plane with a propeller and a 4-cylinder, 12-horsepower engine. They constructed the craft in sections in their bike shop and put the pieces together in Kitty Hawk, North Carolina, where they would make their pioneering flight.

Orville and Wilbur Wright flew into history in their double-winged craft on Dec. 17, 1903. Orville piloted the plane for 12 seconds while Wilbur ran alongside. The plane traveled 120 feet at 26 knots, or approximately 30 miles per hour.

The milestone marked the beginning of the aviation era. The Wright brothers' invention launched a new industry and revolutionized transportation, commerce and communication all over the world.

On Dec. 17, 2003, the 100th anniversary of the first flight, a pilot will re-create the ground-breaking flight in a full-scale replica of the 1903 Wright Flyer. The pilot will fly the plane while lying on his or her stomach, just as Orville did a century before.

SMOOTH RIDING

While the Wright brothers were clearly pioneers in aviation, these other transportation inventions have made travel much easier and more enjoyable.

INVENTION	DATE	LOCATION
hot-air balloon	1783	France
parachute	1783	France
steamship	1783	France
steam-powered locomotive	1804	England
passenger elevator	1852	United States
bicycle	1884	England
car with internal-combustion engine	1885	Germany
motorcycle	1885	Germany
car run by gasoline	1892	United States
zeppelin	1900	Germany
rocket	1926	United States
double-rotor helicopter	1936	Germany
jet	1939	Germany
Rollerblades	1980	United States
Segway human transporter	2001	United States

How to Get a Patent

Got a great idea for a new invention? You should have it patented, which is permission from the government to make, sell or use an invention, so no one else can take credit for or profit from your ingenuity. The process can be complicated. The first step is to file an application with the U.S. Patent and Trademark Office. You must explain your idea clearly to a patent examiner to determine whether it is new and useful. You must have an illustration of the device in action. Many people hire patent attorneys, which can be very expensive, to make sure that their patents conform to the U.S. Patent Office rules. If you get a patent, your invention will be assigned a unique number and you alone will have the right to sell your device. For more information, contact the U.S. Patent and Trademark Office at Crystal Plaza 3, Room 2C02, Washington, D.C., 20231.

To see how you can patent your inventions, go to **www.uspto.gov/**

TFK MYSTERY PERSON

CLUE 1: I was an American inventor born in Ohio in 1847.
CLUE 2: I developed my first invention, the electrical vote recorder, when I was 21.
CLUE 3: Throughout my lifetime, I created more than 1,000 inventions, including an electric pen and motion-picture camera. My most important invention was the electric lightbulb in 1879.

WHO AM I?

(See Answer Key that begins on page 340.)

LANGUAGE

SPEAKING OF HOME

Nearly 18% of Americans speak a language other than English at home. That's about 47 million people! More than 300 languages are spoken in the U.S. today. Here are the 10 most common.

1. Spanish
2. Chinese
3. French
4. German
5. Tagalog (spoken in the Philippines)
6. Vietnamese
7. Italian
8. Korean
9. Russian
10. Polish

Source: U.S. Census Bureau

LANGUAGES SPOKEN AROUND THE WORLD

There are more than 2,700 languages in the world. There are also more than 7,000 dialects. A dialect is a regional variety of a language that has a different pronunciation, vocabulary or meaning. Here are the 10 most widely spoken languages in the world.

LANGUAGE	COUNTRIES WHERE SPOKEN	NUMBER OF PEOPLE
1. Chinese (Mandarin)	China	1.1 billion
2. English	U.S., U.K., Canada, Australia, New Zealand	514 million
3. Hindustani	India	496 million
4. Spanish	Spain, Latin America	425 million
5. Russian	Russia	275 million
6. Arabic	Middle East, North Africa	256 million
7. Bengali	Bangladesh	215 million
8. Portuguese	Portugal, parts of Africa and South America	194 million
9. Malay-Indonesian	Malaysia, Indonesia	176 million
10. French	France, Belgium, Switzerland, Canada, parts of Africa	129 million

Source: Ethnologue

SAY IT IN ZULU

Zulu is the most widely spoken language in South Africa. Zulu uses many tones and clicking sounds. These are made by pressing the tongue against different parts of the mouth. Try out these phrases.

ENGLISH	ZULU	HOW YOU SAY IT
Hello	Sawubona	(sa-woo-boh-na)
Goodbye	Sala kahle	(sah-la kah-leh)
Friend	Umngane	(oom-gan-eh)
My name is ___.	Igama lami ngu __.	(ee-gah-ma lah-me ngoo___.)
Thank you	Ngiyabonga	(ngee-ya-bon-ga)

Bonus: Try saying, "Hello, friend. My name is _____."

go Hear languages from around the world at
www.timeforkids.com/goplaces

Si, you can read Spanish!

Spanish is the second most widely spoken language in the U.S. Use the Word Bank to translate, or turn into English, this letter. Find each Spanish word in the bank, then write its meaning on the line below it.

WORD BANK

amiga = friend
en = in
gato = cat
hola = hello
mi = my
México = Mexico
perro = dog
tengo = have
tu = your
un = a
vivo = live
y = and
yo = I

¡Hola!
_____

mi gato

Yo vivo en México.
___ ___ ___ ___

Yo tengo un gato y
___ ___ ___ ___ ___

un perro.
___ ___

mi perro

Tu amiga,
___ ___

Pilar

(See Answer Key that begins on page 340.)

Word Relationships: Analogies

An analogy is a type of word problem. It is made up of two word pairs, like this:

SOFT : VELVET :: _____ : ballerina

Your goal in solving an analogy is to find a word that correctly completes the second pair. Both pairs of words have the same kind of relationship. To solve the analogy you need to find that relationship. Read the analogy like this:

Soft is to velvet as "blank" is to ballerina.

Ask yourself: What is the relationship between soft and velvet? The relationship between soft and velvet is descriptive—one word describes the other. Therefore, in the second pair of words, one word must describe the other. Graceful describes ballerina.

Here are some other types of relationships the word pairs might have:

Synonyms	or words that have similar meanings, as in WORK : LABOR
Antonyms	or words that have opposite meanings, as in SHORT : TALL
Part to Whole	in which one word is a part of the other, as in ARM : BODY
Item to Category	in which one word names something that falls into the group named by the other word, as in MILK : BEVERAGE

PALINDROMES

A palindrome is a word, phrase or sentence that reads the same forward and backward. Here are some examples of palindromes.

A Santa at NASA.
civic
dad
Dee saw a seed.
Hannah
kayak
madam
never odd or even
Nurses run.
radar
Rise to vote, sir.
Was it a cat I saw?

Can you think of other palindromes?

"ONYMS"

ACRONYM

An acronym is a word or name formed by combining the first letters of words in a phrase. For example, SCUBA comes from self-contained underwater breathing apparatus.

ANTONYM

Antonyms are words with opposite meanings. **Sweet** and **bitter** are antonyms.

HETERONYM

Heteronyms are words with identical spellings but different meanings and pronunciations. For example, **bow** and arrow, and to **bow** on stage.

HOMONYM

Homonyms are words that sound alike (and are sometimes spelled alike) but name different things. **Die** (to stop living) and **dye** (color) are homonyms.

PSEUDONYM

From the Greek **pseud** (false) and **onym** (name), a pseudonym is a false name or pen name used by an author. Mark Twain is a pseudonym for Samuel Langhorne Clemens.

SYNONYMS

Synonyms are words with the same or similar meanings. **Cranky** and **grumpy** are synonyms.

Idioms

If you say, "The cat's out of the bag" instead of "The secret is given away," you're using an idiom. The meaning of an idiom is different from the actual meaning of the words used. Here are some other idioms.

"Let the cat out of the bag"

Sometimes, rural farmers would put a cat in a bag and try to pass it off as a pig, which was more valuable than a cat. If the buyer opened the bag to inspect the animal, he let the cat out of the bag and the trick was exposed. Today, the idiom means to reveal a secret.

"Bury the hatchet"

Native Americans used to bury weapons to show that fighting had ended and enemies were at peace. Today, the idiom means to make up with a friend after an argument or fight.

"A close shave"

In the past, student barbers learned to shave on customers. If they shaved too closely, their clients might be cut or barely escape serious injury. Today, we use this idiom if a person narrowly escapes disaster.

"To take the bull by the horns"

In bullfights, a strong and skilled matador often bravely grasps the horns of an aggressive bull about to attack. The idiom means to fearlessly face danger or a difficult situation.

AMERICAN SIGN LANGUAGE (ASL)
and the AMERICAN MANUAL ALPHABET

American Sign Language (ASL) was developed at the American School for the Deaf, which was founded in 1817 in Hartford, Connecticut. Teachers at the school created ASL by combining French Sign Language with several American visual languages. It includes signs, gestures, facial expressions and the **American Manual Alphabet** shown below. Today, ASL is the fourth most used language in the U.S.

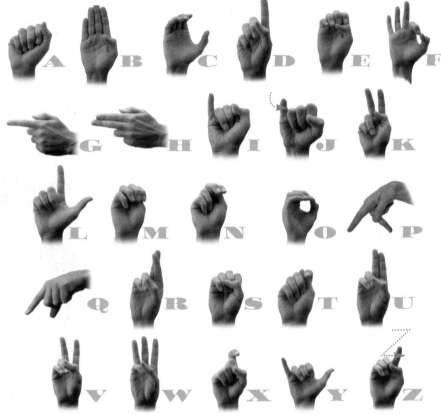

Braille System

In the 1800s **Louis Braille** developed the Braille System to help teach blind children to read and write. Braille, a Frenchman, had himself been blind since an accident at the age of three. His system of letters, numbers and punctuation marks is made up of raised points or dots.

a b c d e f g h i j k l m

n o p q r s t u v w x y z

AMAZING LANGUAGE FACTS

● The most difficult language to learn is Basque, which is spoken in northern Spain and southwestern France. It is not related to any other language in the world. It has an extremely complicated word structure and vocabulary.

● All pilots on international flights identify themselves in English.

● Somalia is the only African country in which the entire population speaks the same language, Somali.

● More than 1,000 different languages are spoken on the continent of Africa.

● The language in which a government conducts business is the official language of that country.

● The Berbers of North Africa have no written form of their language.

TFK TOP 5
MOST STUDIED LANGUAGES IN THE U.S.

According to the U.S. Department of Education, these are the most popular foreign languages studied in schools.

1. Spanish
2. French
3. German
4. Russian
5. Japanese

TFK MYSTERY PERSON

CLUE 1: I was born in 1880 in Tuscumbia, Alabama. At age 1, an illness left me blind and deaf.
CLUE 2: When I was 6, my parents hired Anne Mansfield Sullivan to be my special teacher.
CLUE 3: I soon learned to communicate with sign language and Braille. I spent the rest of my life helping other disabled people.

WHO AM I?
(See Answer Key that begins on page 340.)

161

MATH

Numerical Prefixes

A prefix is an element at the beginning of a word. A numerical prefix lets you know how many there are of a particular thing.

PREFIX	MEANING	EXAMPLE
uni-	1	unicorn: mythical creature with one horn
mono-	1	monorail: train that runs on one track
bi-	2	bicycle: two-wheeled vehicle
tri-	3	triceratops: three-horned dinosaur
quadr-	4	quadruped: four-footed animal
quint-	5	quintuplets: five babies born at a single birth
penta-	5	pentagon: figure with five sides
hex-	6	hexapod: having six legs—an insect, for example
sex-	6	sextet: group of six musicians
hept-	7	heptathlon: athletic contest with seven events
sept-	7	septuagenarian: a person between ages 70 and 80
octo-	8	octopus: sea creature with eight arms
nove-	9	novena: prayers said over nine days
deka- or deca-	10	decade: a period of 10 years
cent-	100	century: a period of 100 years
hecto-	100	hectogram: 100 grams
milli-	1,000	millennium: a period of 1,000 years
kilo-	1,000	kilogram: 1,000 grams
mega-	1,000,000	megaton: one million tons
giga-	1,000,000,000	gigabyte: one billion bytes

ROMAN NUMERALS

The ancient Romans gave us this numbering system. The year 2004 in Roman numerals is **MMIV**.

One	I
Two	II
Three	III
Four	IV
Five	V
Six	VI
Seven	VII
Eight	VIII
Nine	IX
Ten	X
Eleven	XI
Twelve	XII
Thirteen	XIII
Fourteen	XIV
Fifteen	XV
Sixteen	XVI
Seventeen	XVII
Eighteen	XVIII
Nineteen	XIX
Twenty	XX
Thirty	XXX
Forty	XL
Fifty	L
Sixty	LX
Seventy	LXX
Eighty	LXXX
Ninety	XC
One hundred	C
Five hundred	D
One thousand	M

I am VIII years old!

INTEGERS

Integers are **whole numbers. They include positive numbers, negative numbers and zero.** Integers can be shown as a **number line:**

$$\longleftarrow \quad -4 \quad -3 \quad -2 \quad -1 \quad 0 \quad 1 \quad 2 \quad 3 \quad 4 \quad \longrightarrow$$

The arrows on each end of the number line mean that you can keep counting in either direction.

Adding and Subtracting Integers

Whether you are adding or subtracting two integers, **start by using the number line to find the first number.** Put your finger on it. Let's say the first number is 2:

● If you are adding a positive number, move your finger to the right as many places as the value of that number. For example, if you are adding 2, move your finger 2 places to the right.

$2 + 2 = 4$

● If you are adding a negative number, move your finger to the left as many places as the value of that number. For example, if you are adding -4, move your finger 4 places to the left.

$2 + -4 = -2$

● If you are subtracting a positive number, move your finger to the left as many places as the value of that number. For example, if you are subtracting 4, move your finger 4 places to the left.

$2 - 4 = -2$

● If you are subtracting a negative number, move your finger to the right as many places as the value of that number. For example, if you are subtracting -2, move your finger 2 places to the right.

$2 - -2 = 4$

Here are two rules to remember:

● Adding a negative number is the same as subtracting a positive number.

$3 + -4 = 3 - 4$

● Subtracting a negative number is the same as adding a positive number. The two negatives cancel out each other.

$3 - -4 = 3 + 4$

Multiplying and Dividing Integers

● If you multiply or divide two positive numbers, the result will be positive.

$6 \times 2 = 12$

● If you multiply or divide a positive number with a negative number, the result will be negative.

$6 \times -2 = -12$

● If you multiply or divide two negative numbers, the result will be positive—the two negatives will cancel out each other.

$-6 \times -2 = 12$

IS IT AN INTEGER?

Only whole numbers are integers. Therefore, these numbers can never be integers:

● fractions
● decimals
● percents
● exponents

EVEN and Odd Numbers

E ven numbers are numbers that can be divided evenly by 2. Odd numbers are numbers that cannot be divided evenly by 2. Zero is considered an even number.

Is It Even or Odd?

To tell whether a number is even or odd, look at the number in the ones place. That single number will tell you whether the entire number is odd or even.

An even number ends in 0, 2, 4, 6 or 8.

An odd number ends in 1, 3, 5, 7 or 9.

Consider the number 3,842,917. It is an odd number because it ends in 7, an odd number. Likewise, 8,322 is an even number because it ends in 2.

Adding Even and Odd Numbers

even + even = even
4 + 2 = 6

even + odd = odd
4 + 3 = 7

odd + odd = even
5 + 3 = 8

Subtracting Even and Odd Numbers

even − even = even
4 − 2 = 2

even − odd = odd
4 − 3 = 1

odd − odd = even
5 − 3 = 2

Multiplying Even and Odd Numbers

even x even = even
4 x 2 = 8

even x odd = even
4 x 3 = 12

odd x odd = odd
5 x 3 = 15

Division, or The Fraction Problem

As you can see, there are rules that determine what happens when you add, subtract or multiply even and odd numbers. In all of these operations, you will always get a particular kind of whole number.

But when you divide numbers, something tricky can happen—you might be left with a fraction. Fractions are neither even numbers nor odd numbers, because they are not whole numbers. They are only parts of numbers and can be written in different ways.

For example, you can't say the fraction 1/3 is odd because the denominator (the bottom part) is an odd number. You could just as well write that same fraction as 2/6, in which the denominator is an even number.

The terms even number and odd number are only used for whole numbers.

To find the answer to an addition or multiplication problem, pick one number from the top of the box and one number from the left side. Follow each row into the center. The place where they meet is the answer.

Addition Table

+	0	1	2	3	4	5	6	7	8	9	10
0	0	1	2	3	4	5	6	7	8	9	10
1	1	2	3	4	5	6	7	8	9	10	11
2	2	3	4	5	6	7	8	9	10	11	12
3	3	4	5	6	7	8	9	10	11	12	13
4	4	5	6	7	8	9	10	11	12	13	14
5	5	6	7	8	9	10	11	12	13	14	15
6	6	7	8	9	10	11	12	13	14	15	16
7	7	8	9	10	11	12	13	14	15	16	17
8	8	9	10	11	12	13	14	15	16	17	18
9	9	10	11	12	13	14	15	16	17	18	19
10	10	11	12	13	14	15	16	17	18	19	20

Multiplication Table

X	0	1	2	3	4	5	6	7	8	9	10	11	12
0	0	0	0	0	0	0	0	0	0	0	0	0	0
1	0	1	2	3	4	5	6	7	8	9	10	11	12
2	0	2	4	6	8	10	12	14	16	18	20	22	24
3	0	3	6	9	12	15	18	21	24	27	30	33	36
4	0	4	8	12	16	20	24	28	32	36	40	44	48
5	0	5	10	15	20	25	30	35	40	45	50	55	60
6	0	6	12	18	24	30	36	42	48	54	60	66	72
7	0	7	14	21	28	35	42	49	56	63	70	77	84
8	0	8	16	24	32	40	48	56	64	72	80	88	96
9	0	9	18	27	36	45	54	63	72	81	90	99	108
10	0	10	20	30	40	50	60	70	80	90	100	110	120
11	0	11	22	33	44	55	66	77	88	99	110	121	132
12	0	12	24	36	48	60	72	84	96	108	120	132	144

PRIME NUMBERS

A **prime number** is a number that can be divided, without a remainder, only by itself and by 1. For example, 17 is a prime number. It can be divided only by 17 and by 1.

Some facts:

● The only even prime number is 2. All other even numbers can be divided by 2.

● No prime number greater than 5 ends in a 5. Any number greater than 5 that ends in a 5 can be divided by 5.

● Zero and 1 are not considered prime numbers.

● Except for 0 and 1, a number is either a prime number or a composite number. A composite number is any number greater than 1 that is not prime.

To prove whether a number is a prime number, first try dividing it by 2, and see if you get a whole number. If you do, it can't be a prime number. If you don't get a whole number, next try dividing it by 3, then by 5, then by 7 and so on, always dividing by an odd number.

DECIMAL PLACES

O **ne** decimal place to the left of the decimal point is the ones place. One decimal place to the right of the decimal place is the tenths place.

Keep your eye on the **9** to see where the decimal places fall.

millions	9,000,000.0
hundred thousands	900,000.0
ten thousands	90,000.0
thousands	9,000.0
hundreds	900.0
tens	90.0
ones	9.0
tenths	0.9
hundredths	0.09
thousandths	0.009
ten-thousandths	0.0009
hundred-thousandths	0.00009
millionths	0.000009

9.0

To add or subtract decimals, line up the decimal points and use zeros to fill in the blanks:

$$9 - 2.67 =$$

$$
\begin{array}{r}
9.00 \\
-2.67 \\
\hline
6.33
\end{array}
$$

FRACTIONS, DECIMALS & PERCENTS

How to Reduce a Fraction

Divide the numerator (the top part) and the denominator (the bottom part) by their **greatest common factor** (GCF), which is the largest whole number that can be divided evenly into each of the numbers.

> Example: $6/15$ The greatest common factor is 3, so
> $(6 \div 3) / (15 \div 3) = 2/5$

Or

Divide the numerator and the denominator by a common **factor**. A factor is any number that divides a number evenly without a remainder. Keep dividing until you can no longer divide either the numerator or the denominator evenly by the common factor.

> Example: $8/20$, using 2 as the factor:
> $(8 \div 2) / (20 \div 2) = 4/10 =$
> $(4 \div 2) / (10 \div 2) = 2/5$

To change

A fraction to a decimal:
Divide the denominator into the numerator.

> $1/4 = 1.00 \div 4 = 0.25$

A fraction to a percent:
Multiply the fraction by 100 and reduce it. Then, attach a percent sign.

> $1/4 \times 100/1 = 100/4 = 25/1 = 25\%$

A decimal to a fraction:
Starting from the decimal point, count the decimal places. If there is one decimal place, put the number over 10 and reduce. If there are two places, put the number over 100 and reduce. If there are three places, put it over 1,000 and reduce, and so on.

> $0.25 = 25/100 = 1/4$

A decimal to a percent:
Move the decimal point two places to the right. Then, attach a percent sign.

> $0.25 = 25\%$

A percent to a decimal:
Move the decimal point two places to the left. Then, drop the percent sign.

> $25\% = 0.25$

A percent to a fraction:
Put the number over 100 and reduce. Then drop the percent sign.

> $25\% = 25/100 = 1/4$

Did You Know?

A cardinal number shows quantity—it tells how many.
- 8 puppies
- 10 friends

ROUNDING NUMBERS

A rounded number has about the same value as the number you start with, but it is less exact. For example, 341 rounded to the nearest hundred is 300. That is because 341 is closer in value to 300 than to 400.

Rules for Rounding

Here's the general rule for rounding:

● If the number you are rounding ends with 5, 6, 7, 8 or 9, round the number up.

   Example: **38 rounded to the nearest ten is 40**

● If the number you are rounding ends with 0, 1, 2, 3 or 4, round the number down.

   Example: **33 rounded to the nearest ten is 30**

What Are You Rounding To?

When rounding a number, ask: What are you rounding it to? Numbers can be rounded to the nearest ten, the nearest hundred, the nearest thousand and so on.

Consider the number 4,827.

● 4,827 rounded to the nearest ten is 4,830

● 4,827 rounded to the nearest hundred is 4,800

● 4,827 rounded to the nearest thousand is 5,000

Rounding and Decimals

Rounding decimals works exactly the same as rounding whole numbers. The only difference is that you round to tenths, hundredths, thousandths and so on.

● 7.8899 rounded to the nearest tenth is 7.9

● 1.0621 rounded to the nearest hundredth is 1.06

● 3.8792 rounded to the nearest thousandth is 3.879

ROUNDING TIP

When rounding long decimals, look only at the number in the place you are rounding to and the number that follows it. For example, to round 5.3874791 to the nearest hundredth, just look at the number in the hundredths place—8—and the number that follows it—7. Then you can easily round it up to 5.39.

POWERS & EXPONENTS

A power is the product of multiplying a number by itself.

Usually, a power is represented with **a base number** and an **exponent**. The **base number** tells **what number is being multiplied.** The exponent, a small number written above and to the right of the base number, tells how many times the base number is being multiplied.

For example, **"6 to the 5th power"** may be written as 6^5. Here, the base number is 6 and the exponent is 5. This means that 6 is being multiplied by itself 4 times: 6 x 6 x 6 x 6 x 6

6 x 6 x 6 x 6 x 6 = 7,776

or $6^5 = 7,776$

BASE NUMBER	2ND POWER	3RD POWER	4TH POWER	5TH POWER
1	1	1	1	1
2	4	8	16	32
3	9	27	81	243
4	16	64	256	1,024
5	25	125	625	3,125
6	36	216	1,296	7,776
7	49	343	2,401	16,807
8	64	512	4,096	32,768
9	81	729	6,561	59,049
10	100	1,000	10,000	100,000
11	121	1,331	14,641	161,051
12	144	1,728	20,736	248,832

TFK PUZZLES & GAMES

To the Rescue!

The Asian long-horned beetle is a wood-chomping bug that came to the U.S. from China. Now the bug has invaded Snedley Mountains State Park. You've got to act fast! What's the shortest route from Snackburg to Pixley? Add up the miles. Then draw a line along the best route.

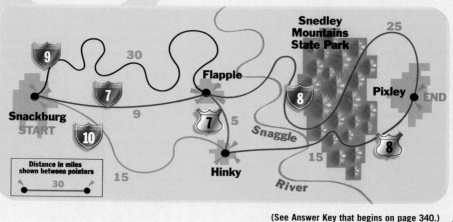

(See Answer Key that begins on page 340.)

169

COMMON FORMULAS

FINDING AREA

Area is the amount of surface within fixed lines.

SQUARE
Multiply the length of the side by itself. (For example, if the side is 6 inches long, multiply 6 x 6.)

RECTANGLE
Multiply the base by the height.

CIRCLE
Multiply the radius by itself, then multiply the result by 3.1416.

TRAPEZOID
Add the two parallel sides, multiply by the height and divide by 2.

TRIANGLE
If you know the base and the height, multiply them and then divide by 2.

FINDING CIRCUMFERENCE and PERIMETER

The CIRCUMFERENCE of a circle is the complete distance around it. To find the circumference of a circle, multiply its diameter by 3.1416.

The PERIMETER of a geometrical figure is the complete distance around that figure. To find the perimeter, simply add up the lengths of the figure's sides.

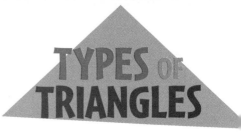

TYPES OF TRIANGLES

A **triangle** has three sides and is made of straight lines. A triangle may be classified by how many of its sides are of equal length.

In an **equilateral** triangle, all three sides are the same length.

In an **isosceles** triangle, two sides are the same length.

In a **scalene** triangle, none of the sides are the same length.

A triangle may also be classified by what kind of angles it has.

In an **equiangular** triangle, all the angles are equal—each one measures 60 degrees. An equiangular triangle is always equilateral.

In a **right** triangle, one of the angles is a right angle—an angle of 90 degrees. A right triangle may be isosceles or scalene.

In an **obtuse** triangle, one angle is greater than a right angle—it is more than 90 degrees. An obtuse triangle may be isosceles or scalene.

In an **acute** triangle, all angles are less than right angles—each one is less than 90 degrees. An acute triangle may be equilateral, isosceles or scalene.

Origins of Measurements

In ancient times, the body ruled when it came to measuring. The length of a foot, the width of a finger and the distance of a step were all accepted measurements.

Inch: At first an inch was the width of a man's thumb. In the 14th century, King Edward II of England ruled that 1 inch equals 3 grains of barley placed end to end lengthwise.

Hand: A hand was approximately 5 inches across. Today, a hand is 4 inches and is used to measure horses (from the ground to the horse's withers, or shoulder).

Span: A span was the length of the hand stretched out, about 9 inches.

Foot: In ancient times, the foot was 11¼₂ inches. Today it is 12 inches.

Yard: A yard was originally the length of a man's belt. Today it is 36 inches, about the distance from the nose to the tip of the outstretched arm of a man.

U.S. WEIGHTS AND MEASURES

MEASURING LENGTH

12 inches = 1 foot
3 feet = 1 yard
5½ yards = 1 rod
40 rods = 1 furlong
8 furlongs = 1 mile

MEASURING AREA

144 square inches = 1 square foot
9 square feet = 1 square yard
30¼ square yards = 1 square rod
160 square rods = 1 acre
640 acres = 1 square mile

MEASURING WEIGHT

16 ounces = 1 pound
2,000 pounds = 1 ton

MEASURING LIQUID

2 cups = 1 pint
2 pints = 1 quart
4 quarts = 1 gallon

COOKING MEASURES

3 teaspoons = 1 tablespoon
4 tablespoons = ¼ cup
5 tablespoons + 1 teaspoon = ⅓ cup
16 tablespoons = 1 cup

171

METRIC WEIGHTS

Most of the world uses the metric system. The only countries not on this system are the U.S., Myanmar (formerly called Burma) and Liberia.

The metric system is based on **10s**. For example, 10 decimeters make a meter.

Units smaller than a meter have Latin prefixes:

Deci- means **10**; 10 decimeters make a meter.
Centi- means **100**; 100 centimeters make a meter.
Milli- means **1,000**; 1,000 millimeters make a meter.

Units larger than a meter have Greek prefixes:

Deka- means **10**; a dekameter is 10 meters.
Hecto- means **100**; a hectometer is 100 meters.
Kilo- means **1,000**; a kilometer is 1,000 meters.

HELPFUL HINTS

Remember:
A meter is a little more than a **yard**.

A kilometer is less than a **mile**.

A liter is a little more than a **quart**.

Length

UNIT	VALUE
millimeter (mm)	0.001 meters
centimeter (cm)	0.01 meters
decimeter (dm)	0.1 meter
meter (m)	1 meter
dekameter (dam)	10 meters
hectometer (hm)	100 meters
kilometer (km)	1,000 meters

Mass and Weight

UNIT	VALUE
milligram (mg)	0.001 grams
centigram (cg)	0.01 grams
decigram (dg)	0.10 grams
gram (g)	1 gram
dekagram (dag)	10 grams
hectogram (hg)	100 grams
kilogram (kg)	1,000 grams
metric ton (t)	1,000,000 grams

Did You Know?

An ordinal number shows rank— the order of a thing in a set.
• 3rd fastest
• 6th in line

Capacity

UNIT	VALUE
milliliter (ml)	0.001 liters
centiliter (cl)	0.01 liters
deciliter (dl)	0.10 liters
liter (l)	1 liter
dekaliter (dal)	10 liters
hectoliter (hl)	100 liters
kiloliter (kl)	1,000 liters

and MEASURES

Metric Conversions

MULTIPLY	BY	TO FIND
centimeters	.3937	inches
feet	.3048	meters
gallons	3.7853	liters
grams	.0353	ounces
inches	2.54	centimeters
kilograms	2.2046	pounds
kilometers	.6214	miles
liters	1.0567	quarts
liters	.2642	gallons
meters	3.2808	feet
meters	1.0936	yards
miles	1.6093	kilometers
ounces	28.3495	grams
pounds	.4536	kilograms
quarts	.946	liters
square kilometers	.3861	square miles
square meters	1.196	square yards
square miles	2.59	square kilometers
square yards	.8361	square meters
yards	.9144	meters

A paper clip weighs about one gram.

Did You Know?

A nominal number identifies or names something.
- Jersey number 2
- ZIP code 02116

TFK
MYSTERY PERSON

CLUE 1: I was born in France in 1623. By age 12, I was an expert in math.

CLUE 2: When I was 19, I developed a gadget to help solve math problems. Numbers were punched in metal wheels and the answer appeared in an area at the top.

CLUE 3: My invention was the first calculator!

WHO AM I?

(See Answer Key that begins on page 340.)

MONEY

Money Troubles

A slow U.S. economy brings tough times

In Washington State, long lines form outside food pantries as people wait their turn to choose from shelves packed with donated cans of soup and tuna. Nearly one in every five people in the state has had to depend on charity because groceries cost too much.

In Florida, soup kitchens that feed the hungry free of charge struggle to keep up with the demand for meals.

The U.S. fell into a recession (see Word Bank) in March 2001. Many things contributed to the economic slowdown. The late 1990s was a period of great economic growth. Nearly every worker had a job. Americans were investing more in the stock market. Many people grew rich by buying and selling stocks in technology companies, including Internet businesses.

But the bubble began to burst in 2000, when Americans started questioning whether Internet companies were worth as much as people said they were. Then, in a wave of business scandals throughout 2002, some major companies misled their stockholders and engaged in dishonest behavior. People lost faith in big businesses. The stock market's value fell.

A survey recently released by the Federal Reserve Bank, the main bank of the U.S., shows Americans are spending less money, especially on big purchases like cars.

"Less spending for clothes and cars can lead to fewer orders at factories and workers losing their jobs," says Allen Sanderson, an economist at the University of Chicago.

The poorest in America have been hit especially hard. For the first time in eight years, the number of children in the U.S. living below the poverty line has increased. Eleven-year-old Terrence Taylor's mother has not been able to find a regular job. She had to move her five children into Chicago's public housing. "If we had money, we'd mo somewhere safer," says Terrence.

Still, economists say that the U.S. will bounce back. The country has recovered fro worse periods. "These economic slumps ter to be mild and short," says Sanderson. "We have every reason to be optimistic."

By Ritu Upadhyay

Soup-kitchen workers in Fort Lauderdale, Florida, are serving needy folks.

Word Bank

Bear market A time when stock prices have been generally falling

Bull market A period when stock prices are mostly rising

Depression A period when business, the employment rate and stock-market values decline sharply and stay at low levels for a long time

Economy The system a country uses to manage money and resources to produce goods (things to buy) and services (work done for others)

Inflation A continuous increase in the price of goods and services. As prices increase, the value of money decreases.

Recession A period of time when people and companies are spending less and unemployment rises. A recession can turn into a depression if it continues for an extended period of time.

Stock Shares, or pieces, of a company that are sold to the public

Unemployment rate The percentage of workers who don't have jobs and are actively seeking employment. For example, if 5 out of every 100 workers need a job, the unemployment rate is 5%.

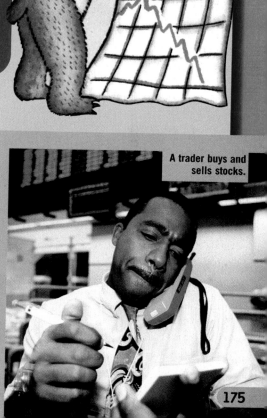

A trader buys and sells stocks.

The Stock Market

Who owns companies like Disney, McDonald's and Wal-Mart? Ordinary people do. For about $19, you can buy one piece, or share, of stock in McDonald's. People buy stock in companies hoping that they can make money by selling it later for a higher price. A stock's price depends on how many people want to buy it. If the demand for a stock is strong (perhaps because the company has a hot new product), then the price goes up. If nobody wants to buy it, the price drops. Shares of companies are bought and sold in a marketplace called the **stock market**.

About half of Americans own stock. Most lost money over the last few years, as stock prices fell. But like the economy, the stock market goes through cycles. When stock prices head up again, it's usually a sign of an improving economy.

U.S. Paper Money

BILL*	PORTRAIT	DESIGN ON BACK
$1	Washington	ONE between the front and back of the Great Seal of the U.S.
$2 (1998)	Jefferson	The signing of the Declaration of Independence
$5 (2000)	Lincoln	Lincoln Memorial
$10 (2000)	Hamilton	U.S. Treasury Building
$20 (1998)	Jackson	White House
$50 (1997)	Grant	U.S. Capitol
$100 (1996)	Franklin	Independence Hall in Philadelphia, Pennsylvania

*Date in parentheses indicates when new versions of bills were introduced.

- The Treasury first printed paper money in 1862, during a coin shortage. The bills were issued in denominations of $1, $5, $25 and 50 cents.

- The $100 bill is the largest that is now in circulation.

- Bills that get worn out from everyday use are taken out of circulation and replaced.

- A $1 bill usually lasts 18 months; $5 bill, two years; $10 bill, three years; $20 bill, four years; and $50 and $100 bills, nine years. Circulating coins last about 25 years.

- About 1% of $5 and $10 bills are counterfeited each week.

U.S. Coins

COIN	PORTRAIT	DESIGN ON BACK
Cent	Lincoln	Lincoln Memorial
Nickel	Jefferson	Monticello
Dime	F.D. Roosevelt	Torch, olive branch, oak branch
Quarter	Washington	Eagle*
Half-dollar	J.F. Kennedy	Presidential coat of arms
Dollar	Sacagawea and her infant son	Eagle in flight

*The 50 State Quarters Program features new quarters with unique designs on the back.

New Money

The U.S. Government introduced the 50 State Quarters Program Act in 1999. It features new quarters with unique state designs on the back. Five coins have debuted each year since 1999, and five new quarters will be released every year until 2008. The quarters are being released in the order that the states joined the union.

Other types of money have had a face-lift. In 2000, the U.S. Treasury introduced redesigned $5 and $10 bills to make counterfeiting more difficult. The new notes feature oversize pictures of Abraham Lincoln and Alexander Hamilton that are slightly off-center. Other anti-counterfeiting measures include watermarks that can be seen under a light, security threads that glow when exposed to ultraviolet light and tiny printing that's visible with the help of a magnifying glass. The $100, $50 and the $20 bills underwent similar makeovers in 1996, 1997 and 1998, respectively.

Did You Know?

A half-gallon of milk cost about $ .14 in 1890 and $ .31 in 1945. Today, we pay about $2.00!

Old Money

- Before coins existed, the ancient Greeks used iron nails as money, the ancient Britons used sword blades and the ancient Chinese used swords and knives. The Hercules coin was introduced by Alexander the Great in 325 B.C.
- **Cowrie shells** have been used as money in many cultures.
- Native Americans used **wampum,** woven material, as money.
- Chinese coins had holes in the center so they could be strung together like beads, which made carrying them easier.
- A Roman coin shows the double-faced god **Janus.** It dates from 240-220 B.C.
- People used banks even before they used paper money and coins! In ancient Mesopotamia, grains and other valuable trade goods were stored in palaces and temples for safekeeping.

Learn more fun facts about money at, www.FACTMONSTER.COM

Budget Keeping

A **budget** is a tool used by people, businesses and governments to predict how much money will come in and how much will be spent over a period of time, usually a year. If you spend more money than you receive, you will experience a "budget deficit."

A **household budget** lists all the sources of money for that household, such as income from a job, loans or rent, and all the ways that money will be spent, usually on things like housing, school, clothes, food, cars and other bills.

The **government's budget** shows how much money it expects to take in from taxes and where it will spend that money—on such things as defense, education, roads, energy and health care. The U.S. Government often spends more than it receives, and the result is a national debt of $5.8 trillion.

go → To manage your own budget, try *www.timeforkids.com/budget*

2002 Federal Budget

In 2002 the government took in about $1.9 trillion in taxes and spent about $2 trillion. As you can see, the government experienced a deficit. Here's a look at where the money went.

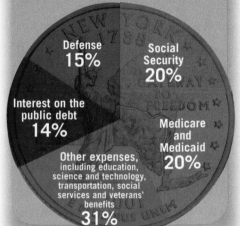

Defense **15%**

Social Security **20%**

Interest on the public debt **14%**

Medicare and Medicaid **20%**

Other expenses, including education, science and technology, transportation, social services and veterans' benefits **31%**

TFK PUZZLES & GAMES

Make Your Own Budget

To make your own budget, write down every single item you spend money on each week and how much it costs. Your list may include movies, CDs and food. Now add up how much you earn each week from an allowance, baby-sitting or a paper route. Subtract the money you spend from the money you earn. You have a budget surplus if there's money left over. You have a deficit if there's no money left or you come up with a negative number. In that case, look at each item on your "spend" list to see if there's anything you can cut.

Eureka! It's the Euro

The **euro** is the official currency of the European Union. It was introduced in 1999 in an effort to unite the member countries economically. In January 2002, euro notes (paper money) and coins replaced the old currency in Austria, Belgium, Finland, France, Germany, Greece, Ireland, Italy, Luxembourg, The Netherlands, Portugal and Spain. The other members of the European Union, Denmark, Great Britain and Sweden, did not adopt the euro.

Euro notes are decorated with elements that symbolize European architecture. The notes come in different sizes and use the colors blue, green, yellow, orange and mauve. Euro coins are made in silver, gold and copper tones and show a common design on one side and various national symbols on the other. Because they are made by mints in different countries, they vary slightly in size.

X07728368033

10 EURO

TFK TOP 5
RICHEST CELEBRITIES

1. George Lucas
2. Oprah Winfrey
3. Steven Spielberg
4. Tiger Woods
5. The rock band U2

Source: Forbes.com

TFK MYSTERY PERSON

CLUE 1: Born in 1706, I was a leader in politics and science—I invented bifocal glasses, the lightning rod and a stove.
CLUE 2: I signed the Declaration of Independence.
CLUE 3: I appear on the $100 bill, and one of my famous quotes is: "A penny saved is a penny earned."

WHO AM I?
(See Answer Key that begins on page 340.)

179

FROM PAGE TO FILM

What's the next big movie? It just might be at the bottom of your book bag!

R on Weasley, Stuart Little, Shrek, Jesse Tuck: What do they have in common? All have made the move from the small, printed page to the big, silver screen—and all with great success!

Children's books can make blockbuster movies. The film based on J.K. Rowlings's first Harry Potter book made more money than any other film in 2001. Its sequel, *Harry Potter and the Chamber of Secrets*, worked similar box-office magic when it swooped into theaters in 2002.

BY
KATHRYN R. HOFFMAN

Making movies from beloved books is not an easy job. Filmmakers have a hard time living up to the images in readers' minds. "When you read, you translate what the author says into your own personal movie that runs in your head," says Natalie Babbitt, the author of *Tuck Everlasting*. It can be hard to accept another version.

Pacing is a big issue. Films usually move faster than books and require more action. The book *Tuck Everlasting*, for example, devotes many pages to an emotional struggle in a character's head.

Wearing the famous hat and amazing makeup, actor Mike Meyers is a close match to the original Cat in the Hat.

Length is an issue, too. When filmmakers tackle a 400-page book, something has to go. While working on the second film, *Harry Potter* director Chris Columbus realized he had to cut the Death Day Party scene—an eerie, ghostly celebration. "I had some heated discussions with my kids," Columbus says. Over their objections, he sacrificed the scene for the good of the movie.

At the other extreme, the creators of *Shrek*, *Jumanji* and *The Cat and the Hat* movies have had to turn short works into 90 minutes of big screen action. To stretch out the story, they added characters and new plot details. The donkey that almost stole the show in *Shrek* barely existed in the book.

Movies draw on the unique talents of actors, set and costume designers and musicians, among others. They have tools that no writer has. "A safe, faithful telling of the book— I think that's a failure," says Chris Van Allsburg, the author of *Jumanji*. "You haven't used the magic of filmmaking."

FROM BOOK TO BLOCKBUSTER

These classics and soon-to-be classics got their start in print.

Harriet the Spy

Based on Louise Fitzhugh's best-selling children's novel. Harriet, a sixth-grader, imagines herself as a spy and records the comings and goings of her classmates in a notebook. Things go from bad to worse when a cruel classmate finds the notebook and shares it with the entire school.

James and the Giant Peach

Based on a story by Roald Dahl. James, a recently orphaned British boy, moves in with his two evil aunts. His dismal life takes a magical turn when a giant peach transports him—and his newfound insect friends—across the ocean to New York City.

Did You Know?

Americans spent $9.3 billion on about 1.6 billion movie tickets in 2002.

The Jungle Book

Based on the story by Rudyard Kipling. In this animated classic, Mowgli, a young boy who has been raised in the jungle by wolves, resists when his father-figure, Bagheera the Panther, tries to take him to a village inhabited by humans. The pair runs into an assortment of creatures that are both threatening and endearing.

A Little Princess

Based on the novel by Frances Hodgson Burnett. In the 1995 film, a wealthy 10-year-old girl attends a New York City boarding school while her father fights in World War I. She goes from riches to rags when her father dies in combat and she becomes a servant.

Mary Poppins

Based on the book by P.L. Travers. The story of the beloved "nearly perfect nanny" introduced the word "supercalifragilisticexpialidocious" into our vocabulary. The ill-behaved Banks children find themselves enchanted and transformed by their charming, magical new nanny, Mary Poppins.

Stuart Little

Based on E.B. White's story. A New York City couple adopts an adorable mouse, Stuart Little, to provide companionship for their son. Snowball the cat, who refuses to share the house with a lesser species, devises a plan to get rid of Stuart.

MOVIE MILESTONES

1889   **William Dickson**, commissioned by Thomas Edison, builds the first movie camera and names it the **Kinetograph**.

1894   **The Edison Corporation** opens the first motion-picture studio. The first **Kinetoscope** parlor opens in New York City, where people can see films for 25¢.

1895   In France, the **Lumière** brothers hold the **first public screening** of a film.

1903   *The Great Train Robbery* is the first film with a plot. It is also the first western.

1905   The first movie theater opens in Pittsburgh, Pennsylvania.

1914   **Winsor McCay** unleashes *Gertie the Dinosaur*, the first animated cartoon.

1923   German shepherd **Rin Tin Tin** becomes film's first dog star.

1924   **Walt Disney** creates his first cartoon, *Alice's Wonderland*.

1927   **Al Jolson** performs his nightclub act in *The Jazz Singer*, the first feature-length talkie.

1928   **Walt Disney** introduces the first cartoons with sound. The Academy Awards are handed out for the first time. *Wings* wins best picture.

1937   **Walt Disney's** first full-length animated feature, *Snow White and the Seven Dwarfs*, hits theaters.

1968   The movie rating system debuts with G, PG, R and X.

1977   *Star Wars* hits theaters.

1998   *Titanic* becomes the highest-grossing film of all time.

1999   *Star Wars: Episode One—The Phantom Menace* opens and breaks a string of box-office records.

2001   The first **Harry Potter** movie premieres.

2002   *My Big Fat Greek Wedding* becomes the most profitable movie of all time. It earns more than $200 million at the box office. It cost about $5 million to make.

NOTHING ON EARTH COULD COME BETWEEN

LEONARDO DiCAPRIO   KATE WINSLET

TITANIC

TELEVISION TIMELINE

1927 Philo Farnsworth transmits the first all-electronic television image.

1928 John Baird beams a television image from England to the U.S. GE introduces a television set with a 3-inch to 4-inch screen.

1931 There are nearly 40,000 television sets in the U.S.; 9,000 of them are in New York City alone.

1947 The Yankees beat the Dodgers in the first televised World Series. *Meet the Press* debuts on NBC. The first news show will become television's longest-running program.

1949 The first Emmy Awards are handed out. *These Are My Children*, a live, 15-minute show, premieres on NBC. It is the first soap opera.

1950 Saturday-morning children's programming begins.

1951 Color television is introduced in the U.S. For the first time, a nationwide program airs: Edward R. Murrow's *See It Now* series.

1952 Television's first magazine-style program, the *Today* show, debuts on NBC.

1960 Seventy million people watch the presidential debate between John F. Kennedy and Richard Nixon. Ninety percent of U.S. homes have a TV set.

1966 The first *Star Trek* episode is broadcast.

1967 Congress creates the Public Broadcasting System (PBS).

1968 *60 Minutes* airs on CBS, beginning its reign as the longest-running prime-time newsmagazine.

1969 Children's Television Workshop introduces Sesame Street.

1973 *An American Family* debuts on PBS. The show follows the real-life Loud family and marks the beginning of reality TV.

1980 Ted Turner launches CNN, the first all-news network.

1988 Ninety-eight percent of U.S. homes have at least one television set.

1990 *The Simpsons* debuts on Fox. It goes on to be TVs longest-running comedy.

2003 The average cost of a 30-second ad during the Super Bowl is $2.1 million.

TOP-RATED PRIME-TIME SHOWS*

Kids 6 to 11
1. *Survivor: Africa* (CBS)
2. *Survivor: Marquesas* (CBS)
3. *Malcolm in the Middle* (Fox)
4. *Wonderful World of Disney* (ABC)
5. *American Idol* (Fox)

Kids 12 to 17
1. *Malcolm in the Middle* (Fox)
2. *The Simpsons* (Fox)
3. *American Idol* (Fox)
4. *Bernie Mac* (Fox)
5. *Survivor: Africa* (CBS)

*2001-2002 season
Source: Nielsen Media Research

TV Facts and Figures

Did you ever count the number of hours you watch TV each week? **Try it.** You may be surprised at the amount of time you spend in front of the tube. Here are some statistics that may encourage you to tune out.

- On average, kids ages 2 to 17 watch 19 hours and 40 minutes of TV each week.
- Hours per year most kids spend in school: **900**
- Hours per year most kids watch TV: **1,023**
- Number of violent acts the average American child sees on TV before age 18: **200,000**
- Number of murders witnessed on TV by age 18: **16,000**
- Number of commercials viewed each year by American children: **2,000**
- Number of teenagers ages 13 to 17 who can name the city where the U.S. Constitution was written: **25%**
- Number of teenagers who can name where you can find the ZIP code 90210: **75%**
- Number of videos rented daily: **6 million**
- Number of books checked out of libraries daily: **3 million**

Source: TV-Turnoff Network

TFK PUZZLES & GAMES

Laugh Trackers!

America has always loved sitcoms. Below are some of TV's all-time funniest shows. Can you put these classic sitcoms in the order they first aired?

___ A. I Love Lucy

___ B. Seinfeld

___ C. The Cosby Show

___ D. Gilligan's Island

___ E. Cheers

___ F. Mork and Mindy

(See Answer Key that begins on page 340.)

TFK TOP 5

ALL-TIME HIGHEST-GROSSING KIDS' MOVIES

RANK	MOVIE	MONEY EARNED	YEAR RELEASED
1.	Star Wars	$461 million	1977
2.	E.T.: The Extra-Terrestrial	$435 million	1982
3.	Star Wars Episode One—The Phantom Menace	$431 million	1999
4.	Harry Potter and the Sorcerer's Stone	$318 million	2001
5.	The Lion King	$313 million	1994

Source: Exhibitor Relations. Through Nov. 17, 2002

TFK MYSTERY PERSON

CLUE 1: I was born in a log cabin in Utah in 1906.
CLUE 2: I created one of the 20th century's most popular machines—the television.
CLUE 3: I was only 21 when I produced the first electronic TV image, a straight line.

WHO AM I?

(See Answer Key that begins on page 340.)

Music

HIGH Notes in American Popular Music

Elvis Presley, the King of Rock, once strummed this guitar.

ca. 1775 British soldiers sing "Yankee Doodle" to mock colonists. Americans adopt it as their own tune.

1814 Francis Scott Key publishes "The Star-Spangled Banner."

1861 Julia Ward Howe writes the poem *Battle Hymn of the Republic;* set to music, it becomes a popular Civil War song.

1893 The "Happy Birthday" tune is written by two teachers in Louisville, Kentucky.

1925 The Grand Ole Opry in Nashville, Tennessee, begins Saturday night radio broadcasts of country-and-western performers.

1936 Electric guitar introduced.

1948 Columbia Records debuts the "long-playing" vinyl record.

1951 Cleveland disc jockey Alan Freed coins the term "rock and roll."

ca. 1955 Elvis Presley becomes the first rock star.

1958 *Billboard* magazine debuts its Hot 100 chart listing popular songs. The National Academy of Recording Arts and Sciences presents the first Grammy Awards.

1964 The Beatles' "I Want to Hold Your Hand" is a sensation, igniting the "British invasion."

1969 The Woodstock Music and Art Fair is attended by hundreds of thousands of fans.

1977 The movie *Saturday Night Fever* brings the Bee Gees' disco music to the silver screen.

1981 (MTV) music television debuts.

1983 Compact discs begin to replace vinyl records.

1984 Ricky Martin starts his five-year stint with Menudo.

1985 Michael Jackson releases his CD and video *Thriller.*

1989 Eight-year-old Britney Spears makes her television debut on *Star Search.*

early 1990s Grunge rock emerges in Seattle, Washington, featuring such bands as Nirvana and Pearl Jam.

1992 Backstreet Boys, a top male group of the 1990s, forms.

1995 The Rock and Roll Hall of Fame and Museum opens in Cleveland, Ohio.

1999 Napster, a computer application that lets people swap music on the Internet, debuts and outrages many in the music industry.

2001 More than 30 years after breaking up, The Beatles top the chart with the greatest-hits album *1.*

Kurt Cobain of Nirvana

Good Vibrations: Families of Instruments

Musical instruments are grouped into families based on how they make sounds. In an orchestra, musicians sit together in these family groupings. But not every instrument fits neatly into a group. For example, the piano has strings that vibrate and hammers that strike. Is it a string instrument or a percussion instrument? Some say it is both!

Brass

Brass instruments are made of brass or some other metal and make sounds when air is blown inside. The musician's lips must buzz, as though making a "raspberry" noise against the mouthpiece. Air then vibrates inside the instrument, which produces a sound.

Brass instruments include the trumpet, trombone, tuba, French horn, cornet and bugle.

Percussion

Most percussion instruments, such as drums and tambourines, make sounds when they are hit. Others are shaken, like maracas, and still others may be rubbed, scratched or whatever else will make the instrument vibrate and thus produce a sound.

Percussion instruments include drums, cymbals, triangles, chimes, bells and xylophones.

Strings

Yes, the sounds of string instruments come from their strings. The strings may be plucked, as with a guitar or harp; bowed, as with a cello or a violin; or struck, as with a dulcimer. This creates a vibration that causes a unique sound.

Stringed instruments include the violin, viola, cello, bass, harp and dulcimer.

Woodwinds

Woodwind instruments produce sound when air (wind) is blown inside. Air might be blown across an edge, as with a flute; between a reed and a surface, as with a clarinet; or between two reeds, as with a bassoon. The sound happens when the air vibrates inside.

Woodwind instruments include the flute, piccolo, clarinet, recorder, bassoon and oboe.

TFK PUZZLES & GAMES

World Music!

You've heard of hip-hop, jazz, classical and country music. But people from across the globe have created many other types of popular music. Can you match the style of music with the country it's most closely associated with?

1. Rumba
2. Samba
3. Flamenco
4. Reggae
5. Calypso

A. Spain
B. Jamaica
C. Cuba
D. Trinidad
E. Brazil

(See Answer Key that begins on page 340.)

Music Genres

blues A style of music that evolved from southern African-American work and secular (non-religious) songs. Blues influenced the development of rock, rhythm and blues and country music. Some blues musicians include Billie Holiday, Muddy Waters, Robert Johnson and Sonny Boy Williamson.

classical Classical music is usually more sophisticated and complex than other styles of music, such as rock and country. Most classical compositions are instrumentals, which means there are no words in the songs. Classical music has its roots in Europe. It includes symphonies, chamber music, sonatas and ballets. Some important classical-music composers are Wolfgang Amadeus Mozart, Ludwig Van Beethoven, Joseph Haydn and Johann Sebastian Bach. Philip Glass and John Williams are modern classical-music composers.

country-and-western music A form of American music that originated in the Southwest and the Southeast in the 1920s. Early country songs often told stories of poor people facing difficult lives. Recent country music is often hard to tell apart from pop music. The Grand Ole Opry, which began broadcasting performances in 1925 from Nashville, Tennessee, helped to popularize country music throughout the nation. Johnny Cash, Tammy Wynette, Willie Nelson, Faith Hill and Dolly Parton are popular country-music singers.

Bob Dylan

folk A style of music that has been passed down orally within cultures or regions. It is known for its simple melodies and the use of acoustic instruments. Contemporary folk music is based on traditional folk music and often contains political lyrics. Bob Dylan, Pete Seeger, Woody Guthrie and the group Peter, Paul and Mary are folk performers.

jazz American music born in the early part of the 20th century from African rhythms and slave chants. It has spread from its African-American roots to a worldwide audience. Jazz forms include improvisation (unrehearsed playing), swing, bebop and cool jazz. Ella Fitzgerald, Benny Goodman, Miles Davis and Thelonius Monk are famous jazz musicians.

opera A drama, or play, in which the parts are sung to instrumental accompaniment played by an orchestra. The libretto, or words to the opera, can be either serious or comic. Some famous operas include *Aïda, La Bohème, Madama Butterfly* and *Don Giovanni*.

pop (popular) music Pop covers a wide range of music styles and is often softer than rock and is driven by melody. Pop usually appeals to a broad assortment of listeners. Some famous pop musicians include Frank Sinatra, Jennifer Lopez, Avril Lavigne and Justin Timberlake.

Jennifer Lopez

punk A form of rock that is often loud, angry and bitter. It emerged in the 1970s as an alternative to rock music. Punk bands include The Clash, Ramones and Buzzcocks.

Music Genres continued

rap Urban, typically African-American music that features spoken lyrics often about social or political issues. The words are usually spoken over a background of sampled sounds, "scratched" records or drum loops. Hip-hop, a style of music similar to rap, blends rock, jazz and soul with sampled sounds. **Grandmaster Flash, Run-D.M.C., Beastie Boys, Jay-Z, 50 Cent, Nelly** and **Ashanti** are rappers.

rock One of the most popular forms of 20th-century music, rock combines African-American rhythms, urban blues, folk and country music. It developed in the early 1950s and has inspired dozens of subgenres, such as grunge, ska and heavy metal. Some important rock bands are **The Beatles, The Rolling Stones** and **Aerosmith. Elvis Presley, Janis Joplin** and **Jimi Hendrix** were pioneering rock musicians.

Top-Selling Albums of All Time

★ *Their Greatest Hits 1971–1975* Eagles (Elektra)
★ *Thriller* Michael Jackson (Epic)
★ *The Wall* Pink Floyd (Columbia)
★ *Led Zeppelin IV* Led Zeppelin (Swan Song)
★ *Greatest Hits Volumes I & II* Billy Joel (Columbia)
★ *Back In Black* AC/DC (Elektra)
★ *The Beatles* The Beatles (Capitol)
★ *Come on Over* Shania Twain (Mercury Nashville)
★ *Rumours* Fleetwood Mac (Warner Bros.)
★ *The Bodyguard* **(Soundtrack)** Whitney Houston (Arista)

Source: The Recording Industry Association of America

TFK MYSTERY PERSON

CLUE 1: I was born on January 27, 1756, in Salzburg, Austria.
CLUE 2: I quickly rose to stardom, and by age 4 had already composed sonatas and concertos. By age 10, I was performing throughout Europe and composing symphonies.
CLUE 3: I was the subject of the movie *Amadeus*.

WHO AM I?

(See Answer Key that begins on page 340.)

189

MYTHOLOGY

Some myths that you know may have been around for hundreds, or even thousands, of years. Although myths are often entertaining, they did not originate just for entertainment. Unlike folklore or fables, myths were once believed to be true. Myths helped to explain human nature and the mysteries of the world.

THE OLYMPIAN GODS AND GODDESSES

In Greek mythology, 12 gods and goddesses ruled the universe from atop Greece's Mount Olympus. All the Olympians are related to one another. The Romans adopted most of these gods and goddesses, but with new names, which are given below in parentheses.

The most powerful of all, **ZEUS (Jupiter)** was god of the sky and the king of Olympus. His temper affected the weather; he threw thunderbolts when he was unhappy. He was married to Hera.

HERA (Juno) was goddess of marriage and the queen of Olympus. She was Zeus's wife and sister. Many myths tell of how she got back at Zeus for his insults.

POSEIDON (Neptune) was god of the sea. He was the most powerful god except for his brother, Zeus. He lived in a beautiful palace under the sea and caused earthquakes when he was in a rage.

Zeus

HADES (Pluto) was king of the dead. He lived in the underworld, the heavily guarded land where he ruled over the dead. He was the brother of Zeus and the husband of Persephone, Demeter's daughter, whom he kidnapped.

APHRODITE (Venus) was the goddess of love and beauty. She may have been the daughter of Zeus, or she may have risen from the sea on a shell.

Hephaestus

APOLLO (same Roman name) was the god of music and healing. He was also an archer and hunted with a silver bow. Apollo was the son of Zeus and the twin of Artemis.

ARES (Mars) was the god of war. He was both cruel and a coward. Ares was the son of Zeus and Hera, but neither of his parents liked him.

HEPHAESTUS (Vulcan) was the god of fire and the forge (a furnace in which metal is heated). Although he made armor and weapons for the gods, he loved peace. He was the son of Zeus and Hera and married Aphrodite.

ARTEMIS (Diana) was the goddess of the hunt and the protector of women in childbirth. She loved all wild animals. Artemis was the daughter of Zeus and the twin of Apollo.

ATHENA (Minerva) was the goddess of wisdom. She was also skilled in the art of war. Athena sprang full-grown from the forehead of Zeus and became his favorite child.

HESTIA (Vesta) was the goddess of the hearth (a fireplace at the center of the home). She was the most gentle of the gods and does not play a role in many myths. Hestia was the sister of Zeus and the oldest of the Olympians.

Diana

HERMES (Mercury) was the messenger god, a trickster and a friend to thieves. He was the son of Zeus. The speediest of all gods, he wore winged sandals and a winged hat.

These Olympians are sometimes included in the list of rulers:

DEMETER (Ceres) was the goddess of the harvest. The word "cereal" comes from her Roman name. She was the sister of Zeus. Her daughter, Persephone, was forced to live with Hades each winter, during which time Demeter let no crops grow.

DIONYSUS (Bacchus) was the god of wine. In ancient Greece Dionysus was honored with springtime festivals that centered on theater. Dionysus was the son of Zeus.

Hermes

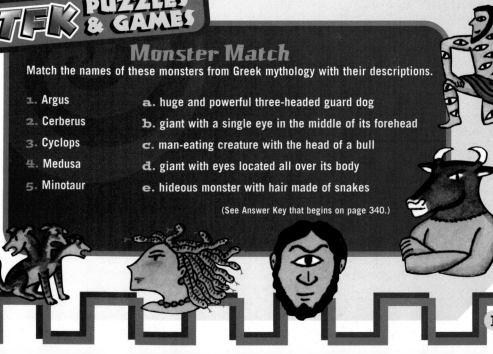

TFK PUZZLES & GAMES

Monster Match

Match the names of these monsters from Greek mythology with their descriptions.

1. Argus   a. huge and powerful three-headed guard dog

2. Cerberus   b. giant with a single eye in the middle of its forehead

3. Cyclops   c. man-eating creature with the head of a bull

4. Medusa   d. giant with eyes located all over its body

5. Minotaur   e. hideous monster with hair made of snakes

(See Answer Key that begins on page 340.)

Gods and Goddesses

Aztec

HUITZILOPOCHTLI was the god of the sun and of war. He was the patron god of the Aztec capital of Tenochtitlán, where Mexico City now stands. The Aztecs built a great temple there in his honor and sacrificed many humans to him.

COATLICUE was the goddess of the earth and the mother of all the gods. She also gave birth to the moon and stars. In Tenochtitlán the Aztecs carved a gigantic stone statue of her wearing a necklace made of human hearts and hands.

CHICOMECOATL was the goddess of corn and fertility. So important was corn to the Aztecs that she was also known as "the goddess of nourishment."

QUETZALCOATL was the god of learning. A wise god, he helped to create the universe and humankind and later invented agriculture and the calendar. He is often shown as a magnificent feathered serpent.

Egyptian

RA was the supreme god and the god of the sun. The early pharaohs claimed to be descended from him. He sometimes took the form of a hawk or a lion.

NUT represented the heavens and helped to put the world in order. She had the ability to swallow stars and the pharaohs and cause them to be born again. She existed before all else had been created.

OSIRIS was the god of the underworld and the judge of the dead. He was associated with the cycle of life and was often shown wearing mummy wrappings.

ISIS invented agriculture. She was the goddess of law, healing, motherhood and fertility. She came to be seen as a kind of Mother Earth figure.

HORUS was a sky god who loved goodness and light. The son of Osiris and Isis, he was sometimes shown as a young child.

THOTH was the god of wisdom and magic. He was believed to have invented writing, astronomy and other arts, and he served as a scribe, or writer, to the gods.

NEPHTHYS was the goddess of the dead. She was a kind and understanding companion to the newly dead as well as to those left behind.

Around the World

Mayan

HUNAHPU was a god of the sun and the father of the first humans. A great hero, with his brother he defeated the forces of death and went on to rule in the heavens.

HURAKAN was the god of storms and winds. When the first humans made him angry, he swept them away in a violent flood. The word "hurricane" comes from his name.

IXCHEL was the goddess of the moon and the protector of pregnant women. She was often shown as an old woman wearing a full skirt and holding a serpent.

CHAC was the god of agriculture and a great friend to humankind. He brought them rain and used his vast tail and fangs to protect planted fields.

ITZAMNA was the official god of the Mayan empire and the founder of its people. Corn, chocolate, writing and calendars were among his many gifts to them.

Norse

ODIN was the supreme god and, along with his brothers Vili and Ve, the creator of the world. He was also the ruler of war and wisdom.

FRIGG was the goddess of the sky, marriage and motherhood. It was believed that she knew the fate of each person but kept it a close secret.

LOKI was the god of mischief and death. He liked to invent horrible ways to harm the other gods. His nastiness and trickery earned him many an enemy.

FREYJA was the goddess of love and fertility. She was very beautiful and enjoyed music and song. Fairies were among her most beloved companions.

BALDER was the god of light, peace and joy. A kind and gentle god, he was slain in a plot hatched by Loki. He was greatly mourned, especially by his parents, Odin and Frigg.

TFK

MYSTERY PERSON

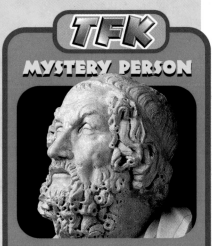

CLUE 1: I was a blind poet born in Greece around 800 B.C. During my lifetime, I traveled the country, reciting my poems from memory.

CLUE 2: I wrote the epic poems the *Odyssey* and the *Iliad*. They told the story of a war between Greece and Troy and the hero Odysseus' return to his homeland.

CLUE 3: My poetry has influenced writers through the ages.

WHO AM I?

(See Answer Key that begins on page 340.)

PRESIDENTS

1 GEORGE WASHINGTON (SERVED 1789-1797)
Born: February 22, 1732, in Westmoreland County, Virginia
Died: December 14, 1799
Political Party: None
Vice President: John Adams
DID YOU KNOW? Washington was the only President unanimously elected. He received all 69 electoral votes.

2 JOHN ADAMS (SERVED 1797-1801)
Born: October 30, 1735, in Braintree, Massachusetts
Died: July 4, 1826
Political Party: Federalist
Vice President: Thomas Jefferson
DID YOU KNOW? Adams was the first President to live in the White House.

3 THOMAS JEFFERSON (SERVED 1801-1809)
Born: April 13, 1743, in Shadwell, Virginia
Died: July 4, 1826
Political Party: Democratic-Republican
Vice Presidents: Aaron Burr, George Clinton
DID YOU KNOW? In signing the 1803 Louisiana Purchase, Jefferson nearly doubled the size of the U.S.

4 JAMES MADISON (SERVED 1809-1817)
Born: March 16, 1751, in Port Conway, Virginia
Died: June 28, 1836
Political Party: Democratic-Republican
Vice Presidents: George Clinton, Elbridge Gerry
DID YOU KNOW? Madison was the only President to have two Vice Presidents die in office. Clinton died in 1812 and Gerry died in 1814.

5 JAMES MONROE (SERVED 1817-1825)
Born: April 28, 1758, in Westmoreland County, Virginia
Died: July 4, 1831
Political Party: Democratic-Republican
Vice President: Daniel D. Tompkins
DID YOU KNOW? The Monroe Doctrine forbade foreign countries like Spain and Russia from expanding into North and South America.

PORTRAITS COURTESY OF THE NATIONAL PORTRAIT GALLERY, SMITHSONIAN INSTITUTION; LIBRARY OF CONGRESS AND THE CARTER, JFK AND REAGAN PRESIDENTIAL LIBRARIES

6 JOHN QUINCY ADAMS (SERVED 1825-1829)

Born: July 11, 1767, in Braintree, Massachusetts
Died: February 23, 1848
Political Party: Democratic-Republican
Vice President: John C. Calhoun

DID YOU KNOW? In 1843, Adams became the first President to have his photograph taken.

7 ANDREW JACKSON (SERVED 1829-1837)

Born: March 15, 1767, in Waxhaw, South Carolina
Died: June 8, 1845
Political Party: Democratic
Vice Presidents: John C. Calhoun, Martin Van Buren

DID YOU KNOW? Jackson took several bullets while fighting in duels—an activity for which he was famous.

8 MARTIN VAN BUREN (SERVED 1837–1841)

Born: December 5, 1782, in Kinderhook, New York
Died: July 24, 1862
Political Party: Democratic
Vice President: Richard M. Johnson

DID YOU KNOW? Van Buren was the first President born a U.S. citizen rather than a British subject.

9 WILLIAM HENRY HARRISON (SERVED 1841)

Born: February 9, 1773, in Berkeley, Virginia
Died: April 4, 1841
Political Party: Whig
Vice President: John Tyler

DID YOU KNOW? Harrison had the shortest presidency: he died after only a month in office.

10 JOHN TYLER (SERVED 1841–1845)

Born: March 29, 1790, in Charles City County, Virginia
Died: January 18, 1862
Political Party: Whig
Vice President: None

DID YOU KNOW? Tyler was the first President to marry in office. He was also the President with the most children (15).

11 JAMES KNOX POLK (SERVED 1845–1849)

Born: November 2, 1795, in Mecklenburg County, North Carolina
Died: June 15, 1849
Political Party: Democratic
Vice President: George M. Dallas

DID YOU KNOW? Polk's inauguration was the first one to be reported by telegraph.

12 ZACHARY TAYLOR (SERVED 1849–1850)
Born: November 24, 1784, in Montebello, Orange County, Virginia
Died: July 9, 1850
Political Party: Whig
Vice President: Millard Fillmore
DID YOU KNOW? Taylor never voted until he was 62 years old.

13 MILLARD FILLMORE (SERVED 1850–1853)
Born: January 7, 1800, in Summerhill, New York
Died: March 8, 1874
Political Party: Whig
Vice President: None
DID YOU KNOW? Fillmore and his first wife, Abigail, started the White House Library.

14 FRANKLIN PIERCE (SERVED 1853–1857)
Born: November 23, 1804, in Hillsborough, New Hampshire
Died: October 8, 1869
Political Party: Democratic
Vice President: William R. King
DID YOU KNOW? Pierce was the only elected President not re-nominated by his party for a second term as President.

15 JAMES BUCHANAN (SERVED 1857–1861)
Born: April 23, 1791, in Cove Gap, Pennsylvania
Died: June 1, 1868
Political Party: Democratic
Vice President: John C. Breckinridge
DID YOU KNOW? Buchanan was the only President to remain a bachelor—he never married.

16 ABRAHAM LINCOLN (SERVED 1861–1865)
Born: February 12, 1809, in Hodgenville, Kentucky
Died: April 15, 1865
Political Party: Republican
Vice Presidents: Hannibal Hamlin, Andrew Johnson
DID YOU KNOW? Lincoln's Gettysburg Address and Second Inaugural Address are among the greatest presidential speeches.

17 ANDREW JOHNSON (SERVED 1865–1869)
Born: December 29, 1808, in Raleigh, North Carolina
Died: July 31, 1875
Political Party: Democratic
Vice President: None
DID YOU KNOW? Johnson was the first President to be impeached. The Senate found him not guilty, however, and he remained President.

18 ULYSSES S. GRANT (SERVED 1869–1877)
Born: April 27, 1822, in Point Pleasant, Ohio
Died: July 23, 1885
Political Party: Republican
Vice Presidents: Schuyler Colfax, Henry Wilson
DID YOU KNOW? Grant's much-praised *Memoirs* has been in print since 1885.

19 RUTHERFORD B. HAYES (SERVED 1877–1881)
Born: October 4, 1822, in Delaware, Ohio
Died: January 17, 1893
Political Party: Republican
Vice President: William A. Wheeler
DID YOU KNOW? The first telephone was installed in the White House while Hayes was President.

20 JAMES A. GARFIELD (SERVED 1881)
Born: November 19, 1831, in Orange, Ohio
Died: September 19, 1881
Political Party: Republican
Vice President: Chester A. Arthur
DID YOU KNOW? Garfield was the first President who campaigned in two languages—English and German.

21 CHESTER A. ARTHUR (SERVED 1881–1885)
Born: October 5, 1829, in Fairfield, Vermont
Died: November 18, 1886
Political Party: Republican
Vice President: None
DID YOU KNOW? A stylish dresser, Arthur was nicknamed "Gentleman Boss" and "Elegant Arthur."

22 GROVER CLEVELAND (SERVED 1885–1889)
Born: March 18, 1837, in Caldwell, New Jersey
Died: June 24, 1908
Political Party: Democratic
Vice President: Thomas A. Hendricks
DID YOU KNOW? Cleveland was the only President to be defeated and then re-elected, serving two non-consecutive terms.

23 BENJAMIN HARRISON (SERVED 1889–1893)
Born: August 20, 1833, in North Bend, Ohio
Died: March 13, 1901
Political Party: Republican
Vice President: Levi P. Morton
DID YOU KNOW? Benjamin Harrison was the only President who was a grandson of a President (William Henry Harrison).

24 GROVER CLEVELAND (SERVED 1893–1897)

Born: March 18, 1837, in Caldwell, New Jersey
Died: June 24, 1908
Political Party: Democratic
Vice President: Adlai E. Stevenson

DID YOU KNOW? Cleveland was the only President to be married in the White House.

25 WILLIAM MCKINLEY (SERVED 1897–1901)

Born: January 29, 1843, in Niles, Ohio
Died: September 14, 1901
Political Party: Republican
Vice Presidents: Garret A. Hobart, Theodore Roosevelt

DID YOU KNOW? McKinley was the first President to use a telephone to organize his campaign.

26 THEODORE ROOSEVELT (SERVED 1901–1909)

Born: October 27, 1858, in New York, New York
Died: January 6, 1919
Political Party: Republican
Vice President: Charles W. Fairbanks

DID YOU KNOW? Theodore Roosevelt was the first President to ride in an automobile, an airplane and a submarine.

27 WILLIAM H. TAFT (SERVED 1909–1913)

Born: September 15, 1857, in Cincinnati, Ohio
Died: March 8, 1930
Political Party: Republican
Vice President: James S. Sherman

DID YOU KNOW? Taft was the only President who went on to serve as Chief Justice of the Supreme Court.

28 WOODROW WILSON (SERVED 1913–1921)

Born: December 28, 1856, in Staunton, Virginia
Died: February 3, 1924
Political Party: Democratic
Vice President: Thomas R. Marshall

DID YOU KNOW? Wilson was the first President to hold a news conference. About 125 members of the press attended the event on March 15, 1913.

29 WARREN G. HARDING (SERVED 1921–1923)

Born: November 2, 1865, in Corsica, Ohio
Died: August 2, 1923
Political Party: Republican
Vice President: Calvin Coolidge

DID YOU KNOW? Harding was a newspaper publisher before he was President.

30 CALVIN COOLIDGE (SERVED 1923–1929)
Born: July 4, 1872, in Plymouth, Vermont
Died: January 5, 1933
Political Party: Republican
Vice President: Charles G. Dawes
DID YOU KNOW? Coolidge was the first President to be sworn in by his father, a justice of the peace.

31 HERBERT C. HOOVER (SERVED 1929–1933)
Born: August 10, 1874, in West Branch, Iowa
Died: October 20, 1964
Political Party: Republican
Vice President: Charles Curtis
DID YOU KNOW? An asteroid, Hooveria, was named for Hoover.

32 FRANKLIN D. ROOSEVELT (SERVED 1933–1945)
Born: January 30, 1882, in Hyde Park, New York
Died: April 12, 1945
Political Party: Democratic
Vice Presidents: John Garner, Henry Wallace, Harry S. Truman
DID YOU KNOW? Franklin D. Roosevelt was the only President elected to four terms.

33 HARRY S. TRUMAN (SERVED 1945–1953)
Born: May 8, 1884, in Lamar, Missouri
Died: December 26, 1972
Political Party: Democratic
Vice President: Alben W. Barkley
DID YOU KNOW? Truman was a farmer, a hatmaker and a judge before entering politics.

34 DWIGHT D. EISENHOWER (SERVED 1953–1961)
Born: October 14, 1890, in Denison, Texas
Died: March 28, 1969
Political Party: Republican
Vice President: Richard M. Nixon
DID YOU KNOW? Eisenhower was a five-star general in World War II before becoming President.

35 JOHN F. KENNEDY (SERVED 1961–1963)
Born: May 29, 1917, in Brookline, Massachusetts
Died: November 22, 1963
Political Party: Democratic
Vice President: Lyndon B. Johnson
DID YOU KNOW? Kennedy was the first Roman Catholic President.

36 LYNDON B. JOHNSON (SERVED 1963-1969)

Born: August 27, 1908, in Stonewall, Texas
Died: January 22, 1973
Political Party: Democratic
Vice President: Hubert H. Humphrey

DID YOU KNOW? Lyndon Johnson was the first person to take the oath of office on an airplane. It was the presidential jet.

37 RICHARD M. NIXON (SERVED 1969-1974)

Born: January 9, 1913, in Yorba Linda, California
Died: April 22, 1994
Political Party: Republican
Vice Presidents: Spiro T. Agnew, Gerald R. Ford

DID YOU KNOW? Nixon was the first President to resign.

38 GERALD R. FORD (SERVED 1974-1977)

Born: July 14, 1913, in Omaha, Nebraska
Political Party: Republican
Vice President: Nelson A. Rockefeller

DID YOU KNOW? After college, Ford was a football coach, a park ranger and a male model.

39 JIMMY CARTER (SERVED 1977-1981)

Born: October 1, 1924, in Plains, Georgia
Political Party: Democratic
Vice President: Walter F. Mondale

DID YOU KNOW? Carter won the Nobel Peace Prize in October 2002.

40 RONALD W. REAGAN (SERVED 1981-1989)

Born: February 6, 1911, in Tampico, Illinois
Political Party: Republican
Vice President: George H.W. Bush

DID YOU KNOW? Reagan worked for nearly 30 years as a Hollywood actor.

41 GEORGE H.W. BUSH (SERVED 1989-1993)

Born: June 12, 1924, in Milton, Massachusetts
Political Party: Republican
Vice President: J. Danforth Quayle

DID YOU KNOW? Bush was the first President to spend a holiday with troops overseas—Thanksgiving in Saudi Arabia.

42 WILLIAM J. CLINTON (SERVED 1993–2001)

Born: August 19, 1946, in Hope, Arkansas
Political Party: Democratic
Vice President: Albert Gore, Jr.

DID YOU KNOW? Clinton was the second of two Presidents to be impeached. The Senate acquitted him.

43 GEORGE W. BUSH (SERVED 2001–)

Born: July 6, 1946, in New Haven, Connecticut
Political Party: Republican
Vice President: Richard B. Cheney

DID YOU KNOW? George W. Bush is the second President who is the son of a former President. (John Quincy Adams was the first.)

★★ ELECTION HEADLINES ★★

Candidate with the highest popular vote: Ronald Reagan (1984)—54,455,075

Candidate with the highest electoral vote: Reagan (1984)—525, out of 538 electors.

Candidates who carried the most states: Richard M. Nixon (1972) and Reagan (1984)—49

Candidates who won the Electoral College but lost the popular vote: Rutherford Hayes (1876), Benjamin Harrison (1888) and George W. Bush (2000)

Candidate who became President but lost BOTH the Electoral College AND the popular vote: John Quincy Adams (1824), who was elected by the House of Representatives

go For biographies of all the Presidents www.FACTMONSTER.COM

Did You Know?

Presidents John Adams, Jefferson and Monroe all died on the Fourth of July. President Coolidge was born on that day.

White House Facts

★ The White House has 132 rooms, including 32 bathrooms. The building features 412 doors, 147 windows, 28 fireplaces, 7 staircases and 3 elevators.

★ The White House has six floors—two basements, two floors for the First Family and two floors for offices and visitors.

★ About 6,000 people visit the White House every day.

★ The British burned the White House during the War of 1812. The building was restored, and the smoke-stained, gray stone walls were painted white.

★ President Theodore Roosevelt gave the White House its official name in 1901. It has also been known as the President's Palace, the President's House and the Executive Mansion.

TFK TOP 5 SHORTEST PRESIDENTS

Think you have to be tall for people to look up to you? Think again! The tallest President was Abraham Lincoln. He was 6 feet, 4 inches tall. But here are some leaders who were much shorter!

1. James Madison . . . . .5 feet, 4 inches

2. Benjamin Harrison . . . . . . .5 feet, 6 inches

3. Martin Van Buren . . . . . . .5 feet, 6 inches

4. John Adams . . . . .5 feet, 7 inches

5. John Quincy Adams . . . . . .5 feet, 7 inches

Happy Birthday, Teddy!

FROM TFK MAGAZINE

DRAWING THE LINE IN MISSISSIPPI

When President Theodore "Teddy" Roosevelt traveled to the state of Mississippi in November 1902, he had no idea that he was about to make history.

Roosevelt was trying to settle a border fight between Mississippi and Louisiana. He also planned to go bear hunting. He found himself face-to-face with a 235-pound bear. It had been trapped by a tracker and tied to a tree for the President to shoot. He refused. Shooting an exhausted, tied-up animal, Roosevelt felt, was unsportsmanlike.

Reporters on the trip were impressed. The *Washington Post* ran a cartoon with the caption, "Drawing the line in Mississippi," referring both to the bear and the border.

The cartoon bear inspired New York City shopkeepers Rose and Morris Michtom. They created a sad-faced stuffed bear and put it in their shop window with a sign that read, "Teddy's Bear."

Teddies became "bear" necessities. Roosevelt made one the mascot of his 1904 election campaign. Meanwhile, in Germany, toymaker Margarete Steiff had also begun making stuffed bears in 1902. They were so popular that by 1907, the Steiff company was making nearly 1 million bears a year!

To this day, people can't decide whether it was Steiff or the Michtoms who made the very first teddy. But there's no question that it happened about 100 years ago and gave rise to a bounty of beloved bears.

TFK MYSTERY PERSON

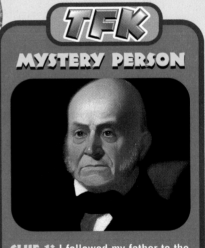

CLUE 1: I followed my father to the White House, becoming the first son of a President to serve as our nation's leader. (George W. Bush is the second.)

CLUE 2: I was Secretary of State under President James Monroe in 1817.

CLUE 3: I later fought against the expansion of slavery.

WHO AM I?

(See Answer Key that begins on page 340.)

	JUDAISM	**CHRISTIANITY**
FOUNDER	The Hebrew leader **Abraham** founded Judaism around 2000 B.C. **Moses** gave the Jews the Torah around 1250 B.C.	**Jesus Christ**, who was crucified around A.D. 30 in Jerusalem
HOW MANY GODS	One	One
HOLY WRITINGS	The most important are the **Torah,** or the five books of Moses. Others include Judaism's oral tradition, which is known as the **Talmud** when it is written down.	**The Bible** is the main sacred text of Christianity.
BELIEFS	Jews believe in the laws of God and the words of the prophets. In Judaism, however, actions are more important than beliefs.	Jesus taught love of God and neighbor and a concern for justice.
TYPES	The three main types today are **Orthodox, Conservative** and **Reform.**	In 1054 Christians separated into the Eastern Orthodox Church and the Roman Catholic Church. In the early 1500s **the major Protestant groups** (Lutheran, Presbyterian and Episcopalian) came into being. A variety of other groups have since developed.
WHERE	There are large Jewish populations in **Israel** and the **U.S.**	Through its missionary activity Christianity has spread to most parts of the globe.

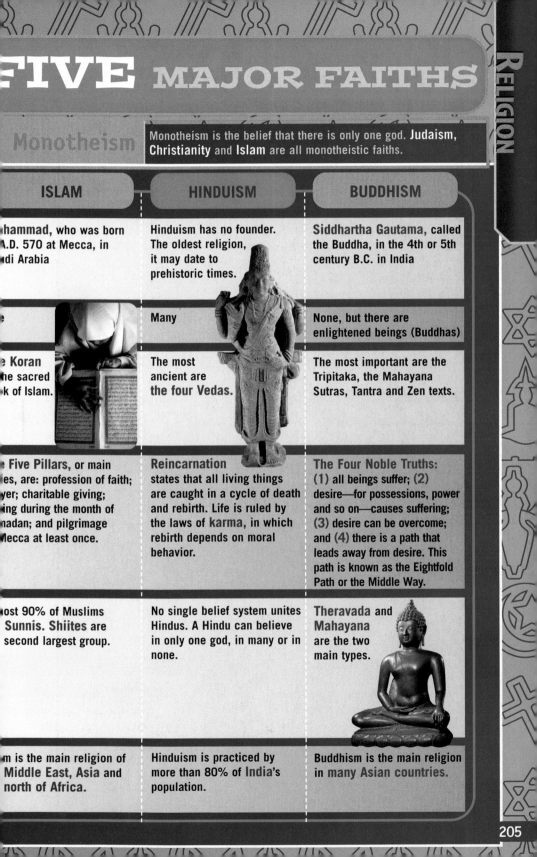

FIVE MAJOR FAITHS

Monotheism

Monotheism is the belief that there is only one god. **Judaism, Christianity** and **Islam** are all monotheistic faiths.

ISLAM	HINDUISM	BUDDHISM
...hammad, who was born ...A.D. 570 at Mecca, in ...di Arabia	Hinduism has no founder. The oldest religion, it may date to prehistoric times.	**Siddhartha Gautama**, called the Buddha, in the 4th or 5th century B.C. in India
...	Many	None, but there are enlightened beings (Buddhas)
...Koran ...he sacred ...k of Islam.	The most ancient are the four Vedas.	The most important are the Tripitaka, the Mahayana Sutras, Tantra and Zen texts.
...Five Pillars, or main ...es, are: profession of faith; ...yer; charitable giving; ...ing during the month of ...nadan; and pilgrimage ...Mecca at least once.	**Reincarnation** states that all living things are caught in a cycle of death and rebirth. Life is ruled by the laws of **karma**, in which rebirth depends on moral behavior.	**The Four Noble Truths:** (1) all beings suffer; (2) desire—for possessions, power and so on—causes suffering; (3) desire can be overcome; and (4) there is a path that leads away from desire. This path is known as the Eightfold Path or the Middle Way.
...ost 90% of Muslims **Sunnis. Shiites** are ... second largest group.	No single belief system unites Hindus. A Hindu can believe in only one god, in many or in none.	**Theravada** and **Mahayana** are the two main types.
...m is the main religion of ...Middle East, Asia and ...north of Africa.	Hinduism is practiced by more than 80% of India's population.	Buddhism is the main religion in many Asian countries.

Holy Places

Throughout the world are places of special significance to different religious groups. Here's just a sampling of the world's sacred spots.

★ **The Holy Land**—a collective name for areas of Israel, Jordan and Egypt—is a place of pilgrimage for Muslims, Jews and Christians.

Pilgrims gather at Mecca

★ **The Ganges River** in India is sacred to Hindus. They drink its water, bathe in it and scatter the ashes of their dead in it.

★ **Mount Fuji**, in Japan, is sacred to Buddhists, who believe it represents a gateway to another world.

★ **The Black Hills** of South Dakota are a holy place for some Native Americans, who travel there in vision quests—searches for peace and oneness with the universe.

★ The **Sacred Mosque in Mecca**, Saudi Arabia, is sacred to Muslims. Muslims around the world face in the direction of Mecca five times a day to pray.

★ **Mount Tai Shan** is China's most sacred mountain. It is thought to be a center of living energy—a holy place for Taoists and Buddhists.

★ **Lourdes, France,** is the home of a Roman Catholic shrine where the Virgin Mary was said to appear to St. Bernadette.

Religious Dress

People from many religions use dress as a sign of their faith. Sometimes a special type of dress is required by religion, while other times it is a matter of custom.

● **Islam** requires both men and women to be modest not only in behavior but in dress. Some Muslim women wear modest dress, or *hijab*, that covers most of the head and body.

● **Sikhs**—followers of Sikhism, a religion from India—also keep their heads covered. Sikh men wrap their heads in cotton turbans, while Sikh women may wear turbans or headscarves.

● Most **Hasidic Jewish** men wear *payos,* curled forelocks, and *tzitzit*, fringed shawls, both of which were worn by some ancient Israelites. Jewish men of all backgrounds may wear yarmulkes (skullcaps).

● **Buddhist** nuns and monks wear robes in a variety of colors, from gray to orange, depending on their region and their tradition. In many cases, both nuns and monks in the Buddhist tradition shave their heads.

● **"Plain people"** such as the Amish and Mennonites dress in simple clothing that reflects a devotion to traditional ways. Men often wear plain hats and long coats, and women wear simple dresses and aprons.

OTHER MAJOR RELIGIONS

There are many religions in the world. In addition to the five major faiths, religions with many followers include Shintoism, Taoism, Confucianism, Sikhism and Ba'hai.

10 Largest World Religions

Estimates of world religions are very rough. Aside from Christianity, few religions keep statistical records.

RELIGION	MEMBERS
1. Christianity	1.9 billion
2. Islam	1.1 billion
3. Hinduism	781 million
4. Buddhism	324 million
5. Sikhism	19 million
6. Judaism	14 million
7. Baha'ism	6.1 million
8. Confucianism	5.3 million
9. Jainism	4.9 million
10. Shintoism	2.8 million

Founded in the U.S.

Religious groups founded in the U.S. include **Christian Scientists, Latter-day Saints (Mormons), Seventh-day Adventists** and **Jehovah's Witnesses.**

Largest Churches in the United States

Denomination name	Number of members
1. Catholic Church	63,683,030
2. Southern Baptist Convention	15,960,308
3. United Methodist Church	8,340,954
4. Church of God in Christ	5,499,875
5. Church of Jesus Christ of Latter-day Saints	5,208,827
6. Evangelical Lutheran Church in America	5,125,919
7. National Baptist Convention of America, Inc.	3,500,000
8. Presbyterian Church (U.S.A.)	3,485,332
9. Assemblies of God	2,577,560
10. Lutheran Church-Missouri Synod (LCMS)	2,554,088

Source: Yearbook of American & Canadian Churches, 2002

TFK MYSTERY PERSON

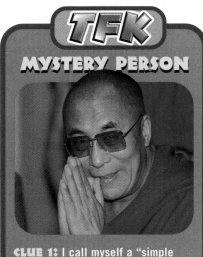

CLUE 1: I call myself a "simple Buddhist monk." But I'm actually the spiritual leader of the Tibetan people and the head of state of Tibet.

CLUE 2: Since China invaded Tibet in 1950, I have worked in a non-violent way to liberate my country.

CLUE 3: I won the 1989 Nobel Peace Prize for my struggle against Chinese rule.

WHO AM I?

(See Answer Key that begins on page 340.)

Atheists and Agnostics

An **atheist** does not believe in God. An **agnostic** believes that it is not known whether God exists. About 7% of Americans say they are either atheist or agnostic.

SCIENCE

BONES FROM THE ICE AGE

What was life like in the Ice Age? Scientists trying to answer that question must often work with less-than-perfect clues. Most fossils of the big, woolly animals that walked the Earth in those days are incomplete, because scavengers scattered their bones.

No wonder a team of British scientists was overjoyed when they found buried in a rock quarry a beautifully preserved cluster of Ice Age fossils dating back 30,000 to 50,000 years. Among them were a mammoth, reindeer, a wild horse, bison and a wolf.

By Martha Pickerill

Hardly any bones were missing. Best of all, they found four nearly perfect fossils of woolly rhinos—the fur-covered ancestors of the rhinoceroses we see today. One even had a little plant from its lunch still stuck in its teeth.

The new discovery wasn't just a pile of bones.

The surrounding field survived too. "The plants are beautifully preserved," said Simon Buteux, director of the University of Birmingham team that made the find. Buteux hopes that with this discovery, scientists will be able to piece together a clear picture of one ecosystem that thrived in the frozen past.

The era of the big freeze started gradually about 2 million years ago and lasted until about 11,000 years ago. During that time, there were periods when the climate grew mild. But at the frostiest point, which we call the Ice Age, glaciers covered Antarctica and large parts of what are now Europe and North and South America. The northernmost quarter of the mainland U.S. was coated in ice! Experts think that changes in ocean currents, the atmosphere or Earth's orbit caused the chilly climate change.

An artist's idea of what a woolly rhino from the Ice Age would have looked like.

Earth's Timeline

Life on Earth began about 2 billion years ago, but there are no good fossils from before the Cambrian Period (see below). The largely unknown past before then is called the Pre-Cambrian Era. It is divided into the Lower (or older) and Upper (or younger) Pre-Cambrian Eras—also called the Archeozoic and Proterozoic Eras.

The history of Earth since the Cambrian Period began is divided into three giant chunks of time, or eras, each of which includes a number of shorter periods.

PALEOZOIC ERA
This era began 550 million years ago and lasted for 305 million years. It is sometimes called Early Life.

Period	Millions of Years Ago	Creatures That Appeared
CAMBRIAN	550-510	INVERTEBRATE SEA LIFE
ORDOVICIAN	510-439	FIRST FISH
SILURIAN	439-409	GIGANTIC SEA SCORPIONS
DEVONIAN	409-363	MORE FISH AND SEA LIFE
CARBONIFEROUS	363-290	EARLY INSECTS AND AMPHIBIANS
PERMIAN	290-245	EARLIEST TURTLES

MESOZOIC ERA
This era began 245 million years ago and lasted for 180 million years. It is sometimes called Middle Life or the Age of Reptiles.

Period	Millions of Years Ago	Creatures That Appeared
TRIASSIC	245-208	EARLY REPTILES AND MAMMALS
JURASSIC	208-146	EARLY DINOSAURS; FIRST BIRDS
CRETACEOUS	146-65	MORE DINOSAURS, BIRDS; FIRST MARSUPIALS

CENOZOIC ERA
This era began 64 million years ago and includes the geological present. It is sometimes called Recent Life or the Age of Mammals.

Period	Millions of Years Ago	Creatures That Appeared
TERTIARY	64-2	LARGER MAMMALS; MANY INSECTS; BATS
PLEISTOCENE (Ice Age)	2-0.01	EARLY HUMANS
HOLOCENE	0.01-now	THE LAST 3,000 YEARS ARE CALLED "HISTORY"

 Read more about dino discoveries at www.timeforkids.com/dinosaurs

The Branches of Science

THE PHYSICAL SCIENCES	**Physics** The study of matter and energy and the interactions between them. Physicists study such subjects as gravity, light and time. Albert Einstein, a famous physicist, developed the Theory of Relativity.
	Chemistry The science that deals with the composition, properties, reactions and the structure of matter. The chemist Louis Pasteur, for example, discovered pasteurization, which is the process of heating liquids such as milk and orange juice to kill harmful germs.
	Astronomy The study of the universe beyond the Earth's atmosphere

THE EARTH SCIENCES	**Geology** The science of the origin, history and structure of the Earth, and the physical, chemical and biological changes that it has experienced or is experiencing
	Oceanography The exploration and study of the ocean
	Paleontology The science of the forms of life that existed in prehistoric or geologic periods
	Meteorology The science that deals with the atmosphere and its phenomena, such as weather and climate

THE LIFE SCIENCES (Biology)	**Botany** The study of plants
	Zoology The science that covers animals and animal life
	Genetics The study of heredity
	Medicine The science of diagnosing, treating and preventing illness, disease and injury

Did You Know?

DNA

(deoxyribonucleic acid)
is a long molecule located in living cells that
carries hereditary information, which includes
the traits we inherit from our parents.
DNA is shaped like a very tiny,
twisted ladder. DNA is found in **genes**,
which are sets of chemical instructions
in every cell of every creature.
The genes we inherit from our parents
determine things like skin color
and the shape of our nose.

Our Human Ancestors

Here are a few major discoveries about our ancestors.

YEARS AGO	SPECIES	DISCOVERED	NOTES
ca. 5.2–5.8 million	*Ardipithecus ramidus kadabba*	1997–1998 in Alayla, Ethiopia	Oldest-known human ancestor. Stood about 4 feet tall. Walked upright.
ca. 4.2 million	*Australopithecus anamensis*	1995, two sites at Lake Turkana in Kenya	Possible ancestor of *A. afarensis* (Lucy). Walked upright.
ca. 3.2 million	*Australopithecus afarensis*	1974 at Hadar in the Afar Triangle of eastern Ethiopia	Nicknamed Lucy. Her skeleton was 3.5 feet tall. She had an apelike skull and walked fully upright. She lived in family groups throughout eastern Africa.
ca. 2.5 million	*Australopithecus africanus*	1924 in Cape Province, South Africa	Descendant of Lucy. Lived in social groups.
ca. 2 million	*Homo habilis* (skillful or handy man)	1960 in Olduvai Gorge, Tanzania	First brain enlargement. Believed to have used stone tools.
ca. 1.8 million	*Homo erectus* (upright man or Java Man)	1891 in Java, Indonesia	Brain size twice that of *australopithecine* species. Java Man may have been a direct ancestor of *Homo sapiens* or may have developed on a separate evolutionary track. He is the first hominid to use fire and the hand ax and the first to live in caves.
ca. 100,000	*Homo sapiens* (knowing or wise man)	1868 Cro-Magnon, in France	Anatomically modern humans

The Food Chain

Plants, animals and people need each other to survive. They are linked together by their dependence on food. In a food chain, the smallest creature is eaten by a larger one, which in turn feeds a still larger one, and so on. Food chains exist both on land and in water. Here's an example of the food chain at work:

Grass eaten by grasshoppers,) (grasshoppers eaten by frogs,) (frogs eaten by snakes,) (snakes eaten by eagles.

The Elements

Elements are the building blocks of nature. Water, for example, is built from two basic ingredients: hydrogen elements and oxygen elements. Each element is a pure substance—it cannot be split up into any simpler pure substances.

The smallest part of an element is an **atom.** An atom, however, is made up of even smaller particles. These are known as subatomic particles. The most important are:

● **protons, which have positive electrical charges**

● **electrons, which have negative electrical charges**

● **neutrons, which are electrically neutral**

The atomic number of an element is the number of protons in one atom of the element. Each element has a different atomic number. For example, the atomic number of hydrogen is 1, and the atomic number of oxygen is 8.

1
H
Hydrogen

6
C
Carbon

8
O
Oxygen

16
S
Sulfur

26
Fe
Iron

53
I
Iodine

47
Ag
Silver

Ra
Radium

TYPES OF ELEMENTS

As of 2003, scientists have discovered at least **112** different elements.

● Elements with atomic numbers 1 (hydrogen) to 92 (uranium) are found naturally on Earth.

● Those with atomic numbers 93 (neptunium) or greater are artificial elements. They have to be synthesized, that is, created by combining two or more elements with lower atomic numbers.

● Elements with atomic numbers 101 and up are known as the transfermium elements. They are also known as heavy elements because their atoms have very large masses compared with atoms of hydrogen, the lightest of all elements.

HOW THE ELEMENTS ARE NAMED

Names for new elements are approved by the International Union of Pure and Applied Chemistry (IUPAC) in Geneva, Switzerland. They are often named for scientists, places or Greek or Latin words. For example, krypton (atomic number 36) is from the Greek word *kryptos*, meaning hidden, because it is colorless and odorless.

go For information on all the elements WWW.FACTMONSTER.COM

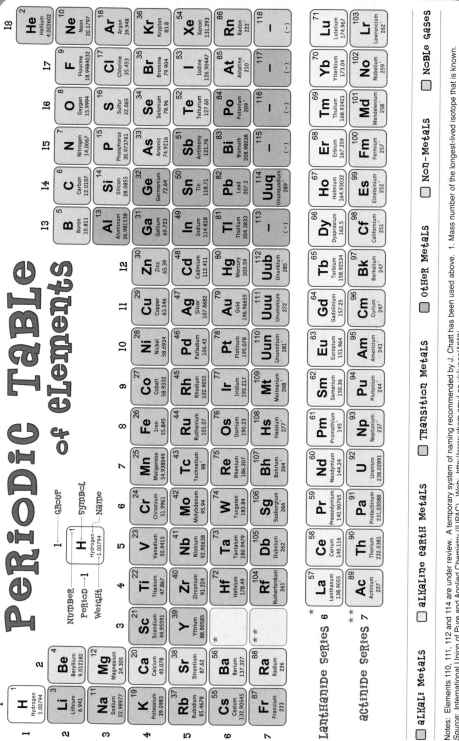

PeRioDic TaBLe
of eLements

Group																	
1																	18

NUMBER ← 1 → **GROUP**

PeRioD → 1 **H** ← **SYMBoL**
Hydrogen
1.00794 ← **NaMe**
WeIGHt

1 H Hydrogen 1.00794	2											13	14	15	16	17	2 He Helium 4.002602
3 Li Lithium 6.941	4 Be Beryllium 9.012182											5 B Boron 10.811	6 C Carbon 12.0107	7 N Nitrogen 14.0067	8 O Oxygen 15.9994	9 F Flourine 18.9984032	10 Ne Neon 20.1797
11 Na Sodium 22.98977	12 Mg Magnesium 24.305	3	4	5	6	7	8	9	10	11	12	13 Al Aluminum 26.981538	14 Si Silicon 28.0855	15 P Phosphorus 30.973761	16 S Sulfur 32.065	17 Cl Chlorine 35.453	18 Ar Argon 39.948
19 K Potassium 39.0983	20 Ca Calcium 40.078	21 Sc Scandium 44.95591	22 Ti Titanium 47.867	23 V Vanadium 50.9415	24 Cr Chromium 51.9961	25 Mn Manganese 54.938049	26 Fe Iron 55.845	27 Co Cobalt 58.9332	28 Ni Nickel 58.6934	29 Cu Copper 63.546	30 Zn Zinc 65.39	31 Ga Gallium 69.723	32 Ge Germanium 72.64	33 As Arsenic 74.9216	34 Se Selenium 78.96	35 Br Bromine 79.904	36 Kr Krypton 83.8
37 Rb Rubidium 85.4678	38 Sr Strontium 87.62	39 Y Yttrium 88.90585	40 Zr Zirconium 91.224	41 Nb Niobium 92.90638	42 Mo Molybdenum 95.94	43 Tc Technetium 98	44 Ru Ruthenium 101.07	45 Rh Rhodium 102.9055	46 Pd Palladium 106.42	47 Ag Silver 107.8682	48 Cd Cadmium 112.411	49 In Indium 114.818	50 Sn Tin 118.71	51 Sb Antimony 121.76	52 Te Tellurium 127.60	53 I Iodine 126.90447	54 Xe Xenon 131.293
55 Cs Cesium 132.90545	56 Ba Barium 137.327	★	72 Hf Hafnium 178.49	73 Ta Tantalum 180.9479	74 W Tungsten 183.84	75 Re Rhenium 186.207	76 Os Osmium 190.23	77 Ir Iridium 192.217	78 Pt Platinum 195.078	79 Au Gold 196.96655	80 Hg Mercury 200.59	81 Tl Thallium 204.3833	82 Pb Lead 207.2	83 Bi Bismuth 208.98038	84 Po Polonium 209˙	85 At Astatine 210˙	86 Rn Radon 222˙
87 Fr Francium 223˙	88 Ra Radium 226˙	★★	104 Rf Rutherfordium 261˙	105 Db Dubnium 262˙	106 Sg Seaborgium 266˙	107 Bh Bohrium 264˙	108 Hs Hassium 277˙	109 Mt Meitnerium 268˙	110 Uun Ununnilium 281˙	111 Uuu Unununium 272˙	112 Uub Ununbium 285˙	113 – (–)	114 Uuq Ununquadium 289˙	115 – (–)	116 – (–)	117 – (–)	118 – (–)

LaNtHaNiDe SeRieS 6 ★

| 57 La Lanthanum 138.9055 | 58 Ce Cerium 140.116 | 59 Pr Praseodymium 140.90765 | 60 Nd Neodymium 144.24 | 61 Pm Promethium 145˙ | 62 Sm Samarium 150.36 | 63 Eu Europium 151.964 | 64 Gd Gadolinium 157.25 | 65 Tb Terbium 158.92534 | 66 Dy Dysprosium 162.5 | 67 Ho Holmium 164.93032 | 68 Er Erbium 167.259 | 69 Tm Thulium 168.93421 | 70 Yb Ytterbium 173.04 | 71 Lu Lutetium 174.967 |

actiniDe SeRieS 7 ★★

| 89 Ac Actinium 227˙ | 90 Th Thorium 232.0381 | 91 Pa Protactinium 231.03588 | 92 U Uranium 238.02891 | 93 Np Neptunium 237˙ | 94 Pu Plutonium 244˙ | 95 Am Americium 243˙ | 96 Cm Curium 247˙ | 97 Bk Berkelium 247˙ | 98 Cf Californium 251˙ | 99 Es Einsteinium 252˙ | 100 Fm Fermium 257˙ | 101 Md Mendelevium 258˙ | 102 No Nobelium 259˙ | 103 Lr Lawrencium 262˙ |

☐ aLKaLi MetaLs   ☐ aLKaLine eaRtH MetaLs   ☐ TRansition MetaLs   ☐ OtHeR MetaLs   ☐ Non-MetaLs   ☐ NoBLe GaSes

Notes: Elements 110, 111, 112 and 114 are under review. A temporary system of naming recommended by J. Chatt has been used above. 1. Mass number of the longest-lived isotope that is known.
Source: International Union of Pure and Applied Chemistry (IUPAC). Web: http://www.chem.qmul.ac.uk/iupac/AtWt/

What Makes a GOOD Science Project?

Maybe you already know what you want to do, or maybe you're clueless.
Whatever you decide, here are steps you should consider when doing your project.

BE FRESH

Judges and teachers always look for original ideas. Your project could be original in the scientific concept, or maybe you've come up with a new way to solve an old problem or a new and better way to interpret the data.

PASSING THE "HUH?" TEST

It may be a super idea for a project but it won't impress others if you don't have a well-defined goal or objective of what you're doing. Just what scientific concept are you trying to prove or disprove with your project?

UNDERSTAND IT—IT'S YOUR PROJECT, NOT YOUR FOLKS'

Your project must show that YOU understand and know how to use scientific theory, terms, techniques and methodologies properly. Chances are if it doesn't make sense to you, it won't make sense to others.

PROVE YOUR POINT

Judges and teachers look for complete projects. As a scientist, it is your responsibility to provide all evidence to support whatever claims you are making. Without data or results that support your claims, it's not a completed work.

PUT IN SOME TIME (and FUN)

How much time and energy have you put into your project? Was it a one-hour wonder or did you actually put in some effort and time? Either way, it will show. Pick a topic you like. Science is found everywhere. Think "outside the box" and have some fun!

CLEAR AS GLASS

Your ideas should be clearly presented and easy to understand. Remember, the more you understand about the scientific principles, the easier it is for you to explain them in terms everyone understands.

Source: U.S. Government, California Energy Commission

Build Your Own Volcano

Ready for some backyard activity—volcanic activity, that is? Here's what you need:

Materials:
- Baking pan or cover of a large bucket
- Soda bottle (16 ounce or 20 ounce)
- Moist soil or sand
- 1 tablespoon baking soda
- 1 cup vinegar
- Red food coloring

1. Color the vinegar with red food coloring.

2. Put the baking pan (or cover) on the ground and place the soda bottle in the middle of it.

3. Shape the moist soil (or sand) around the bottle to form a mountain. Bring the soil to the bottle's opening, but don't get the soil inside the bottle.

4. Pour the baking soda into the bottle.

5. Pour the colored vinegar into the bottle.

Watch red foam spray out of the top and down the mountain like lava from a volcano.

Why it happened:
The baking soda reacted with the vinegar to produce carbon dioxide gas. The gas built up enough pressure to push the foaming liquid out of the top of the bottle.

ROCKS

Rocks are classified in **three** types based on how they are formed.

Igneous rocks are formed when molten rock (magma) from within Earth cools and solidifies. There are two kinds: intrusive igneous rocks solidify beneath Earth's surface; extrusive igneous rocks solidify at the surface.
Examples: granite, basalt, obsidian

Sedimentary rocks are formed when sediment (bits of rock plus material such as shells and sand) gets packed together. They can take millions of years to form. Most rocks that you see on the ground are sedimentary.
Examples: limestone, sandstone, shale

Metamorphic rocks are sedimentary or igneous rocks that have been transformed by heat, pressure or both. Metamorphic rocks are usually formed deep within the Earth, during a process such as mountain building.
Examples: schist, marble, slate

Minerals and Gems

Minerals are solid, inorganic (not living) substances that are found in and on Earth. Most are chemical compounds, which means they are made up of two or more elements. For example, the mineral sapphire is made up of aluminum and oxygen. A few minerals, such as gold, silver and copper, are made from a single element. Minerals are considered the building blocks of rocks. Rocks can be made up of as many as six minerals.

Many minerals, such as gold and silver, are very valuable because they are beautiful and rare. Limestone, clay and quartz are other examples of minerals.

Gems are minerals or pearls that have been cut and polished. They are used as ornaments, like jewelry. Precious stones are the most valuable gems. They include diamonds, rubies and emeralds.

Journey to the Center of the Earth

Inner core: The center of the Earth. It is made up of solid iron and nickel. It is about 800 miles thick.

Outer core: The outer core surrounds the inner core. It is composed mostly of liquid iron and nickel and is about 1,400 miles thick.

Mantle: The mantle is 1,800 miles thick and extends nearly to the surface of Earth. It is made up of rock.

Crust: The outer layer of the Earth, made mostly of rock, measures between 5 and 25 miles thick.

Plants

Without plants, nearly all life on Earth would end. Plants provide oxygen for humans and animals to breathe, and they provide food for many animals. There are about 260,000 plant species in the world today. They are found on land, in oceans and in fresh water. They were the first living things on Earth.

Like animals, plants are organisms, or living things. These three features distinguish plants from animals: plants have chlorophyll, a green pigment necessary for photosynthesis; they are fixed in one place (they don't move); and their cell walls are made sturdy by a material called cellulose.

Plants are broadly divided into two groups: flower- and fruit-producing plants and those that do not produce flowers or fruits. Flowering and fruit plants include all garden flowers, agricultural crops, grasses, shrubs and most leaf trees. Non-flowering plants include pines, ferns, mosses and conifers (evergreen trees or shrubs that produce cones).

Carnivorous Plants

Some plants live in soil that doesn't provide adequate nutrients, so they eat insects for nourishment. Here are some insect-eating plants.

Pitcher plants have trumpet-shaped leaves that contain a liquid. When the insect enters the leaf, tiny, stiff hairs prevent it from escaping. Juices secreted in the leaves help the plant to digest the insects.

Sundew plants have sticky hairs on their leaves that trap insects. The digestive juices in the leaves help the plant "swallow" its helpless victim.

Venus's-flytrap has bristled leaves shaped like bear traps. When an insect touches the bristles, the "trap" slams shut, trapping the insect.

Plant Hall of Fame

Biggest Flower
Rafflesia arnoldii
Each bloom is as big as 3 feet wide and can weigh up to 24 pounds. The reddish-brown flower, which gives off a horrible odor, is found in Southeast Asia.

Oldest Tree
Bristlecone pines These trees are found in California, Nevada and Utah. Some in California's White Mountains are more than 4,500 years old. The oldest-known living bristlecone pine is more than 4,700 years old.

Biggest Fungus
Not only is the *Armillaria ostoyae,* or the honey mushroom, the largest fungus, it's also probably the biggest living organism in the world. Located in Malheur National Forest in eastern Oregon, the fungus lives three feet underground and spans 3.5 miles.

Photosynthesis

Photosynthesis is a process in which green plants (and some bacteria) use **energy** from the Sun, **carbon dioxide** from the air and **water** from the ground to make **oxygen** and **glucose.** Glucose is a sugar that plants use for energy and growth.

Chlorophyll is what makes the process of photosynthesis work. Chlorophyll, a green pigment, traps the energy from the Sun and helps to change it into glucose.

Photosynthesis is one example of how people and plants depend on each other. It provides us with most of the oxygen we need in order to breathe. We, in turn, exhale the carbon dioxide needed by plants.

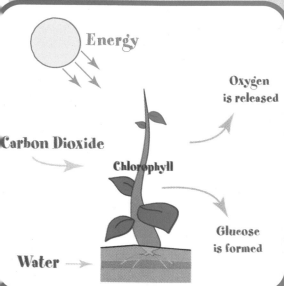

Energy

Oxygen is released

Carbon Dioxide

Chlorophyll

Glucose is formed

Water

Did You Know?

About 64 million years ago, Colorado may have been home to a lush rain forest. Recent excavations yielded fossils of tropical-looking blooms, giant fronds and trees 6 feet across—more than 100 kinds of flora in all.

Scientists believe the plants were nurtured in a hot, humid climate with an annual rainfall of about 100 inches. A vast inland sea may have provided some of the moisture.

TFK MYSTERY PERSON

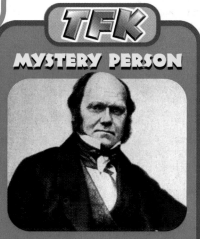

CLUE 1: I'm a British scientist who was born in 1809.

CLUE 2: After attending Cambridge University in England, I sailed the world and studied new species on the H.M.S. *Beagle.*

CLUE 3: I developed the theory of evolution after studying finches on the Galápagos Islands.

WHO AM I?

(See Answer Key that begins on page 340.)

Beyond Pluto

A distant object is orbiting the Sun. Is it a planet?

An artist created this image of icy Quaoar. It is based on pictures taken by the Hubble Space Telescope.

When the object first showed up in Michael Brown's telescope during the summer of 2002, it looked like a plain, dim star. Then he and fellow astronomer Chadwick Trujillo saw it move slowly across the sky. That meant it was much closer than a star and much more unusual.

The two scientists from the California Institute of Technology had discovered a giant ball of dirty ice, 800 miles across and orbiting the Sun 1 billion miles beyond Pluto. It's the biggest thing to turn up in our solar system since Pluto was discovered in 1930.

But it wasn't a total surprise. Scientists have known for about 10 years that the outer part of the solar system is full of icy chunks. This region, which is called the Kuiper (ky-per) Belt, begins at Neptune's orbit and stretches tens of billions of miles into deep space.

When small pieces of the Kuiper Belt fall in toward the Sun, we call them comets. This one, which Brown and Trujillo named Quaoar (kwah-oh-wahr) after a Native American god, is huge—half as big as Pluto. "There could be something out there as big as Mars!" says astronomer David Jewitt.

Kuiper Belt objects are thought to be leftovers from the time the solar system was born. Studying them will tell us plenty about the stuff our system of planets was made from.

But Quaoar is also sure to revive a debate that began a few years ago, when some experts declared that Pluto wasn't really a planet. It was more like an overgrown Kuiper Belt object, they said. If astronomers keep finding huge Kuiper Belt objects, they'll have to decide whether these should be called planets or whether Pluto should lose its title as a planet.

BY MICHAEL D. LEMONICK

Quaoar orbits in the Kuiper Belt, a ring of dusty, icy objects at the edge of the solar system.

Sun
Mercury
Venus
Earth
Mars
Jupiter
Saturn
Uranus
Neptune
Pluto
Quaoar
Kuiper Belt

Our Solar System

MERCURY

VENUS

EARTH

MARS

JUPITER

SATURN

The Sun

The solar system is made up of the **Sun** (*solar* means sun) at its center, nine planets and the various moons, asteroids, comets and meteors controlled by the Sun's gravitational pull.

Our closest star, the Sun, is thought to be about 4.6 billion years old. This fiery ball is 870,000 miles (1,392,000 km) across and is estimated to be more than 27,000,000°F (15,000,000°C) at its core. Did you know that more than a million Earth-sized planets could fit inside the Sun? The Sun is so massive that it exerts a powerful gravitational pull on everything in our solar system, including Earth.

The Planets

Our solar system has nine planets: **Mercury, Venus, Earth, Mars, Jupiter, Saturn, Uranus, Neptune** and **Pluto**. The planets travel around the Sun in an oval-shaped path called an **orbit**. One journey around the Sun is called a **revolution**. As each planet orbits the Sun, it also spins on its axis.

NEPTUNE

URANUS

PLUTO

The Universe

Astronomers think that the universe could contain 40 to 50 billion galaxies—huge systems with billions of stars. Our own galaxy is the **Milky Way**. It contains about 200 billion stars.

Did You Know?

Light travels at about 186,000 miles per second when nothing gets in its way.

New Moon

Crescent Moon

First Quarter

Full Moon

Last Quarter

The Moon

The moon travels around Earth at 22,900 miles (36,800 km) per hour. Temperatures range from -299°F (-184°C) during its night to 417°F (214°C) during its day, except at the poles, where the temperature is a constant -141°F (-96°C). The gravitational pull of the moon on the Earth affects the ocean tides on Earth. The closer the moon is to Earth, the greater the effect. The time between high tides is about 12 hours and 25 minutes.

Crescent

New

Source: NASA

The Planets

MERCURY

Named for a Roman god, a winged messenger, this planet zooms around the Sun at 30 miles per second!

Size
Two-fifths the size of Earth

Diameter
3,032.4 miles (4,880 km)

Surface
Covered by a dusty layer of minerals, the surface is made up of plains, cliffs and craters.

Atmosphere
A thin mixture of helium (95%) and hydrogen

Temperature
The sunlit side can reach 950°F (510°C). The dark side can drop to -346°F (-210°C).

Mean Distance from the Sun
36 million miles (57.9 million km)

Revolution Time (in Earth days or years)
88 Earth days

Moons: 0
Rings: 0

VENUS

Named after the Roman goddess of love and beauty, Venus is also known as the "morning star" and "evening star" since it is visible at these times.

Size
About 650 miles smaller in diameter than Earth

Diameter
7,519 miles (12,100 km)

Surface
A rocky, dusty expanse of mountains, canyons and plains, with a 200-mile river of hardened lava

Atmosphere
Carbon dioxide (95%), nitrogen, sulfuric acid and traces of other elements

Temperature
Ranges from 55°F (13°C) to 396°F (202°C) at the surface

Mean Distance from the Sun
67.24 million miles (108.2 million km)

Revolution Time (in Earth days or years)
243.1 Earth days

EARTH

Our planet is not perfectly round. It bulges at the equator and is flatter at the poles.

Size
Four planets in our solar system are larger and four are smaller than Earth.

Diameter
7,926.2 miles (12,756 km)

Surface
Earth is made up of water (70%), air and solid ground.

Atmosphere
Nitrogen (78%), oxygen (21%), other gases

Temperature
Averages 59°F (15°C) at sea level

Mean Distance from the Sun
92.9 million miles (149.6 million km)

Revolution Time (in Earth days or years)
365 days, 5 hours, 46 seconds

Moons: 1
Rings: 0

Jupiter's "Great Red Spot" is a raging storm of gases, mainly red phosphorus. The storm is larger in size than Earth and has continued for centuries with no sign of dying down.

MARS

Because of its blood-red color (which comes from iron-rich dust), this planet was named for the Roman god of war.

Size
About one-quarter the size of Earth

Diameter
4,194 miles (6,794 km)

Surface
Canyons, dunes, volcanoes and polar caps of water ice and carbon dioxide ice

Atmosphere
Carbon dioxide (95%)

Temperature
As low as -305°F (-187°C)

Mean Distance from the Sun
141.71 million miles (227.9 million km)

Revolution Time
(in Earth days or years)

687 Earth days

Moons: 2
Rings: 0

JUPITER

The largest planet in our solar system was named for the most important Roman god.

Size
11 times the diameter of Earth

Diameter
88,736 miles (142,800 km)

Surface
A hot ball of gas and liquid

Atmosphere
Whirling clouds of colored dust, hydrogen, helium, methane, water and ammonia

Temperature
-234°F (-148°C) average

Mean Distance from the Sun
483.88 million miles (778.3 million km)

Revolution Time
(in Earth days or years)

11.9 Earth years

Moons: 16
Rings: 1

SATURN

Named for the Roman god of farming, the second-largest planet has many majestic rings surrounding it.

Size
About 10 times larger than Earth

Diameter
74,978 miles (120,660 km)

Surface
Liquid and gas

Atmosphere
Hydrogen and helium

Temperature
-288°F (-178°C) average

Mean Distance from the Sun
887.14 million miles (1,427 million km)

Revolution Time
(in Earth days or years)

29.5 Earth years

Moons: 19
Rings: 1,000?

The Planets

URANUS

This greenish-blue planet is named for an ancient Greek sky god.

Size
About 4 times larger than Earth

Diameter
Diameter: 32,193 miles (51,810 km)

Surface
Little is known.

Atmosphere
Hydrogen, helium and methane

Temperature
Uniform temperature of -353°F (-214°C)

Mean Distance from the Sun
1,783.98 million miles (2,870 million km)

Revolution Time
(in Earth days or years)

84 Earth years

Moons: 21
Rings: 11

NEPTUNE

This stormy blue planet is named for an ancient Roman sea god.

Size
About 4 times the size of Earth

Diameter
30,775 miles (49,528 km)

Surface
A liquid layer covered with thick clouds and raging storms

Atmosphere
Hydrogen, helium, methane and ammonia

Temperature
-353°F (-214°C)

Mean Distance from the Sun
2,796.46 million miles (4,497 million km)

Revolution Time
(in Earth days or years)

164.8 Earth years

Moons: 8
Rings: 4

PLUTO

Named for the Roman god of the underworld, Pluto is the coldest and smallest planet. Some astronomers think it is actually a large comet orbiting the Sun.

Size
Less than one-fifth the size of Earth

Diameter
1,423 miles? (2,290 km?)

Surface
A giant snowball of methane and water mixed with rock

Atmosphere
Methane

Temperature
Between -369° and -387°F (-223° and -233°C)

Mean Distance from the Sun
3,666 million miles (5,900 million km)

Revolution Time
(in Earth days or years)

248.5 Earth years

Moons: 1
Rings: ?

Our Base in Space

This is what the International Space Station will look like when it is completely built.

Thousands of people from 16 nations are working together to build the biggest structure ever to float above our planet: the **International Space Station (ISS)**. The ISS is a giant Lego project in the sky. More than 100 major pieces are being assembled 230 miles above Earth, where gravity is much lower than it is on the surface.

In November 1998, the Russian *Proton* rocket made the first flight to the ISS, delivering the first module, Zarya Control Module. The United States's space shuttle *Endeavour* followed in December 1998, when astronauts attached the Unity Node to Zarya. The first crew, consisting of one American and two Russians, arrived at ISS in October 2000. From that point on, ISS has been permanently staffed.

Because of the low gravity in space, the 70 major sections of the ISS are being put together in space instead of on Earth. NASA expects the final pieces to be assembled by April 2006. When finished, the ISS will be as large as two football fields and will include six separate science labs. Astronauts, who will work on the ISS for up to six months at a time, will conduct experiments on board. They plan to study the long-term effects of weightlessness on humans, invent substances that work best in very low gravity and more. One day, the ISS may be a launching place for exploratory missions to other planets, like Mars.

Crews from the International Space Station and the space shuttle *Discovery* share a meal in a module of the space station.

Participating countries are: the United States, Canada, Japan, Russia, Belgium, Denmark, France, Germany, Italy, the Netherlands, Norway, Spain, Sweden, Switzerland, the United Kingdom and Brazil.

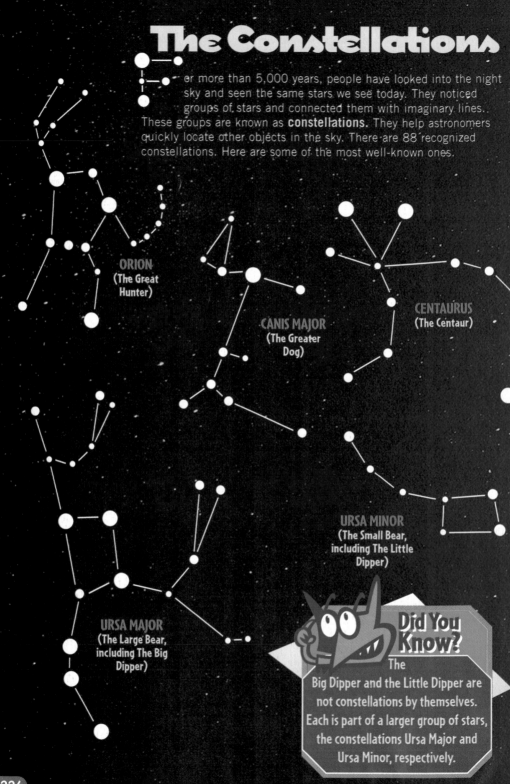

The Constellations

or more than 5,000 years, people have looked into the night sky and seen the same stars we see today. They noticed groups of stars and connected them with imaginary lines. These groups are known as **constellations.** They help astronomers quickly locate other objects in the sky. There are 88 recognized constellations. Here are some of the most well-known ones.

ORION
(The Great Hunter)

CANIS MAJOR
(The Greater Dog)

CENTAURUS
(The Centaur)

URSA MINOR
(The Small Bear, including The Little Dipper)

URSA MAJOR
(The Large Bear, including The Big Dipper)

Did You Know?

The Big Dipper and the Little Dipper are not constellations by themselves. Each is part of a larger group of stars, the constellations Ursa Major and Ursa Minor, respectively.

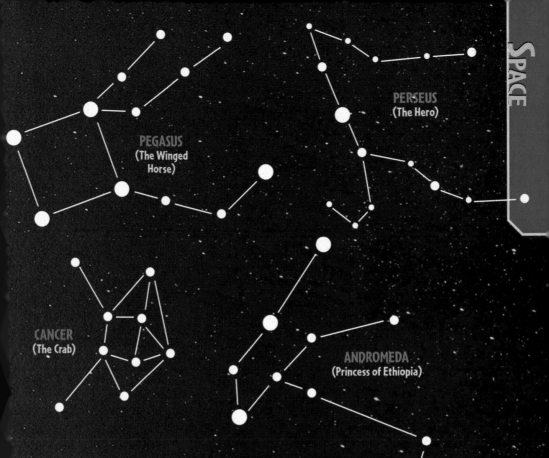

PEGASUS
(The Winged Horse)

PERSEUS
(The Hero)

CANCER
(The Crab)

ANDROMEDA
(Princess of Ethiopia)

TFK TOP 5 PLANETS WITH THE LONGEST DAYS

A day is the amount of time it takes for a planet to complete a single rotation on its axis. In our solar system, these planets take the longest to rotate once. The length of a single day for each planet is measured in Earth days and hours.

1. Venus: 243 Earth days

2. Mercury: 59 Earth days

3. Pluto: 6 Earth days

4. Mars: 25 Earth hours

5. Earth: 24 hours

Friday

Astronomical Terms

 Between the orbits of Mars and Jupiter are an estimated 30,000 pieces of rocky debris, known collectively as the **asteroids,** or planetoids (small planets). **Ceres,** the largest asteroid, measures about 600 miles across. It was the first asteroid discovered, during the New Year's night of 1801.

A **comet** is an enormous "snowball" of frozen gases (mostly carbon dioxide, methane and water vapor). Comets originate in the outer solar system. As comets move toward the Sun, heat from the Sun turns some of the snow into gas, which begins to glow. Halley's comet was discovered more than 2,000 years ago. It appears every 76 years.

Gravity is the force that draws objects to each other. On Earth, gravity pulls things down, toward the center of the planet. That's why things fall down.

A **light year** is the distance light travels in one year. It equals 5.88 trillion miles.

A **meteor** is a small piece of cosmic matter. When a meteor enters our atmosphere, it is called a **meteoroid.** It is also known as a shooting star, because it burns while passing through the air. Larger meteoroids that survive the journey through the atmosphere and land on Earth are called **meteorites.**

A meteorite made this crater in Arizona.

A **solar eclipse** occurs when the moon is in its new phase and it moves between the Sun and the Earth, blocking the Sun's light from a small part of the Earth. In a **total solar eclipse,** the moon completely obscures the Sun. During an **annular eclipse,** the moon blocks out most of the Sun's disk, leaving just a ring of light that is still visible around the edge. In a **lunar eclipse,** the Earth blocks the Sun's light from the moon.

Space Exploration TIMELINE

1957 The Soviet Union launches *Sputnik,* the first satellite.

1961 Soviet Yuri Gagarin is the first space traveler.

1962 John Glenn is the first American to orbit Earth.

1963 Soviet Valentina Tereshkova becomes the first woman in space.

1965 Soviet cosmonaut Alexei Leonov makes the first space walk.

1969 *Apollo 11* astronaut Neil Armstrong becomes the first human to walk on the moon.

1971 The Soviet Union launches the world's first space station, *Salyut 1.*

1973 The United States sends its first space station, *Skylab,* into orbit.

1976 *Viking I* is the first spacecraft to land on Mars.

1981 U.S. space shuttle *Columbia,* the world's first reusable spacecraft, is launched.

1986 The space shuttle *Challenger* explodes 73 seconds after liftoff. Six astronauts and civilian Christa McAuliffe die.

1990 The Hubble Space Telescope is put into orbit.

2003 The space shuttle *Columbia* breaks up over Texas during re-entry; seven astronauts die.

Famous Star Gazers

ERÁTOSTHENES
(276-195 B.C.)
This Greek astronomer was the first to accurately measure the size of Earth.

NICOLAUS COPERNICUS
(1473-1543)
Polish astronomer Copernicus was the first to theorize that the Sun, not Earth, was the center of our universe—a controversial idea that was strongly denounced.

PTOLEMY
(A.D. 120-189)
The ancient Greek astronomer Ptolemy theorized that Earth was the center of the universe, and the Sun, moon, planets and stars revolved around it.

GALILEO GALILEI
(1564-1642)
The Italian astronomer Galileo is considered the first to use the telescope. With it he discovered craters on our moon and proved that the planets circle the Sun.

EDWIN HUBBLE
(1889-1953)
This American astronomer classified the different types of galaxies in the universe and developed the theory that the universe is expanding. This theory is called Hubble's Law.

JOHANNES KEPLER
(1571-1630)
The German astronomer Kepler discovered that the orbits of the planets are elliptical (oval) rather than round.

SIR ISAAC NEWTON
(1643-1727)
The British astronomer Newton discovered the principle of gravity. He used the theory of gravity to explain how the moon is held in its orbit around Earth.

EDMOND HALLEY
(1656-1742)
This British astronomer was the first to calculate the orbit of a comet. The comet named for him, Halley's comet, passes close enough to Earth to be seen about every 76 years.

MYSTERY PERSON

CLUE 1: I was born in Streator, Illinois, in 1906.
CLUE 2: In 1930, as an assistant at the Lowell Observatory in Arizona, I discovered the planet Pluto.
CLUE 3: I also discovered several stars, a comet and a supercluster of galaxies.

WHO AM I?
(See Answer Key that begins on page 340.)

SPORTS

THE OTHER OLYMPICS

Athletes with disabilities go for the gold

BY RITU UPADHYAY

The Winter Olympics in Salt Lake City, Utah, excited the world. But even more Olympic thrills came after the closing ceremonies, when 7,500 athletes from 36 countries streamed into Salt Lake City's Olympic Stadium to the cheers of more than 40,000 spectators. Some athletes were in wheelchairs, others were led by guide dogs. But they were all there to participate in the 2002 Winter Paralympic Games.

The Paralympics are just like the Olympics, but these Games are for athletes with physical disabilities. The Paralympics, which began in 1960, take place right after the Olympics.

Paralympic athletes are categorized by their type of disability, and they compete with other athletes in the same category. Paralympians use many of the same courses as Olympic athletes but have special equipment that is custom-designed for their disabilities.

In the Winter Paralympic Games, there are 25 events, including downhill and cross-country skiing and ice sledge hockey—a fast-paced sport played by athletes with lower-limb disabilities. Players sit in sleds and push themselves around the ice using two short hockey sticks.

In the 2000 summer games, athletes competed in 18 events, including contests in track and field, weight lifting and swimming. Wheelchair rugby will debut as a medal event in the 2004 games in Athens.

One goal of the Games is to change the way the public sees people with disabilities. Paralympians are great athletes. Their disabilities do not hold them back.

American mono-skier Muffy Davis, a silver medalist in the women's slalom, is paralyzed from the chest down. "The limits we have are the ones we put on ourselves," she says. "If you want something bad enough, you'll find a way to do it."

Paralympic alpine skiing is an event for athletes who are visually impaired or missing a limb.

BASEBALL

It is believed that baseball is based on an old English game called rounders. The first baseball games in the U.S. were played in the 1840s.

Major League Stadium Fun Facts

The oldest Major League Baseball stadium is Fenway Park in Boston. It opened on April 20, 1912.

Qualcomm Stadium in San Diego holds the most people: 66,307.

 Comerica Park in Detroit features a merry-go-round and Ferris wheel under the stands.

Yankee Stadium is known as "The House That Ruth Built" because Babe Ruth attracted so many fans that additional seats were installed to accommodate them.

Bank One Ballpark in Phoenix, Arizona, opened on March 31, 1998. It has a swimming pool for fans in the outfield stands. Architects designed a retractable roof so fans don't have to sit in the hot sun for more than three hours. The roof weighs more than 9 million pounds and opens or closes in four minutes.

Minute Maid Park, in Houston, Texas, was known as Enron Field during its first two seasons, but the name was changed at the beginning of the 2002 season in light of Enron's downfall.

The Little League World Series

The Little League World Series—the sport's annual world-championship tournament—has been played in Williamsport, Pennsylvania, every year since 1947. Taiwan has won 16 times, more than any other foreign country.

Louisville, Kentucky, grabbed the 2002 crown with a 1-0 win over Sendai, Japan. Teams representing towns in the U.S. have won 27 times. California has five championship wins; Connecticut, New Jersey and Pennsylvania each have four wins and New York and Texas have two each.

Top Players of 2002

Most Valuable Player
A.L.—Miguel Tejada, SS, Oakland Athletics
N.L.—Barry Bonds, LF, San Francisco Giants

Cy Young Award (Best Pitcher)
A.L.—Barry Zito, Oakland Athletics
N.L.—Randy Johnson, Arizona Diamondbacks

Rookie of the Year
A.L.—Eric Hinske, 3B, Toronto Blue Jays
N.L.—Jason Jennings, P, Colorado Rockies

The Negro Leagues

From the 1920s through the 1940s, black professional ballplayers played for the segregated teams of the legendary Negro Leagues. The leagues included such Hall of Famers as **Josh Gibson**, Cool Papa Bell and Satchel Paige. The color barrier was finally broken when African-American baseball player Jackie Robinson joined the Brooklyn Dodgers in 1947.

A League of Their Own

Most strikeouts thrown in one game: 21, by Tom Cheney of the Washington Senators on September 12, 1962, in 16 innings.

Most runs scored in a game:
- By one team: 29 (tie). The Boston Red Sox vs. St. Louis Browns, June 8, 1950; Chicago White Sox vs. Oakland A's, April 23, 1955
- By two teams: 49. The Chicago Cubs beat the Philadelphia Phillies, 26–23 on Aug. 25, 1922, at Wrigley Field (then Cubs Park) in Chicago.

Longest game (in innings): 26. The Brooklyn Dodgers defeated the Boston Braves, 1–1, on May 1, 1920.

Basketball

Rocket Man

The Houston Rockets' Yao Ming has taken off as the team's big man at center. At 7 ft. 5 in., the graceful, fluid Yao (Ming is his given name, and Yao is his family name) is a force to be reckoned with.

Yao began his professional career in China with the Shanghai Sharks and was the No. 1 draft pick in the 2002 NBA draft. He is only the third Chinese player to play in the U.S. His mother was a former Chinese national-team basketball player.

HOT SHOTS

• **Most points scored in a game (by a team):** 186. Detroit Pistons vs. Denver Nuggets, Dec. 13, 1983 (3 overtimes). The game also resulted in the all-time highest number of points scored by two teams: 370. The Pistons beat the Nuggets, 186-184.

• **Most points scored in a game (by a player):** 100. Wilt Chamberlain of the Philadelphia Warriors, against the New York Knicks, in Hershey, Pennsylvania, on March 2, 1962.

• **Tallest player:** 7 ft. 7 in. (tie). Gheorghe Muresan and Manute Bol. Muresan played from 1993–2000. Bol played parts of 10 years.

• **Shortest player:** 5 ft 3 in. Tyrone (Muggsy) Bogues played in the NBA from 1987 to 2001.

TOP 5 CAREER NBA SCORERS	
	AVERAGE POINTS PER GAME
MICHAEL JORDAN	31.0
WILT CHAMBERLAIN	30.1
SHAQUILLE O'NEAL	27.6
ELGIN BAYLOR	27.4
JERRY WEST	27.0

TFK PUZZLES & GAMES

Bizarre Basketball!

This is one wacky game of hoops! Can you spot all the mistakes in picture? If you find at least 12 things wrong, consider it a slam dun!

230

(See Answer Key that begins on page 340.)

FOOTBALL

Originally a game played by colleges, professional football became popular in America in the 1920s. The National Football League (NFL) was established in 1922 and merged with the American Football League in 1970 to form a 26-team league. The NFL now consists of 32 teams with the addition of the Houston Texans in 2002.

2002 Top Players

Passing Leader
Rich Gannon, Oakland Raiders (4,689 yards)

Rushing Leader
Ricky Williams, Miami Dolphins (1,853 yards)

Receiving Leader
Marvin Harrison, Indianapolis Colts (1,722 yards)

Touchdowns
Priest Holmes, Kansas City Chiefs (24)

Interceptions
Rod Woodson, Oakland Raiders (8)
Brian Kelly, Tampa Bay Buccaneers (8)

Sacks
Jason Taylor, Miami Dolphins (18.5)

FUTURE SUPER BOWL SITES

2004	SUPER BOWL XXXVIII (38)	Houston, Texas
2005	SUPER BOWL XXXIX (39)	Jacksonville, Florida
2006	SUPER BOWL XXXX (40)	Detroit, Michigan

The Buc Stops Here

The Tampa Bay Buccaneers outplayed the Oakland Raiders on every level to win 48-21 in Super Bowl XXXVII. But Bucs coach Jon Gruden enjoyed a distinct advantage over Oakland coach Bill Callahan: Gruden coached the Raiders for three years before he joined the Bucs for the 2002 season. Oakland quarterback Rich Gannon threw five interceptions, a Super Bowl record. The Bucs returned three of them for touchdowns.

Football Phenomena

Most points scored in a game: 113. The Washington Redskins defeated the New York Giants, 72–41, on November 27, 1966.

Longest field goal: 63 yards (tie) Tom Dempsey, New Orleans Saints vs. Detroit Lions, November 8, 1970. Jason Elam, Denver Broncos vs. Jacksonville Jaguars, October 25, 1998.

Longest touchdown run: 99 yards. Tony Dorsett, Dallas Cowboys vs. Minnesota Vikings, January 3, 1983.

TFK TOP 5 BIGGEST SUPER BOWL VICTORIES

1. 1990 San Francisco 49ers 55, Denver Broncos 10
2. 1986 Chicago Bears 46, New England Patriots 10
3. 1993 Dallas Cowboys 52, Buffalo Bills 17
4. 1988 Washington Redskins 42, Denver Broncos 10
5. 1984 Los Angeles Raiders 38, Washington Redskins 9

Source: National Football League

College Basketball
March Madness

Fans describe the end of college-basketball season as "March Madness." That's because the men's and women's championship tournaments are held in March and feature more than 100 of the best teams in the country. Most of the games are exciting and many have dramatic finishes. The biggest tournament is the NCAA tournament, which began in 1939. UCLA has won the most men's titles (11) and Tennessee has won the most women's titles (6). In 2002, the University of Maryland won the men's title, and the University of Connecticut won the women's title.

TFK SPOTLIGHT

This Team's on the Ball!

What a winning streak! On January 18, 2003, the University of Connecticut's women's basketball team made history. The UConn Huskies defeated the Georgetown Hoyas 72-49 for a 55th straight win. They broke the old record of 54 wins set by Louisiana Tech from 1980 to 1982.

"Winning 55 in a row—that's pretty special," said All-American junior Diana Taurasi, who scored 22 points in the big game. In the 2002 season, the Huskies went 39-0 and won their third national title in seven years. The team had not lost a game since March 30, 2001. The team's streak ended at 70 wins on March 11, 2003, when Villanova defeated the Huskies.

Hoop Heavyweights

Here are the NCAA Division I men's basketball teams with the best records for each decade.

Decade	Team	W-L	Pct.
1950s	Kentucky	224-33	.872
1960s	UCLA	234-52	.818
1970s	UCLA	273-27	.910
1980s	North Carolina	281-63	.817
1990s	Kansas	286-60	.827
2000s	Stanford	58-7	.892

College Football

Fiesta Time

Undefeated **Ohio State University** became the 2002 Division I-A national champion after defeating last year's No. 1 team, the **University of Miami,** in the Fiesta Bowl. The Buckeyes' 31-24 victory didn't come easy, however. The team won in double overtime. It was the only I-A team to end with a perfect 14-0 season.

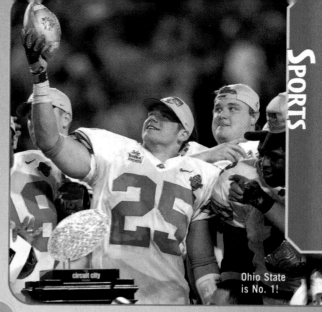

Ohio State is No. 1!

Other 2003 Bowl Game Results

Rose Bowl (Pasadena, California)
Oklahoma 34, Washington State 14
Orange Bowl (Miami, Florida)
USC 38, Iowa 17
Sugar Bowl (New Orleans, Louisiana)
Georgia 26, Florida State 13

A Full Bowl

While the Fiesta, Rose and Orange Bowls may be the most famous, there are more than two dozen college-football bowl games played each year! Here's a list of all of them.

Rose	Music City	GMAC
Fiesta	Houston	San Francisco
Orange	Insight	Capital One
Sugar	Liberty	Peach
Holiday	Continental	Independence
Cotton	Tire	Las Vegas
Seattle	Silicon Valley	Tangerine
Sun	Classic	Humanitarian
Outback	Motor City	New Orleans
Gator	Alamo	Hawaii

Top Dog

The Heisman Trophy is an annual award given since 1935 to the most outstanding college-football player in the country. Several Heisman winners have gone on to success in the NFL and have been elected to the Pro Football Hall of Fame after retiring. Current NFL stars Eddie George (1995), Charles Woodson (1997) and Ricky Williams (1998) are recent winners. In 2002, USC quarterback **Carson Palmer** won the award.

Carson Palmer was college football's best in 2002.

COLLEGE CODE FOR FOOTBALL NUMBERS

1-49	**Quarterbacks, running backs, defensive backs, some wide receivers and linebackers**
50-59	**Offensive and defensive linemen and linebackers**
60-69	**Offensive and defensive linemen**
70-79	**Offensive and defensive linemen**
80-89	**Wide receivers and tight ends**
90-99	**Defensive ends, tackles and linemen**

233

HOCKEY

Who Was That Masked Man?

The first goaltender to regularly wear a face mask was Montreal's Jacques Plante. A shot broke his nose in 1959 and he wore a mask after that. He was ridiculed at first, but now every goaltender wears a mask. Thanks to Plante, many broken bones and stitches have been avoided.

Boom Boom

One of the most feared (and certainly the most powerful) shots used by hockey players is the slap shot. Some players can unleash accurate blasts at more than 100 miles an hour. The slap shot was invented and popularized by Hall of Famer **Bernie (Boom Boom) Geoffrion** in the 1950s. With his booming shot, Geoffrion, along with teammate Maurice (Rocket) Richard, led the Montreal Canadiens to six Stanley Cup titles.

Hot Shots

Most goals in a game: 7. Joe Malone, Quebec Bulldogs vs. Toronto St. Pats, Jan. 21, 1920.

Most points in a game: 10 (6 goals, 4 assists). Darryl Sittler, Toronto Maple Leafs vs. Boston Bruins, Feb. 7, 1976.

Most goals in a season: 92. Wayne Gretzky, Edmonton Oilers, 1981–1982.

TFK TOP 5
NHL ALL-TIME CAREER POINT SCORERS

		Goals	Assists	Points
1.	Wayne Gretzky	894	1,963	2,857
2.	Gordie Howe	801	1,049	1,850
3.	Mark Messier	672	1,158	1,830
4.	Marcel Dionne	731	1,040	1,771
5.	Ron Francis	532	1,204	1,736

(Through January 28, 2003)

The Stanley Cup

Each player on the team that wins the NHL championship gets his name engraved on the **Stanley Cup** along with all the previous winners. The original cup was only seven inches high; now it stands about three feet tall. The Montreal Canadiens have won the most titles with 23.

Original Six

Between 1942 and 1967, the NHL consisted of just six teams—Boston Bruins, Chicago Blackhawks, Detroit Red Wings, Montreal Canadiens, New York Rangers and Toronto Maple Leafs. As you might expect, the teams got to know one another pretty well. They had to play each other 14 times during the regular season. Today there are 30 teams in the NHL.

TFK Q&A

Tiger Woods

Tiger Woods is the youngest golfer in history to win all four major championships. TIME For Kids Kid Reporter Mia Kabasakalis spoke with Tiger Woods about his life—and his new video game, Tiger Woods PGA Tour 2003.

Q: What's the best part of being a professional golfer?

A: Playing against the best around the world—and beating them too!

Q: What will kids like most about your video game?

A: How realistic it is. The courses are exactly how they are in person.

Q: What's your favorite childhood memory?

A: When I was 11, I had straight A's, three recesses a day and I won 33 tournaments. My life peaked at 11. It's been downhill ever since.

Q: Did you ever want to quit golf or get mad at your dad [his coach]?

A: I never got mad at my dad, but I got mad at myself a lot. I just can't stand not playing up to my abilities.

Tee Time

The four major events in men's professional golf (the Grand Slam) are:

The Masters
British Open
U.S. Open
PGA Championship

The four major events in women's professional golf (the Women's Grand Slam) are:

LPGA Championship
U.S. Women's Open
Nabisco Championship
Women's British Open

The **Ryder Cup** is the most prestigious team golf event in the world. It is played every two years between a team of American golfers and a team of European golfers.

Boy Wonder

In 2002 13-year-old Lo Shih-Kai of Taiwan won the Hong Kong Men's Amateur Tournament and qualified for the Hong Kong Open, becoming the youngest player to enter a European Tour event.

Did You Know?

Odds of hitting a hole-in-one: 8,400 to 1

Oldest golfer to hit a hole-in-one: 101 years old, Harold Stilson, Deerfield Beach, Florida, 108 yards, May 2001

Youngest golfer to hit a hole-in-one: 3 years old, Jake Paine, Lake Forest, California, 66 yards, July 2001

Longest hole-in-one (non-dogleg): 447 yards, Robert Mitera, Omaha, Nebraska, October 1965

Longest hole-in-one (dogleg): 496 yards, Shawn Lynch, Exeter, England, July 1995

235

Olympics

What Do the Olympic Rings Symbolize?

The rings represent the five major regions of the world: Africa, Asia, Australia, Europe and the Americas.

And You Thought They Just Used a Match

The Olympic flame in Olympia, Greece, is rekindled every two years using a mirror and the Sun's rays.

Weary Warriors

A 1912 wrestling match between Alfred Asikainen and Martin Klein lasted 11 hours. Klein won but was too tired to participate in the next round.

Athletes from around the world gather to watch the lighting of the flame to start each Olympic Games.

The Olympics will return to its roots in 2004. The very first Olympics was held in Greece in 776 B.C. In 1896, more than 2,000 years later, Athens was the site of the first Modern Olympics as 245 athletes from 14 nations came together to compete. Athens is currently the site of massive building preparations for the 2004 Games. Unlike other recent Olympics, no new sports will be added for the 2004 Games, but you can be sure that there will be a lot more than 245 competitors this time. More than 10,000 athletes from more than 200 nations will assemble in Athens August 13-29, 2004, to compete for gold.

Upcoming Olympic Games

2004	(SUMMER)	Athens, Greece
2006	(WINTER)	Turin, Italy
2008	(SUMMER)	Beijing, China

Countries with the Most All-Time Medals

Summer	Gold	Silver	Bronze	Total
1. U.S.A.	872	658	586	2,116
2. U.S.S.R.* (1952-88)	395	319	296	1,010
3. Great Britain	180	233	225	638

Winter	Gold	Silver	Bronze	Total
1. Norway	94	94	75	263
2. U.S.S.R.* (1956-88)	78	57	59	194
3. U.S.A.	69	72	52	193

*In 1991 the U.S.S.R. (Union of Soviet Socialist Republics) broke up into several countries, including Russia.

Gymnastics

Gymnastics is one of the world's most physically demanding sports, not to mention one of the most popular sports at the Summer Olympics.

The Féderation Internationale de Gymnastique (FIG) is the organization that oversees gymnastics throughout the world. The FIG recognizes seven gymnastic areas: men's artistic gymnastics, women's artistic gymnastics, rhythmic gymnastics, trampoline, sports aerobics, sports acrobatics and non-competitive general gymnastics. Artistic, rhythmic and trampoline gymnasts will compete in the 2004 Olympics in Athens.

Here's a look at some of the most popular events.

Artistic Gymnastics
Men and Women

Floor exercise: Gymnasts should use all of the 40-ft. by 40-ft. mat. The men's exercises require strength, flexibility and balance. Women combine dance movements, tumbling and acrobatics and use music in their routines.

Vault: The gymnast runs 82 feet and somersaults over the vaulting table.

Men
Pommel horse: The gymnast performs a series of circular and scissor movements over the horse. The hands are the only part of the body that should touch the apparatus. Great upper-body strength is needed.

Rings: Backward and forward swings and holds are performed while keeping the rings as still as possible. Great balance and an acrobatic dismount are important.

Parallel bars: The athlete works along the bars and swings above and below them.

Horizontal (high) bar: The athlete performs several swinging movements and grip changes. It's important that the body does not touch the bar. Spectacular dismounts rate high.

Kerri Strug

Women
Balance beam: Gymnasts do leaps, turns, jumps and more—on a beam 16 feet long and only four inches wide!

Uneven bars: The athletes perform continuous swinging movements in both directions, above and below the bars. Twists, somersaults, high flight and smooth dismounts will help to earn a high score.

Rhythmic Gymnastics
Rhythmic gymnasts combine sport and artistic interpretation. They use ropes, hoops, balls, clubs and ribbons, which must be kept in constant motion.

Gymnastic Stars
Olga Korbut, a Soviet gymnast, inspired many girls to take up gymnastics after she won three gold medals at the 1972 Olympics in Munich. Romanian gymnast **Nadia Comaneci** became the first woman to score a perfect 10, at the 1976 summer games in Montreal, Canada. **Kerri Strug** provided us with one of the most exciting events of the 1996 Olympics—and gymnastics history—when she nailed her vault on an injured ankle to ensure a gold medal for the U.S. team.

The current U.S. team is full of rookies, but keep an eye on Ashley Postell and Courtney Kupets in the 2004 Olympics in Athens.

Nadia Comaneci

Track and Field

Did you ever wonder...

. . . why the distance of a marathon is 26 miles, 385 yards? At the 1908 Olympic marathon in London, the royal family wanted a better view of the finish line. Organizers added 385 yards to the 26-mile race so the finish would be in front of the royal box. It's been that way ever since.

Vaulting to the Top

One of the most popular and successful American track-and-field stars is women's pole vaulter **Stacy Dragila.** She won the pole-vaulting competition at the 1999 and 2001 World Championships. When the sport made its Olympic debut at Sydney in 2000, Dragila won the gold there, too. In 2001 alone, she broke eight world records!

Give Him a Speeding Ticket

The world-record holder of the 100-meter dash is widely considered the "World's Fastest Man." American **Tim Montgomery** claimed that title in September 2002 in Paris with a time of 9.78 seconds. He shaved one-hundredth of a second off the previous record, which had been held by his countryman, **Maurice Greene.**

Cycling

Four in a Row for Lance

In 2002, **Lance Armstrong** again showed the world that he was "K of the Mountains," as he roared his rivals in the grueling mounta climbs to win his fourth consecutive Tour de France. His closest competitor finished minutes and 17 seconds behind h Amazingly, in 199 Armstrong had be diagnosed with ca and was given on 50% chance to li

Swimming

The Thorpedo

Australia's **Ian Thorpe** is one of the most dominant male swimmers ever. He was just 17 when he won five medals at the 2000 Olympics in Sydney, Australia. Then, at the 2001 World Swimming Championships, Thorpe broke three world records and won an unprecedented six gold medals. At 6 feet, 4 inches with huge hands and size 17 feet, Thorpe has a body made for the pool.

Did You Know?

In order to fill an Olympic-size pool (50 meters by 25 yards or meters), it takes anywhere from 700,000 to 850,000 gallons of water.

Style Points

The five swimming areas used in competition are:

Breaststroke

Backstroke

Butterfly

Freestyle

Medley (combination of all)

Seven Up

Mark Spitz won a record seven gold medals at the 1972 Olympics in Munich—and he set world records in each event! He has nine Olympic gold medals in all, more than any other swimmer.

Extreme Sports

"Extreme sports" refers to sports as different as skateboarding and ice climbing. Probably the most famous "extreme" athlete is skateboarder Tony Hawk. At the 1999 Summer X Games, Hawk became the first skateboarder to land a 900 trick in the half-pipe competition. A 900 is 2½ complete midair rotations on the skateboard. It's called a 900 because one complete spin is 360 degrees around (like a circle), and 2½ x 360 = 900.

Americans made an **"extreme"** statement with their success in the snowboarding half-pipe at the 2002 Winter Olympics in Salt Lake City, Utah. Kelly Clark won gold in the women's event while Ross Powers, Danny Kass and J.J. Thomas took gold, silver and bronze, respectively, in the men's half-pipe.

go For more on all the sports in this chapter, go to www.FACTMONSTER.COM

Soccer

Soccer is the world's most popular sport. Known widely as football throughout the rest of the world, soccer is played by boys and girls and men and women of nearly all ages. In all, hundreds of millions of people play around the world.

The World Cup

The world's biggest soccer tournament is called the World Cup. It's played every four years by teams made up of each country's best players.

The U.S. won the last women's World Cup in 1999, while Brazil was the winner of the last men's World Cup in 2002. The next men's World Cup tournament will be held in 2006 in Germany. China will host the women's World Cup in 2003.

World Cup Champions

Men	Women
1930 Uruguay	1991 U.S.A.
1934 Italy	1995 Norway
1938 Italy	1999 U.S.A.
1942-1946 not held	
1950 Uruguay	
1954 West Germany	
1958 Brazil	
1962 Brazil	
1966 England	
1970 Brazil	
1974 West Germany	
1978 Argentina	
1982 Italy	
1986 Argentina	
1990 West Germany	
1994 Brazil	
1998 France	
2002 Brazil	

Hamm It Up

Mia Hamm, the captain of the U.S. national soccer team, is the best female soccer player in the world. And she has the trophies to prove it. Hamm won the first two FIFA World Women's Player of the Year awards in 2001 and 2002. She added the awards to the long list of honors she's already received, including a 1996 Olympic gold medal, a 1999 Women's World Cup title and four consecutive NCAA national championships at the University of North Carolina. Hamm is also one of the big-name players in the Women's United Soccer Association, or WUSA.

TENNIS

The four tournaments of tennis's Grand Slam are:

Australian Open
French Open
Wimbledon
U.S. Open

Love Means Zero

Learn how to speak and score like a tennis pro.
Love is zero points.
15, 30, 40 are tennis terms for one point, two points and three points.
Game point is the fourth point. The first player to win the fourth point (and lead by two) wins the game.
Deuce is the term for the game being tied 40-40. Play continues until one player wins by 2 points.
Set To win a set a player must win six games and lead by at least two. If each player wins six games there is a seven-point tiebreaker game to decide the winner.
Match The match usually ends when one player wins two out of three sets.

Sibling Rivalry

Serena and **Venus Williams**, powerhouse professional tennis players, dominated the courts throughout 2002 and into 2003, helping to make women's professional tennis tournaments must-see events. Serena won four consecutive Grand Slam tournaments: the French Open in June 2002, Wimbledon in July, the U.S. Open in September and the Australian Open in January 2003, earning herself a No. 1 ranking. She's the fifth woman in history to hold all four Grand Slam titles at once.

Venus was also on fire. She earned a No. 2 ranking, and made it to the finals in three of 2002's four Grand Slam events. She placed No. 2, behind little sister Serena, in Wimbledon, the U.S and French Opens and then again in the 2003 Australian Open.

Some of Tennis' Best Rivalries

	Matchup	Era	Leader
M E N	Pete Sampras vs. Andre Agassi	1980s–	Sampras leads, 20-14
	Jim Courier vs. Michael Chang	1990s	Tied, 12-12
	Ivan Lendl vs. John McEnroe	1980s	Lendl, 21-15
	John McEnroe vs. Jimmy Connors	1970s–'90s	McEnroe, 20-13
	Jimmy Connors vs. Bjorn Borg	1970s–'80s	Borg, 10-8
W O M E N	Venus Williams vs. Serena Williams	1990s–	Venus leads, 6-5
	Martina Hingis vs. Lindsay Davenport	1990s–	Davenport, 14-11
	Steffi Graf vs. Monica Seles	1980s–'90s	Graf, 10-5
	Martina Navratilova vs. Chris Evert	1970s–'80s	Navratilova, 43-37
	Margaret Smith Court vs. Billie Jean King	1960s–'70s	Smith Court, 22-10

RACING

Automobile racing originated in France in 1894 and appeared in the U.S. the next year.

Racing Anyone?
The National Association for Stock Car Racing's **Winston Cup Series** is the most popular auto racing series in the U.S. The NASCAR season runs from February to November. The biggest Winston Cup race of the year is the **Daytona 500.**

Our Need for Speed
The biggest and oldest race held in the U.S. is the **Indianapolis 500.** It's held every year at the oval-shaped Indianapolis Motor Speedway in Indiana. The track is nicknamed the Brickyard because it was originally made of brick. Cars race around the track at average speeds of up to 225 miles per hour.

Who's Who in Pit Row
When a car pulls off the track for a pit stop, it might look like chaos, but it is actually a precise routine. Here's a list of the key pit-crew men and women.
Jack man—the crew "quarterback" is in charge of jacking up the car so its tires can be changed.
Gas-can man—refills the gas tank with a giant gas can that can weigh 90 lbs. when full; most pit stops require two cans.
Catch-can man—catches overflow of gas in a special canister; lets jack man know when fueling is complete.
Front/rear tire carrier—carries new tires to the car; carries old ones back over the wall; tires can weigh 75 pounds and are extremely hot.
Front/rear tire changer—takes off the five lug nuts holding each tire in place with an air gun in less than two seconds and secures the new tires.

What Do the Flags Mean?
Race officials use flags to instruct drivers during a race. Here's what they mean:
Green—Go!
Yellow—Caution. There is a problem on the track, and drivers must go slow and not pass.
Red—Stop. Something has made the track unusable (maybe an accident or bad weather).
White—Last lap.
Checkered—Finish. The race is over

World Champions
Germany's **Michael Schumacher** won his fifth Formula One driver's world championship in 2002, moving him into a tie for first place on the all-time list. Here are the drivers with the most world titles, listed with their home countries.
5– **Juan-Manuel Fangio (Argentina)**
   Michael Schumacher (Germany)
4– **Alain Prost (France)**
3– **Jack Brabham (Australia)**
   Niki Lauda (Austria)
   Nelson Piquet (Brazil)
   Ayrton Senna (Brazil)
   Jackie Stewart (Great Britain)

Animal Sports

Horse Racing

Animals are a big part of the sports world, and horses in particular play a large role. The history of horse racing can be traced to ancient Egypt and Greece, where horse-and-chariot races were part of the Olympic Games. It is often called "the sport of kings" because breeding and racing horses was a popular hobby of the royal family in England during the 12th century.

Triple Crown

Horse racing in the U.S. reaches its peak each spring with the running of the **Triple Crown.** The Triple Crown is a series of three prestigious races starting with the Kentucky Derby, which is held each year on the first Saturday in May at Churchill Downs in Louisville, Kentucky. The next race is the Preakness Stakes, followed by the Belmont Stakes.

Here is a list of the 11 horses that have won the Triple Crown—that is, won all three races in the same year. Notice that it hasn't been done in more than 20 years!

1919 **Sir Barton**	1946 **Assault**
1930 **Gallant Fox**	1948 **Citation**
1935 **Omaha**	1973 **Secretariat**
1937 **War Admiral**	1977 **Seattle Slew**
1941 **Whirlaway**	1978 **Affirmed**
1943 **Count Fleet**	

Sled-Dog Racing

Dogs are great athletes. In the annual Iditarod Trail Sled Dog Race, an average team uses 16 dogs. Each team pulls a large sled (and driver!) more than 1,100 miles through the snowy Alaskan wilderness. The race from Anchorage to Nome, first run in 1973, commemorates a 1925 lifesaving delivery of medicine to the village of Nome by sled dogs.

TFK

MYSTERY PERSON

CLUE 1: I brought home the U.S.'s only gold medal, in figure skating, from the 1968 Winter Olympics.
CLUE 2: I won three World and five U.S. Figure Skating Championships.
CLUE 3: At the opening ceremonies of the 2002 Winter Olympic Games, held at Salt Lake City, I took to the ice to carry the Olympic torch.

WHO AM I?

(See Answer Key that begins on page 340.)

Seattle Slew

Seattle Slew was born with an outwardly curved right foot and was so clumsy as a colt that his trainer nicknamed him "Baby Huey." But the big, black horse went on to become one of thoroughbred racing's greatest animals. He was one of only 11 horses to win the coveted Triple Crown. When Seattle Slew was only four years old, he retired to a pampered and happy life on a Kentucky farm. He died on May 7, 2002, at age 28, exactly 25 years after his spectacular Kentucky Derby win.

COME TO THE FAIR!

Where does the biggest cowboy in the nation keep watch over the biggest Ferris wheel in North America and the biggest crowd at any state fair? In Texas, of course, where the state fair is a big, big deal! Most Dallas kids get a day off from school to attend the fair.

The nation's first agricultural fair took place in 1807 in Pittsfield, Massachusetts, where farmer Elkanah Watson displayed sheep under a tree. Americans still celebrate the bounty of their farms, gardens and homes at 49 state fairs across the U.S. These days, fairgoers also take a spin on thrill rides, rock out to live music and eat deep-fried Twinkies and pickles! But some kids still prefer the old traditions. "I go for the animals straightaway," said Lauren Pattinson of Dallas.

Most of the nation's state fairs are held from July through the end of the harvest season in October. Fair visitors spend millions of dollars, says Max Willis of the International Association of Fairs and Expositions.

By
Laura C. Girardi

Big Tex and North America's highest Ferris wheel stand tall in Dallas.

Play the Great State Race at
www.timeforkids.com/stategame

The *Great Seal* of the United States

Benjamin Franklin, John Adams and Thomas Jefferson began designing the Great Seal in 1776. The Great Seal is printed on the back of the $1 bill and is used on certain government documents, such as foreign treaties.

The bald eagle, our national bird, is at the center of the seal. It holds a banner in its beak. The motto says *E pluribus unum*, which is Latin for "out of many, one." This refers to the colonies that united to make a nation. In one claw, the eagle holds an olive branch for peace; in the other claw, arrows for war.

Other SYMBOLS of the United States

The **bald eagle** has been our national bird since 1872. The Founding Fathers had been unable to agree on which native bird should have the honor—Benjamin Franklin strongly preferred the turkey! Besides appearing on the Great Seal, the bald eagle is pictured on coins, the dollar bill, all official U.S. seals and the President's flag.

The image of **Uncle Sam,** with his white hair and top hat, first became famous on World War I recruiting posters. The artist, James Montgomery Flagg, used himself as a model. But the term dates back to the War of 1812, when a meat packer nicknamed Uncle Sam supplied beef to the troops. The initials for his nickname were quite appropriate!

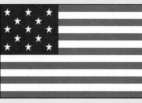

The **U.S.** Flag

In 1777 the Continental Congress decided that the flag would have 13 alternating red and white stripes, for the 13 colonies, and 13 white stars on a blue background. A new star has been added for every new state. Today the flag has 50 stars.

The Pledge of Allegiance to the Flag

The original pledge was published in the September 8, 1892, issue of *The Youth's Companion* in Boston. For years, there was a dispute over who should get credit for writing the pledge, James B. Upham or Francis Bellamy, both members of the magazine's staff. In 1939, the United States Flag Association decided that Bellamy should get the credit. **Here's the original version of the pledge.**

I pledge allegiance to my Flag and the Republic for which it stands—one nation indivisible—with liberty and justice for all.

State Regions

New England Connecticut, Maine, Massachusetts, New Hampshire, Rhode Island, Vermont

From the 17th century until well into the 19th, New England was the country's cultural and economic center. The mainstays of the region became shipbuilding, fishing and trade.

Middle Atlantic Delaware, Maryland, New Jersey, New York, Pennsylvania

Philadelphia was the birthplace of the Declaration of Independence in 1776 and the U.S. Constitution in 1787. New York City is the nation's most populous city and its financial hub.

South Alabama, Arkansas, Florida, Georgia, Kentucky, Louisiana, Mississippi, Missouri, North Carolina, South Carolina, Tennessee, Virginia, West Virginia

The South was first settled by English Protestants. Especially in coastal areas, settlers grew wealthy by raising and selling cotton and tobacco on large farms called plantations.

Midwest Illinois, Indiana, Iowa, Kansas, Michigan, Minnesota, Nebraska, North Dakota, Ohio, South Dakota, Wisconsin

Starting in the early 1800s, easterners moved to the Midwest in search of better farmland. The fertile soil made it possible for farmers to produce harvests of cereal crops.

Southwest Arizona, New Mexico, Oklahoma, Texas

The Southwest differs from the adjoining Midwest in weather (drier), population (less dense) and ethnicity (strong Spanish-American and Native-American components).

West Alaska, California, Colorado, Hawaii, Idaho, Montana, Nevada, Oregon, Utah, Washington, Wyoming

The West is a region of scenic beauty on a grand scale. All of its states are partly mountainous, and the mountain ranges are the sources of startling contrasts.

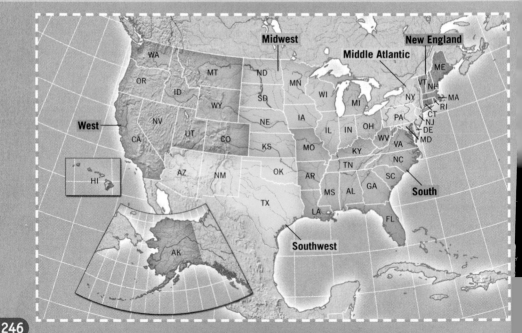

Source: The U.S. Department of State

LARGEST CITIES IN THE U.S.

RANK	CITY	POPULATION*
1.	New York, New York	8,008,278
2.	Los Angeles, California	3,694,820
3.	Chicago, Illinois	2,896,016
4.	Houston, Texas	1,953,631
5.	Philadelphia, Pennsylvania	1,517,550
6.	Phoenix, Arizona	1,321,045
7.	San Diego, California	1,223,400
8.	Dallas, Texas	1,188,580
9.	San Antonio, Texas	1,144,646
10.	Detroit, Michigan	951,270
11.	San Jose, California	894,943
12.	Indianapolis, Indiana	781,870
13.	San Francisco, California	776,733
14.	Jacksonville, Florida	735,617
15.	Columbus, Ohio	711,470
16.	Austin, Texas	656,562
17.	Baltimore, Maryland	651,154
18.	Memphis, Tennessee	650,100
19.	Milwaukee, Wisconsin	596,974
20.	Boston, Massachusetts	589,141

*Figures based on Census 2000

Did You Know?

Alaska is the largest state. It measures 570,374 square miles. Rhode Island is the smallest. It's a mere 1,045 square miles.

FAMOUS FIRST	CITY	DATE
Aquarium	New York, New York	1896
Baseball stadium	Pittsburgh, Pennsylvania	1909
Computer	Philadelphia, Pennsylvania	1946
Elevator	New York, New York	1852
Ferris wheel	Chicago, Illinois	1893
Hospital	Philadelphia, Pennsylvania	1752
Lighthouse	Boston, Massachusetts	1716
Movie theater	Pittsburgh, Pennsylvania	1905
Parking meter	Oklahoma City, Oklahoma	1935
Public museum	Charleston, South Carolina	1773
Public zoo	Philadelphia, Pennsylvania	1874
Railroad station	Baltimore, Maryland	1830
Revolving restaurant	Seattle, Washington	1961
Skyscraper	Chicago, Illinois	1885
Subway	Boston, Massachusetts	1897
Traffic light	Cleveland, Ohio	1914

Washington, D.C.
MEMORIALS and LANDMARKS

In addition to the White House, several architectural masterpieces and symbolic landmarks adorn our nation's capital. Here are some of them.

Capitol Building

This is where Congress meets and conducts business. Construction of the building started in 1793, and its design was changed several times, until it was finally finished more than 75 years later, in 1865. The Capitol's most recognizable feature is the 180-foot-high cast iron dome of the Great Rotunda.

Jefferson Memorial

In 1934, Congress authorized the construction of a memorial to honor Thomas Jefferson. The memorial, like Jefferson's home in Monticello, Virginia, is based on the Roman Pantheon. Construction of the circular marble building was finished in 1943.

Lincoln Memorial

Construction of this memorial started in 1914 and was completed in 1922. Architect Henry Bacon modeled the marble, granite and limestone building after the Greek Parthenon. The inside of the memorial is divided into three chambers: central, north and south. A white marble statue of President Lincoln sits in the central chamber. The Gettysburg Address is carved into the walls of the south chamber, and Lincoln's famous Second Inaugural speech is on the the north-chamber wall. The 36 Doric columns on the outside of the memorial represent the number of states in the Union at the time of Lincoln's death in 1865.

National Archives

The National Archives is the official library where the records of the three branches of the U.S. government are kept and preserved. The Declaration of Independence, the Constitution and the Bill of Rights are on display here. A collection of Civil War pictures taken by the famous photographer Mathew Brady is also on display.

National Mall

No, this isn't the official shopping center of the U.S. It's a 146-acre lawn that stretches from the Potomac River to the Capitol building. The area hosts political rallies, festivals and other events.

Smithsonian Institution

A wealthy English researcher, James Smithson, left all his money to create a museum in Washington, D.C. And he never even visited the United States! He also left his scientific library and his collection of minerals to the new museum. The Smithsonian is a network of museums and art galleries, research projects and special performances. Among its 14 museums are the National Air and Space Museum, the Museum of Natural History and the National Portrait Gallery.

U.S. Holocaust Memorial Museum

The Holocaust Museum opened in 1993. The museum is America's national institution for the documentation, study and interpretation of Holocaust history. The memorial houses the largest collection of material about the murder of more than 6 million Jews by Nazi Germany between 1933 and 1945. It cost more than $168 million to build the museum.

Vietnam Veterans Memorial

More than 1,400 people submitted design ideas for this memorial to the men and women who died in the Vietnam War. A 21-year-old Yale University student, Maya Lin, won the contest. The V-shaped memorial is made of black granite. The names of more than 58,000 veterans who lost their lives in the war are etched in the wall.

Washington Monument

Construction of this magnificent monument involved nearly a century of planning, building and controversy. The first plans called for a large statue of George Washington on a horse. After Washington's death in 1797, a memorial was discussed, only to be delayed again. Finally, in 1848, work started on the monument that stands today. After more fits and starts, the monument was finished in 1884 and opened to the public in 1888. The narrowing shaft, or obelisk, is made of stone and is covered with white marble. The monument stands just over 555 feet. Memorial stones from the 50 states, foreign countries and organizations line the inside walls.

A Look at the U.S. Population*

U.S. Population: 281,421,906

Males: 138,053,563
(49.1% of population)
Females: 143,368,343
(50.9% of population)
Number of kids ages 5 to 9: 20,549,505
Number of kids ages 10 to 14: 20,528,072
**Number of centenarians
(people over age 100):** 50,454
It's estimated that by the year 2050, there will be about 834,000 Americans over the age of 100!

Race

75.1% of Americans are white.
12.5% are of Hispanic origin
(they may be of any race).
12.3% are black.
3.6% are Asian, Native Hawaiian or
Pacific Islander.
0.9% are Native American or Alaskan Native.
*Figures based on Census 2000.

Life Expectancy

When the nation was founded, the average American could expect to live to age 35. By 1900, life expectancy had increased to 47.3. In 2000, the life expectancy was 74.1 for men and 79.5 for women.

Kids at Home

About 71% of kids live with two parents.
About 25% live with one parent.
Nearly 4% live with neither parent.
About 5.5% live in a home maintained by a grandparent.

A Look Back at the U.S. Population

1790	3,929,214	1900	75,994,575
1800	5,308,483	1920	105,710,620
1820	9,638,453	1950	150,697,361
1850	23,191,876	1980	226,545,805
1880	50,155,783	1990	248,709,873

Figures do not include armed forces overseas.

NATIVE AMERICANS

There are more than 550 federally recognized Indian tribes in the United States, including 223 village groups in Alaska. "Federally recognized" means these tribes and groups have a special legal relationship with the U.S. government.

Largest American Indian Tribes

1. Cherokee
2. Navajo
3. Chippewa
4. Sioux
5. Choctaw
6. Pueblo
7. Apache
8. Iroquois
9. Lumbee
10. Creek

Indian Reservations

The largest reservation is the Navajo Reservation, which has about 16 million acres of land in Arizona, New Mexico and Utah. Many of the smaller reservations are less than 1,000 acres with the smallest less than 100 acres.

Here are the reservations with the largest populations:

1. **Navajo (Arizona, New Mexico and Utah)**
2. **Pine Ridge (Nebraska and South Dakota)**
3. **Fort Apache (Arizona)**
4. **Gila River (Arizona)**
5. **Papago (Arizona)**
6. **Rosebud (South Dakota)**
7. **San Carlos (Arizona)**
8. **Zuni Pueblo (Arizona and New Mexico)**
9. Hopi (Arizona)
10. Blackfeet (Montana)

Foreign-Born Americans

The term "foreign born" refers to Americans who were not born in this country. More than one-third of foreign-born Americans came from Central America, which includes Belize, Guatemala, Honduras, El Salvador, Nicaragua, Costa Rica and Panama.

8.1% Other Regions

6.6% South America

9.8% Caribbean

34.5% Central America

25.5% Asia

15.3% Europe

Note: Because numbers are rounded, figures do not add up to 100%.

Source: U.S. Census Bureau

Where Immigrants Come From

According to U.S. Census figures, the number of people born in other countries reached 31.1 million in 2000, up from about 13 million in 1990. Here are the top countries for U.S. immigration.

1. **Mexico**
2. **China**
3. **Philippines**
4. **India**
5. **Cuba**
6. **Vietnam**
7. **El Salvador**
8. **Korea**
9. **Dominican Republic**
10. **Canada**

Source: Immigration and Naturalization Service (INS)

TFK TOP 5

STATES WITH THE MOST HISPANICS

Celebrate Hispanic Heritage Month! It begins on September 15, the date when five countries in Central America—Costa Rica, El Salvador, Guatemala, Honduras and Nicaragua—gained their independence from Spain. More than 30 million people living in the U.S. trace their roots to Spanish-speaking countries. Here are the states with the most Hispanic people.

1. California ------------>10,966,556
2. Texas ----------------> 6,669,666
3. New York ----------> 2,867,583
4. Florida -------------> 2,682,715
5. Illinois ---------------> 1,530,262

Source: U.S. Census Bureau

Naturalization

When immigrants enter the United States, they are not American citizens. In order to enjoy many of the privileges of being an American, such as the right to vote and hold public office, a person must gain citizenship. The process for becoming a citizen is called naturalization. To become a naturalized citizen, a person must fill out an application with the Immigration and Naturalization Service and meet language and residency requirements, among other conditions.

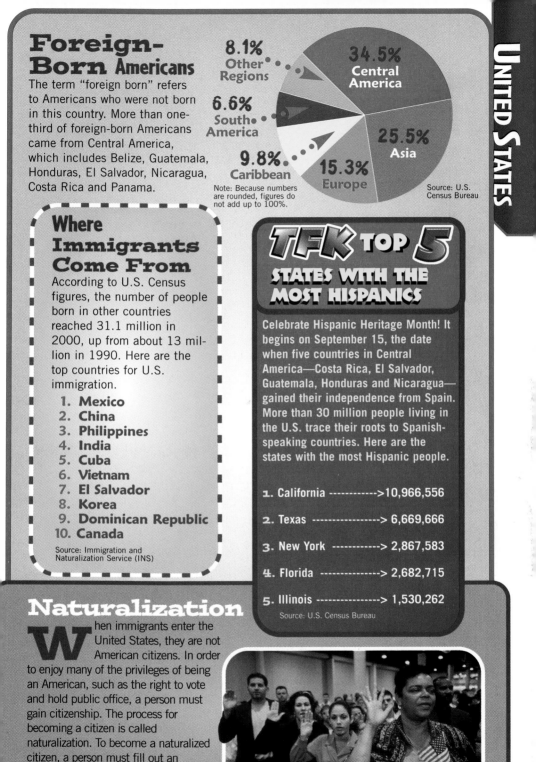

251

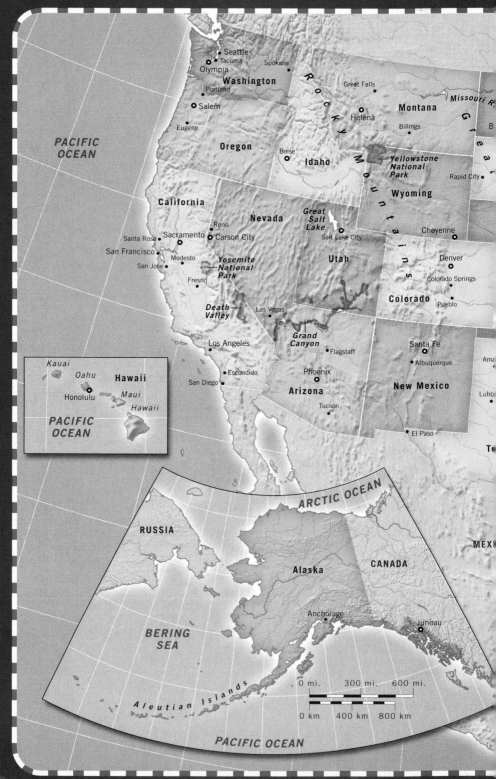

PACIFIC
OCEAN

Seattle
Tacoma
Olympia
Portland
Washington
Spokane
Great Falls

Salem
Eugene

Oregon
Boise
Idaho

Rocky
Helena
Montana
Billings
Great

Missouri R.

B

Yellowstone
National
Park

Rapid City

California
Reno
Nevada
Santa Rosa
Sacramento
Carson City
San Francisco
Modesto
San Jose
Fresno
*Yosemite
National
Park*

*Great
Salt
Lake*
Salt Lake City

Utah

Mountains

Wyoming

Cheyenne

Denver
Colorado Springs
Colorado
Pueblo

*Death
Valley*
Las Vegas

*Grand
Canyon*
Flagstaff

Santa Fe
Albuquerque

Los Angeles

Hawaii

Kauai
Oahu
Honolulu
Maui
Hawaii

PACIFIC
OCEAN

Escondido
San Diego

Phoenix
Arizona
Tucson

El Paso

New Mexico

Ama

Lubb

Te

MEX

ARCTIC OCEAN

RUSSIA

Alaska

CANADA

Anchorage

Juneau

*BERING
SEA*

Aleutian Islands

0 mi.   300 mi.   600 mi.

0 km   400 km   800 km

PACIFIC OCEAN

252

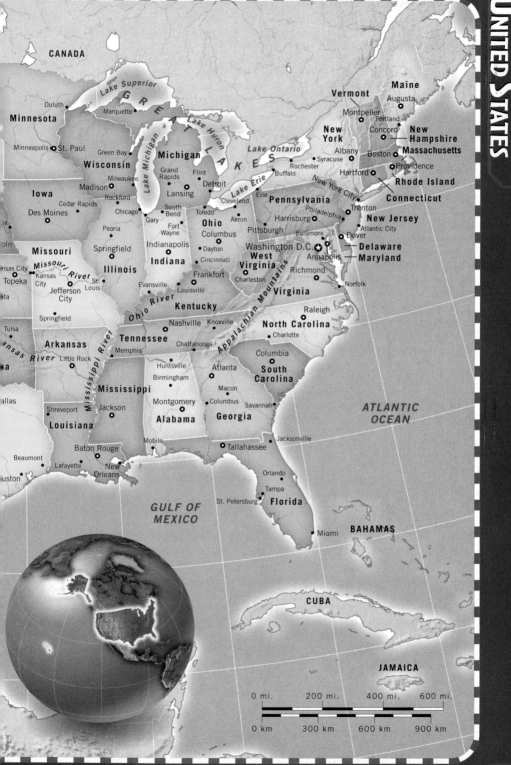

CANADA

Lake Superior

G R E A T

Duluth
Marquette

Minnesota

Minneapolis ○ St. Paul

Green Bay

L A K E S

Lake Huron

Wisconsin

Madison ○

Milwaukee

Rockford

Grand
Rapids

Flint

Michigan

Lansing

Maine

Augusta

Vermont

Montpelier

Portland

Concord

New
Hampshire

New
York

Albany

Syracuse

Rochester

Lake Ontario

Lake Erie

Buffalo

Boston

Massachusetts

Providence

Rhode Island

Hartford

Iowa

Cedar Rapids

Des Moines ○

Detroit

Cleveland

Erie

Pennsylvania

New York City

Trenton

Connecticut

Chicago

South
Bend

Toledo

Akron

New Jersey

Peoria

Gary

Fort
Wayne

Ohio

Harrisburg

Philadelphia

Atlantic City

oln

Missouri

Springfield ○

Indianapolis ○

Columbus

Pittsburgh

Baltimore

Dover

Delaware

○ Dayton

Cincinnati

Washington D.C. ★

Maryland

nsas City,

Illinois

Indiana

West

Annapolis

Missouri River

Kansas
City

St.
Louis

Evansville

Frankfort

Virginia

Richmond ○

Virginia

ta

Topeka ○

Jefferson
City

Louisville

Charleston

Norfolk

Springfield ○

Ohio River

Kentucky

Raleigh ○

Tulsa ○

Nashville ○

Knoxville

North Carolina

nsas

Arkansas

Mississippi River

Tennessee

Chattanooga

Charlotte ●

River

Memphis

a

Little Rock ○

Columbia ○

South

Huntsville ●

Atlanta ○

Carolina

Birmingham ●

Mississippi

Macon ●

allas

Shreveport ●

Jackson ○

Montgomery ○

Columbus ●

Savannah ●

ATLANTIC
OCEAN

Louisiana

Alabama

Georgia

Beaumont ●

Mobile ○

Lafayette ●

Baton Rouge ○

uston

New
Orleans

Tallahassee ○

Jacksonville ●

Orlando ●

Tampa ●

GULF OF
MEXICO

St. Petersburg ●

Florida

BAHAMAS

Miami ●

CUBA

JAMAICA

0 mi.   200 mi.   400 mi.   600 mi.

0 km   300 km   600 km   900 km

Appalachian Mountains

253

ALABAMA

Origin of name: May come from a Choctaw word meaning "thicket-clearers"

Entered union (rank): December 14, 1819 (22)

Motto: *Audemus jura nostra defendere* (We dare defend our rights)

Tree: southern longleaf pine

Flower: camellia

Bird: yellowhammer

Other: dance: square dance; nut: pecan

Song: "Alabama"

Nickname: Yellowhammer State

Residents: Alabamian, Alabaman

Land area: 50,750 square miles (131,443 sq km)

Population (2002): 4,486,508

Capital: Montgomery
Largest city: Birmingham
Abbreviation: Ala.
Postal code: AL

Home of: George Washington Carver, who discovered more than 300 uses for peanuts

ALASKA

Origin of name: From an Aleut word meaning "great land" or "that which the sea breaks against"

Entered union (rank): January 3, 1959 (49)

Motto: North to the future

Tree: sitka spruce

Flower: forget-me-not

Bird: willow ptarmigan

Other: fossil: woolly mammoth; sport: dog mushing

Song: "Alaska's Flag"

Nicknames: The Last Frontier and Land of the Midnight Sun

Residents: Alaskan

Land area: 570,374 square miles (1,477,267 sq km)

Population (2002): 643,786

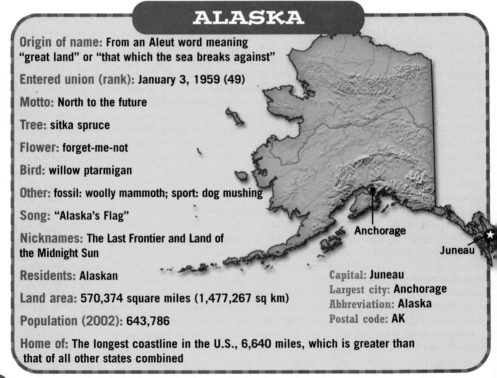

Capital: Juneau
Largest city: Anchorage
Abbreviation: Alaska
Postal code: AK

Home of: The longest coastline in the U.S., 6,640 miles, which is greater than that of all other states combined

ARIZONA

Origin of name: From the Native American *Arizonac,* meaning "little spring"

Entered union (rank): February 14, 1912 (48)

Motto: *Ditat deus* (God enriches)

Tree: palo verde

Flower: flower of saguaro cactus

Bird: cactus wren

Other: gemstone: turquoise; neckwear: bola tie

Song: "Arizona"

Nickname: Grand Canyon State

Residents: Arizonan, Arizonian

Land area: 113,642 square miles (296,400 sq km)

Population (2002): 5,456,453

Home of: The most telescopes in the world, in Tucson

Phoenix

Capital: Phoenix
Largest city: Phoenix
Abbreviation: Ariz.
Postal code: AZ

ARKANSAS

Origin of name: From the Quapaw Indians

Entered union (rank): June 15, 1836 (25)

Motto: *Regnat populus* (The people rule)

Tree: pine

Flower: apple blossom

Bird: mockingbird

Other: fruit and vegetable: pink tomato; insect: honeybee

Song: "Arkansas"

Nickname: The Natural State

Residents: Arkansan

Land area: 52,075 square miles (134,874 sq km)

Population (2002): 2,710,079

Home of: The only active diamond mine in the U.S.

Little Rock

Capital: Little Rock
Largest city: Little Rock
Abbreviation: Ark.
Postal code: AR

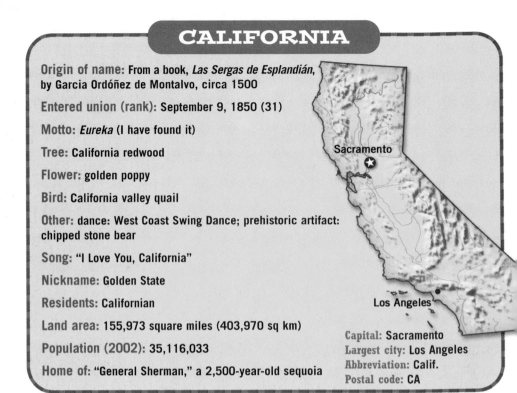

Origin of name: From a book, *Las Sergas de Esplandián*, by Garcia Ordóñez de Montalvo, circa 1500

Entered union (rank): September 9, 1850 (31)

Motto: *Eureka* (I have found it)

Tree: California redwood

Flower: golden poppy

Bird: California valley quail

Other: dance: West Coast Swing Dance; prehistoric artifact: chipped stone bear

Song: "I Love You, California"

Nickname: Golden State

Residents: Californian

Land area: 155,973 square miles (403,970 sq km)

Population (2002): 35,116,033

Home of: "General Sherman," a 2,500-year-old sequoia

Sacramento

Los Angeles

Capital: Sacramento
Largest city: Los Angeles
Abbreviation: Calif.
Postal code: CA

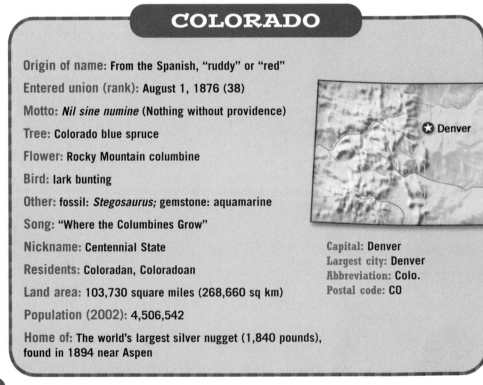

Origin of name: From the Spanish, "ruddy" or "red"

Entered union (rank): August 1, 1876 (38)

Motto: *Nil sine numine* (Nothing without providence)

Tree: Colorado blue spruce

Flower: Rocky Mountain columbine

Bird: lark bunting

Other: fossil: *Stegosaurus;* gemstone: aquamarine

Song: "Where the Columbines Grow"

Nickname: Centennial State

Residents: Coloradan, Coloradoan

Land area: 103,730 square miles (268,660 sq km)

Population (2002): 4,506,542

Home of: The world's largest silver nugget (1,840 pounds), found in 1894 near Aspen

Denver

Capital: Denver
Largest city: Denver
Abbreviation: Colo.
Postal code: CO

CONNECTICUT

Origin of name: From a Quinnehtukqut Indian word meaning "beside the long tidal river"

Entered union (rank): January 9, 1788 (5)

Motto: *Qui transtulit sustinet* (He who transplanted still sustains)

Tree: white oak

Flower: mountain laurel

Bird: American robin

Other: hero: Nathan Hale; heroine: Prudence Crandall

Song: "Yankee Doodle"

Nickname: Nutmeg State

Residents: Nutmegger

Land area: 4,845 square miles (12,550 sq km)

Population (2002): 3,460,503

Capital: Hartford
Largest city: Bridgeport
Abbreviation: Conn.
Postal code: CT

Home of: The first American cookbook, *American Cookery* by Amelia Simmons, published in Hartford in 1796

DELAWARE

Origin of name: From Delaware River and Bay, named for Sir Thomas West, Baron De La Warr

Entered union (rank): December 7, 1787 (1)

Motto: Liberty and independence

Tree: American holly

Flower: peach blossom

Bird: blue hen chicken

Other: colors: colonial blue and buff; insect: ladybug

Song: "Our Delaware"

Nicknames: Diamond State, First State and Small Wonder

Residents: Delawarean

Land area: 1,955 square miles (5,153 sq km)

Population (2002): 807,385

Capital: Dover
Largest city: Wilmington
Abbreviation: Del.
Postal code: DE

Home of: The first log cabins in North America, built in 1683 by Swedish immigrants

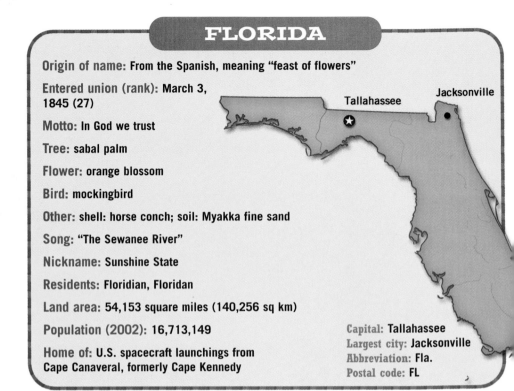

FLORIDA

Origin of name: From the Spanish, meaning "feast of flowers"

Entered union (rank): March 3, 1845 (27)

Motto: In God we trust

Tree: sabal palm

Flower: orange blossom

Bird: mockingbird

Other: shell: horse conch; soil: Myakka fine sand

Song: "The Sewanee River"

Nickname: Sunshine State

Residents: Floridian, Floridan

Land area: 54,153 square miles (140,256 sq km)

Population (2002): 16,713,149

Home of: U.S. spacecraft launchings from Cape Canaveral, formerly Cape Kennedy

Jacksonville

Tallahassee

Capital: Tallahassee
Largest city: Jacksonville
Abbreviation: Fla.
Postal code: FL

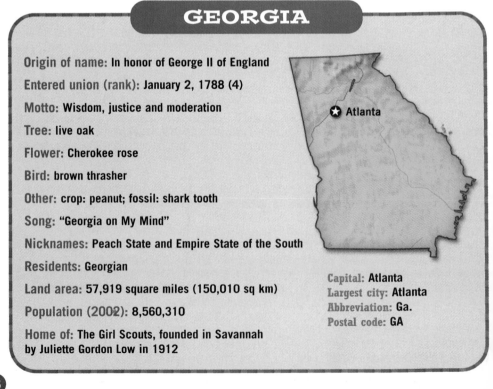

GEORGIA

Origin of name: In honor of George II of England

Entered union (rank): January 2, 1788 (4)

Motto: Wisdom, justice and moderation

Tree: live oak

Flower: Cherokee rose

Bird: brown thrasher

Other: crop: peanut; fossil: shark tooth

Song: "Georgia on My Mind"

Nicknames: Peach State and Empire State of the South

Residents: Georgian

Land area: 57,919 square miles (150,010 sq km)

Population (2002): 8,560,310

Home of: The Girl Scouts, founded in Savannah by Juliette Gordon Low in 1912

Atlanta

Capital: Atlanta
Largest city: Atlanta
Abbreviation: Ga.
Postal code: GA

HAWAII

Origin of name: Probably from a Polynesian word meaning "ancestral home"

Entered union (rank): August 21, 1959 (50)

Motto: *Ua mau ke ea o ka aina i ka pono* (The life of the land is perpetuated in righteousness)

Tree: kukui (candlenut)

Flower: yellow hibiscus

Bird: nene (Hawaiian goose)

Other: gem: black coral; marine mammal: humpback whale

Song: "Hawaii Ponoi"

Nickname: Aloha State

Residents: Hawaiian

Land area: 6,423 square miles (16,637 sq km)

Population (2002): 1,244,898

Home of: The only royal palace in the U.S. (Iolani)

Honolulu

Capital: Honolulu (on Oahu)
Largest city: Honolulu
Abbreviation: Hawaii
Postal code: HI

IDAHO

Origin of name: Though popularly believed to be a Native American word, it is an invented name whose meaning is unknown.

Entered union (rank): July 3, 1890 (43)

Motto: *Esto perpetua* (It is forever)

Tree: white pine

Flower: syringa (lilac)

Bird: mountain bluebird

Other: fish: cutthroat trout; horse: Appaloosa

Song: "Here We Have Idaho"

Nickname: Gem State

Residents: Idahoan

Land area: 82,751 square miles (214,325 sq km)

Population (2002): 1,341,131

Home of: The longest main street in America, 33 miles, in Island Park

Capital: Boise
Largest city: Boise
Abbreviation: Idaho
Postal code: ID

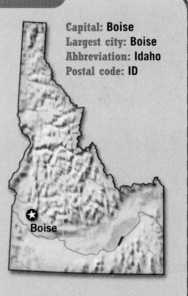

Boise

ILLINOIS

Origin of name: Algonquian for "tribe of superior men"

Entered union (rank): December 3, 1818 (21)

Motto: State sovereignty, national union

Tree: white oak

Flower: violet

Bird: cardinal

Other: animal: white-tailed deer; prairie grass: big bluestem

Song: "Illinois"

Nickname: Prairie State

Residents: Illinoisan

Land area: 55,593 square miles (143,987 sq km)

Population (2002): 12,600,620

Home of: The tallest building in the country, Sears Tower, in Chicago

Capital: Springfield
Largest city: Chicago
Abbreviation: Ill.
Postal code: IL

INDIANA

Origin of name: Means "land of Indians"

Entered union (rank): December 11, 1816 (19)

Motto: The crossroads of America

Tree: tulip tree

Flower: peony

Bird: cardinal

Other: river: Wabash; stone: limestone

Song: "On the Banks of the Wabash, Far Away"

Nickname: Hoosier State

Residents: Indianan, Indianian

Land area: 35,870 sq miles (92,904 sq km)

Population (2002): 6,159,068

Home of: The famous car race, the Indianapolis 500

Capital: Indianapolis
Largest city: Indianapolis
Abbreviation: Ind.
Postal code: IN

IOWA

Origin of name: Probably from an Indian word meaning "this is the place"

Entered union (rank): December 28, 1846 (29)

Motto: Our liberties we prize and our rights we will maintain

Tree: oak

Flower: wild rose

Bird: eastern goldfinch

Other: fossil: crinoid; rock: geode

Song: "Song of Iowa"

Nickname: Hawkeye State

Residents: Iowan

Land area: 55,875 square miles (144,716 sq km)

Population (2002): 2,936,760

Des Moines ✪

Capital: Des Moines
Largest city: Des Moines
Abbreviation: Iowa
Postal code: IA

Home of: The shortest and steepest railroad in the U.S., in Dubuque, 60° incline, 296 feet

KANSAS

Origin of name: From a Sioux word meaning "people of the south wind"

Entered union (rank): January 29, 1861 (34)

Motto: *Ad astra per aspera*
(To the stars through difficulties)

Tree: cottonwood

Flower: sunflower

Bird: western meadowlark

Other: animal: buffalo; reptile: ornate box turtle

Song: "Home on the Range"

Nicknames: Sunflower State and Jayhawk State

Residents: Kansan

Land area: 81,823 square miles (211,922 sq km)

Population (2002): 2,715,884

Topeka ✪

● Wichita

Capital: Topeka
Largest city: Wichita
Abbreviation: Kans.
Postal code: KS

Home of: Helium, discovered in 1905 at the University of Kansas

KENTUCKY

Origin of name: From an Iroquoian word (Kentahten) meaning "land of tomorrow"

Entered union (rank): June 1, 1792 (15)

Motto: United we stand, divided we fall

Tree: tulip poplar

Flower: goldenrod

Bird: Kentucky cardinal

Other: bluegrass song: "Blue Moon of Kentucky"; horse: Thoroughbred

Song: "My Old Kentucky Home"

Nickname: Bluegrass State

Residents: Kentuckian

Land area: 39,732 square miles (102,907 sq km)

Population (2002): 4,092,891

Home of: The largest underground cave in the world, the Mammoth-Flint Cave system, over 300 miles long

Louisville • ★ Frankfort

Capital: Frankfort
Largest city: Louisville
Abbreviation: Ky.
Postal code: KY

LOUISIANA

Origin of name: In honor of Louis XIV of France

Entered union (rank): April 30, 1812 (18)

Motto: Union, justice and confidence

Tree: bald cypress

Flower: magnolia

Bird: eastern brown pelican

Other: crustacean: crawfish; dog: Catahoula leopard hound

Songs: "Give Me Louisiana" and "You Are My Sunshine"

Nickname: Pelican State

Residents: Louisianan, Louisianian

Land area: 43,566 square miles (112,836 sq km)

Population (2002): 4,482,646

Home of: About 98% of the world's crawfish

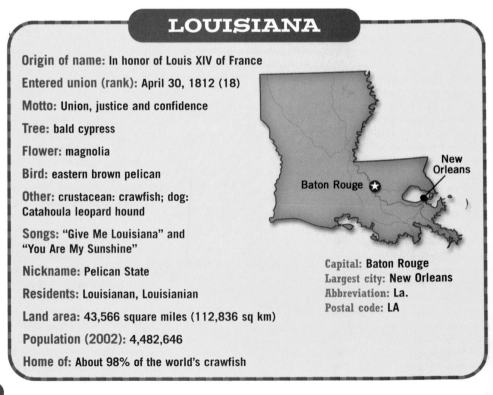

New Orleans

Baton Rouge ★

Capital: Baton Rouge
Largest city: New Orleans
Abbreviation: La.
Postal code: LA

MAINE

Origin of name: First used to distinguish the mainland from the offshore islands

Entered union (rank): March 15, 1820 (23)

Motto: *Dirigo* (I lead)

Tree: white pine tree

Flower: white pine cone and tassel

Bird: chickadee

Other: animal: moose; cat: Maine coon cat

Song: "State of Maine Song"

Nickname: Pine Tree State

Residents: Mainer

Land area: 30,865 square miles (79,939 sq km)

Population (2002): 1,294,464

Augusta

Portland

Capital: **Augusta**
Largest city: **Portland**
Abbreviation: **Maine**
Postal code: **ME**

Home of: The most easterly point in the U.S., West Quoddy Head

MARYLAND

Origin of name: In honor of Henrietta Maria (queen of Charles I of England)

Entered union (rank): April 28, 1788 (7)

Motto: *Fatti maschii, parole femine*
(Manly deeds, womanly words)

Tree: white oak

Flower: black-eyed Susan

Bird: Baltimore oriole

Other: crustacean: Maryland blue crab; sport: jousting

Song: "Maryland! My Maryland!"

Nicknames: Free State and Old Line State

Residents: Marylander

Land area: 9,775 square miles (25,316 sq km)

Population (2002): 5,458,137

Baltimore

Annapolis

Capital: **Annapolis**
Largest city: **Baltimore**
Abbreviation: **Md.**
Postal code: **MD**

Home of: The first umbrella factory in the U.S., opened 1928, in Baltimore

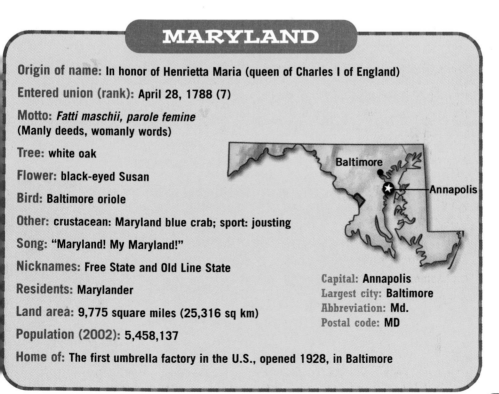

MASSACHUSETTS

Origin of name: From the Massachusett Indian tribe, meaning "at or about the great hill"

Entered union (rank): February 6, 1788 (6)

Motto: *Ense petit placidam sub libertate quietem* (By the sword we seek peace, but peace only under liberty)

Tree: American elm

Flower: mayflower

Bird: chickadee

Other: beverage: cranberry juice; dessert: Boston cream pie

Song: "All Hail to Massachusetts"

Nicknames: Bay State and Old Colony State

Residents: Bay Stater

Land area: 7,838 square miles (20,300 sq km)

Population (2002): 6,427,801

Home of: The first World Series, played between the Boston Pilgrims and the Pittsburgh Pirates in 1903

Boston ✪

Capital: Boston
Largest city: Boston
Abbreviation: Mass.
Postal code: MA

MICHIGAN

Origin of name: From an Indian word (Michigana) meaning "great or large lake"

Entered union (rank): January 26, 1837 (26)

Motto: *Si quaeris peninsulam amoenam circumspice* (If you seek a pleasant peninsula, look around you)

Tree: white pine

Flower: apple blossom

Bird: robin

Other: reptile: painted turtle; wildflower: Dwarf Lake iris

Song: "Michigan, My Michigan"

Nickname: Wolverine State

Residents: Michigander, Michiganite

Land area: 56,809 square miles (147,135 sq km)

Population (2002): 10,050,446

Home of: Battle Creek, "Cereal City," produces most of the breakfast cereal in the U.S.

Capital: Lansing
Largest city: Detroit
Abbreviation: Mich.
Postal code: MI

Lansing ✪

Detroit

MINNESOTA

Origin of name: From a Dakota Indian word meaning "sky-tinted water"

Entered union (rank): May 11, 1858 (32)

Motto: *L'Étoile du nord* (The north star)

Tree: red (or Norway) pine

Flower: lady slipper

Bird: common loon

Other: drink: milk; mushroom: morel

Song: "Hail Minnesota"

Nicknames: North Star State, Gopher State and Land of 10,000 Lakes

Residents: Minnesotan

Land area: 79,617 square miles (206,207 sq km)

Population (2002): 5,019,720

Minneapolis
St. Paul

Capital: St. Paul
Largest city: Minneapolis
Abbreviation: Minn.
Postal code: MN

Home of: The world's oldest rock, 3.8 billion years old, found in the Minnesota River valley

MISSISSIPPI

Origin of name: From an Indian word meaning "Father of Waters"

Entered union (rank): December 10, 1817 (20)

Motto: *Virtute et armis* (By valor and arms)

Tree: magnolia

Flower: flower or bloom of the magnolia or evergreen magnolia

Bird: mockingbird

Other: stone: petrified wood; water mammal: bottlenosed dolphin

Song: "Go, Mississippi"

Nickname: Magnolia State

Residents: Mississippian

Land area: 46,914 square miles (121,506 sq km)

Population (2002): 2,871,782

Home of: Coca-Cola, first bottled in 1894 in Vicksburg

Jackson

Capital: Jackson
Largest city: Jackson
Abbreviation: Miss.
Postal code: MS

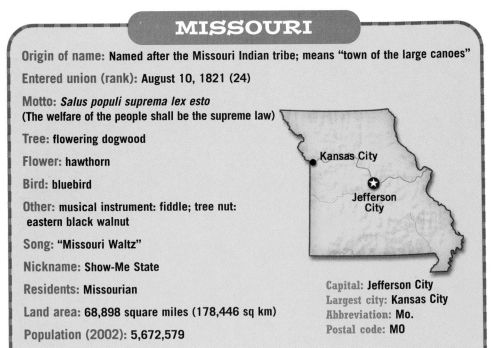

MISSOURI

Origin of name: Named after the Missouri Indian tribe; means "town of the large canoes"

Entered union (rank): August 10, 1821 (24)

Motto: *Salus populi suprema lex esto*
(The welfare of the people shall be the supreme law)

Tree: flowering dogwood

Flower: hawthorn

Bird: bluebird

Other: musical instrument: fiddle; tree nut: eastern black walnut

Song: "Missouri Waltz"

Nickname: Show-Me State

Residents: Missourian

Land area: 68,898 square miles (178,446 sq km)

Population (2002): 5,672,579

Capital: Jefferson City
Largest city: Kansas City
Abbreviation: Mo.
Postal code: MO

Home of: Mark Twain and some of his characters, such as Tom Sawyer and Huckleberry Finn

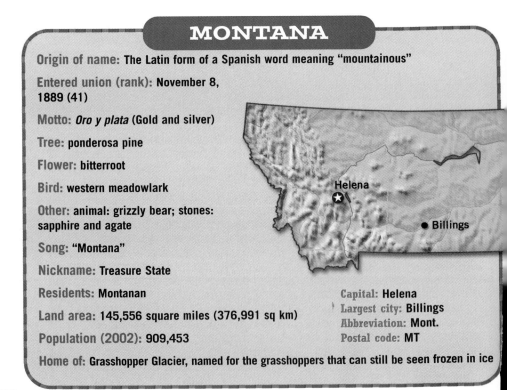

MONTANA

Origin of name: The Latin form of a Spanish word meaning "mountainous"

Entered union (rank): November 8, 1889 (41)

Motto: *Oro y plata* (Gold and silver)

Tree: ponderosa pine

Flower: bitterroot

Bird: western meadowlark

Other: animal: grizzly bear; stones: sapphire and agate

Song: "Montana"

Nickname: Treasure State

Residents: Montanan

Land area: 145,556 square miles (376,991 sq km)

Population (2002): 909,453

Capital: Helena
Largest city: Billings
Abbreviation: Mont.
Postal code: MT

Home of: Grasshopper Glacier, named for the grasshoppers that can still be seen frozen in ice

NEBRASKA

Origin of name: From an Oto Indian word meaning "flat water"

Entered union (rank): March 1, 1867 (37)

Motto: Equality before the law

Tree: cottonwood

Flower: goldenrod

Bird: western meadowlark

Other: ballad: "A Place Like Nebraska"; soft drink: Kool-Aid

Song: "Beautiful Nebraska"

Nicknames: Cornhusker State and Beef State

Residents: Nebraskan

Land area: 76,878 square miles (199,113 sq km)

Population (2002): 1,729,180

Home of: The only roller-skating museum in the world, in Lincoln

Capital: Lincoln
Largest city: Omaha
Abbreviation: Nebr.
Postal code: NE

NEVADA

Origin of name: From the Spanish, "snowcapped"

Entered union (rank): October 31, 1864 (36)

Motto: All for our country

Trees: single-leaf piñon and bristlecone pine

Flower: sagebrush

Bird: mountain bluebird

Other: metal: silver; reptile: desert tortoise

Song: "Home Means Nevada"

Nicknames: Sagebrush State, Silver State and Battle Born State

Residents: Nevadan, Nevadian

Land area: 109,806 square miles (284,397 sq km)

Population (2002): 2,173,491

Home of: The Devil's Hole pupfish, found only in Devil's Hole, an underground pool near Death Valley

Capital: Carson City
Largest city: Las Vegas
Abbreviation: Nev.
Postal code: NV

NEW HAMPSHIRE

Origin of name: From the English county of Hampshire

Entered union (rank): June 21, 1788 (9)

Motto: Live free or die

Tree: white birch

Flower: purple lilac

Bird: purple finch

Other: amphibian: spotted newt; sport: skiing

Songs: "Old New Hamshire" and "New Hampshire, My New Hampshire"

Nickname: Granite State

Residents: New Hampshirite

Land area: 8,969 square miles (23,231 sq km)

Population (2002): 1,275,056

Home of: Artificial rain, first used near Concord in 1947 to fight a forest fire

Concord

Manchester

Capital: Concord
Largest city: Manchester
Abbreviation: N.H.
Postal code: NH

NEW JERSEY

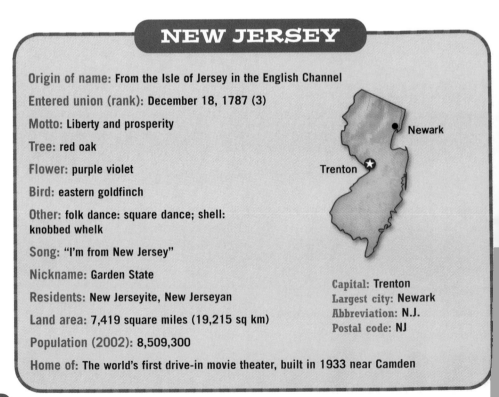

Origin of name: From the Isle of Jersey in the English Channel

Entered union (rank): December 18, 1787 (3)

Motto: Liberty and prosperity

Tree: red oak

Flower: purple violet

Bird: eastern goldfinch

Other: folk dance: square dance; shell: knobbed whelk

Song: "I'm from New Jersey"

Nickname: Garden State

Residents: New Jerseyite, New Jerseyan

Land area: 7,419 square miles (19,215 sq km)

Population (2002): 8,509,300

Newark

Trenton

Capital: Trenton
Largest city: Newark
Abbreviation: N.J.
Postal code: NJ

Home of: The world's first drive-in movie theater, built in 1933 near Camden

NEW MEXICO

Origin of name: From Mexico

Entered union (rank): January 6, 1912 (47)

Motto: *Crescit eundo* (It grows as it goes)

Tree: piñon

Flower: yucca

Bird: roadrunner

Other: cookie: biscochito; vegetables: chili and frijole

Song: "O Fair New Mexico"

Nickname: Land of Enchantment

Residents: New Mexican

Land area: 121,365 square miles (314,334 sq km)

Population (2002): 1,855,059

Home of: Smokey Bear, a cub orphaned by fire in 1950, buried in Smokey Bear Historical State Park in 1976

Santa Fe
Albuquerque

Capital: **Santa Fe**
Largest city: **Albuquerque**
Abbreviation: **N.M.**
Postal code: **NM**

NEW YORK

Origin of name: In honor of the Duke of York

Entered union (rank): July 26, 1788 (11)

Motto: *Excelsior* (Ever upward)

Tree: sugar maple

Flower: rose

Bird: bluebird

Other: animal: beaver; muffin: apple

Song: "I Love New York"

Nickname: Empire State

Residents: New Yorker

Land area: 47,224 square miles (122,310 sq km)

Population (2002): 19,157,532

Home of: The first presidential Inauguration. George Washington took the oath of office in New York City on April 30, 1789.

Albany

New York City

Capital: **Albany**
Largest city: **New York**
Abbreviation: **N.Y.**
Postal code: **NY**

NORTH CAROLINA

Origin of name: In honor of Charles I of England

Entered union (rank): November 21, 1789 (12)

Motto: *Esse quam videri* (To be rather than to seem)

Tree: pine

Flower: dogwood

Bird: cardinal

Other: dog: plott hound; historic boat: shad boat

Song: "The Old North State"

Nickname: Tar Heel State

Residents: North Carolinian

Land area: 48,718 square miles (126,180 sq km)

Population (2002): 8,320,146

Capital: Raleigh
Largest city: Charlotte
Abbreviation: N.C.
Postal code: NC

Home of: Virginia Dare, the first English child born in America, on Roanoke Island in 1587

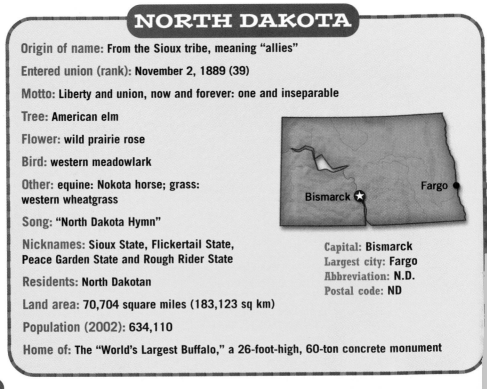

NORTH DAKOTA

Origin of name: From the Sioux tribe, meaning "allies"

Entered union (rank): November 2, 1889 (39)

Motto: Liberty and union, now and forever: one and inseparable

Tree: American elm

Flower: wild prairie rose

Bird: western meadowlark

Other: equine: Nokota horse; grass: western wheatgrass

Song: "North Dakota Hymn"

Nicknames: Sioux State, Flickertail State, Peace Garden State and Rough Rider State

Residents: North Dakotan

Land area: 70,704 square miles (183,123 sq km)

Population (2002): 634,110

Capital: Bismarck
Largest city: Fargo
Abbreviation: N.D.
Postal code: ND

Home of: The "World's Largest Buffalo," a 26-foot-high, 60-ton concrete monument

OHIO

Origin of name: From an Iroquoian word meaning "great river"

Entered union (rank): March 1, 1803 (17)

Motto: With God all things are possible

Tree: buckeye

Flower: scarlet carnation

Bird: cardinal

Other: beverage: tomato juice; fossil: trilobite

Song: "Beautiful Ohio"

Nickname: Buckeye State

Residents: Ohioan

Land area: 40,953 square miles (106,067 sq km)

Population (2002): 11,421,267

Home of: The first electric traffic lights, invented and installed in Cleveland in 1914

Columbus

Capital: Columbus
Largest city: Columbus
Abbreviation: Ohio
Postal code: OH

OKLAHOMA

Origin of name: From two Choctaw Indian words meaning "red people"

Entered union (rank): November 16, 1907 (46)

Motto: *Labor omnia vincit* (Labor conquers all things)

Tree: redbud

Flower: mistletoe

Bird: scissor-tailed flycatcher

Other: furbearer: raccoon; waltz: "Oklahoma Wind"

Song: "Oklahoma"

Nickname: Sooner State

Residents: Oklahoman

Land area: 68,679 square miles (177,877 sq km)

Population (2002): 3,493,714

Home of: The first parking meter, installed in Oklahoma City in 1935

Oklahoma City

Capital: Oklahoma City
Largest city: Oklahoma City
Abbreviation: Okla.
Postal code: OK

OREGON

Origin of name: Unknown

Entered union (rank): February 14, 1859 (33)

Motto: *Alis volat propriis* (She flies with her own wings)

Tree: Douglas fir

Flower: Oregon grape

Bird: western meadowlark

Other: fish: Chinook salmon; nut: hazelnut

Song: "Oregon, My Oregon"

Nickname: Beaver State

Residents: Oregonian

Land area: 96,003 square miles (248,647 sq km)

Population (2002): 3,521,515

Capital: Salem
Largest city: Portland
Abbreviation: Ore.
Postal code: OR

Home of: The world's smallest park, totaling 452 square inches, created in Portland on St. Patrick's Day in 1948 for leprechauns and snail races

PENNSYLVANIA

Origin of name: In honor of Sir William Penn, father of state founder William Penn. It means "Penn's Woodland."

Entered union (rank): December 12, 1787 (2)

Motto: Virtue, liberty and independence

Tree: hemlock

Flower: mountain laurel

Bird: ruffed grouse

Other: dog: Great Dane; insect: firefly

Song: "Pennsylvania"

Nickname: Keystone State

Residents: Pennsylvanian

Land area: 44,820 square miles (116,083 sq km)

Population (2002): 12,335,091

Capital: Harrisburg
Largest city: Philadelphia
Abbreviation: Pa.
Postal code: PA

Home of: The first magazine in America, the *American Magazine*, published in Philadelphia for three months in 1741

RHODE ISLAND

Origin of name: From the Greek Island of Rhodes

Entered union (rank): May 29, 1790 (13)

Motto: Hope

Tree: red maple

Flower: violet

Bird: Rhode Island Red hen

Other: shell: quahog; stone: cumberlandite

Song: "Rhode Island"

Nickname: Ocean State

Residents: Rhode Islander

Land area: 1,045 square miles (2,706 sq km)

Population (2002): 1,069,725

Home of: Rhode Island Red chickens, first bred in 1854; the start of poultry as a major American industry

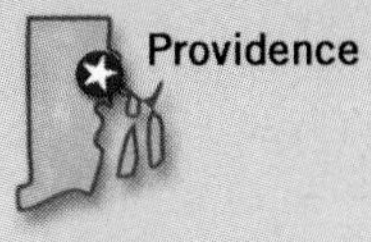

Providence

Capital: Providence
Largest city: Providence
Abbreviation: R.I.
Postal code: RI

SOUTH CAROLINA

Origin of name: In honor of Charles I of England

Entered union (rank): May 23, 1788 (8)

Mottoes: *Animis opibusque parati* (Prepared in mind and resources) and *Dum spiro spero* (While I breathe, I hope)

Tree: palmetto

Flower: yellow jessamine

Bird: Carolina wren

Other: hospitality beverage: tea; music: the spiritual

Song: "Carolina"

Nickname: Palmetto State

Residents: South Carolinian

Land area: 30,111 square miles (77,988 sq km)

Population (2002): 4,107,183

Home of: The first tea farm in the U.S., created in 1890 near Summerville

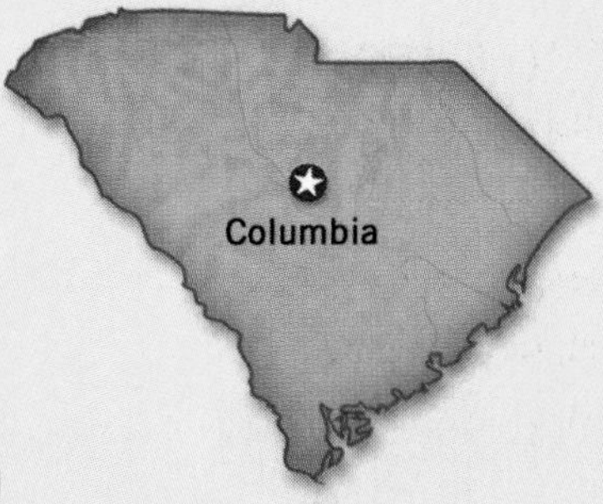

Columbia

Capital: Columbia
Largest city: Columbia
Abbreviation: S.C.
Postal code: SC

SOUTH DAKOTA

Origin of name: From the Sioux tribe, meaning "allies"

Entered union (rank): November 2, 1889 (40)

Motto: Under God the people rule

Tree: black hills spruce

Flower: American pasqueflower

Bird: ring-necked pheasant

Other: dessert: kuchen; jewelry: Black Hills gold

Song: "Hail! South Dakota"

Nicknames: Mount Rushmore State and Coyote State

Residents: South Dakotan

Land area: 75,898 square miles (196,575 sq km)

Population (2002): 761,063

Home of: The world's largest natural indoor warm-water pool, Evans' Plunge in Hot Springs

Capital: Pierre
Largest city: Sioux Falls
Abbreviation: S.D.
Postal code: SD

TENNESSEE

Origin of name: Of Cherokee origin; the exact meaning is unknown

Entered union (rank): June 1, 1796 (16)

Motto: Agriculture and commerce

Tree: tulip poplar

Flower: iris

Bird: mockingbird

Other: amphibian: Tennessee cave salamander; animal: raccoon

Songs: "Tennessee Waltz," "My Homeland, Tennessee," "When It's Iris Time in Tennessee," "My Tennessee," "Rocky Top" and "Tennessee"

Nickname: Volunteer State

Residents: Tennessean, Tennesseean

Land area: 41,220 square miles (106,759 sq km)

Population (2002): 5,797,289

Home of: Graceland, the estate and grave site of Elvis Presley

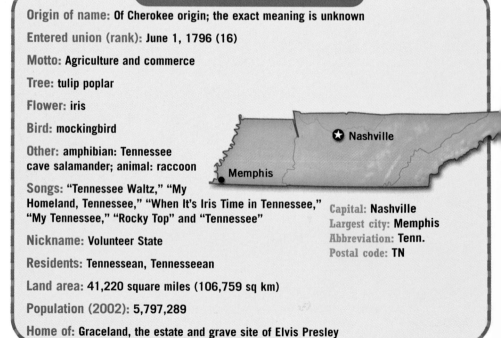

Capital: Nashville
Largest city: Memphis
Abbreviation: Tenn.
Postal code: TN

TEXAS

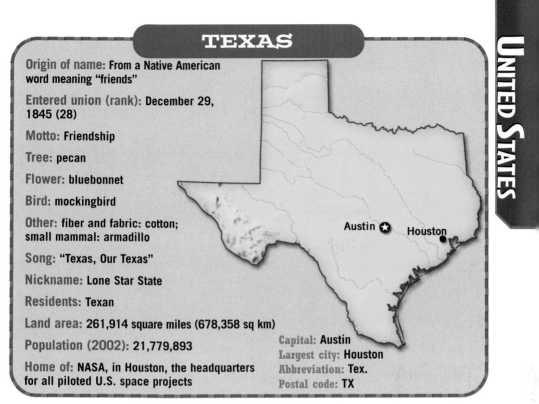

Origin of name: From a Native American word meaning "friends"

Entered union (rank): December 29, 1845 (28)

Motto: Friendship

Tree: pecan

Flower: bluebonnet

Bird: mockingbird

Other: fiber and fabric: cotton; small mammal: armadillo

Song: "Texas, Our Texas"

Nickname: Lone Star State

Residents: Texan

Land area: 261,914 square miles (678,358 sq km)

Population (2002): 21,779,893

Home of: NASA, in Houston, the headquarters for all piloted U.S. space projects

Capital: Austin
Largest city: Houston
Abbreviation: Tex.
Postal code: TX

UTAH

Origin of name: From the Ute tribe, meaning "people of the mountains"

Entered union (rank): January 4, 1896 (45)

Motto: Industry

Tree: blue spruce

Flower: sego lily

Bird: California gull

Other: cooking pot: dutch oven; fruit: cherry

Song: "Utah, We Love Thee"

Nickname: Beehive State

Residents: Utahan, Utahn

Land area: 82,168 square miles (212,816 sq km)

Population (2002): 2,316,256

Capital: Salt Lake City
Largest city: Salt Lake City
Abbreviation: Utah
Postal code: UT

Home of: Rainbow Bridge, the largest natural stone bridge in the world, 290 feet high, 275 feet across

VERMONT

Origin of name: From the French *vert mont,* meaning "green mountain"

Entered union (rank): March 4, 1791 (14)

Motto: Vermont, freedom and unity

Tree: sugar maple

Flower: red clover

Bird: hermit thrush

Other: animal: Morgan horse; insect: honeybee

Song: "Hail, Vermont!"

Nickname: Green Mountain State

Residents: Vermonter

Land area: 9,249 square miles (23,956 sq km)

Population (2002): 616,592

Capital: Montpelier
Largest city: Burlington
Abbreviation: Vt.
Postal code: VT

Home of: The largest production of maple syrup in the U.S.

VIRGINIA

Origin of name: In honor of Elizabeth I, "Virgin Queen" of England

Entered union (rank): June 25, 1788 (10)

Motto: *Sic semper tyrannis* (Thus always to tyrants)

Tree: dogwood

Flower: American dogwood

Bird: cardinal

Other: dog: American foxhound; shell: oyster shell

Song: "Carry Me Back to Old Virginia"

Nicknames: The Old Dominion and Mother of Presidents

Residents: Virginian

Land area: 39,598 square miles (102,558 sq km)

Population (2002): 7,293,542

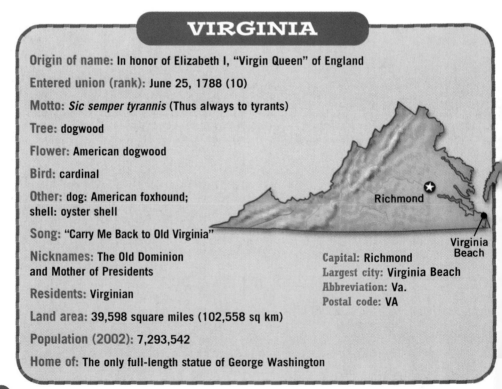

Capital: Richmond
Largest city: Virginia Beach
Abbreviation: Va.
Postal code: VA

Home of: The only full-length statue of George Washington

WASHINGTON

Origin of name: In honor of George Washington

Entered union (rank): November 11, 1889 (42)

Motto: *Al-ki* (Indian word meaning "by and by")

Tree: western hemlock

Flower: coast rhododendron

Bird: willow goldfinch

Other: fossil: Columbian mammoth; fruit: apple

Song: "Washington, My Home"

Nickname: Evergreen State

Residents: Washingtonian

Land area: 66,582 square miles (172,447 sq km)

Population (2002): 6,068,996

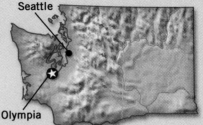

Seattle

Olympia

Capital: Olympia
Largest city: Seattle
Abbreviation: Wash.
Postal code: WA

Home of: The Lunar Rover, the vehicle used by astronauts on the moon. Boeing, in Seattle, makes aircraft and spacecraft.

WEST VIRGINIA

Origin of name: In honor of Elizabeth I, "Virgin Queen" of England

Entered union (rank): June 20, 1863 (35)

Motto: *Montani semper liberi* (Mountaineers are always free)

Tree: sugar maple

Flower: rhododendron

Bird: cardinal

Other: animal: black bear; fruit: golden delicious apple

Songs: "West Virginia," "My Home Sweet Home," "The West Virginia Hills" and "This Is My West Virginia"

Nickname: Mountain State

Residents: West Virginian

Land area: 24,087 square miles (62,384 sq km)

Population (2002): 1,801,873

Charleston

Capital: Charleston
Largest city: Charleston
Abbreviation: W.Va.
Postal code: WV

Home of: Marbles. Most of the country's glass marbles are made around Parkersburg.

WISCONSIN

Origin of name: French corruption of an Indian word whose meaning is disputed

Entered union (rank): May 29, 1848 (30)

Motto: Forward

Tree: sugar maple

Flower: wood violet

Bird: robin

Other: dance: polka; symbol of peace: mourning dove

Song: "On Wisconsin"

Nickname: Badger State

Residents: Wisconsinite

Land area: 54,314 square miles (140,673 sq km)

Population (2002): 5,441,196

Capital: Madison
Largest city: Milwaukee
Abbreviation: Wis.
Postal code: WI

Home of: The typewriter, invented in Milwaukee in 1867

WYOMING

Origin of name: From a Delaware Indian word meaning "mountains and valleys alternating"

Entered union (rank): July 10, 1890 (44)

Motto: Equal rights

Tree: cottonwood

Flower: Indian paintbrush

Bird: meadowlark

Other: dinosaur: *Triceratops*; gemstone: jade

Song: "Wyoming"

Nickname: Equality State

Residents: Wyomingite

Land area: 97,105 square miles (251,501 sq km)

Population (2002): 498,703

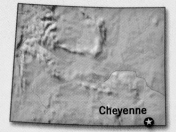

Capital: Cheyenne
Largest city: Cheyenne
Abbreviation: Wyo.
Postal code: WY

Home of: The Register of the Desert, a huge granite boulder that covers 27 acres and has 5,000 early pioneer names carved on it

WASHINGTON, D.C.

The District of Columbia, which covers the same area as the city of Washington, is the capital of the United States. It is located between Virginia and Maryland on the Potomac River. The district is named after Columbus. The Federal Government and tourism are the mainstays of its economy. Many unions as well as business, professional and nonprofit organizations have headquarters there.

   D.C. history began in 1790 when Congress took charge of organizing a new site for the capital. George Washington chose the spot, midway between the northern and southern states on the Potomac River. The seat of government was transferred from Philadelphia, Pennsylvania, to Washington, D.C., on December 1, 1800, and President John Adams became the first resident of the White House.

   A petition asking for the district's admission to the Union as the 51st state was filed in Congress on September 9, 1983. The district is continuing this drive for statehood.

Motto: *Justitia omnibus* (Justice to all)

Flower: American Beauty rose

Tree: scarlet oak

Land area: 68.25 square miles (177 sq km)

Population (2000): 570,898

The U.S. Capitol building

The NATIONAL PARK System

The National Park System of the U.S. is run by the National Park Service, a bureau of the Department of the Interior. Yellowstone, which was opened in 1872, was the first national park in the world. The system includes not only the most extraordinary and spectacular scenic exhibits in the U.S., but also a large number of sites distinguished either for their historic importance, prehistoric importance, scientific interest or for their superior recreational assets.

   The National Park System is made up of 378 areas covering more than 83 million acres in every state except Delaware. It also includes areas in the District of Columbia, American Samoa, Guam, Puerto Rico and the Virgin Islands. For a complete listing of National Park areas, visit the website of the Park Service: www.nps.gov

Yosemite National Park in California has beautiful scenery.

go ▸ For fun facts and trivia on all the states, go to WWW.FACTMONSTER.COM

The U.S. Territories

A territory is a region that belongs to the U.S., but which is not one of the 50 states. Although territories govern themselves to a limited extent, they are really governed by the U.S. Territories sometimes become states; Alaska and Hawaii were the last two territories admitted to the Union as states.

THE COMMONWEALTH OF PUERTO RICO

Puerto Rico is located in the Caribbean Sea, about 1,000 miles east-southeast of Miami, Florida. A U.S. possession since 1898, it consists of the island of Puerto Rico plus the adjacent islets of Vieques, Culebra and Mona.

Capital: San Juan
Land area: 3,459 square miles (8,959 sq km)
Population estimate (2002): 3,885,877
Languages: Spanish and English

GUAM

Guam, the largest and southernmost island in the Marianas Island chain (see "Northern Mariana Islands," below), became a U.S. territory in 1898.

Capital: Agaña
Land area: 212 square miles (549 sq km)
Population estimate (2002): 163,941
Languages: English and Chamorro; Japanese is also widely spoken

THE COMMONWEALTH OF THE NORTHERN MARIANA ISLANDS (CNMI)

The Northern Mariana Islands, east of the Philippines and south of Japan, have been part of the U.S. since 1986. They include the islands of Rota, Saipan, Tinian, Pagan, Guguan, Agrihan and Aguijan.

Capital: Chalan Kanoa (on Saipan)
Total area: 184.17 square miles (477 sq km)
Population estimate (2002): 80,006
Languages: English, Chamorro, Carolinian

THE U.S. VIRGIN ISLANDS

The Virgin Islands consist of nine main islands and some 75 islets. Since 1666, Britain has ruled six of the main islands; the remaining three (St. Croix, St. Thomas and St. John), as well as about 50 of the islets, were acquired by Denmark, and then purchased by the U.S in 1917.

Capital: Charlotte Amalie (on St. Thomas)
Land area: 140 square miles (363 sq km): St. Croix, 84 square miles (218 sq km); St. Thomas, 32 square miles (83 sq km); St. John, 20 square miles (52 sq km)
Population estimate (2002): 124,778
Languages: English, but Spanish and French are also spoken

AMERICAN SAMOA

American Samoa is a group of five volcanic islands and two coral atolls. It is located some 2,600 miles south of Hawaii in the South Pacific. It includes the eastern Samoan islands of Tutuila, Aunu'u and Rose; three islands (Ta'u, Olosega and Ofu) of the Manu'a group; and Swains Island. The territory became part of the U.S. in 1900, except for Swains Island, which was acquired in 1925.

Capital: Pago Pago
Land area: 77 square miles (199 sq km)
Population estimate (2002): 70,260
Languages: Samoan (closely related to Hawaiian) and English

THE MIDWAY ISLANDS

The Midway Islands lie about 1,150 miles west-northwest of Hawaii. They became part of the U.S. in 1867.

Total area: 2 square miles (5.2 sq km)
Population estimate (2002): no indigenous inhabitants; about 40 people make up the staff of the U.S. Fish and Wildlife Service.

WAKE ISLAND

Wake Island, between Midway and Guam, is an atoll consisting of the three islets of Wilkes, Peale and Wake. It was annexed by Hawaii in 1899.

Total area: 2.5 square miles (6.5 sq km)
Population estimate (1995): no indigenous inhabitants; 302 U.S. military personnel and civilian contractors

JOHNSTON ATOLL

Johnston is a coral atoll about 700 miles southwest of Hawaii. It consists of four small islands—Johnston Island, Sand Island, Hikina Island and Akau Island—which lie on a 9-mile-long reef. It was claimed by Hawaii in 1858.

Land area: 1.08 square miles (2.8 sq km)
Population estimate (2002): no indigenous inhabitants. In previous years, there was an average of 1,100 U.S. military and civilian contractor personnel present; they left in September 2001.

BAKER, HOWLAND AND JARVIS ISLANDS

These Pacific islands were claimed by the U.S. in 1936. **Baker Island** is an atoll of approximately 1 square mile (2.6 sq km) located about 1,650 miles from Hawaii. **Howland Island,** 36 miles to the northwest, is 1 mile long. Tiny **Jarvis Island** is several hundred miles to the east.

KINGMAN REEF

Kingman Reef, located about 1,000 miles south of Hawaii, has been a U.S. possession since 1922. Triangular in shape, it is about 9.5 miles long.

Did You Know?

An atoll is a coral island made up of a reef surrounding a lagoon (shallow pool).

NAVASSA ISLAND

Navassa Island is located in the Caribbean Sea, between Cuba, Haiti and Jamaica. It has an area of 2 square miles (5.2 sq km) and was claimed for the U.S. in 1857.

PALMYRA ATOLL

Palmyra Atoll has a total area of 4.6 square miles (11.9 sq km) and is located 994 miles (1,600 km) southwest of Honolulu.

TFK MYSTERY PERSON

CLUE 1: One of 13 children, I was born into slavery in 1797. Forty years later, I gained my freedom.
CLUE 2: Although I could neither read nor write, I was a great speaker. I traveled the country giving speeches that demanded equal rights for women and African Americans.
CLUE 3: After the Civil War, I helped newly freed slaves and tried to convince the government to give them land.

WHO AM I?

(See Answer Key that begins on page 340.)

ISIDORE BLOWS ASHORE

A fierce storm pounds the southern U.S.
By Ritu Upadhyay

The pounding rain and 65-mile-an-hour winds left cars toppled and streets submerged. Screen doors, mailboxes and furniture bobbed in three feet of water. "I don't know whose they are, but I've got three recliner chairs in my yard," said Susan Serpas, who lives in Delacroix, Louisiana.

In late September 2002, tropical storm Isidore blew across parts of the U.S., soaking Louisiana, Alabama and Mississippi. Some residents had to evacuate their homes when the storm hit. "I woke up and found two feet of water in my apartment," said Laquincy Nixon as he carried his son and daughter to a shelter in Houma, Louisiana.

But despite the flooding, the U.S. was spared the worst of Isidore's wrath. Days earlier, hurricane Isidore ripped through Mexico, killing two people, destroying villages and leaving 70,000 people homeless. By the time Isidore arrived on the Gulf Coast, it was a weaker—though still forceful—tropical storm.

Scientists track hurricanes as they approach land. The months from June through November are considered hurricane season in the Atlantic region. Weather experts say that the season reaches its peak in the fall. "We're on high alert because this is when we see the worst of them come through," said Martin Nelson, a meteorologist at the National Hurricane Center.

Though they can track a storm's path, scientists cannot predict how hard it will hit. Many cities had been bracing themselves for days, fearful of Isidore's arrival. This time, what started off as a monstrous hurricane lost power and ended up being a big storm. But there's always a next time!

The storm whipped up giant waves along Alabama's shore.

Gathering Speed

Tropical wind systems are classified according to their wind speed. The faster a storm blows, the more destructive it gets. When Isidore hit Mexico, it was a Category 3 hurricane. Luckily, it slowed to a tropical storm when it struck the U.S.

TROPICAL STORM Winds 40 to 73 miles per hour
Category 1 Hurricane winds 74 to 95 miles per hour
Category 2 Hurricane winds 96 to 110 miles per hour
Category 3 Hurricane winds 111 to 130 miles per hour
Category 4 Hurricane winds 131 to 155 miles per hour
Category 5 Hurricane winds greater than 155 miles per hour

Hang on to Your Hat! It's a HURRICANE!

A storm is declared a hurricane when winds reach speeds of 74 miles an hour. Wind speeds can exceed 190 miles per hour in some hurricanes. In the U.S., the official hurricane season lasts from June 1 to November 30, but hurricanes can happen at any time of the year. Cyclones, hurricanes and typhoons are the same kind of tropical storm but are called different names in different parts of the world.

What's Your Name?

Because hurricanes often occur at the same time, officials assign short, distinctive names to the storms to avoid confusion among weather stations, coastal bases and ships at sea. A storm is given a name once its winds reach 40 miles per hour. These are the names that have been chosen for Atlantic storms in 2003 and 2004:

2003: Ana, Bill, Claudette, Danny, Erika, Fabian, Grace, Henri, Isabel, Juan, Kate, Larry, Mindy, Nicholas, Odette, Peter, Rose, Sam, Teresa, Victor and Wanda

2004: Alex, Bonnie, Charley, Danielle, Earl, Frances, Gaston, Hermine, Ivan, Jeanne, Karl, Lisa, Matthew, Nicole, Otto, Paula, Richard, Shary, Tomas, Virginie and Walter

An Early Retirement

When hurricanes are particularly destructive, their names are retired from the list of usable names. A retired name cannot be reused for at least 10 years. Here is a list of some of the infamous hurricane names that have settled into retirement.

NAME	YEAR	LOCATION(S) AFFECTED
Alicia	1983	North Texas
Andrew	1992	Bahamas, Florida, Louisiana
Bob	1991	North Carolina, Northeast U.S.
Camille	1969	Louisiana, Mississippi, Alabama
Carla	1961	Texas
Carol	1954	Northeast U.S.
Connie	1955	North Carolina
Frederic	1979	Alabama, Mississippi
Gloria	1985	North Carolina, Northeast U.S.
Hattie	1961	Belize, Guatemala
Hazel	1954	Antilles, North and South Carolina
Hilda	1964	Louisiana
Hugo	1989	Antilles, South Carolina
Ione	1995	North Carolina
Mitch	1998	Nicaragua, Honduras, Guatemala

How's the WEATHER?

Temperature

Air temperature is measured by a mercury thermometer. When the temperature rises, the mercury expands and rises in the thermometer tube. When the temperature falls, the mercury contracts and falls.

In the U.S., the **Fahrenheit** scale is used most often. On this scale, 32° is the freezing point of water, and 212° is the boiling point.

The **Celsius,** or centigrade, scale is used by the World Meteorological Organization and most countries in the world. On this scale, 0° is freezing, and 100°is boiling.

To convert Fahrenheit to Celsius, subtract 32, multiply by 5, and divide the result by 9.
   Example: To convert 50°F to °C: 50 − 32 = 18; 18 x 5 = 90; 90 ÷ 9 = 10

To convert Celsius to Fahrenheit, multiply by 9, divide by 5, and add 32.
   Example: To convert 10°C to °F: 10 x 9 = 90; 90 ÷ 5 = 18; 18 + 32 = 50

°Celsius	°Fahrenheit
−50	−58
−40	−40
−30	−22
−20	−4
−10	14
0	32
5	41
10	50
15	59
20	68
25	77
30	86
35	95
40	104
45	113
50	122

Air Pressure and Humidity

Air pressure is the weight of the atmosphere pressing down on Earth. It is measured by a **barometer** in units called millibars. Most barometers use mercury in a glass column, like a thermometer, to measure the change in air pressure.

Air pressure changes with altitude. When you move to a higher place, say a tall mountain, air pressure decreases because there are fewer air molecules as you move higher up.

Relative humidity is the amount of moisture the air can hold before it rains. The most the air can hold is 100 percent. Humidity is measured by a **psychrometer,** which indicates the amount of water in the air at any one temperature.

Did You Know?

On January 22, 1945, in Spearfish, South Dakota, the temperature rose 49°F (9.4°C) in two minutes! At 7:30 A.M. the temperature was -4.5°F. By 7:32 A.M., it had risen to 45°F.

SEND IN THE CLOUDS

Clouds are little drops of water hanging in the atmosphere. A ceilometer measures the height of clouds. When clouds become heavy with humidity, water falls from them. This is called precipitation. In warmer clouds, precipitation falls as rain. In colder clouds, precipitation falls as snow. Thunderstorm clouds can bring another kind of precipitation—hail. When ice crystals in a cloud get tossed around by strong air currents and then become stuck together by water that freezes on them, hail forms.

Cloud	Nickname	Height	Appearance
CIRRUS	Mare's tails	4 miles or more	thin, feathery
CIRROCUMULUS	Mackerel sky	4 miles or more	small patches of white
CIRROSTRATUS	Bedsheet clouds	4 miles	thin, white sheets
STRATUS (RAIN OR SNOW CLOUDS)	High fogs	0-1 mile	low, gray blanket
CUMULUS	Cauliflowers	¼-4 miles	flat-bottomed, white puffy
CUMULONIMBUS (RAIN OR SNOW CLOUDS)	Thunderheads	¼-4 miles	mountains of heavy, dark clouds

go Hot or cold, crunch the numbers at
www.timeforkids.com/numbers

It's a Twister!

A tornado is a dark, funnel-shaped cloud made up of violently churning winds that can reach speeds of up to 300 miles an hour. A tornado can be from a few feet wide to a mile wide, and its track can extend from less than a mile to several hundred miles. Tornadoes generally travel in a northeast direction at speeds ranging from 20 to 60 miles an hour.

Tornadoes are most often caused by giant thunderstorms known as "supercells." These powerful, highly organized storms form when warm, moist air along the ground rushes upward, meeting cooler, drier air. As the rising warm air cools, the moisture it carries condenses, forming a massive thundercloud, sometimes growing to as much as 50,000 feet in height. Winds at different levels of the atmosphere feed the updraft and cause the formation of the tornado's characteristic funnel shape.

The Fujita scale classifies tornadoes according to the damage they cause. Almost half of all tornadoes fall into the F1 or "moderate damage" category. These tornadoes reach speeds of 73 to 112 miles per hour and can overturn automobiles and uproot trees. Only about 1% of tornadoes are classified as F5, causing "incredible damage." With wind speeds in excess of 261 miles per hour, these tornadoes can hurl houses very far.

Did You Know?

Although tornadoes can happen any time of the year, they are especially common during the spring and early summer. May and June are the peak months in terms of numbers, and April appears to be the deadliest month.

THUNDERSTORMS

Nearly 1,800 thunderstorms are happening at any moment around the world. That's 16 million a year!

You can estimate how many miles away a storm is by counting the number of seconds between the flash of lightning and the clap of thunder. Divide the number of seconds by five to get the distance in miles. The lightning is seen before the thunder is heard because light travels faster than sound.

Thunderstorms affect small areas when compared with hurricanes and winter storms. The typical thunderstorm is 15 miles in diameter and lasts an average of 30 minutes.

Thunderstorms need three things:
* Moisture—to form clouds and rain
* Unstable air—relatively warm air that can rise rapidly
* Lift—fronts, sea breezes and mountains that are capable of lifting air to help form thunderstorms

Safety Zone

During a thunderstorm, avoid open spaces, trees and ballparks. The safest place to be is in a building, preferably one with a lightning rod. The rod offers protection by intercepting lightning— an electrical discharge—and transmitting its current to the ground. The other safe place to be is in a car with the windows rolled up, as long as you don't touch any of the metal parts. Rubber-soled shoes and rubber tires provide NO protection from lightning.

LIGHTNING

The action of rising and descending air within a thunderstorm separates positive and negative electric charges. Water and ice particles also affect the distribution of electrical charge. Lightning results from the buildup and discharge of electrical energy between positively and negatively charged areas.

The average flash of lightning could turn on a 100-watt light bulb for more than three months. The air near a lightning strike is hotter than the surface of the Sun!

The rapid heating and cooling of air near the lightning channel causes a shock wave that results in thunder.

Did You Know?

Lightening *can* strike the same place twice! It has "favorite" sites that it may hit many times during one storm.

BLIZZARD BLITZ

A blizzard is a winter storm with high winds, low temperatures and driving snow. According to the U.S. Weather Bureau's official definition, the winds must exceed 35 miles (56 km) per hour and the temperature must drop to 20°F (-7°C) or lower.

The worst winter storm in U.S. history
The Blizzard of 1888 surprised the northeastern U.S. with as much as five feet of snow in some areas. Two hundred boats sank and more than 400 people died due to very powerful winds and frigid temperatures.

Greatest Snowfalls in North America

Duration	Place	Date	Inches
24 hours	Silver Lake, Colo.	April 14–15, 1921	76
1 month	Tamarack, Calif.	Jan. 1911	390
1 storm	Mt. Shasta Ski Bowl, Calif.	Feb. 13-19, 1959	189
1 season	Mount Baker, Wash.	1998-1999	1,140

Snow Kidding!

- Snow covers either permanently or temporarily about 23% of the Earth's surface.
- A falling snowflake can take up to about two hours to reach the ground.
- The heaviest snowflake falls at a speed of about one mile per hour.
- There are six types of snowflakes: needles, columns, plates, columns topped with plates, dendrites and stars.
- The type of snow crystal that forms depends on the humidity and temperature.
- Six-sided snowflakes occur only about 25% of the time—they usually break while falling.

Did You Know?

A snowflake usually starts out as a particle of dust. The dust absorbs water, which, when it freezes, forms the heart of a growing ice crystal.

EXTREMEs of Climate

Greatest Rainfalls

Duration/Place	Date	Inches	Centimeters
1 day, world: Foc-Foc, La Réunion (African island)	Jan. 7–8, 1966	72	182.5
1 day, U.S.: Alvin, Texas	July 25–26, 1979	43	109
1 year, world: Cherrapunji, India	Aug. 1860–Aug. 1861	1,042	2,647
1 year, U.S.: Kukui, Maui, Hawaii	Dec. 1981–Dec. 1982	739	1,878

Highest Recorded Temperatures

Place	Date	°F	°C
World: El Azizia, Libya, Africa	September 13, 1922	136	58
U.S.: Death Valley, California	July 10, 1913	134	57

Lowest Recorded Temperatures

Place	Date	°F	°C
World: Vostok, Antarctica	July 21, 1983	−129	−89
U.S.: Prospect Creek, Alaska	January 23, 1971	−80	−62

PUZZLES & GAMES

Weather or Not

Each sentence has a weather-related word hidden within it. Can you find the five words below that are buried in the sentences? We did one to get you started:

I spent a month undergoing tests.

Words: mist rain centigrade wind barometer

1. I wrote down the amount of thaw in degrees, as usual.
2. Handing in my weather report to him is trouble, but I must do it.
3. According to Reba, Rome terrifies some tourists.
4. I saw Sara inside the store.
5. Jim wants a raise. I wouldn't give him a cent. I grade his work an F!

(See Answer Key that begins on page 340.)

TFK MYSTERY PERSON

CLUE 1: Born in Sweden in 1859, I won a Nobel Prize in Chemistry in 1903 for my work in electrochemistry.
CLUE 2: Later, I said the burning of fossil fuels will increase the level of carbon dioxide in the air, which will cause Earth's temperature to rise.
CLUE 3: Many scientists now think that the greenhouse effect, which I predicted, is causing global warming.

WHO AM I?
(See Answer Key that begins on page 340.)

FATHER OF HIS COUNTRY

Interview with Nelson Mandela, winner of the 1993 Nobel Peace Prize

Nelson Mandela dedicated his life to the struggle for racial equality in South Africa. He spent 27 years in prison for opposing the South African system of segregating the white race from the black and other races called apartheid (a-par-tide). Mandela negotiated an end to apartheid in 1990, and in 1994 he became the country's first democratically elected president. He stepped down in 1999 at age 80. He won the Nobel Peace Prize in 1993.

Time For Kids caught up with Mandela at his home in Johannesburg.

TFK: What do children mean to you?

Mandela: Children are a treasure, the wealth of any country. They are the future leaders of society. But they must be given support. They must be given education. Their health must be looked after. Above all, they must be given love.

TFK: What is life like for children in South Africa?

Mandela: We have emerged from one of the most brutal systems of oppression ever seen. We were deprived of the opportunity to send our children to the best schools. Nevertheless, our people are caring for and looking after their children.

TFK: What work is your charity, the Nelson Mandela Children's Fund, doing?

Mandela: We're concentrating on raising the status of disabled children. I organized occasions to entertain disabled children. When parents see the president of the country sitting at a table with disabled children, they stop being ashamed of their own disabled children. They see that their children are human beings, but with disabilities that can be attended to.

TFK: What has kept you going throughout your long struggle?

Mandela: The support I have gotten from society is very encouraging. And the fact that I've got more to accomplish keeps me going.

Other Nobel Peace Prize Winners Who Have Changed the World

Jimmy Carter (2002), former U.S. president, won the award for his efforts to find peaceful solutions to international conflicts and for advancing democracy and human rights.

The United Nations and Kofi Annan (2001) The U.N. and its leader were honored for working to build a more just and peaceful world.

Mother Teresa (1979), Catholic nun, won the prize for helping the poorest of the world's poor in Calcutta, India, for 50 years.

The World's Nations from A to Z

On the following pages you will find information about the world's nations. Here's an example.

If you divide the population by the area, you can find out the population density—how many people there are per square mile.

This tells the main languages and the official languages (if any) spoken in a nation. In this case, most people in the nation speak English, and a smaller number speak Maori.

This is the type of money used in the nation.

New Zealand

Where?
Pacific Islands

Capital: Wellington

Area: 103,737 sq mi (268,680 sq km)

Population estimate (2003): 3,951,307

Government: Parliamentary democracy

Languages: English (official); a smaller number speak Maori

Monetary unit: New Zealand dollar

Per capita GDP: $19,500

Literacy rate: 99%

The per capita GDP is a way to estimate the wealth of a nation. It represents the value of all goods and services produced by a nation in one year, divided by that nation's population.

This tells the percentage of people who can read and write.

Afghanistan

Where? Asia
Capital: Kabul
Area: 251,737 sq mi (652,000 sq km)
Population estimate (2003): 28,717,213
Government: Multiparty republic
Languages: Pushtu, Dari Persian, other Turkic and minor languages
Monetary unit: Afghani
Per capita GDP: $800
Literacy rate: 29%

Albania

Where? Europe
Capital: Tiranë
Area: 11,100 sq mi (28,750 sq km)
Population estimate (2003): 3,582,205
Government: Emerging democracy
Languages: Albanian (Tosk is the official dialect), Greek
Monetary unit: Lek
Per capita GDP: $3,800
Literacy rate: 72%

Algeria

Where? Africa
Capital: Algiers
Area: 919,590 sq mi (2,381,740 sq km)
Population estimate (2003): 32,818,500
Government: Republic
Languages: Arabic (official), French, Berber dialects
Monetary unit: Dinar
Per capita GDP: $5,600
Literacy rate: 57%

Andorra

Where? Europe
Capital: Andorra la Vella
Area: 181 sq mi (468 sq km)
Population estimate (2003): 69,150
Government: Parliamentary democracy
Languages: Catalán (official), French, Spanish
Monetary units: French franc and Spanish peseta
Per capita GDP: $19,000
Literacy rate: 100%

Go Places with TFK! Take a country tour, hear the language, explore the history at *www.timeforkids.com/goplaces*

Angola

Where? Africa
Capital: Luanda
Area: 481,350 sq mi (1,246,700 sq km)
Population estimate (2003): 10,766,471
Government: Transitional, nominally a multiparty democracy
Languages: Bantu, Portuguese (official)
Monetary unit: Kwanza
Per capita GDP: $1,330
Literacy rate: 42%

Antigua and Barbuda

Where? North America
Capital: St. John's
Area: 171 sq mi (443 sq km)
Population estimate (2003): 67,897
Government: Constitutional monarchy
Language: English
Monetary unit: East Caribbean dollar
Per capita GDP: $10,000
Literacy rate: 89%

Argentina

Where? South America
Capital: Buenos Aires
Area: 1,068,296 sq mi (2,766,890 sq km)
Population estimate (2003): 38,740,807
Government: Republic
Languages: Spanish (official), English, Italian, German, French
Monetary unit: Peso
Per capita GDP: $12,000
Literacy rate: 96%

Armenia

Where? Asia
Capital: Yerevan
Area: 11,500 sq mi (29,800 sq km)
Population estimate (2003): 3,326,448
Government: Republic
Language: Armenian
Monetary unit: Dram
Per capita GDP: $3,350
Literacy rate: 99%

Australia

Where? Pacific Islands
Capital: Canberra
Area: 2,967,893 sq mi (7,686,850 sq km)
Population estimate (2003): 19,731,984
Government: Democratic
Language: English
Monetary unit: Australian dollar
Per capita GDP: $24,000
Literacy rate: 100%

Austria

Where? Europe
Capital: Vienna
Area: 32,375 sq mi (83,850 sq km)
Population estimate (2003): 8,188,207
Government: Federal republic
Language: German
Monetary unit: Euro (formerly schilling)
Per capita GDP: $27,000
Literacy rate: 99%

Azerbaijan

Where? Asia
Capital: Baku
Area: 33,400 sq mi (86,600 sq km)
Population estimate (2003): 7,830,764
Government: Republic
Languages: Azerbaijani Turkic, Russian, Armenian
Monetary unit: Manat
Per capita GDP: $3,100
Literacy rate: 97%

Bahamas

Where? North America
Capital: Nassau
Area: 5,380 sq mi (13,940 sq km)
Population estimate (2003): 297,477
Government: Constitutional parliamentary democracy
Language: English
Monetary unit: Bahamian dollar
Per capita GDP: $16,800
Literacy rate: 90%

Bahrain

Where? Asia
Capital: Manamah
Area: 257 sq mi (665 sq km)
Population estimate (2003): 667,238
Government: Constitutional monarchy
Languages: Arabic (official), English, Farsi, Urdu
Monetary unit: Bahrain dinar
Per capita GDP: $13,000
Literacy rate: 77%

Bangladesh

Where? Asia
Capital: Dhaka
Area: 55,598 sq mi (144,000 sq km)
Population estimate (2003): 138,448,210
Government: Parliamentary democracy
Languages: Bangla (official), English
Monetary unit: Taka
Per capita GDP: $1,750
Literacy rate: 36%

Barbados

Where? North America
Capital: Bridgetown
Area: 166 sq mi (431 sq km)
Population estimate (2003): 277,264
Government: Parliamentary democracy
Language: English
Monetary unit: Barbados dollar
Per capita GDP: $14,500
Literacy rate: 99%

Belarus

Where? Europe
Capital: Minsk
Area: 80,154 sq mi (207,600 sq km)
Population estimate (2003): 10,322,151
Government: Republic
Language: Belarussian
Monetary unit: Belarussian ruble
Per capita GDP: $8,200
Literacy rate: 100%

Belgium

Where? Europe
Capital: Brussels
Area: 11,781 sq mi (30,510 sq km)
Population estimate (2003): 10,289,088
Government: Federal parliamentary democracy under a constitutional monarch
Languages: Dutch (Flemish), French, German (all official)
Monetary unit: Euro (formerly Belgian franc)
Per capita GDP: $26,100
Literacy rate: 99%

Belize

Where? Central America
Capital: Belmopan
Area: 8,865 sq mi (22,960 sq km)
Population estimate (2003): 266,440
Government: Parliamentary democracy
Languages: English (official), Creole, Spanish, Garifuna, Mayan
Monetary unit: Belize dollar
Per capita GDP: $3,250
Literacy rate: 91%

Benin

Where? Africa
Capital: Porto-Novo (official)
Area: 43,483 sq mi (112,620 sq km)
Population estimate (2003): 7,041,490
Government: Republic under multiparty democratic rule
Languages: French (official), African languages
Monetary unit: CFA franc
Per capita GDP: $1,040
Literacy rate: 23%

Bhutan

Where? Asia
Capital: Thimphu
Area: 18,147 sq mi (47,000 sq km)
Population estimate (2003): 2,139,549
Government: Monarchy
Language: Dzongkha
Monetary unit: Ngultrum
Per capita GDP: $1,200
Literacy rate: 42%

Bolivia

Where? South America
Capital: Sucre
Area: 424,162 sq mi (1,098,580 sq km)
Population estimate (2003): 8,586,443
Government: Republic
Languages: Spanish (official), Quechua, Aymara, Guarani
Monetary unit: Boliviano
Per capita GDP: $2,600
Literacy rate: 82%

Bosnia and Herzegovina

Where? Europe
Capital: Sarajevo
Area: 19,741 sq mi (51,129 sq km)
Population estimate (2003): 3,989,018
Government: Emerging democracy
Languages: The language is called Serbian, Croatian or Bosnian depending on the speaker.
Monetary unit: Dinar
Per capita GDP: $1,800
Literacy rate: NA

Botswana

Where? Africa
Capital: Gaborone
Area: 231,800 sq mi (600,370 sq km)
Population estimate (2003): 1,573,267
Government: Parliamentary republic
Languages: English (official), Setswana
Monetary unit: Pula
Per capita GDP: $7,800
Literacy rate: 69%

Brazil

Where? South America
Capital: Brasília
Area: 3,286,470 sq mi (8,511,965 sq km)
Population estimate (2003): 182,032,604
Government: Federative republic
Language: Portuguese
Monetary unit: Real
Per capita GDP: $7,400
Literacy rate: 81%

Brunei

Where? Asia
Capital: Bandar Seri Begawan
Area: 2,228 sq mi (5,770 sq km)
Population estimate (2003): 358,098
Government: Constitutional sultanate
Languages: Malay (official), Chinese, English
Monetary unit: Brunei dollar
Per capita GDP: $18,000
Literacy rate: 80%

Bulgaria

Where? Europe
Capital: Sofia
Area: 48,822 sq mi (110,910 sq km)
Population estimate (2003): 7,537,929
Government: Parliamentary democracy
Language: Bulgarian
Monetary unit: Lev
Per capita GDP: $6,200
Literacy rate: 93%

Burkina Faso

Where? Africa
Capital: Ouagadougou
Area: 105,870 sq mi (274,200 sq km)
Population estimate (2003): 13,228,460
Government: Parliamentary
Languages: French (official), tribal languages
Monetary unit: CFA franc
Per capita GDP: $1,040
Literacy rate: 18%

Burundi

Where? Africa
Capital: Bujumbura
Area: 10,745 sq mi (27,830 sq km)
Population estimate (2003): 6,096,156
Government: Republic
Languages: Kirundi and French (both official), Swahili
Monetary unit: Burundi franc
Per capita GDP: $600
Literacy rate: 41%

Cambodia

Where? Asia
Capital: Phnom Penh
Area: 69,900 sq mi (181,040 sq km)
Population estimate (2003): 13,124,764
Government: Multiparty liberal democracy under a constitutional monarchy
Languages: Khmer (official), French, English
Monetary unit: Riel
Per capita GDP: $1,500
Literacy rate: 69%

Cameroon

Where? Africa
Capital: Yaoundé
Area: 183,567 sq mi (475,440 sq km)
Population estimate (2003): 15,746,179
Government: Unitary republic
Languages: French and English (both official), African languages
Monetary unit: CFA franc
Per capita GDP: $1,700
Literacy rate: 54%

Canada

Where? North America
Capital: Ottawa, Ontario
Area: 3,851,788 sq mi (9,976,140 sq km)
Population estimate (2003): 32,207,113
Government: Confederation with parliamentary democracy
Languages: English and French (both official)
Monetary unit: Canadian dollar
Per capita GDP: $27,700
Literacy rate: 96%

Cape Verde

Where? Africa
Capital: Praia
Area: 1,557 sq mi (4,033 sq km)
Population estimate (2003): 412,137
Government: Republic
Languages: Portuguese, Crioulo
Monetary unit: Cape Verdean escudo
Per capita GDP: $1,500
Literacy rate: 67%

Central African Republic

Where? Africa
Capital: Bangui
Area: 240,534 sq mi (622,984 sq km)
Population estimate (2003): 3,683,538
Government: Republic
Languages: French (official), Sangho, Arabic, Hansa, Swahili
Monetary unit: CFA franc
Per capita GDP: $1,300
Literacy rate: 38%

Chad

Where? Africa
Capital: N'Djamena
Area: 495,752 sq mi (1,284,000 sq km)
Population estimate (2003): 9,253,493
Government: Republic
Languages: French (official), Sangho, Arabic, Hansa, Swahili
Monetary unit: CFA franc
Per capita GDP: $1,030
Literacy rate: 40%

Chile

Where?
South America
Capital: Santiago
Area: 292,258 sq mi (756,950 sq km)
Population estimate (2003): 15,665,216
Government: Republic
Language: Spanish
Monetary unit: Peso
Per capita GDP: $10,000
Literacy rate: 95%

China

Where? Asia
Capital: Beijing
Area: 3,705,386 sq mi (9,596,960 sq km)
Population estimate (2003): 1,286,975,468
Government: Communist state
Languages: Chinese (Mandarin), local dialects
Monetary unit: Yuan
Per capita GDP: $4,300
Literacy rate: 84%

Colombia

Where? South America
Capital: Bogotá
Area: 439,733 sq mi (1,138,910 sq km)
Population estimate (2003): 41,662,073
Government: Republic
Language: Spanish
Monetary unit: Peso
Per capita GDP: $6,300
Literacy rate: 87%

Comoros

Where? Africa
Capital: Moroni
Area: 838 sq mi (2,170 sq km)
Population estimate (2003): 632,948
Government: Independent republic
Languages: French and Arabic (both official), Shaafi Islam (Swahili dialect), Malagasu
Monetary unit: CFA franc
Per capita GDP: $710
Literacy rate: 48%

Congo, Democratic Republic of the

Where? Africa
Capital: Kinshasa
Area: 905,562 sq mi (2,345,410 sq km)
Population estimate (2003): 56,625,039
Government: Dictatorship
Languages: French (official), Swahili, Lingala, Ishiluba, Kikongo, others
Monetary unit: Congolese franc
Per capita GDP: $590
Literacy rate: 72%

Congo, Republic of the

Where? Africa
Capital: Brazzaville
Area: 132,046 sq mi (342,000 sq km)
Population estimate (2003): 2,954,258
Government: Dictatorship
Languages: French (official), Lingala, Kikongo, others
Monetary unit: CFA franc
Per capita GDP: $900
Literacy rate: 57%

Costa Rica

Where? Central America
Capital: San José
Area: 19,730 sq mi (51,100 sq km)
Population estimate (2003): 3,896,092
Government: Democratic republic
Language: Spanish
Monetary unit: Colón
Per capita GDP: $8,500
Literacy rate: 93%

Côte d'Ivoire

Where? Africa
Capital: Yamoussoukro
Area: 124,502 sq mi (322,460 sq km)
Population estimate (2003): 16,962,491
Government: Republic
Languages: French (official), African languages
Monetary unit: CFA franc
Per capita GDP: $1,550
Literacy rate: 54%

Croatia

Where? Europe
Capital: Zagreb
Area: 21,829 sq mi (56,538 sq km)
Population estimate (2003): 4,422,248
Government: Presidential/parliamentary democracy
Language: Croatian
Monetary unit: Kuna
Per capita GDP: $8,300
Literacy rate: 97%

Cuba

Where? North America
Capital: Havana
Area: 42,803 sq mi (110,860 sq km)
Population estimate (2003): 11,263,429
Government: Communist state
Language: Spanish
Monetary unit: Peso
Per capita GDP: $2,300
Literacy rate: 94%

Cyprus

Where? Middle East
Capital: Lefkosia (Nicosia)
Area: 3,572 sq mi (9,250 sq km)
Population estimate (2003): 771,657
Government: Republic
Languages: Greek, Turkish
Monetary unit: Cyprus pound
Per capita GDP: Greek Cypriot area: $15,000; Turkish Cypriot area: $7,000
Literacy rate: 94%

Czech Republic

Where? Europe
Capital: Prague
Area: 30,450 sq mi (78,866 sq km)
Population estimate (2003): 10,249,216
Government: Parliamentary democracy
Language: Czech
Monetary unit: Koruna
Per capita GDP: $14,400
Literacy rate: 99%

Denmark

Where? Europe
Capital: Copenhagen
Area: 16,639 sq mi (43,094 sq km)
Population estimate (2003): 5,384,384
Government: Constitutional monarchy
Languages: Danish, Faeroese, Greenlandic, German
Monetary unit: Krone
Per capita GDP: $28,000
Literacy rate: 99%

Djibouti

Where? Africa
Capital: Djibouti
Area: 8,800 sq mi (23,000 sq km)
Population estimate (2003): 457,130
Government: Republic
Languages: Arabic and French (both official), Afar, Somali
Monetary unit: Djibouti franc
Per capita GDP: $1,400
Literacy rate: 46%

Dominica

Where? North America
Capital: Roseau
Area: 290 sq mi (750 sq km)
Population estimate (2003): 69,655
Government: Parliamentary democracy
Languages: English (official), French patois
Monetary unit: East Caribbean dollar
Per capita GDP: $3,700
Literacy rate: 94%

Dominican Republic

Where? North America
Capital: Santo Domingo
Area: 18,815 sq mi (48,730 sq km)
Population estimate (2003): 8,715,602
Government: Representative democracy
Languages: Spanish, English
Monetary unit: Peso
Per capita GDP: $5,800
Literacy rate: 84%

East Timor

Where? Asia
Capital: Dili
Area: 5,814 sq mi (15,057 sq km)
Population estimate (2003): 997,853
Government: Republic
Languages: Tetum, Portuguese (official), Bahasa Indonesia, English
Monetary unit: U.S. dollar
Per capita GDP: $500
Literacy rate: 48%

Ecuador

Where? South America
Capital: Quito
Area: 109,483 sq mi (283,560 sq km)
Population estimate (2003): 13,710,234
Government: Republic
Languages: Spanish (official), Quechua
Monetary unit: U.S. dollar
Per capita GDP: $3,000
Literacy rate: 90%

Egypt

Where? Africa
Capital: Cairo
Area: 386,660 sq mi (1,001,450 sq km)
Population estimate (2003): 74,718,797
Government: Republic
Language: Arabic
Monetary unit: Egyptian pound
Per capita GDP: $3,700
Literacy rate: 48%

El Salvador

Where? Central America
Capital: San Salvador
Area: 8,124 sq mi (21,040 sq km)
Population estimate (2003): 6,470,379
Government: Republic
Language: Spanish
Monetary unit: Colón
Per capita GDP: $4,600
Literacy rate: 73%

Equatorial Guinea

Where? Africa
Capital: Malabo
Area: 10,830 sq mi (28,050 sq km)
Population estimate (2003): 510,473
Government: Republic
Languages: Spanish (official), French (second official), pidgin English, Fang, Bubi, Creole
Monetary unit: CFA franc
Per capita GDP: $2,100
Literacy rate: 50%

Eritrea

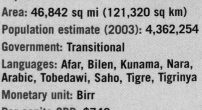

Where? Africa
Capital: Asmara
Area: 46,842 sq mi (121,320 sq km)
Population estimate (2003): 4,362,254
Government: Transitional
Languages: Afar, Bilen, Kunama, Nara, Arabic, Tobedawi, Saho, Tigre, Tigrinya
Monetary unit: Birr
Per capita GDP: $740
Literacy rate: 20%

Estonia

Where? Europe
Capital: Tallinn
Area: 17,462 sq mi (45,226 sq km)
Population estimate (2003): 1,408,556
Government: Parliamentary democracy
Languages: Estonian (official), Russian, Finnish, English
Monetary unit: Kroon
Per capita GDP: $10,000
Literacy rate: 100%

Ethiopia

Where? Africa
Capital: Addis Ababa
Area: 485,184 sq mi (1,127,127 sq km)
Population estimate (2003): 66,557,553
Government: Federal republic
Languages: Amharic (official), English, Orominga, Tigrigna, others
Monetary unit: Birr
Per capita GDP: $700
Literacy rate: 28%

Fiji

Where? Oceania
Capital: Suva
Area: 7,054 sq mi (18,270 sq km)
Population estimate (2003): 868,531
Government: Republic
Languages: Fijian, Hindustani, English (official)
Monetary unit: Fiji dollar
Per capita GDP: $5,200
Literacy rate: 79%

Finland

Where? Europe
Capital: Helsinki
Area: 130,127 sq mi (337,030 sq km)
Population estimate (2003): 5,190,785
Government: Republic
Languages: Finnish and Swedish (both official)
Monetary unit: Euro (formerly markka)
Per capita GDP: $25,800
Literacy rate: 100%

France

Where? Europe
Capital: Paris
Area: 211,208 sq mi (547,030 sq km)
Population estimate (2003): 60,180,529
Government: Republic
Language: French
Monetary unit: Euro (formerly French franc)
Per capita GDP: $25,400
Literacy rate: 99%

Gabon

Where? Africa
Capital: Libreville
Area: 103,347 sq mi (267,670 sq km)
Population estimate (2003): 1,321,560
Government: Republic
Languages: French (official), Fang, Myene, Bateke, Bapounou/Eschira, Bandjabi
Monetary unit: CFA franc
Per capita GDP: $5,500
Literacy rate: 61%

The Gambia

Where? Africa
Capital: Banjul
Area: 4,363 sq mi (11,300 sq km)
Population estimate (2003): 1,501,050
Government: Republic
Languages: English (official), native tongues
Monetary unit: Dalasi
Per capita GDP: $1,770
Literacy rate: 27%

Georgia

Where? Asia
Capital: T'bilisi
Area: 26,911 sq mi (69,700 sq km)
Population estimate (2003): 4,934,413
Government: Republic
Languages: Georgian (official), Russian, Armenian, Azerbaijani
Monetary unit: Lari
Per capita GDP: $3,100
Literacy rate: 99%

Germany

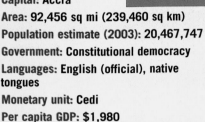

Where? Europe
Capital: Berlin
Area: 137,846 sq mi (357,021 sq km)
Population estimate (2003): 82,398,326
Government: Federal republic
Language: German
Monetary unit: Euro (formerly Deutsche mark)
Per capita GDP: $26,200
Literacy rate: 99%

Ghana

Where? Africa
Capital: Accra
Area: 92,456 sq mi (239,460 sq km)
Population estimate (2003): 20,467,747
Government: Constitutional democracy
Languages: English (official), native tongues
Monetary unit: Cedi
Per capita GDP: $1,980
Literacy rate: 60%

Greece

Where? Europe
Capital: Athens
Area: 50,942 sq mi (131,940 sq km)
Population estimate (2003): 10,665,989
Government: Parliamentary republic
Language: Greek
Monetary unit: Euro (formerly drachma)
Per capita GDP: $17,900
Literacy rate: 93%

Grenada

Where? North America
Capital: Saint George's
Area: 133 sq mi (344 sq km)
Population estimate (2003): 89,258
Government: Constitutional monarchy
Language: English
Monetary unit: East Caribbean dollar
Per capita GDP: $4,750
Literacy rate: 98%

Guatemala

Where? Central America
Capital: Guatemala City
Area: 42,042 sq mi (108,890 sq km)
Population estimate (2003): 13,909,384
Government: Constitutional democratic republic
Languages: Spanish (official), Indian languages
Monetary unit: Quetzal
Per capita GDP: $3,700
Literacy rate: 55%

Guinea

Where? Africa
Capital: Conakry
Area: 94,925 sq mi (245,860 sq km)
Population estimate (2003): 9,030,220
Government: Republic
Languages: French (official), native tongues
Monetary unit: Guinean franc
Per capita GDP: $1,970
Literacy rate: 24% in French; 48% in local languages

Guinea-Bissau

Where? Africa
Capital: Bissau
Area: 13,946 sq mi (36,120 sq km)
Population estimate (2003): 1,360,827
Government: Republic
Languages: Portuguese (official), African languages
Monetary unit: Guinea-Bissau peso
Per capita GDP: $900
Literacy rate: 37%

Guyana

Where? South America
Capital: Georgetown
Area: 83,000 sq mi (214,970 sq km)
Population estimate (2003): 702,100
Government: Republic
Languages: English (official), Amerindian dialects
Monetary unit: Guyana dollar
Per capita GDP: $3,600
Literacy rate: 96%

Haiti

Where? North America
Capital: Port-au-Prince
Area: 10,714 sq mi (27,750 sq km)
Population estimate (2003): 7,527,817
Government: Elected government
Languages: Creole and French (both official)
Monetary unit: Gourde
Per capita GDP: $1,700
Literacy rate: 53%

Honduras

Where? Central America
Capital: Tegucigalpa
Area: 43,278 sq mi (112,090 sq km)
Population estimate (2003): 6,669,789
Government: Democratic constitutional republic
Languages: Spanish, Amerindian dialects
Monetary unit: Lempira
Per capita GDP: $2,600
Literacy rate: 73%

Hungary

Where? Europe
Capital: Budapest
Area: 35,919 sq mi (93,030 sq km)
Population estimate (2003): 10,045,407
Government: Parliamentary democracy
Language: Magyar (Hungarian)
Monetary unit: Forint
Per capita GDP: $12,000
Literacy rate: 98%

Iceland

Where? Europe
Capital: Reykjavik
Area: 39,768 sq mi (103,000 sq km)
Population estimate (2003): 280,798
Government: Constitutional republic
Language: Icelandic
Monetary unit: Icelandic króna
Per capita GDP: $24,800
Literacy rate: 100%

Go Places with TFK! Take a country tour, hear the language, explore the history at *www.timeforkids.com/goplaces*

India

Where? Asia
Capital: Delhi
Area: 1,269,338 sq mi (3,287,590 sq km)
Population estimate (2003): 1,049,700,118
Government: Federal republic
Languages: Hindi (national), English; 24 major languages plus more than 1,600 dialects
Monetary unit: Rupee
Per capita GDP: $2,500
Literacy rate: 52%

Indonesia

Where? Asia
Capital: Jakarta
Area: 741,096 sq mi (1,919,440 sq km)
Population estimate (2003): 234,893,4531
Government: Republic
Languages: Bahasa Indonesia (official), Dutch, English; more than 500 languages and dialects
Monetary unit: Rupiah
Per capita GDP: $3,000
Literacy rate: 84%

Iran

Where? Middle East
Capital: Tehran
Area: 636,293 sq mi (1,648,000 sq km)
Population estimate (2003): 68,278,826
Government: Theocratic republic
Languages: Farsi (Persian), Azari, Kurdish, Arabic
Monetary unit: Rial
Per capita GDP: $6,400
Literacy rate: 54%

Iraq

Where? Middle East
Capital: Baghdad
Area: 168,753 sq mi (437,072 sq km)
Population estimate (2003): 24,683,313
Government: Republic
Languages: Arabic, Kurdish
Monetary unit: Iraqi dinar
Per capita GDP: $2,500
Literacy rate: 60%

Ireland

Where? Europe
Capital: Dublin
Area: 27,136 sq mi (70,280 sq km)
Population estimate (2003): 3,924,140
Government: Republic
Languages: English, Irish Gaelic
Monetary units: Euro (formerly Irish pound [punt])
Per capita GDP: $27,300
Literacy rate: 98%

Israel

Where? Middle East
Capital: Jerusalem
Area: 8,020 sq mi (20,770 sq km)
Population estimate (2003): 6,116,533
Government: Parliamentary democracy
Languages: Hebrew (official), Arabic, English
Monetary unit: Shekel
Per capita GDP: $20,000
Literacy rate: 92%

Italy

Where? Europe
Capital: Rome
Area: 116,305 sq mi (301,230 sq km)
Population estimate (2003): 57,998,353
Government: Republic
Language: Italian
Monetary unit: Euro (formerly lira)
Per capita GDP: $24,300
Literacy rate: 97%

Jamaica

Where? North America
Capital: Kingston
Area: 4,244 sq mi (10,991 sq km)
Population estimate (2003): 2,695,867
Government: Constitutional parliamentary democracy
Languages: English, Jamaican Creole
Monetary unit: Jamaican dollar
Per capita GDP: $3,700
Literacy rate: 98%

Japan

Where? Asia
Capital: Tokyo
Area: 145,882 sq mi (377,835 sq km)
Population estimate (2003): 127,214,499
Government: Constitutional monarchy with a parliamentary government
Language: Japanese
Monetary unit: Yen
Per capita GDP: $27,200
Literacy rate: 99%

Jordan

Where? Middle East
Capital: Amman
Area: 34,445 sq mi (89,213 sq km)
Population estimate (2003): 5,460,265
Government: Constitutional monarchy
Languages: Arabic (official), English
Monetary unit: Jordanian dinar
Per capita GDP: $4,200
Literacy rate: 86%

Kazakhstan

Where? Asia
Capital: Astana
Area: 1,049,150 sq mi (2,717,300 sq km)
Population estimate (2003): 16,763,795
Government: Republic
Languages: Kazak (Qazaq) and Russian (both official)
Monetary unit: Tenge
Per capita GDP: $5,900
Literacy rate: 98%

Kenya

Where? Africa
Capital: Nairobi
Area: 224,960 sq mi (582,650 sq km)
Population estimate (2003): 31,639,091
Government: Republic
Languages: English (official), Swahili, several others
Monetary unit: Kenyan shilling
Per capita GDP: $1,000
Literacy rate: 69%

Kiribati

Where? Pacific Islands
Capital: Tarawa
Area: 313 sq mi (811 sq km)
Population estimate (2003): 98,549
Government: Republic
Languages: English (official), I-Kiribati (Gilbertese)
Monetary unit: Australian dollar
Per capita GDP: $840
Literacy rate: 90%

Korea, North

Where? Asia
Capital: Pyongyang
Area: 46,540 sq mi (120,540 sq km)
Population estimate (2003): 22,466,481
Government: Authoritarian socialist; one-man dictatorship
Language: Korean
Monetary unit: Won
Per capita GDP: $1,000
Literacy rate: 100%

Korea, South

Where? Asia
Capital: Seoul
Area: 38,023 sq mi (98,480 sq km)
Population estimate (2003): 48,289,037
Government: Republic
Language: Korean
Monetary unit: Won
Per capita GDP: $18,000
Literacy rate: 98%

Kuwait

Where? Middle East
Capital: Kuwait
Area: 6,880 sq mi (17,820 sq km)
Population estimate (2003): 2,183,161
Government: Nominal constitutional monarchy
Languages: Arabic (official), English
Monetary unit: Kuwaiti dinar
Per capita GDP: $15,100
Literacy rate: 73%

Kyrgyzstan

Where? Asia
Capital: Bishkek
Area: 76,641 sq mi (198,500 sq km)
Population estimate (2003): 4,892,808
Government: Republic
Languages: Kyrgyz (official), Russian
Monetary unit: Som
Per capita GDP: $2,800
Literacy rate: 97%

Laos

Where? Asia
Capital: Vientiane
Area: 91,429 sq mi (236,800 sq km)
Population estimate (2003): 5,921,545
Government: Communist state
Languages: Lao (official), French, English
Monetary unit: Kip
Per capita GDP: $1,630
Literacy rate: 45%

Latvia

Where? Europe
Capital: Riga
Area: 24,938 sq mi (64,589 sq km)
Population estimate (2003): 2,348,784
Government: Parliamentary democracy
Language: Latvian
Monetary unit: Lats
Per capita GDP: $7,800
Literacy rate: 99%

Lebanon

Where? Middle East
Capital: Beirut
Area: 4,015 sq mi (10,400 sq km)
Population estimate (2003): 3,727,703
Government: Republic
Languages: Arabic (official), French, English
Monetary unit: Lebanese pound
Per capita GDP: $5,200
Literacy rate: 80%

Lesotho

Where? Africa
Capital: Maseru
Area: 11,720 sq mi (30,350 sq km)
Population estimate (2003): 1,861,959
Government: Parliamentary constitutional monarchy
Languages: English and Sesotho (both official), Zulu, Xhosa
Monetary unit: Loti
Per capita GDP: $2,450
Literacy rate: 56%

Liberia

Where? Africa
Capital: Monrovia
Area: 43,000 sq mi (111,370 sq km)
Population estimate (2003): 3,317,176
Government: Republic
Languages: English (official), tribal dialects
Monetary unit: Liberian dollar
Per capita GDP: $1,100
Literacy rate: 40%

Libya

Where? Africa
Capital: Tripoli
Area: 679,358 sq mi (1,759,540 sq km)
Population estimate (2003): 5,499,074
Government: Military dictatorship
Languages: Arabic, Italian, English
Monetary unit: Libyan dinar
Per capita GDP: $7,600
Literacy rate: 64%

Liechtenstein

Where? Europe
Capital: Vaduz
Area: 62 sq mi (160 sq km)
Population estimate (2003): 33,145
Government: Hereditary constitutional monarchy
Languages: German (official), Alemmanic dialect
Monetary unit: Swiss franc
Per capita GDP: $23,000
Literacy rate: 100%

Lithuania

Where? Europe
Capital: Vilnius
Area: 25,174 sq mi (65,200 sq km)
Population estimate (2003): 3,592,561
Government: Parliamentary democracy
Languages: Lithuanian (official), Polish, Russian
Monetary unit: Litas
Per capita GDP: $7,600
Literacy rate: 98%

Luxembourg

Where? Europe
Capital: Luxembourg
Area: 999 sq mi (2,586 sq km)
Population estimate (2003): 454,157
Government: Constitutional monarchy
Languages: Luxembourgian, French, German
Monetary unit: Euro (formerly Luxembourg franc)
Per capita GDP: $43,400
Literacy rate: 100%

Macedonia

Where? Europe
Capital: Skopje
Area: 9,781 sq mi (25,333 sq km)
Population estimate (2003): 2,063,122
Government: Emerging democracy
Languages: Macedonian, Albanian
Monetary unit: Denar
Per capita GDP: $4,400
Literacy rate: NA

Madagascar

Where? Africa
Capital: Antananarivo
Area: 226,660 sq mi (587,040 sq km)
Population estimate (2003): 16,979,744
Government: Republic
Languages: Malagasy and French (both official)
Monetary unit: Malagasy franc
Per capita GDP: $870
Literacy rate: 80%

Malawi

Where? Africa
Capital: Lilongwe
Area: 45,745 sq mi (118,480 sq km)
Population estimate (2003): 11,651,239
Government: Multiparty democracy
Languages: English and Chichewa (both official)
Monetary unit: Kwacha
Per capita GDP: $660
Literacy rate: 49%

Malaysia

Where? Asia
Capital: Kuala Lumpur
Area: 127,316 sq mi (329,750 sq km)
Population estimate (2003): 23,092,940
Government: Constitutional monarchy
Languages: Malay (official), Chinese, Tamil, English
Monetary unit: Ringgit
Per capita GDP: $9,000
Literacy rate: 78%

Maldives

Where? Asia
Capital: Malé
Area: 116 sq mi (300 sq km)
Population estimate (2003): 329,684
Government: Republic
Languages: Dhivehi (official), Arabic, Hindi, English
Monetary unit: Maldivian rufiyaa
Per capita GDP: $3,870
Literacy rate: 91%

Mali

Where? Africa
Capital: Bamako
Area: 478,764 sq mi (1,240,000 sq km)
Population estimate (2003): 11,626,219
Government: Republic
Languages: French (official), African languages
Monetary unit: CFA franc
Per capita GDP: $840
Literacy rate: 32%

Malta

Where? Europe
Capital: Valletta
Area: 122 sq mi (316 sq km)
Population estimate (2003): 400,420
Government: Republic
Languages: Maltese and English (both official)
Monetary unit: Maltese lira
Per capita GDP: $15,000
Literacy rate: 88%

Marshall Islands

Where? Pacific Islands
Capital: Majuro
Area: 70 sq mi (181.3 sq km)
Population estimate (2002): 73,630
Government: Constitutional government
Languages: Marshallese and English (both official)
Monetary unit: U.S. dollar
Per capita GDP: $1,600
Literacy rate: 91%

Mauritania

Where? Africa
Capital: Nouakchott
Area: 397,953 sq mi (1,030,700 sq km)
Population estimate (2003): 2,912,584
Government: Republic
Languages: Arabic (official), French
Monetary unit: Ouguiya
Per capita GDP: $1,800
Literacy rate: 34%

Mauritius

Where? Africa
Capital: Port Louis
Area: 788 sq mi (2,040 sq km)
Population estimate (2003): 1,210,447
Government: Parliamentary democracy
Languages: English (official), French, Creole, Hindi, Urdu, Hakka, Bojpoori
Monetary unit: Mauritian rupee
Per capita GDP: $10,800
Literacy rate: 81%

Mexico

Where? North America
Capital: Mexico City
Area: 761,600 sq mi (1,972,550 sq km)
Population estimate (2003): 104,907,991
Government: Federal republic
Languages: Spanish, Indian languages
Monetary unit: Peso
Per capita GDP: $9,000
Literacy rate: 87%

Micronesia

Where? Pacific Islands
Capital: Palikir
Area: 271 sq mi (702 sq km)
Population estimate (2003): 136,973
Government: Constitutional government
Languages: English (official), native languages
Monetary unit: U.S. dollar
Per capita GDP: $2,000
Literacy rate: 85%

Moldova

Where? Europe
Capital: Chisinau
Area: 13,067 sq mi (33,843 sq km)
Population estimate (2003): 4,439,502
Government: Republic
Languages: Moldovan (official), Russian, Gagauz
Monetary unit: Moldovan lem
Per capita GDP: $2,550
Literacy rate: 97%

Monaco

Where? Europe
Capital: Monaco
Area: 0.75 sq mi (1.95 sq km)
Population estimate (2003): 32,130
Government: Constitutional monarchy
Languages: French (official), English, Italian, Monégasque
Monetary unit: French franc
Per capita GDP: $27,000
Literacy rate: 99%

Mongolia

Where? Asia
Capital: Ulaan Baatar
Area: 604,250 sq mi (1,565,000 sq km)
Population estimate (2003): 2,712,315
Government: Parliamentary republic
Languages: Mongolian (official), Turkic, Russian, Chinese
Monetary unit: Tugrik
Per capita GDP: $1,770
Literacy rate: 97%

Morocco

Where? Africa
Capital: Rabat
Area: 172,413 sq mi (446,550 sq km)
Population estimate (2003): 31,689,265
Government: Constitutional monarchy
Languages: Arabic (official), French, Berber dialects, Spanish
Monetary unit: Dirham
Per capita GDP: $3,700
Literacy rate: 50%

Mozambique

Where? Africa
Capital: Maputo
Area: 309,494 sq mi (801,590 sq km)
Population estimate (2003): 17,479,266
Government: Republic
Languages: Portuguese (official), Bantu languages
Monetary unit: Metical
Per capita GDP: $900
Literacy rate: 33%

Myanmar (Burma)

Where? Asia
Capital: Rangoon
Area: 261,969 sq mi (678,500 sq km)
Population estimate (2003): 42,510,537
Government: Military regime
Languages: Burmese, minority languages
Monetary unit: Kyat
Per capita GDP: $1,500
Literacy rate: 81%

Namibia

Where? Africa
Capital: Windhoek
Area: 318,694 sq mi (825,418 sq km)
Population estimate (2003): 1,927,447
Government: Republic
Languages: Afrikaans, German, English (official), native languages
Monetary unit: Namibian dollar
Per capita GDP: $4,500
Literacy rate: 38%

Nauru

Where? Pacific Islands
Capital: Yaren District (unofficial)
Area: 8.2 sq mi (21 sq km)
Population estimate (2003): 12,570
Government: Republic
Languages: Nauruan (official), English
Monetary unit: Australian dollar
Per capita GDP: $5,000
Literacy rate: 99%

Nepal

Where? Asia
Capital: Kathmandu
Area: 54,363 sq mi (140,800 sq km)
Population estimate (2003): 26,469,569
Government: Parliamentary democracy and constitutional monarchy
Languages: Nepali (official), Newari, Bhutia, Maithali
Monetary unit: Nepalese rupee
Per capita GDP: $1,400
Literacy rate: 38%

The Netherlands

Where? Europe
Capital: Amsterdam
Area: 16,036 sq mi (41,532 sq km)
Population estimate (2003): 16,150,511
Government: Constitutional monarchy
Language: Dutch
Monetary unit: Euro (formerly guilder)
Per capita GDP: $25,800
Literacy rate: 99%

New Zealand

Where?
Pacific Islands
Capital: Wellington
Area: 103,737 sq mi (268,680 sq km)
Population estimate (2003): 3,951,307
Government: Parliamentary democracy
Languages: English (official), Maori
Monetary unit: New Zealand dollar
Per capita GDP: $19,500
Literacy rate: 99%

Nicaragua

Where?
Central America
Capital: Managua
Area: 49,998 sq mi (129,494 sq km)
Population estimate (2003): 5,128,517
Government: Republic
Language: Spanish
Monetary unit: Cordoba
Per capita GDP: $2,500
Literacy rate: 57%

Niger

Where? Africa
Capital: Niamey
Area: 489,189 sq mi (1,267,000 sq km)
Population estimate (2003): 11,058,590
Government: Republic
Languages: French (official), Hausa,
Songhai, Arabic
Monetary unit: CFA franc
Per capita GDP: $820
Literacy rate: 28%

Nigeria

Where? Africa
Capital: Abuja
Area: 356,700 sq mi (923,770 sq km)
Population estimate (2003): 133,881,703
Government: Republic transitioning from
military to civilian rule
Languages: English (official), Hausa,
Yoruba, Ibo, more than 200 others
Monetary unit: Naira
Per capita GDP: $840
Literacy rate: 51%

Norway

Where? Europe
Capital: Oslo
Area: 125,181 sq mi (324,220 sq km)
Population estimate (2003): 4,546,123
Government: Constitutional monarchy
Languages: Two official forms of
Norwegian, Bokmål and Nynorsk
Monetary unit: Krone
Per capita GDP: $30,800
Literacy rate: 99%

Oman

Where? Middle East
Capital: Muscat
Area: 82,030 sq mi (212,460 sq km)
Population estimate (2003): 2,807,125
Government: Monarchy
Languages: Arabic (official), English,
Indian languages
Monetary unit: Omani rial
Per capita GDP: $8,200
Literacy rate: 80%

Pakistan

Where? Asia
Capital: Islamabad
Area: 310,400 sq mi (803,940 sq km)
Population estimate (2003): 150,694,740
Government: Federal republic
Languages: Punjabi, Sindhi, Siraiki, Pashtu, Urdu (official), others
Monetary unit: Pakistan rupee
Per capita GDP: $2,100
Literacy rate: 35%

Palau

Where? Pacific Islands
Capital: Koror
Area: 177 sq mi (458 sq km)
Population estimate (2003): 19,717
Government: Constitutional government
Languages: Palauan, English (official)
Monetary unit: U.S. dollar
Per capita GDP: $9,000
Literacy rate: 86%

Panama

Where? Central America
Capital: Panama City
Area: 30,193 sq mi (78,200 sq km)
Population estimate (2003): 2,960,784
Government: Constitutional democracy
Languages: Spanish (official), English
Monetary unit: Balboa
Per capita GDP: $5,900
Literacy rate: 89%

Papua New Guinea

Where? Pacific Islands
Capital: Port Moresby
Area: 178,703 sq mi (462,840 sq km)
Population estimate (2003): 5,295,816
Government: Constitutional monarchy with parliamentary democracy
Languages: English, Tok Pisin, Hiri Motu, 717 native languages
Monetary unit: Kina
Per capita GDP: $2,400
Literacy rate: 50%

Paraguay

Where? South America
Capital: Asunción
Area: 157,046 sq mi (406,750 sq km)
Population estimate (2003): 6,036,900
Government: Constitutional republic
Languages: Spanish (official), Guaraní
Monetary unit: Guaraní
Per capita GDP: $4,600
Literacy rate: 90%

Peru

Where? South America
Capital: Lima
Area: 496,223 sq mi (1,285,220 sq km)
Population estimate (2003): 28,409,897
Government: Constitutional republic
Languages: Spanish and Quechua (both official), Aymara, other native languages
Monetary unit: Nuevo sol
Per capita GDP: $4,800
Literacy rate: 85%

The Philippines

Where? Asia
Capital: Manila
Area: 115,830 sq mi (300,000 sq km)
Population estimate (2003): 84,619,974
Government: Republic
Languages: Filipino (based on Tagalog) and English (both official), regional languages
Monetary unit: Peso
Per capita GDP: $4,000
Literacy rate: 94%

Poland

Where? Europe
Capital: Warsaw
Area: 120,727 sq mi (312,683 sq km)
Population estimate (2003): 38,622,660
Government: Republic
Language: Polish
Monetary unit: Zloty
Per capita GDP: $8,800
Literacy rate: 98%

Portugal

Where? Europe
Capital: Lisbon
Area: 35,672 sq mi (92,391 sq km)
Population estimate (2003): 10,102,022
Government: Parliamentary democracy
Language: Portuguese
Monetary unit: Euro (formerly escudo)
Per capita GDP: $17,300
Literacy rate: 85%

Qatar

Where? Middle East
Capital: Doha
Area: 4,416 sq mi (11,439 sq km)
Population estimate (2003): 817,052
Government: Traditional monarchy
Languages: Arabic (official), English
Monetary unit: Qatari riyal
Per capita GDP: $21,200
Literacy rate: 76%

Romania

Where? Europe
Capital: Bucharest
Area: 91,700 sq mi (237,500 sq km)
Population estimate (2003): 22,271,839
Government: Republic
Languages: Romanian (official), Hungarian, German
Monetary unit: Leu
Per capita GDP: $6,800
Literacy rate: 96%

Russia

Where? Europe and Asia
Capital: Moscow
Area: 6,592,735 sq mi (17,075,200 sq km)
Population estimate (2003): 144,526,278
Government: Federation
Languages: Russian, others
Monetary unit: Ruble
Per capita GDP: $8,300
Literacy rate: 98%

Rwanda

Where? Africa
Capital: Kigali
Area: 10,169 sq mi (26,338 sq km)
Population estimate (2003): 7,810,056
Government: Republic
Languages: Kinyarwanda, French, English (all official)
Monetary unit: Rwandan franc
Per capita GDP: $1,000
Literacy rate: 50%

Saint Kitts and Nevis

Where? North America
Capital: Basseterre
Area: 101 sq mi (261 sq km)
Population estimate (2003): 38,763
Government: Constitutional monarchy
Language: English
Monetary unit: East Caribbean dollar
Per capita GDP: $8,700
Literacy rate: 98%

Saint Lucia

Where? North America
Capital: Castries
Area: 239 sq mi (620 sq km)
Population estimate (2003): 162,157
Government: Parliamentary democracy
Languages: English (official), patois
Monetary unit: East Caribbean dollar
Per capita GDP: $4,400
Literacy rate: 67%

Saint Vincent and the Grenadines

Where? North America
Capital: Kingstown
Area: 150 sq mi (389 sq km)
Population estimate (2003): 116,812
Government: Parliamentary democracy
Languages: English (official), French patois
Monetary unit: East Caribbean dollar
Per capita GDP: $2,900
Literacy rate: 96%

Samoa

Where? Pacific Islands
Capital: Apia
Area: 1,104 sq mi (2,860 sq km)
Population estimate (2003): 178,173
Government: Constitutional monarchy under native chief
Languages: Samoan, English
Monetary unit: Tala
Per capita GDP: $3,500
Literacy rate: 98%

San Marino

Where? Europe
Capital: San Marino
Area: 24 sq mi (61 sq km)
Population estimate (2003): 28,119
Government: Independent republic
Language: Italian
Monetary unit: Italian lira
Per capita GDP: $34,600
Literacy rate: 96%

São Tomé and Príncipe

Where? Africa
Capital: São Tomé
Area: 386 sq mi (1,001 sq km)
Population estimate (2003): 175,883
Government: Republic
Language: Portuguese
Monetary unit: Dobra
Per capita GDP: $1,200
Literacy rate: 57%

Saudi Arabia

Where? Middle East
Capital: Riyadh
Area: 756,981 sq mi (1,960,582 sq km)
Population estimate (2003): 24,293,844
Government: Monarchy
Language: Arabic
Monetary unit: Riyal
Per capita GDP: $10,600
Literacy rate: 62%

Senegal

Where? Africa
Capital: Dakar
Area: 75,749 sq mi (196,190 sq km)
Population estimate (2003): 10,580,307
Government: Republic under multiparty democratic rule
Languages: French (official), Wolof, Serer, other dialects
Monetary unit: CFA franc
Per capita GDP: $1,580
Literacy rate: 38%

Serbia and Montenegro*

Where? Europe
Capital: Belgrade
Area: 39,517 sq mi (102,350 sq km)
Population estimate (2003): 10,655,774
Government: Republic
Languages: Serbian, Albanian
Monetary unit: Yugoslav new dinar
Per capita GDP: $2,250
Literacy rate: 91%

*Formerly Yugoslavia

Seychelles

Where? Africa
Capital: Victoria
Area: 176 sq mi (455 sq km)
Population estimate (2003): 80,469
Government: Republic
Languages: English and French (both official), Seselwa
Monetary unit: Seychelles rupee
Per capita GDP: $7,600
Literacy rate: 58%

Sierra Leone

Where? Africa
Capital: Freetown
Area: 27,699 sq mi (71,740 sq km)
Population estimate (2003): 5,732,681
Government: Constitutional democracy
Languages: English (official), Mende, Temne, Krio
Monetary unit: Leone
Per capita GDP: $500
Literacy rate: 21%

Singapore

Where? Asia
Capital: Singapore
Area: 267 sq mi (692.7 sq km)
Population estimate (2003): 4,608,595
Government: Parliamentary republic
Languages: Malay, Chinese (Mandarin), Tamil, English (all official)
Monetary unit: Singapore dollar
Per capita GDP: $24,700
Literacy rate: 90%

Slovakia

Where? Europe
Capital: Bratislava
Area: 18,859 sq mi (48,845 sq km)
Population estimate (2003): 5,430,033
Government: Parliamentary democracy
Languages: Slovak (official), Hungarian
Monetary unit: Koruna
Per capita GDP: $11,500
Literacy rate: 99%

Slovenia

Where? Europe
Capital: Ljubljana
Area: 7,820 sq mi (20,253 sq km)
Population estimate (2003): 1,935,677
Government: Parliamentary democratic republic
Languages: Slovenian, Serbo-Croatian
Monetary unit: Slovenian tolar
Per capita GDP: $16,000
Literacy rate: 99%

Solomon Islands

Where? Pacific Islands
Capital: Honiara
Area: 10,985 sq mi (28,450 sq km)
Population estimate (2003): 509,190
Government: Parliamentary democracy
Languages: English, Solomon Pidgin, more than 60 Melanesian languages
Monetary unit: Solomon Islands dollar
Per capita GDP: $1,700
Literacy rate: 30%

Somalia

Where? Africa
Capital: Mogadishu
Area: 246,199 sq mi (637,657 sq km)
Population estimate (2003): 8,025,190
Government: Parliamentary
Languages: Somali (official), Arabic, English, Italian
Monetary unit: Somali shilling
Per capita GDP: $550
Literacy rate: 24%

South Africa

Where? Africa
Capital (administrative): Pretoria
Area: 471,008 sq mi (1,219,912 sq km)
Population estimate (2003): 42,768,678
Government: Republic
Languages: 11 official languages: Afrikaans, English, Ndebele, Pedi, Sotho, Swazi, Tsonga, Tswana, Venda, Xhosa, Zulu
Monetary unit: Rand
Per capita GDP: $9,400
Literacy rate: 60%

Spain

Where? Europe
Capital: Madrid
Area: 194,896 sq mi (504,782 sq km)
Population estimate (2003): 40,217,413
Government: Parliamentary monarchy
Languages: Castilian Spanish (official), Catalan, Galician, Basque
Monetary unit: Euro (formerly peseta)
Per capita GDP: $18,900
Literacy rate: 95%

Sri Lanka

Where? Asia
Capital: Colombo
Area: 25,332 sq mi (65,610 sq km)
Population estimate (2003): 19,742,439
Government: Republic
Languages: Sinhala (official), Tamil, English
Monetary unit: Sri Lankan rupee
Per capita GDP: $3,250
Literacy rate: 88%

Sudan

Where? Africa
Capital: Khartoum
Area: 967,493 sq mi (2,505,810 sq km)
Population estimate (2003): 38,114,160
Government: Transitional
Languages: Arabic (official), English, tribal dialects
Monetary unit: Sudanese pound
Per capita GDP: $1,360
Literacy rate: 27%

Suriname

Where? South America
Capital: Paramaribo
Area: 63,039 sq mi (163,270 sq km)
Population estimate (2003): 435,449
Government: Constitutional democracy
Languages: Dutch (official), Surinamese, English
Monetary unit: Suriname guilder
Per capita GDP: $3,500
Literacy rate: 95%

Swaziland

Where? Africa
Capital: Mbabane
Area: 6,704 sq mi (17,360 sq km)
Population estimate (2003): 1,161,219
Government: Monarchy
Languages: Swazi (official), English
Monetary unit: Lilangeni
Per capita GDP: $4,200
Literacy rate: 70%

Sweden

Where? Europe
Capital: Stockholm
Area: 173,731 sq mi (449,964 sq km)
Population estimate (2003): 8,878,085
Government: Constitutional monarchy
Language: Swedish
Monetary unit: Krona
Per capita GDP: $24,700
Literacy rate: 99%

Switzerland

Where? Europe
Capital: Bern
Area: 15,942 sq mi (41,290 sq km)
Population estimate (2003): 7,318,638
Government: Federal republic
Languages: German, French, Italian (all official), Romansch
Monetary unit: Swiss franc
Per capita GDP: $31,100
Literacy rate: 99%

Syria

Where? Middle East
Capital: Damascus
Area: 71,498 sq mi (185,180 sq km)
Population estimate (2003): 17,585,540
Government: Republic under military regime
Languages: Arabic (official), French, English
Monetary unit: Syrian pound
Per capita GDP: $3,200
Literacy rate: 65%

Taiwan

Where? Asia
Capital: Taipei
Area: 13,892 sq mi (35,980 sq km)
Population estimate (2003): 22,603,000
Government: Multiparty democratic regime
Language: Chinese (Mandarin)
Monetary unit: New Taiwan dollar
Per capita GDP: $17,200
Literacy rate: 92%

Tajikistan

Where? Asia
Capital: Dushanbe
Area: 55,251 sq mi (143,100 sq km)
Population estimate (2003): 6,863,752
Government: Republic
Language: Tajik
Monetary unit: Tajik ruble
Per capita GDP: $1,140
Literacy rate: 98%

Tanzania

Where? Africa
Capital: Dar es Salaam
Area: 364,898 sq mi (945,087 sq km)
Population estimate (2003): 35,922,454
Government: Republic
Languages: Swahili and English (both official), local languages
Monetary unit: Tanzanian shilling
Per capita GDP: $610
Literacy rate: 52%

Thailand

Where? Asia
Capital: Bangkok
Area: 198,455 sq mi (514,000 sq km)
Population estimate (2003): 64,265,276
Government: Constitutional monarchy
Languages: Thai (Siamese), Chinese, English
Monetary unit: Baht
Per capita GDP: $6,600
Literacy rate: 93%

Togo

Where? Africa
Capital: Lomé
Area: 21,925 sq mi (56,790 sq km)
Population estimate (2003): 5,429,299
Government: Republic under transition to multiparty democratic rule
Languages: French (official), Éwé, Mina, Kabyé, Cotocoli
Monetary unit: CFA franc
Per capita GDP: $1,500
Literacy rate: 43%

Tonga

Where? Pacific Islands
Capital: Nuku'alofa
Area: 290 sq mi (748 sq km)
Population estimate (2003): 108,141
Government: Hereditary constitutional monarchy
Languages: Tongan, English
Monetary unit: Pa'anga
Per capita GDP: $2,200
Literacy rate: 47%

Trinidad and Tobago

Where? North America
Capital: Port-of-Spain
Area: 1,980 sq mi (5,130 sq km)
Population estimate (2003): 1,104,209
Government: Parliamentary democracy
Languages: English (official), Hindi, French, Spanish
Monetary unit: Trinidad and Tobago dollar
Per capita GDP: $9,000
Literacy rate: 95%

Tunisia

Where? Africa
Capital: Tunis
Area: 63,170 sq mi (163,610 sq km)
Population estimate (2003): 9,924,742
Government: Republic
Languages: Arabic (official), French
Monetary unit: Tunisian dinar
Per capita GDP: $6,600
Literacy rate: 65%

Turkey

Where? Europe and Asia
Capital: Ankara
Area: 301,388 sq mi (780,580 sq km)
Population estimate (2003): 68,109,469
Government: Republican parliamentary democracy
Language: Turkish
Monetary unit: Turkish lira
Per capita GDP: $6,700
Literacy rate: 81%

Turkmenistan

Where? Asia
Capital: Ashgabat
Area: 188,455 sq mi (488,100 sq km)
Population estimate (2003): 4,775,544
Government: Republic
Languages: Turkmen, Russian, Uzbek
Monetary unit: Manat
Per capita GDP: $4,700
Literacy rate: 98%

Tuvalu

Where?
Pacific Islands

Capital: Funafuti

Area: 10 sq mi (26 sq km)

Population estimate (2003): 11,305

Government: Constitutional monarchy with a parliamentary democracy

Languages: Tuvaluan, English

Monetary unit: Tuvaluan dollar

Per capita GDP: $1,100

Literacy rate: Less than 50%

Uganda

Where? Africa

Capital: Kampala

Area: 91,135 sq mi (236,040 sq km)

Population estimate (2003): 25,632,794

Government: Republic

Languages: English (official), Swahili, Luganda, Ateso, Luo

Monetary unit: Ugandan shilling

Per capita GDP: $1,200

Literacy rate: 54%

Ukraine

Where? Europe

Capital: Kyiv (Kiev)

Area: 233,089 sq mi (603,700 sq km)

Population estimate (2003): 48,055,439

Government: Republic

Language: Ukrainian

Monetary unit: Hryvnia

Per capita GDP: $4,200

Literacy rate: 100%

United Arab Emirates

Where? Middle East

Capital: Abu Dhabi

Area: 32,000 sq mi (82,880 sq km)

Population estimate (2003): 2,484,818

Government: Federation

Languages: Arabic (official), English

Monetary unit: U.A.E. dirham

Per capita GDP: $21,100

Literacy rate: 68%

United Kingdom

Where? Europe

Capital: London

Area: 94,525 sq mi (244,820 sq km)

Population estimate (2003): 60,094,648

Government: Constitutional monarchy

Languages: English, Welsh, Scots, Gaelic

Monetary unit: Pound sterling

Per capita GDP: $24,700

Literacy rate: 99%

United States

Where? North America

Capital: Washington, D.C.

Area: 3,717,792 sq mi (9,629,091 sq km)

Population estimate (2003): 290,342,554

Government: Federal republic

Languages: English, Spanish spoken by a sizable minority

Monetary unit: U.S. dollar

Per capita GDP: $36,300

Literacy rate: 97%

Uruguay

Where? South America
Capital: Montevideo
Area: 68,040 sq mi
(176,220 sq km)
Population estimate (2003): 3,413,329
Government: Constitutional republic
Language: Spanish
Monetary unit: Peso
Per capita GDP: $9,200
Literacy rate: 96%

Uzbekistan

Where? Asia
Capital: Tashkent
Area: 172,741 sq mi (447,400 sq km)
Population estimate (2003): 25,981,647
Government: Republic
Languages: Uzbek, Russian, Tajik
Monetary unit: Uzbekistani som
Per capita GDP: $2,500
Literacy rate: 99%

Vanuatu

Where?
Pacific Islands
Capital: Port Vila
Area: 5,700 sq mi (14,760 sq km)
Population estimate (2003): 199,414
Government: Republic
Languages: English and French (both
official), Bislama
Monetary unit: Vatu
Per capita GDP: $1,300
Literacy rate: 55%

Vatican City (Holy See)

Where? Europe
Capital: none
Area: 0.17 sq mi (0.44 sq km)
Population estimate (2003): 890
Government: Ecclesiastical
Languages: Latin, Italian, various others
Monetary unit: Italian lira
Per capita GDP: NA
Literacy rate: 100%

Venezuela

Where? South America
Capital: Caracas
Area: 352,143 sq mi
(912,050 sq km)
Population estimate (2003): 24,654,694
Government: Federal republic
Languages: Spanish (official), native
languages
Monetary unit: Bolivar
Per capita GDP: $6,100
Literacy rate: 91%

Vietnam

Where? Asia
Capital: Hanoi
Area: 127,243 sq mi (329,560 sq km)
Population estimate (2003): 81,624,716
Government: Communist state
Languages: Vietnamese (official), French,
English, Khmer, Chinese
Monetary unit: Dong
Per capita GDP: $2,100
Literacy rate: 94%

Go Places with TFK! Take a country tour, hear the langua
explore the history at *www.timeforkids.com/goplaces*

Yemen

Where? Middle East
Capital: Sanaa
Area: 203,850 sq mi (527,970 sq km)
Population estimate (2003): 19,349,881
Government: Republic
Language: Arabic
Monetary unit: Rial
Per capita GDP: $820
Literacy rate: 39%

Zambia

Where? Africa
Capital: Lusaka
Area: 290,584 sq mi (752,610 sq km)
Population estimate (2003): 10,307,333
Government: Republic
Languages: English (official), local dialects
Monetary unit: Kwacha
Per capita GDP: $870
Literacy rate: 73%

Zimbabwe

Where? Africa
Capital: Harare
Area: 150,803 sq mi (390,580 sq km)
Population estimate (2003): 12,576,742
Government: Parliamentary democracy
Languages: English (official), Ndebele, Shona
Monetary unit: Zimbabwean dollar
Per capita GDP: $2,450
Literacy rate: 80%

The U.N. sits on 18 acres of land in New York City.

The United Nations

The **United Nations (U.N.)** was created after World War II to provide a meeting place to help develop good relationships between countries, promote peace and security around the world and encourage international cooperation in solving problems.

The major organizations of the U.N. are the Secretariat, the Security Council and the General Assembly.

The Secretariat is the management center of U.N. operations and is headed by the Secretary-General, who is the director of the U.N.

The Security Council is responsible for making and keeping international peace. Its main purpose is to prevent war by settling disputes between nations. The Security Council has 15 members. There are five permanent members: the U.S., the Russian Federation, Britain, France and China. There are also 10 temporary members that serve two-year terms.

The General Assembly is the world's forum for discussing matters affecting world peace and security, and for making recommendations concerning them. It has no power of its own to enforce decisions. It is made up of the 51 members nations and those admitted since, for a total of 191.

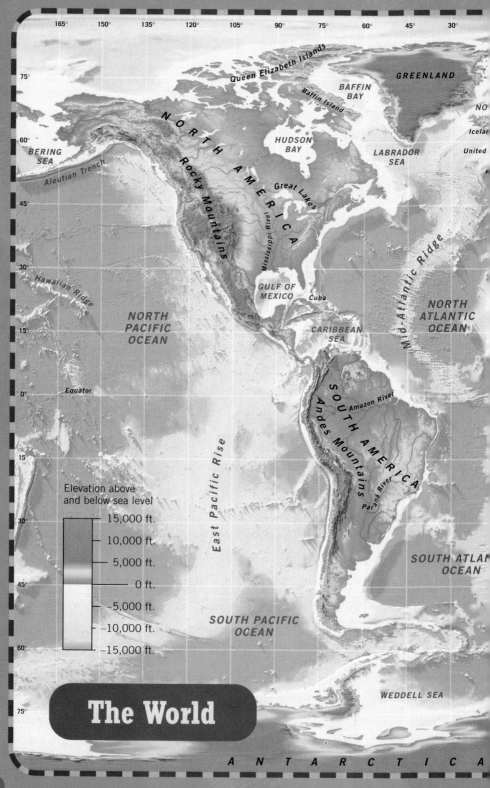

165° 150° 135° 120° 105° 90° 75° 60° 45° 30°

75°

Queen Elizabeth Islands

GREENLAND

BAFFIN
BAY

Baffin Island

NO

60°

BERING
SEA

HUDSON
BAY

LABRADOR
SEA

Icelan

United

Aleutian Trench

45°

Rocky Mountains

NORTH AMERICA

Great Lakes

Mid-Atlantic Ridge

Mississippi River

30°

Hawaiian Ridge

GULF OF
MEXICO

Cuba

NORTH
ATLANTIC
OCEAN

15°

NORTH
PACIFIC
OCEAN

CARIBBEAN
SEA

0°

Equator

SOUTH AMERICA

Amazon River

Andes Mountains

15°

East Pacific Rise

Paraná River

Elevation above
and below sea level

30°

— 15,000 ft.
— 10,000 ft.
— 5,000 ft.
— 0 ft.
— −5,000 ft.
— −10,000 ft.
— −15,000 ft.

SOUTH ATLAN
OCEAN

45°

SOUTH PACIFIC
OCEAN

60°

WEDDELL SEA

75°

The World

A N T A R C T I C A

15°   30°   45°   60°   75°   90°   105°   120°   135°   150°   165°

ARCTIC OCEAN

75°

S i b e r i a

60°

Baltic
Sea

Ural Mts.

River

Ob

Lena River

Sea of
Okhotsk

45°

E U R O P E

A

S

I

A

Mt. Everest
World's
highest point
29,035 ft.

Gobi

Kuril-Kamchatka
Trench

Black
Sea

Caspian
Sea

Aral
Sea

Huang River

Honshu

Japan Trench

**NORTH
PACIFIC
OCEAN**

30°

Mediterranean Sea

Euphrates R.

Persian
Gulf

Indus River

Himalayas

Ganges R.

Chang River

hara

Nile River

Red Sea

**ARABIAN
SEA**

**BAY OF
BENGAL**

Mekong R.

South
China
Sea

Challenger Deep
World's greatest
ocean depth
-36,198 ft.

15°

Equator

0°

F R I C A

Congo River

Central Indian Ridge

**INDIAN
OCEAN**

Ninety East Ridge

Sumatra

Java Trench

Java

Borneo

New Guinea

15°

**Kalahari
Desert**

Madagascar

Great Barrier Reef

A U S T R A L I A

30°

Southwest Indian Ridge

North
Island

South
Island

45°

**Maps always show a
distorted view of the
Earth because they
are not curved in
three dimensions.**

60°

EAN

75°

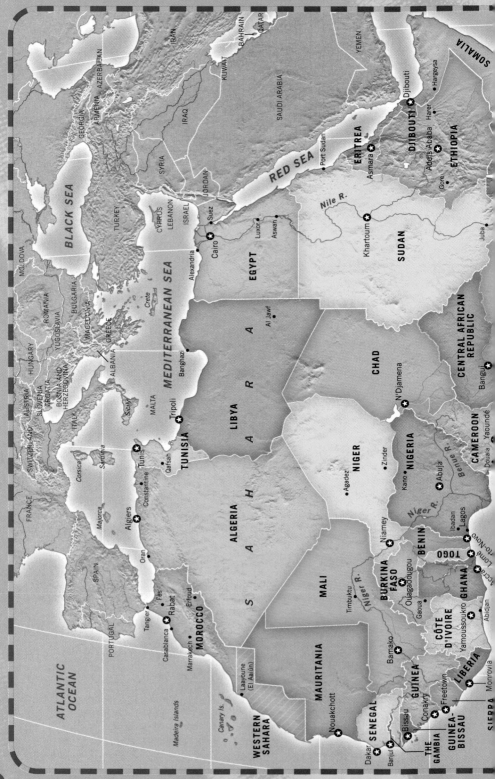

INDIAN OCEAN

ATLANTIC OCEAN

MADAGASCAR

Antananarivo ✪

Moroni ✪

COMOROS

Mozambique Channel

Mombasa ●
Dar es Salaam ✪
Zanzibar ●

TANZANIA

Kigoma ●

Lake Tanganyika

MOZAMBIQUE

Cidade de Nacala ●

Lake Nyasa

MALAWI
Lilongwe ✪

Blantyre ●

Beira ●

Lubumbashi ●

Kitwe ●

Harare ✪

ZIMBABWE

Maputo ●

Pretoria ✪
Mbabane ✪
SWAZILAND

Durban ●

THE CONGO

Kananga ●

Kinshasa ✪

Lusaka ✪

ZAMBIA

Johannesburg ●

Maseru ✪
LESOTHO

Port Elizabeth ●

Pointe-Noire ●

Luanda ✪

ANGOLA

Lubango ●

BOTSWANA

Gaborone ✪

SOUTH AFRICA

Cape Town ●

Namibe ●

NAMIBIA

Windhoek ✪

Walvis Bay ●

Africa

1,000 mi.

500 mi.

0 mi.

1,000 km

500 km

0 km

ARCTIC OCEAN

Bering
Sea

Cherskiy

Tiksi

Verkhoyansk

Magadan

Kamchatka
Peninsula

RUSSIA

Yakutsk

Sea of
Okhotsk

Petropavlovsk-
Kamchatskiy

B E R I A

Sakhalin

Irkutsk

Khabarovsk

Sapporo

Ulaanbaatar

Harbin

MONGOLIA

G o b i

Changchun

Vladivostok

JAPAN

Shenyang

N. KOREA

PACIFIC
OCEAN

Hohhot

Jinxi

P'yongyang

Tokyo

Beijing

Seoul

Nagoya

Tianjin

Taegu

Kyoto

Osaka

Taiyuan

Jinan

Pusan

Kobe

Lanzhou

S. KOREA

Hiroshima

Qingdao

Fukuoka

Xi'an

CHINA

Nagasaki

Chengdu

Hefei

Shanghai

Chongqing

Wuhan

Naha

Fuzhou

Taipei

Xiamen

Liuzhou

TAIWAN

DESH

Nanning

Guangzhou

Kao-hsiung

Mandalay

Macao

Hong Kong

Hanoi

LAOS

Luzon

Vientiane

Baguio

Quezon City

Chiang Mai

Da Nang

Manila

on

THAILAND

VIETNAM

PHILIPPINES

Bangkok

CAMBODIA

Cebu

Phnom
Penh

Ho Chi Minh City

Phuket

Songkhla

Borneo

Asia and the
Middle East

JAPAN

CHINA

TAIWAN

PHILIPPINE
SEA

LAOS

PHILIPPINES

VIETNAM

THAILAND

CAMBODIA

NORTHERN
MARIANA
ISLANDS
Saipan ★ (U.S.)

Agana ★ Guam
(U.S.)

Yap Islands

Caroline Islands

Koror
✪

MICRONESIA

Palik

PALAU

Bandar Seri Begawan

BRUNEI Kota Kinabalu
✪

M A L A Y S I A

Ipoh

Kuala Lumpur Kuching

Medan

SINGAPORE Pontianak

Manado

Borneo

Samarinda

Palu

Sorong

Jayapura
Wewak

PAPUA NEW G

Pakanbaru

Palembang

Banjarmasin

Ujungpandang

Celebes

Irian
Jaya

Sumatra

Jakarta

Surabaya

Semarang

I N D O N E S I A

New Guinea

Honia
Guada

Java

Denpasar (Bali)

Kupang

EAST TIMOR

Timor

Port Moresby
✪

Ashmore and Cartier Islands
(Australia)

Timor Sea

Darwin

Gulf of
Carpentaria

Great Barrier Reef

Coral Sea Islands (Australia)

CORAL
SEA

West Island

Derby

Cairns

INDIAN OCEAN

Townsville

Mackay

Alice Springs

Rockhampton Gladstone

A U S T R A L I A

Brisbane

Tropic of Capricorn

Geraldton

Broken Hill

Lor
I
(Au

Kalgoorlie

Whyalla

Sydney

Perth

Esperance

Adelaide

Canberra

Bunbury

Melbourne

TASM
SE

Hobart

Tasmania

Asia, Australia and the Pacific Islands

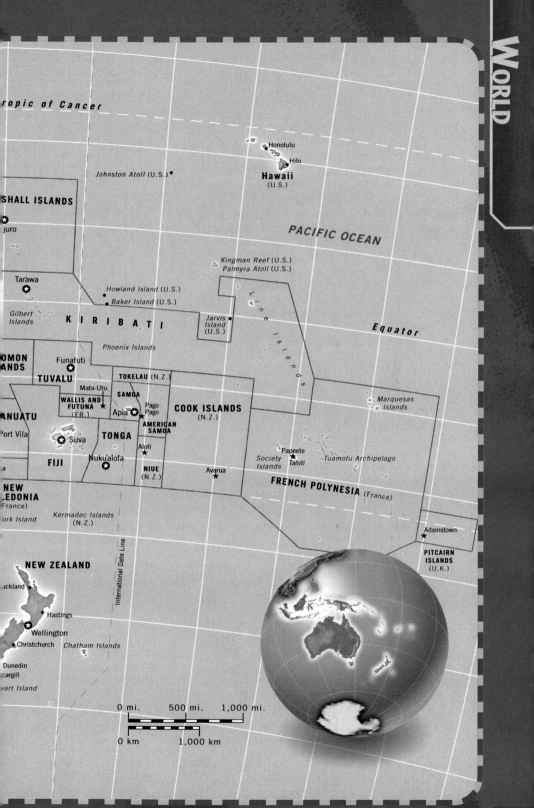

Tropic of Cancer

Honolulu
Hilo
Hawaii
(U.S.)

Johnston Atoll (U.S.)

PACIFIC OCEAN

SHALL ISLANDS

juro

Kingman Reef (U.S.)
Palmyra Atoll (U.S.)

Tarawa

Howland Island (U.S.)
Baker Island (U.S.)

Gilbert
Islands

K I R I B A T I

Jarvis
Island
(U.S.)

Line Islands

Equator

Phoenix Islands

OMON
NDS

Funafuti

TUVALU

TOKELAU (N.Z.)

Marquesas
Islands

Mata-Utu

SAMOA

ANUATU

WALLIS AND
FUTUNA
(FR.)

Apia
Pago
Pago

AMERICAN
SAMOA

COOK ISLANDS
(N.Z.)

ort Vila

Suva

TONGA

Alofi

Papeete

Society Tahiti
Islands

Tuamotu Archipelago

FIJI

Nuku'alofa

NIUE
(N.Z.)

Avarua

FRENCH POLYNESIA (France)

NEW
LEDONIA
France)

Kermadec Islands
(N.Z.)

ork Island

Adamstown

PITCAIRN
ISLANDS
(U.K.)

NEW ZEALAND

uckland

Hastings

International Date Line

Wellington
Christchurch *Chatham Islands*

Dunedin
cargill
wart Island

0 mi.   500 mi.   1,000 mi.

0 km   1,000 km

Europe

Reykjavik
ICELAND

Arctic Circle

FAROE ISLANDS
(Denmark)
Torshavn

SHETLAND ISLANDS

ORKNEY
ISLANDS

HEBRIDES

NORWAY

Trondheim

Bergen

Oslo

Stavanger

SWEDE

Göteborg

Aberdeen

DENMARK

Alborg

Glasgow

Edinburgh

NORTH
SEA

Copenhagen

Malmö

Belfast

UNITED
KINGDOM

Dublin

IRELAND

Liverpool

Leeds

Manchester

Sheffield

NETHERLANDS

Hamburg

Bremen

Berlin

Poz

Birmingham

Amsterdam
The Hague

London

Rotterdam

GUERNSEY (U.K.)

JERSEY (U.K.)

Calais

Lille

Antwerp

Essen

Dusseldorf
Cologne

Le Havre

Brussels

BELGIUM

Bonn

Frankfurt

Prag

Paris

LUXEMBOURG

Luxembourg

Stuttgart

CZECH
REPUBLIC

Brat

Nantes

Strasbourg

Dijon

LIECHTENSTEIN

Munich

Vienna

ATLANTIC OCEAN

FRANCE

Zürich

Vaduz

AUSTRIA

BAY OF
BISCAY

Bordeaux

Bern

Geneva

Lyon

SWITZERLAND

Ljubljana

SLOVEN

Porto

Bilbao

Turin

Milan

Trieste

Za

Toulouse

Genoa

CROATIA

Lisbon

PORTUGAL

Madrid

Andorra
la Vella

Marseille

MONACO

Florence

SAN
MARINO

BOSN
HERZI

Bastia

ITALY

Sara

SPAIN

Barcelona

ANDORRA

Corsica

Vatican
City

Rome

ADRIATI

Seville

Valencia

Majorca

Bari

Faro

Málaga

Palma

Sardinia

Naples

Gibraltar

MEDITERRANEAN SEA

Cagliari

MOROCCO

ALGERIA

A F R I C A

TUNISIA

Palermo

Messina

Sicily

Valletta

MALTA

0 mi.   300 mi.   600 mi.

0 km   300 km   600 km

Murmansk

Pechora

ASIA

Arkhangel'sk

RUSSIA

Oulu

FINLAND

Izhevsk

mpere

Helsinki

St. Petersburg

Kazan

Tallinn

ESTONIA

Nizhniy Novgorod

Moscow

Samara

LATVIA

UANIA

Smolensk

Saratov

Vilnius

Lipetsk

KAZAKHSTAN

Minsk

BELARUS

Homyel'

Voronezh

Brest

Kiev

Kharkiv

Volgograd

L'viv

Derazhnya

Voroshilovgrad

UKRAINE

Gorlovka

Makeyevka

Chisinau

Zhdanov

Rostov

Iasi

Odessa

Mykolavia

MOLDOVA

Kerch'

Groznyy

ROMANIA

Simferopol

aiova

Bucharest

Sevastopol'

Constanta

BLACK SEA

O

Varna

BULGARIA

NIA

Istanbul

niki

T U R K E Y

os

Izmir

Athens

SYRIA

IRAN

Crete

CYPRUS

IRAQ

LEBANON

ICELAND

Greenland Sea

Tasiilaq
(Ammassalik)

Narsarsuaq

GREENLAND
(Denmark)

Labrador
Sea

Island of
Newfoundland

St. John's

Happy Valley
Goose Bay

Nuuk (Godthab)

Davis Strait

Baffin Bay

Iqaluit

CANADA

Qaanaaq (Thule)

Chisasibi
(Fort George)

Alert

Baffin Island

Moosonee

Queen Elizabeth Islands

Resolute

Kajuutoq

HUDSON
BAY

ARCTIC
OCEAN

Victoria Island

Arctic Circle

Churchill

Winnipeg

Banks Island

Beaufort
Sea

Echo Bay

Yellowknife

Regina

Saskatoon

Barrow

Prudhoe Bay

Inuvik

Edmonton

Calgary

Helena

RUSSIA

Alaska (U.S.)

Fairbanks

Whitehorse

Nome

Valdez

Juneau

Vancouver

Seattle

Bethel

Anchorage

Victoria

Olympia

Portland

Kodiak

Salem

Bering
Sea

Aleutian Islands

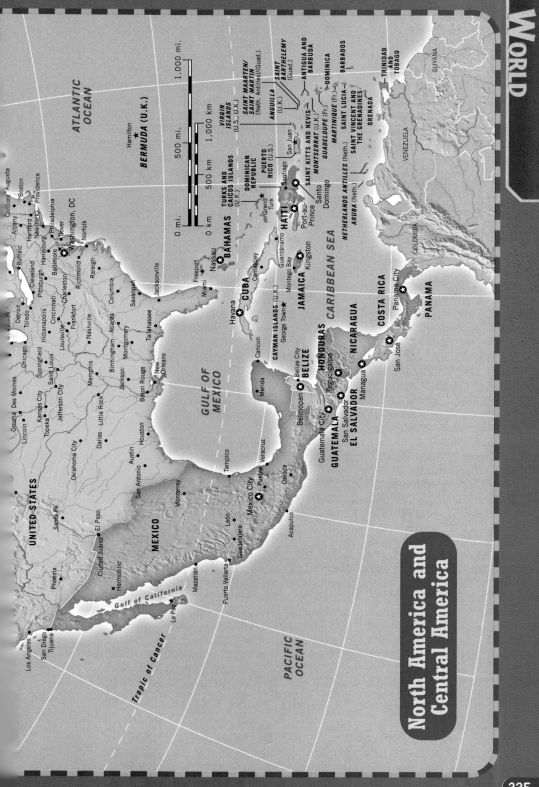

North America and Central America

UNITED STATES

Los Angeles
San Diego
Tijuana
Phoenix
Santa Fe
El Paso
Ciudad Juárez
Hermosillo
Mazatlán
Puerto Vallarta
La Paz
Guadalajara
Acapulco
León
MEXICO
Monterrey
Mexico City
Puebla
Oaxaca
Veracruz
Tampico
Mérida
Cancún

Gulf of California

Tropic of Cancer

PACIFIC OCEAN

GULF OF MEXICO

Omaha
Des Moines
Lincoln
Kansas City
Topeka
Jefferson City
Oklahoma City
Austin
San Antonio
Houston
Dallas
Little Rock
Jackson
Baton Rouge
New Orleans
Memphis
Nashville
Birmingham
Montgomery
Atlanta
Columbia
Savannah
Tallahassee
Jacksonville
Miami
Chicago
Springfield
Saint Louis
Louisville
Frankfort
Indianapolis
Cincinnati
Detroit
Toledo
Cleveland
Pittsburgh
Columbus
Buffalo
Albany
Boston
Providence
Hartford
New York
Philadelphia
Dover
Washington, DC
Baltimore
Harrisburg
Richmond
Norfolk
Raleigh
Charleston
Concord
Augusta

ATLANTIC OCEAN

BERMUDA (U.K.)
Hamilton

BAHAMAS
Freeport
Nassau

CUBA
Havana
Camagüey
Guantánamo

CAYMAN ISLANDS (U.K.)
George Town

JAMAICA
Montego Bay
Kingston

HAITI
Port-au-Prince

DOMINICAN REPUBLIC
Santiago
Santo Domingo

PUERTO RICO (U.S.)
San Juan

TURKS AND CAICOS ISLANDS (U.K.)
Grand Turk

VIRGIN ISLANDS (U.S., U.K.)

SAINT MAARTEN/ SAINT MARTIN (Neth. Antilles/(Guad.)

ANGUILLA (U.K.)

SAINT BARTHÉLEMY (Guad.)

ANTIGUA AND BARBUDA

DOMINICA

GUADELOUPE (Fr.)

MARTINIQUE (Fr.)

SAINT LUCIA

BARBADOS

SAINT VINCENT AND THE GRENADINES

GRENADA

SAINT KITTS AND NEVIS

MONTSERRAT (U.K.)

NETHERLANDS ANTILLES (Neth.)

ARUBA (Neth.)

TRINIDAD AND TOBAGO

CARIBBEAN SEA

BELIZE
Belmopan
Belize City

GUATEMALA
Guatemala City

HONDURAS
Tegucigalpa

EL SALVADOR
San Salvador

NICARAGUA
Managua

COSTA RICA
San José

PANAMA
Panama City

VENEZUELA

COLOMBIA

GUYANA

1,000 mi.
500 mi.
0 mi.
0 km
500 km
1,000 km

335

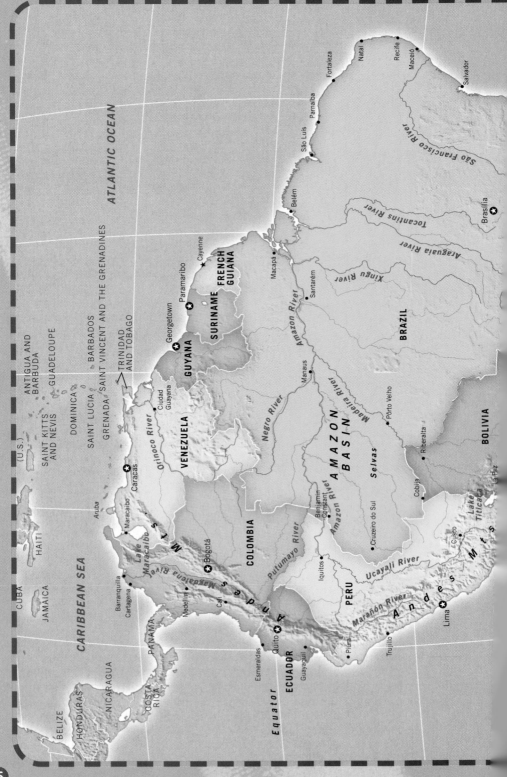

ATLANTIC OCEAN

Fortaleza
Natal
Recife
Maceió
Parnaíba
Salvador

São Luís
São Francisco River

Belém

Macapá
Tocantins River
Araguaia River
Xingu River

Cayenne
FRENCH GUIANA
Brasília

Paramaribo
SURINAME
Georgetown
GUYANA
Santarém

Amazon River

Ciudad Guayana
Negro River
Manaus
BRAZIL

VENEZUELA
Madeira River
Pôrto Velho

Caracas
Aruba
Maracaibo
AMAZON
BASIN
Riberalta
BOLIVIA

Lake Maracaibo
Selvas
Cobija

COLOMBIA
Benjamin Constant
Cruzeiro do Sul
La Paz
Lake Titicaca

Barranquilla
Bogotá
Amazon River
Putumayo River

Cartagena
Medellín
Cali
Iquitos
Ucayali River
Cusco

Andes Mts

PANAMA
ECUADOR
PERU
Marañón River
Lima

Esmeraldas
Quito
Guayaquil
Piura
Trujillo

Equator

NICARAGUA
COSTA RICA

BELIZE
HONDURAS

CARIBBEAN SEA

CUBA
JAMAICA
HAITI

(U.S.)
SAINT KITTS AND NEVIS
ANTIGUA AND BARBUDA
GUADELOUPE
DOMINICA
SAINT LUCIA
BARBADOS
GRENADA
SAINT VINCENT AND THE GRENADINES
TRINIDAD AND TOBAGO

Orinoco River

Magdalena River

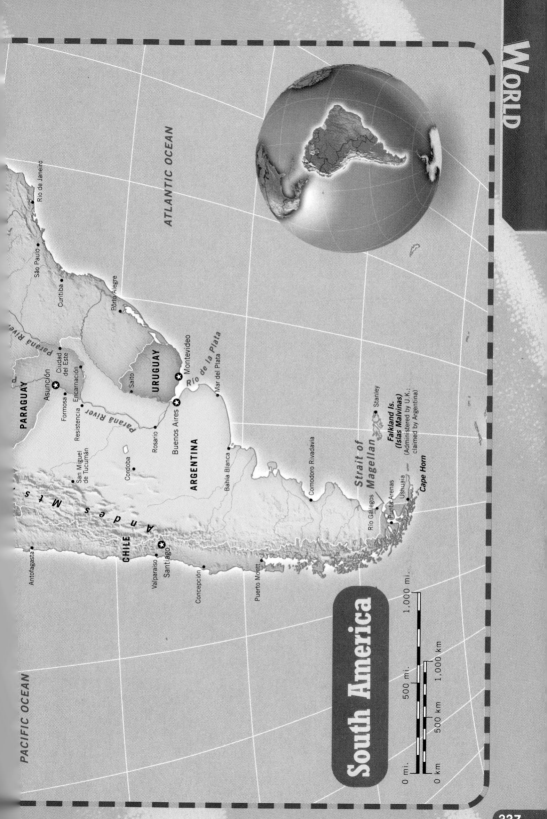

ATLANTIC OCEAN

Rio de Janeiro

São Paulo

Curitiba

Pôrto Alegre

Paraná River

PARAGUAY

Asunción ★

Ciudad del Este

Encarnación

Formosa

Resistencia

Paraná River

San Miguel de Tucumán

Córdoba

Antofagasta

A n d e s   M t s .

CHILE

Santiago ★

Valparaíso

Concepción

Puerto Montt

URUGUAY

Montevideo ★

Salto

Río de la Plata

Mar del Plata

Buenos Aires ★

Rosario

ARGENTINA

Bahía Blanca

Comodoro Rivadavia

Strait of Magellan

Río Gallegos

Punta Arenas

Ushuaia

Cape Horn

Stanley

Falkland Is.
(Islas Malvinas)
(Administered by U.K.;
claimed by Argentina)

PACIFIC OCEAN

South America

1,000 mi.

500 mi.

1,000 km

500 km

0 mi.

0 km

500 km

1,000 km

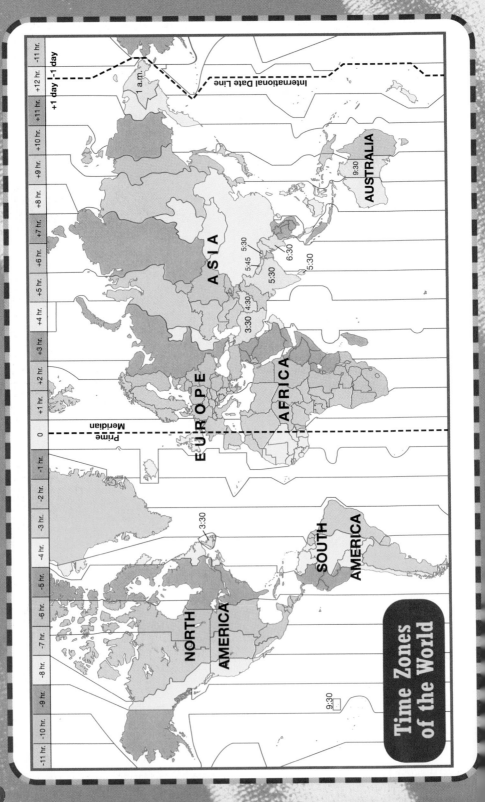

Time Zones
of the World

Did You Know?

In 2003 Yugoslavia was renamed Serbia and Montenegro, reflecting the two republics that remained united after Yugoslavia's 10-year civil war.

World Facts and Figures

The world population jumped from five billion in 1987 to six billion in 1999—12 years. It took 123 years for the population to increase from one billion (1804) to two billion (1927).

Population: 6,267,634,348 (January 2003 estimate)
Most populous nation: China, 1.3 billion people
Least populous country: Tuvalu, 11,305 people
Most populous city: Mumbai (Bombay), India, 11.9 million people

TFK MYSTERY PERSON

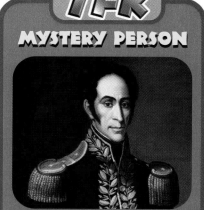

CLUE 1: I was a revolutionary leader born in Caracas, Venezuela, on July 24, 1783.
CLUE 2: Called the Liberator, I helped six South American nations—Venezuela, Colombia, Panama, Ecuador, Bolivia and Peru—gain their independence from Spain.
CLUE 3: Bolivia, once known as Upper Peru, is named after me.

WHO AM I?

(See Answer Key that begins on page 340.)

TFK PUZZLES & GAMES

Wear Are You?

Draw a line from each type of traditional clothing to the country in which people wear it.

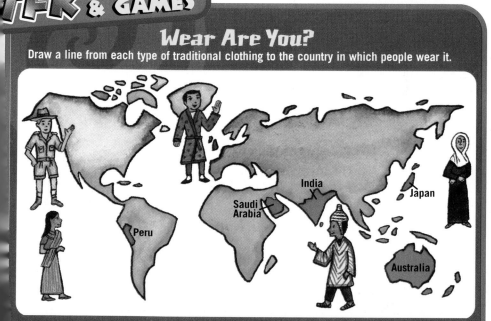

India
Saudi Arabia
Japan
Peru
Australia

(See Answer Key that begins on page 340.)

ANSWER KEY

ANIMALS
Page 31, Mystery Person: Anna Sewell

ART
Page 35, Mystery Person: Chuck Jones

BOOKS
Page 41, Harry and Hogwarts: 1. a; 2. c;
3. b; 4. a; 5. c; 6. b
Page 41, Mystery Person: C.S. Lewis

BUILDINGS & LANDMARKS
Page 47, Mystery Person: Frank Gehry

CALENDARS
Page 51, The Chinese Calendar:
1. rooster; 2. energetic; 3. rabbit. Bonus:
The next Year of the Rooster is 2005.
Page 53, Mystery Person: Cleopatra

COMPUTERS & THE INTERNET
Page 56, Video-game Invasion:
PlayStation 2 (2000), Nintendo
Entertainment System (1985), Sega
Dreamcast (1999), Microsoft Xbox (2001),
Atari 2600 (1977), Nintendo 64 (1996)
Sega Genesis (1989). The game was
PONG.
Page 57, Short Cuts: 1. a; 2. b; 3. b
Page 59, Mystery Person: Bill Gates

DANCE & THEATER
Page 63, Mystery Person: Matthew
Broderick

DINOSAURS
Page 69, Mystery Persons: Meriwether
Lewis and William Clark

DISASTERS
Page 77, Mystery Person: Rudolph Giuliani

ENVIRONMENT
Page 83, Mystery Person: John Chapman

FASHION
Page 85, Mystery Person: Giorgio Armani

GEOGRAPHY
Page 92, Explore the Past!: 1. about
220 years before Columbus; 2. about
500 years before Columbus; 3. about 300
years after Eriksson
Page 93, Mystery Person: Charles
Lindburgh

GOVERNMENT
Page 99, Famous Female Firsts:
Jeannette Rankin—first woman member
of Congress; Hillary Clinton—first First
Lady elected to Senate; Hattie
Caraway—first woman elected to the U.S.
Senate; Frances Perkins—first woman to
hold a Cabinet post; Shirley Chisholm—
first black woman elected to the U.S.
House of Representatives.
Page 105, Mystery Person: Ella Grasso

HEALTH & BODY
Page 113, Mystery Person: Albert
Schweitzer

HISTORY
Page 115, Mystery Person: Queen Isabella

HOLIDAYS
Page 127, Pumpkin Patch Match 1. 14;
2. 4; 3. 12; 4. 5
Page 129, Mystery Person: Martin Luther
King Jr.

HOMEWORK HELPER
Page 131, Rhyme Time: Hook/book,
fish/dish, sock/rock, hat/mat, whale/tail,
boy/toy, girl/pearl, shell/bell,
sandal/handle, hair/air, float/boat,
sand/hand.
Page 149, Mystery Person: Mary McLeod
Bethune

INVENTIONS
Page 155, Mystery Person: Thomas Edison

LANGUAGE
Page 157, Sí, You Can Read Spanish: "Hello! I live in Mexico. I have a cat and a dog. Your friend, Pilar"
Page 161, Mystery Person: Helen Keller

MATH
Page 169, To the Rescue!:

Page 173, Mystery Person: Blaise Pascal

MONEY
Page 179, Mystery Person: Benjamin Franklin

MOVIES & TV
Page 185, Laugh Trackers!: 1. a (*I Love Lucy*—1951); 2. d (*Gilligan's Island*—1964); 3. f (*Mork and Mindy*—1978); 4. e (*Cheers*—1982); 5. c (*The Cosby Show*—1984); 6. b (*Seinfeld*—1989)
Page 185, Mystery Person: Philo Farnsworth

MUSIC
Page 187, World Music!: 1. c; 2. e; 3. a; 4. b; 5. d
Page 189, Mystery Person: Wolfgang Amadeus Mozart

MYTHOLOGY
Page 191, Monster Match: 1. d; 2. a; 3. b; 4. e; 5. c
Page 193, Mystery Person: Homer

PRESIDENTS
Page 203, Mystery Person: John Quincy Adams

RELIGION
Page 207, Mystery Person: Dalai Lama

SCIENCE
Page 217, Mystery Person: Charles Darwin

SPACE
Page 227, Mystery Person: Clyde Tombaugh

SPORTS
Page 230, Bizarre Basketball:

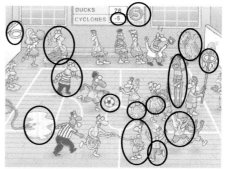

Page 243, Mystery Person: Peggy Fleming

WEATHER
Page 289, Weather or Not?: 1. wind; 2. mist; 3. barometer; 4. rain; 5. centigrade
Page 289, Mystery Person: Svante Arrhenius

WORLD
Page 239, Wear Are You?: Bush outfit, Australia; sari, India; kimono, Japan; chullo (hat) and poncho, Peru; abayah, Saudi Arabia.

Page 239, Mystery Person: Simón Bolívar

INNER BACK COVER
The Numbers Game: 2004

INDEX

L

M

W

Y

Z

We've got all the information you need, from A to Z!

CREDITS

KEY:
LOC—Library of Congress
NARA—National Archives and Records
　　　Administration
NPG—National Portrait Gallery
PD—PhotoDisc
SI—Smithsonian Institution
TPC—Time Picture Collection

All photos clockwise from top left:
Cover: PD (giraffe); NASA (Mars); Eyewire/Punch Stock (trumpet); Reuters New Media Inc. (Bryant); Courtesy Sport-Fun (SpongeBob); Rubberball (girl); NASA (Earth); Bernd Obermann/Ovoworks Time Pix (Statue of Liberty); Newscom (Frodo).
Inside Front Cover: Courtesy the White House (Bush); John Kabasakalis (Woods); Courtesy TIME For Kids (Timberlake).
Inside Back Cover: Puzzle by R studio T.
Title Page: NASA.
Credits Page: Ted Thai for TFK Almanac.
Who's News: 8-9: NASA. **10:** Getty Images/Newscom. **11:** Pat and Rosemarie Keough/Nahanni Productions. **12:** Robert Galbraith/Reuters. **13:** Andrew Cutraro/AP (Kwan); Michael J. LeBrecht II (James). **14:** AFP/Corbis. **15:** Zuma Press/Newscom. **16:** Courtesy Warner Bros. (Potter); Time Picture Collection. **17:** Getty Images/Newscom. **18:** Zuma Press/Newscom. **19:** Newscom (2).
Animals: 20: Ed Wray/AP. **21:** Scott Camazine/Photo Researchers (mussel); George Lepp/Corbis (nutria); Frank Dimeo/Cornell University (beetle); Kevin Schafer/Corbis (coqui); Lennox McLendon/AP (carp). **22:** G.K. & Vikki Hart/Getty Images (reptile); PD; Nicole Duplaix/Getty Images (platypus). **23:** John Shaw/Getty Images (oyster); George Grall/Getty Images (anemone); PD. **24:** Art Wolfe/Getty Images (gorilla); Royalty-Free/Corbis (condor); Ho/Reuters (crane); Joel W. Rogers/Corbis (salmon); Greg Vaughn/Getty Images (owl); Layne Kennedy/Corbis (wolf). **25:** PD; Art Wolfe/Getty Images (wolf). **26:** Royalty-Free/Corbis. **27:** Michael S. Yamashita/Corbis (kangaroo); Digital Vision/Picture Quest (2); PD. **28:** Randy Green/Getty Images; PD. **29:** Tui De Roy/Minden Pictures. **30:** Newscom; Felipe Galindo illustration. **31:** Ken Usami/Photo Disc/Picture Quest (fish); Grace Beahm/The Post and Courier (Sewell).
Art: 32: Ted Thai for TFK Almanac. **33:** Elio Ciol/Corbis; © 2001 Estate Pablo Picasso/ARS; Werner Forman/Corbis; Geoffrey Clements/Corbis. **34:** Christie's Images/Corbis (2); Geoffrey Clements/Corbis; Francis G. Mayer/Corbis; Archivo Iconografico/S.A./Corbis. **35:** Burstein Collection/Corbis (Kooning); Archivo Iconografico, S.A./Corbis (Rembrandt); Francis G. Mayer/Corbis (Renoir); Christie's Image/Corbis (Lichtenstein); Rose Prouser/Reuters (Jones).

Books: 36: Newscom (2); Courtesy Bob Graham. **37:** Felipe Galindo (illustration). **38:** Newscom; Time Picture Collection; Archivo Iconografico, S.A./Corbis. **39:** Motoko Inoue. **40:** Felipe Galindo (illustration). **41:** Bettmann/Corbis (Lewis); Peter Goldberg.
Buildings & Landmarks: 42: Courtesy Charlie DeLeo (2). **43:** Philip Gould/Corbis (Lin); BIll Ross/Corbis (Pei). **44:** Fergus O'Brien/Getty Images; Royalty-Free/Corbis. **45:** Glen Allison/Getty Images (Wat); John Slater/Corbis (Great Wall); Vladimir Pcholkin/Getty Images (Stonehenge). **46:** Bettmann/Corbis; Henry Groskinsky/TPC (Twin Towers). **47:** Larry Lee/Corbis (Petronas Towers); John Scheiber/Corbis (Sears); Earl & Nazima Kowall/Corbis (dam); Newscom (Gehry).
Calendars: 49: Ted Thai for TFK Almanac. **51:** Jen Kraemer/Smith; Andy Caulfield/Image Bank (birthstones). **52:** Encarnacion Lopez (zodiac chart); Ted Thai for TFK Almanac. **53:** EIT Consortium/NASA (Sun); Antonio Cidadao (moon); NASA (Mars, Mercury, Venus); JPL/NASA (Jupiter, Saturn); Corbis Bettmann (Cleopatra).
Computers & The Internet: 54: Felipe Galindo (illustrations); Michael Llewellyn/Onyx (Gibson). **55:** Andy Freeberg; Jane Sanders (illustrations). **56:** Apple Computer Inc; Newscom. **57:** Felipe Galindo (illustration). **58:** Jane Sanders (illustration). **59:** Peter Turnley/Corbis.
Dance: 60: Kent Barker/Image Bank; Newscom. **61:** Ted Spiegal/Corbis; Kevork Djansezian-AP/Wide World Photos (hip-hop); Bettmann/Corbis (Native American); Felipe Galindo (illustration). **62:** Martha Swope/Time Picture Collection (*Nutcracker*); David Gray/Reuters (*Swan Lake*). **63:** Martha Swope/Time Picture Collection (2); Jim Spellman/Wire Image (Broderick).
Dinosaurs: 64: Getty Images/Newscom. **65:** National Museum of Natural History (2). **66:** Carlyn Iverson/Photo Researchers; Photo Researchers. **67:** Stephen J. Krasemann/Photo Researchers; John Weinstein/The Field Museum. **68:** Ted Thai for TFK Almanac. **69:** Portia Sloan For IVPP; Bettmann/Corbis (2); Stephen Blue.
Disasters: 70: Jess Christensen/Reuters (9/11); Newscom (coal miners). **71:** Newscom; Felipe Galindo (illustration). **72:** The Mariners Museum-AP/Wide World Photos; Ralph White/Corbis. **73:** Corbis (Chicago); Reuters New Media Inc/Corbis. **74:** Bernardo De Niz/Reuters. **75:** Gary Braasch/Corbis; Jim Zuckerman/Corbis. **76:** Newscom. **77:** William James Warren/Corbis; Newscom.
Environment: 78: Steve Liss; map courtesy of the National Drought Mitigation Center. **79:** Jane Sanders (illustration). **80:** Kennan Ward/Corbis; Joe McDonald/Corbis. **81:** David Samuel Robbins/Corbis; John Conrad/Corbis (goat).

82: A & L Sinibaldi/Getty Images. **83:** Corbis (Chapman); Dorling Kindersley (maple); John Serrao/Photo Researchers (cherry); Dorling Kindersley (elder).
Fashion: 84: Ted Thai for TFK Almanac; Hulton-Deutsch Collection/Corbis; Corbis/Bettmann (76). **85:** Corbis/Bettmann (Beatles); Gary Hershorn/Reuters; Henry Diltz/Corbis (Madonna); London Features (TLC); Rick Diamond/Image Direct/Newscom (Nelly Furtado); Rufus F. Folkks (Armani).
Geography: 86: Corbis Bettmann; American Museum of Natural History. **87:** Corbis Bettman; Corbis; Tennessee Library & Archives/AP/Wide World Photos (Lewis); AP/ Wide World Photos (Clark); Gianni Dagliorti/Corbis (Magellan). **92:** Len Tweeten for TIME. **93:** Guido Alberto Rossi/Getty Images (Everest); Bettmann/Corbis.
Government: 94: NARA. **95:** Bettmann/Corbis. **96:** AFP/Corbis. **97:** David Phillip-AP/Wide World Photos (Bush); Newscom (Chaney, Snow, Ridge); AP/Wide World Photos (the rest of the Cabinet). **98:** Richard Strauss-SI/Supreme Court of the United States. **99:** Felipe Galindo (illustration). **100:** Joseph Sohm-Chromosohm/Corbis. **101:** Felipe Galindo (illustration). **103:** Joe Lertola (map). **104:** Galen Rowell/Corbis; Ted Thai for TFK Almanac. **105:** Reuters New Media Inc/Corbis; Corbis Bettmann.
Health & Body: 106: Andrew Kaufman/Contact Press Images (3). **107:** Jane Sanders (illustration). **108:** Felipe Galindo (illustration). **109:** Courtesy of the U.S. Department of Agriculture. **111:** Ted Thai for TFK Almanac. **113:** PD; Hulton-Deutsch Collection (Schweitzer).
History: 114: Gianni Daglio Orti/Corbis; Erich Lessing/Art Resource. **115:** Atlantic Productions; Archivo Iconografico, S.A./Corbis. **116:** Roger Wood/Corbis (Sphinx); Bettmann/Corbis (Homer); Yann Arthus-Bertrand/Corbis (Trojan Horse); Joseph Van Os/Getty Images (Great Wall). **117:** Corbis; Bettmann/Corbis; Ted Spiegel/Corbis. **118:** Getty Images (Angor Wat); Bettmann/Corbis (Chaucer); Bettmann/Corbis (2). **119:** Vittoriano Rastelli-Bettmann/Corbis; Bettmann/Corbis (2). **120:** Bettmann/Corbis (2).**121:** Bettmann/Corbis (Vietnam); Ted Horowitz/Corbis (scientist); AP/Wide World Photos (Tiananmen); Peter Turnley/Corbis. **122:** LOC; Bettmann/Corbis (2). **123:** D. Boone/Corbis (Alamo); Bettmann/Corbis. **124:** Bettmann/Corbis (3). **125:** NASA; Bettmann/Corbis; Corbis Sygma.
Holidays: 126: Jane Sanders (illustration); Joseph Sohm; Chromosohm Inc/Corbis. **127:** Jane Sanders (illustration). **128:** Jane Sanders (illustrations); Rita Maas/Getty Images; Gary Buss/Getty Images; Bettmann/Corbis. **129:** Ted Spiegel/Corbis; Peter Turnley/Corbis (Bastille); Bettmann/Corbis.
Homework Helper: 130: Tim Sloan/AP; Geoff Franklin/Getty Images; Mike Simons/Getty Images. **131, 132, 139, 147:** Felipe Galindo (illustrations). **133:** Amy Vangsgard for TIME For Kids (puzzle). **149:** Urbano de Valle (3);

Jed Collectibles; Urbano de Valle (books); Corbis (Bethune).
Inventions: 150: Felipe Galindo (illustration); Dennis Galante (Trikke); General Motors (Hy-wire). **151:** Jens Mortensen (bubbles); Japan Marine Science & Technology Center (Roomba). **152:** Eileen Darby (piano); James Baigrie/Getty Images (ice cream); Friday Associates (fridge); Felipe Galindo (illustration). **153:** Felipe Galindo (illustrations); Digital Art/Corbis (DNA); Corbis (phone); AP/ Wide World Photos (Dolly). **154:** Underwood & Underwood/Corbis. **155:** Felipe Galindo (illustration); Mansell/Time Picture Collection.
Language: 156, 158, 159: Felipe Galindo (illustration). **160:** PD. **161:** Nik Wheller/Corbis; Bettmann/Corbis.
Math: 162: Ted Thai for TFK Almanac. **164:** PD. **168, 171:** Felipe Galindo (illustrations). **173:** Stefano Bianchetti/Corbis.
Money: 174: Judy Sloan Reich/Sun Sentinel. **175:** Jonathan Kirn/Getty Images; Felipe Galindo (illustration). **176:** U.S. Mint. **177:** Newscom; Bettmann/Corbis (yap); David Arky (3); Berheim-Rapho/Getty Images (cowrie shells); Mansell/Timepix (wampum). **178:** R studio T (graph); Felipe Galindo (illustration). **179:** Borri Roessler/AP (euro); Bettmann/Corbis.
Movies & TV: 180: Courtesy Melinda Sue Gordon/Universal Studios. **181:** Newscom (*Jungle Book*); Sony Pictures Image Works (*Stuart Little*). **182:** Bettmann/Corbis (kinetograph). **183:** Bettmann/Corbis (*Star Trek*); *The Simpsons*™ © 2001 Twentieth Century Fox Film Corp. **184:** Dorothy Low; Jane Sanders (illustration). **185:** Bettmann/Corbis (2).
Music: 186: Courtesy Rock and Roll Hall of Fame (guitar); Kevin Mazur/Wire Image.com (Cobain). **187:** Royalty-Free/Corbis; Jane Sanders (illustration). **188:** Dave Hogan/All Action/Retna (Dylan); Newscom (Lopez). **189:** Archivo Iconografico, S.A./Corbis.
Mythology: 190: Christel Gerstenberg/Corbis (Zeus); Araldo de Luca/Corbis (Vulcan). **191:** Bettmann/Corbis (Diana); Araldo de Luca (Hermes); Felipe Galindo (illustration). **192:** Joe Lertola (maps); Charles & Josette Lenars/Corbis (Quetzalcoatl); Gianni Dagli Orti/Corbis (Osiris).**192, 193:** Joe Lertola (maps); Araldo de Luca/Corbis (Homer).
Presidents: 194: Christie's Images/Corbis (Washington); John Trumbull/NPG/SI (Adams); Mather Brown/NPG/SI beq. of Charles Francis Adams (Jefferson); Chester Harding/NPG/SI (Madison); John Vanderlyn/NPG/SI (Monroe). **195:** George Caleb Bingham/NPG/SI (Adams); Ralph Eleaser Whiteside Earl/NPG/SI gift of Andrew W. Mellon (Jackson); Mathew B. Brady/NPG/SI (Van Buren); Albert Gallatin Hoit/NPG/SI (Harrison); LOC (Tyler); Max Westfield/NPG/SI (Polk). **196:** James Reid Lambdin/ NPG/SI gift of Barry Bingham Sr. (Taylor); NPG/SI (Fillmore); George Peter Healy/NPG/SI gift of Andrew W. Mellon (Pierce); George Peter Healy/NPG/SI gift of Andrew W. Mellon (Buchanan); William Judkins Thomson; George Peter Healy/NPG/SI

(Lincoln); Washington Bogart Cooper/NPG/SI.
197: Thomas Le Clear/NPG/SI gift of Mrs.
Grant (Grant); Bettmann/Corbis (Hayes); Ole
Peter Hansen Balling/NPG/SI gift of IBM; Ole
Peter Hansen Balling/NPG/SI gift of Mrs. H.N.
Blue; Anders Zorn/NPG/SI (Cleveland); LOC
(Harrison). **198:** LOC (Cleveland); Adolfo
Muller-Ury/NPG/SI (McKinley); Adrian
Lamb/NPG/SI gift of T.R. Assoc. (Roosevelt);
William Valentine Schevill/NPG/SI gift of W.E.
Schevill (Taft); Edmund Tarbell/ NPG/SI
(Wilson); Margaret Lindsay Williams/NPG/SI
(Harding). **199:** Joseph E. Burgess/NPG/SI gift
of Phi Gamma Delta (Coolidge); Douglas
Chandor/NPG/SI (Hoover); Oscar White/Corbis
(FDR); Greta Kempton/NPG/SI (Truman);
Thomas Edgar Stephens/NPG/SI gift of Ailsa
Mellon Bruce (Eisenhower); JFK Presidential
Library (Kennedy). **200:** Peter Hurd/NPG/SI gift
of the artist (Johnson); Norman Rockwell/
NPG/SI gift of Nixon Foundation (Nixon);
Everett R. Kinstler/NPG/SI gift of Ford
Foundation (Ford); Jimmy Carter Presidential
Library (Carter); Ronald Reagan Presidential
Library (Reagan); Ronald N. Sherr/NPG/SI gift
of Mr. & Mrs. R.E. Krueger (Bush).
201: Bettmann/Corbis (Clinton); Eric
Draper/White House (G.W. Bush); Ronald
Reagan Presidential Library. **202:** Dallas & John
Heaton/Corbis (White House); Felipe Galindo
(illustration). **203:** Cartoon © 1902, The
Washington Post. Reprinted with permission;
Brown Brothers (Teddy Roosevelt); E. Long-
National Museum of American
History/Smithsonian (bear); Addison
Scurlock/Time Picture Collection.
Religion: 204: Phil Schermeister/Corbis
(crucifix); Werner H. Miller/Corbis.
205: Steve Raymer/Asia Images (Koran);
Michael S. Yamashita/Corbis; Luca I.
Tettoni/Corbis. **206:** Bazuki Muhammad/Reuters
(Mecca); Peter Sibbald/TPC; Nathan
Benn/Corbis; Mahfouz Abu Turk/TPC.
207: Galen Rowell/Corbis.
Science: 208: Michael Long/NHMPL.
210: Digital Art/Corbis. **211:** Michael & Patricia
Fogden/Corbis. **214:** PD. **215:** Henry Groskinsky
(gold); Brad Hamann (diagram). **216:** Fletcher &
Baylis/Photo Researchers (rafflesia); Neil Miller-
Papilio/Corbis (flytrap). **217:** Sean M.
Dessureau/Information Please (diagram);
Time Picture Collection.
Space: 218: NASA. **219:** NASA; Antonio
Cidadao (Moon). **220, 221:** NASA (Mercury,
Venus, Earth); NASA (Mars); Univ. of

Arizona/JPL/NASA (Jupiter); Reta Beebe,
D. Gilmore, L. Bergeron and NASA (Saturn).
222: JPL/NASA (Uranus); NASA (Neptune);
Dr. Albrecht, ESA/ESO/NASA. **222:** NASA;
AFP/Corbis. **224, 225:** Encarnacion Lopez;
Jane Sanders (illustration). **226:** Jonathan
Blair/Corbis (crater); George Shelten/NASA
(Glenn); Roger Ressmeyer/Corbis.
227: Bettmann/Corbis (3).
Sports: 228: Douglas C. Piza/AP (opening
ceremonies); John G. Mabanglo/AFP (skiier No.
45); Brian Nicholson-*Standard Examiner*/AP.
229: Bettmann/Corbis. **230:** AFP/Corbis (Yao);
Chris Pizzell/AP World Wide Photos; Steve
Skelton (puzzle). **231:** Newscom. **232:** PD;
Bob Child/AP; Bill Vaughan/Icon
SMI/Newscom. **233:** Icon Sports/Newscom;
Newscom; Jane Sanders (ilustraton). **234:** PD
(3); Bettmann/Corbis (Geoffrion). **235:** John
Kabasakalis; PD. **236:** Reuters New Media
Inc./Corbis (2). **237:** Mike King/Corbis (Strug);
John Feingersh/Corbis (pommel horse);
Bevilacqua Guiliano/Corbis Sygma (Comaneci).
238: AFP/Corbis (2). **239:** AFP/Corbis (2).
240: PD; John Bazemore/AP. **241:** PD;
AFP/Newscom (Williams sisters); AFP/Corbis
(Sampras/Agassi). **242:** Reuters New Media
Inc./Corbis. **243:** AP (Fleming);
Bettmann/Corbis (Seattle Slew).
U.S.: 244: L.M. Otero/AP (cowboy); Courtesy
Angelique le Doux (Ferris wheel).
245: AFP/Corbis (pledge); Felipe Galindo
(illustration). **246:** Joe Lertola (map).
247: Bill Ross/Corbis (Times Square); Joel W.
Rogers/Corbis (space needle). **248:** James P.
Blair/Corbis. **249:** AFP/Corbis. **251:** Jeff
Greenberg/Photoedit. **252-278:** Joe Lertola
(maps). **279:** AFP/Robyn Beck/ Newscom
(Capitol); Index Stock/Newscom (Yosemite).
281: Bettmann/Corbis.
Weather: 282: John David Mercer-*Mobile
Register*/AP (storm at dock); David J. Phillip/AP.
283: Dave Martin/AP/Wide World Photos.
285: Scott T. Smith/Corbis; Tom Bean/Corbis;
Bryan Pickering/Eye Ubiquitous/Corbis; Richard
Hamilton Smith/Corbis; Macduff Everton/Corbis;
Larry Lee/Corbis. **286:** Jim Zuckerman/Corbis.
287: Ted Thai for TFK Almanac; William James
Warren/Corbis. **288:** AFP Photo/Florin Aneculaesi/
Newscom. **289:** Jane Sanders (illustration);
Hulton-Deutsch Collection/Corbis (Arrhenius).
World: 290: Mike Hutchings/Reuters.
323: David Pollack/Corbis. **324-338:** Joe Lertola
(maps). **339:** Corbis/Bettmann; Felipe Galindo
(puzzle).

We're giving credit where credit is due!